ENGLAND
UNDER THE TUDORS AND STUARTS
1485–1689

ENGLAND UNDER
THE
TUDORS AND STUARTS

1485–1689

BY

M. A. R. GRAVES

Senior Lecturer in History,
University of Auckland, New Zealand

LONDON
G. BELL & SONS LTD
1969

First published 1965
Reprinted 1969

SBN 7135 0504 4

Printed in Great Britain by
NEILL & CO. LTD., EDINBURGH

PREFACE

I OFFER no apology for adding a fresh volume to the existing literature on Tudor and Stuart England. It is designed specifically for candidates who are preparing for the Ordinary Level of the General Certificate of Education Examination and takes into account the notable advances made in our knowledge and understanding of this period in recent years. Too often, fresh ideas and new evidence are placed at the disposal of university undergraduates or 'Advanced Level' candidates, but fail to filter down to fifth-forms. I have tried to remedy this deficiency by embodying, in a simple form, the accepted results of research undertaken by such historians as J. E. Neale, G. R. Elton, W. Notestein, H. Trevor-Roper, R. H. Tawney, C. Read, and C. Hill.

Several aims have been firmly fixed in my mind during the writing of this book: to give particular attention to the neglected cultural, social, and economic fields; to dispense with oft-repeated but false notions such as Tudor despotism, and 'the eleven years' tyranny of Charles I'; to treat England as an integral part of Europe (which involves a thorough treatment of Continental developments); to divide the period into clearly defined historical phases, rather than into reigns which constitute convenient but arbitrary and often artificial divisions; to place special stress on the motives underlying actions and the forces underlying historical developments.

This book is the product of my own past experience in teaching history to fifth formers. It is my belief that the difficulties which I have encountered have been experienced by other teachers. I can only hope that this book offers a solution to at least some of those difficulties. Its prime purpose is to provide the fifth-form student with an up-to-date account of the Tudors and Stuarts, adequate for examination purposes, and sufficiently interesting to stimulate him to pursue historical studies beyond the limited horizons of an examination syllabus.

Dunedin, 1964   M. A. R. GRAVES

CONTENTS

THE EARLY STUARTS

CIVIL WAR AND REVOLUTION

RESTORATION TO REVOLUTION

STUART ENGLAND

LIST OF MAPS

GENEALOGICAL TABLES

ILLUSTRATIONS

following page 216

A List of Plates and Explanatory Notes on them will be found on pp. 213–6.

THE EARLY TUDORS
1485–1529

I

THE COMING OF THE TUDORS

EDWARD III ruled for fifty years (1327–77) which were of great importance in the history of England. His long reign had passing moments of military glory. It raised England's prestige, and for the first time men became aware and proud of the fact that they were English. However, his reign had harmful effects which remained when the glory had been forgotten. Ruling a strong and united nation, Edward wished to bully and plunder his weaker but richer French neighbour. His claim to the throne of France, through his mother Isabella, was a mere excuse for attacking her. So began the series of wars, known as the Hundred Years' War (1340–1453). Until the final expulsion of English troops from France in 1453, England devoted her energies to the futile task of forcing the French to accept an English king.

In order to raise enough troops for his campaigns, Edward allowed his nobles to enlist armed retainers to serve under them in France. This practice became widespread. When the Hundred Years' War came to an end, many nobles kept their private armies and used them in the civil wars which followed. These retainers, loyal only to their noble employers who protected them from the king's courts, were one of the greatest threats to law and order in the country.

Edward III's children were added to the ranks of the nobility. The king had five sons. Edward, the 'Black Prince', his eldest son and heir, died the year before him. The youngest, Thomas, was murdered. The other sons, Lionel, John of Gaunt, and Edmund, were endowed with the dukedoms of Clarence, Lancaster, and York, together with great estates. This action created three powerful noble families, closely related by blood to the crown. Eventually these families were to quarrel over the possession of that crown.

A wasteful war with France, the evil practice of retainers, and the creation of powerful rivals to the crown: these were the legacies of Edward III. But in 1377 the crown passed peacefully enough to Richard, son of the Black Prince. Trouble was not delayed for many years. A struggle developed between Richard II and his cousins, the sons of those royal dukes whom Edward had created. Henry Bolingbroke, the son of John of Gaunt, led a rebellion which unseated Richard (1399). The king was forced to abdicate and was later murdered in Pontefract Castle. The rightful heir to the throne was Edmund, Earl of March, but Henry ignored his claim. Instead he successfully claimed the throne for himself, and parliament recognised him as king by the name of Henry IV.

The reign of Henry IV was spent in the suppression of rebellions by nobles, who resented his seizure of the throne. His son, Henry V, took the advice, which Shakespeare put into the mouth of his father, 'to busy giddy minds with foreign quarrels'. He renewed the war with France and so gained the wholehearted support of the nobles, who hoped for gains in France. After his great victory at Agincourt Henry forced upon the French a treaty, by which he was to marry the Princess Katherine, and the eldest son born to them was to become the king of France.

Everything seemed rosy; yet after Henry's early death everything went wrong. His son, Henry VI, became king of England and France in 1422, but the French, inspired by Joan of Arc, expelled the English. By 1453 only Calais remained in English hands. Henry VI himself was only an infant on his accession. During his long minority (1422–37) the nobles gained control of the king's council, which they used to increase their power and wealth. When Henry grew to manhood he lacked the strong character necessary to resume control of it. Furthermore the loss of France made the Lancastrians unpopular. The Yorkists took advantage of this. They put forward the better hereditary claim of their leader, Edward, the duke of York, and deposed Henry VI. Edward became King Edward IV.

The struggle which followed was a prolonged fight between Yorkists and Lancastrians over the possession of the crown. During these wars between the White Rose of York and the Red Rose of Lancaster, the power and prestige of the crown sank to their lowest point. The support or opposition of great nobles could make or break kings. Rewards of money, land, and privileges had to be given to them in order to retain their support. The crown grew poorer and therefore weaker. A weak monarchy could not enforce law and order. Justice was perverted by local magnates and their armed retainers. Gradually the nation lost respect for both the king and his laws.

An attempt was made by Edward IV to restore law and order. He prevented ambitious nobles from controlling his council, and he revived the council's right to act as a law-court. As he feared the overmighty nobles and needed money, Edward preferred to gain the friendship of the rich merchants of London. He rarely summoned parliament where the nobles had great influence, relying instead on compulsory gifts or loans from wealthy individuals. Many of these practices were revived later by Henry VII, the first of the Tudors.

The revival of trade during Edward IV's reign was a result of his success in restoring peace. But this success was limited. He was unable to put an end to private warfare between local nobles and gentry. He freed the crown from debt, but it remained poor. On several occasions he was forced to fight pitched battles in defence of his throne. When he died, a strong Lancastrian party under Henry Tudor's leadership was in Brittany, waiting its chance to overthrow the Yorkist monarchy (1483). That chance came soon for Edward IV at his death left two young sons, Edward and Richard, and five daughters. The late king's brother, Richard of Gloucester, became regent for the little king, Edward V. He placed the young king and his brother 'under protection' in the Tower of London, where they were probably murdered. Richard of Gloucester then usurped the throne. The disappearance of the two young princes caused widespread discontent and opposition to Richard III's rule. This encouraged Henry Tudor to invade England and try his luck. His luck held out and on 22 August 1485 Henry met and defeated Richard III near Market Bosworth in Leicestershire. Richard was killed and the crown passed once more to the Lancastrian party.

THE DESCENDANTS OF EDWARD III

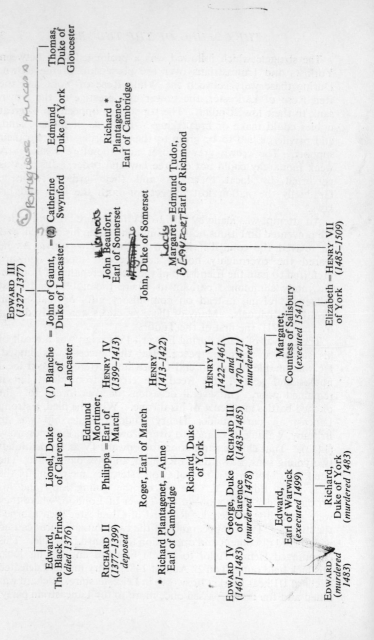

EDWARD III
(1327–1377)

Edward, The Black Prince *(died 1376)*

RICHARD II *(1377–1399) deposed*

Lionel, Duke of Clarence

Philippa = Edmund Mortimer, Earl of March

Roger, Earl of March

Richard Plantagenet, = Anne Earl of Cambridge *

Blanche (1) = John of Gaunt, Duke of Lancaster = (2) Catherine Swynford *(3)*

Portuguese princess

HENRY IV *(1399–1413)*

HENRY V *(1413–1422)*

HENRY VI *(1422–1461 and 1470–1471) murdered*

John Beaufort, James Earl of Somerset

John, Duke of Somerset Joan

Margaret = Edmund Tudor, Beaufort Earl of Richmond

Edmund, Duke of York

Richard * Plantagenet, Earl of Cambridge

EDWARD IV *(1461–1483)*

George, Duke of Clarence *(murdered 1478)*

RICHARD III *(1483–1485)*

Richard, Duke of York

Edward, Earl of Warwick *(executed 1499)*

Margaret, Countess of Salisbury *(executed 1541)*

Edward *(murdered 1483)*

Richard, Duke of York *(murdered 1483)*

Elizabeth = HENRY VII of York *(1485–1509)*

Thomas, Duke of Gloucester

II

HENRY VII

INTRODUCTION

WHEN Richard III's coronet was placed on the head of Henry
Tudor, earl of Richmond, at Bosworth Field, Englishmen did
not realise that this day marked the beginning of the end of the
Wars of the Roses. This was understandable. English kings
had been deposed on five occasions since 1460; there was no
reason to suppose that Henry VII would not suffer the same
fate.

The new king was faced with great difficulties. England was
suffering from the effects not only of civil war, but also of
outbreaks of the plague. His claim to the throne was weak.
The crown was poverty-stricken, whilst its strength was rivalled
by that of the greater nobles; the law-courts had been weakened
by threats and corruption; the Yorkist party had not given up
its claim to the throne and its supporters were numerous and
powerful. On the other hand Henry had certain advantages.
The number of nobles had been reduced by executions and
death in battle. The nation was prepared to support any king
who showed that he could end the civil wars. Even some of the
surviving Yorkists, such as the earl of Surrey, now faithfully
supported Henry.

HENRY VII's CLAIM TO THE THRONE

Henry's most pressing need was to secure his right to the
throne, for his hereditary claim was very weak. He claimed
through his mother, Margaret, last of the Beauforts, who had
been debarred from the throne because they were descended
from an illegitimate son of John of Gaunt. Two Yorkist
claimants had a much stronger hereditary right: the young earl
of Warwick, nephew of Edward IV, and Edward's eldest
daughter, Elizabeth. In addition there was the earl of Lincoln,
the man appointed by the childless Richard III to succeed him.

The weakness of Henry's claim was shown by an act passed

5

by the parliament which he summoned after the battle of Bosworth. It simply stated that Henry was king and made no mention of his hereditary claim. Henry himself declared that he had become king with God's approval, which had been shown by his victory at Bosworth.

He now took steps to remove the rival claimants. He married Elizabeth, thus uniting the claims of Lancaster and York. The young earl of Warwick was imprisoned in the Tower of London, whilst the earl of Lincoln submitted and recognised Henry as king.

THE YORKIST PRETENDERS

A strong Yorkist party still existed. Henry meted out severe punishments to the leaders, but tried to win the support of their followers by a policy of leniency. Those in his power were punished by heavy fines and the loss of lands rather than by imprisonment and execution. To some extent he was successful, but the extreme Yorkists would never accept a Lancastrian king, even though he had a Yorkist queen. They gathered around Edward IV's sister Margaret, the duchess of Burgundy. Their great difficulty was that they had no genuine claimants who were free from Henry's control. So they were forced to put their trust in impostors or pretenders.

In 1487 the Yorkists put forward an impostor, Lambert Simnel, as the earl of Warwick. Henry paraded Warwick through the streets of London, but there was no proof that his prisoner was the real earl. Simnel was supported by Margaret of Burgundy and controlled by the earl of Lincoln who had deserted Henry. He was taken to Ireland where the Yorkists had always been popular. With a small army he set sail for England, landed in Lancashire, and marched south towards London. However the country gave little support to Simnel's army. It was destroyed by the king's forces on 16 June 1487 at Stoke near Newark. All the Yorkist leaders were killed with the exception of Simnel, who was captured. Showing contempt for the Yorkist plotters and realising that Simnel was really harmless, Henry did not harm him. Instead he made him a scullion in the royal household.

The second Yorkist pretender was more dangerous. He was a Fleming named Perkin Warbeck, who had previously been a servant to a French merchant. In 1491 Warbeck claimed that he was Richard, duke of York, the younger of the princes who had been murdered in the Tower. He gained the support of Margaret of Burgundy, who was Henry VII's lifelong enemy. The Holy Roman Emperor and the kings of Scotland and France recognised him as the rightful king of England. He even had supporters at Henry VII's court. Their ringleader was Sir William Stanley who had helped Henry to victory at Bosworth. When this was discovered in 1495, Stanley and the other conspirators were executed.

At first Warbeck was protected by Charles VIII of France, who was at war with England. However, when England and France signed the Treaty of Etaples in 1492, Charles VIII agreed to expel Warbeck. The pretender withdrew to Flanders where he was welcomed by Margaret of Burgundy. She supported his attempted invasion of Kent, in 1495, but it failed. He then transferred his activities to Scotland. Whilst Henry's forces were guarding the border between England and Scotland a serious rebellion occurred in Cornwall. It was caused by heavy taxes, which had been imposed to pay for the defence of North England. It was a dangerous moment. The Cornishmen marched unopposed almost to London before Henry managed to raise forces to defeat them in June 1497. In the following month Warbeck left Scotland, and landed in Cornwall. The English gave him little support and he was forced to surrender to the king's forces.

Unlike Simnel, Perkin Warbeck was not the harmless tool of Yorkists. He was an ambitious adventurer, who had made use of the feud between the White and Red Roses to further his ambition. Yet Henry was lenient with him, and Warbeck remained in custody at the royal court. He tried to escape in 1498, but was imprisoned in the Tower. In 1499 a further attempt resulted in the execution of Warbeck and also of the young earl of Warwick on a vague charge of treason. This charge of treason was simply the excuse for execution. The real reason was that Henry was negotiating for a marriage between his eldest son Arthur (born in 1486) and the Spanish princess, Catherine. Ferdinand, the Spanish ruler, was unwilling to agree to the marriage whilst rivals to Henry VII were still alive. In any case, so long as he lived Warwick remained a threat to Henry. So this second attempt to escape gave Henry the chance to get rid of the last surviving Yorkist claimants, genuine or false.

HENRY VII AND THE CROWN'S POVERTY

The removal of pretenders and rival claimants was only half the battle. To restore good government Henry had to make himself strong. The weakness of the crown had been due to its poverty. Henry realised that money was power, and recognised the necessity of making the crown so rich and strong that no subject would dare to challenge it.

The crown was potentially very rich. So long as the king was able to obtain all that was due to him, he had no need to fear poverty. In addition he could obtain grants of money from parliament, but these were only intended to help him in emergencies. It was generally accepted that the king 'should live of his own' in normal times. For this purpose he had several sources of ordinary revenue: rents from the crown lands; the customs revenue, especially the duty on wool; fines and fees from the law courts. There were also feudal dues, a relic of the feudal society of early medieval England. They were many and varied. When an heir took over his estates, he had to pay a fine. If he was a minor, his lands were held 'in wardship' by the king who received the profits from them. When the heir came of age, he had to pay a fine to recover them. If there were no heirs at all the lands escheated (returned to the crown). The king could also demand payments from his feudal tenants when he went to war, his eldest son was knighted, or his eldest daughter married.

These sources had yielded less and less money during the Wars of the Roses. The kings had been too absorbed in defending their position to worry about their financial rights. They had even given away crown lands to the nobles to keep their support. So the treasury was empty when Henry VII became king.

At first he was forced to rely on loans and parliamentary grants, but as his financial position improved he called parliament as seldom as possible. He did not wish to depend on it and preferred to make do with his normal income. The rents from the royal estates formed the most important source of money. To the old crown lands Henry added the estates of treasonable nobles, the lands of the Yorkist and Lancastrian kings and his own earldom of Richmond. He also reclaimed the estates which had been given away during the civil wars. As a result Henry more than trebled the income from rents. However, he was less successful with customs duties. Although he encouraged trade, the customs only increased slightly, because of smuggling, and wars which interrupted trade. More money was raised from the law-courts, because of the heavy fines imposed on Yorkists and disobedient nobles. However, Henry had the greatest success with feudal dues. The civil wars had enabled many to escape payment of them, but he now sent commissioners round the shires to discover who owed dues and to make them pay.

Apart from his normal revenue the king also took benevolences (which were supposed to be free gifts offered by rich subjects out of goodwill towards their king) and forced loans. In his later years he used two of his councillors, Richard Empson and Edmund Dudley, to help him in the task of making the crown rich. They searched out old forgotten laws and heavily fined people who had unwittingly broken them. This extortion was unpopular, but it was legal. In any case it only hurt those who could afford to pay. Empson and Dudley became notorious because they carried out their work with such great enthusiasm.

As a result of these practices Henry VII has often been called a miserly and greedy king. Yet he was simply trying to re-establish the crown's rights and to build up a rich monarchy. His parsimony was not a personal weakness but the attitude of a wise king who built up his wealth. When it was necessary, he was prepared to spend lavishly. During his reign his annual income rose from £50,000 to £140,000. Henry also accumulated a treasure worth about £1,500,000, most of which was in gold and silver plate and jewels. Indeed he was the last English king to leave a surplus in the treasury when he died.

THE OVERMIGHTY SUBJECTS

Some of the nobles had become 'overmighty' during the fifteenth century. Their power was derived from: (*1*) Their estates which had increased at the crown's expense, for Lancastrian and Yorkist kings had given away lands as rewards to their followers. (*2*) Their control of the king's council, which enabled them to obtain further rewards for themselves and their friends. (*3*) Their employment of armed retainers, the practice known as livery (wearing the lord's uniform as a sign of loyalty to him) and maintenance (the lord's protection of his retainers from punishment in the king's courts, if they broke the law). The retainers were used by the nobles, not only to support the White or Red Rose, but also to settle private disputes, to bully the local abbot or to seize the land of a weaker neighbour. Despite several acts of parliament against livery and maintenance, the evil had increased during the Wars of the Roses. By bribing and threatening juries, retainers prevented the law from being enforced, and they spread the habit of lawlessness and violence throughout the upper classes.

The nobles had unwittingly helped Henry by killing each other in the civil wars. They were exhausted and reduced in numbers, whilst the heads of many surviving noble families were minors, and so became the king's wards. Henry took advantage of the situation to prevent a revival of their power. He struck at their wealth, when he took back all crown lands which had been given away, and fined them heavily for breaches of the peace. The control of the council by the nobles also came to an end. But Henry did not exclude them altogether. He was not opposed to nobles on principle, but only wished to reduce them to obedience. Loyal and capable men, like the earls of Oxford and Shrewsbury and even the ex-Yorkist earl of Surrey, served in his council. Henry simply prevented the nobles from dominating it. Instead, most of his councillors were chosen from the middle class or the Church. Edward Poynings, Richard Empson and Edmund Dudley were members of the middle class, whilst Cardinal Morton and Bishop Fox represented the Church.[1]

Henry also brought to an end the evil of livery and maintenance. Acts were passed against it in 1487 and 1504, and, what was more important, these acts were enforced and breaches of them were punished by heavy fines in the prerogative courts. In such ways Henry forced the nobles into obedience. By the end of his reign the problem of the overmighty subjects no longer existed.

THE PREROGATIVE COURTS

As the king was 'the fountain of all justice', he had the right to ensure that justice was done in the law-courts. Those who could not afford the great expenses of a law suit, or failed to get fair treatment in the courts, could appeal to the king for justice. He could answer this appeal by setting up courts, which would provide justice cheaply and quickly. Henry used this power to

[1] Henry VII was on good terms with the Church and its head, the pope.

the full by reviving old courts. These prerogative courts, so called because they were established by the prerogative or special power of the crown, were used to restore law and order.

The most famous was the court of star chamber. Henry revived the old practice whereby some of his councillors sat as judges in the star chamber in Whitehall Palace. They heard cases with which the ordinary law-courts were unable to deal. Their most important task was to keep order by checking the power of the nobles and the violence of the retainers. In 1487 an act was passed, defining more clearly the power and duties of star chamber: to punish riots, livery and maintenance, unlawful assemblies and other breaches of the peace. The councillors in star chamber carried out these tasks with great success. The nobles found that they were too powerful to be bullied or bribed. Furthermore the local justices of the peace acted more vigorously because they knew that they were supported by star chamber. Gradually the nobles began to realise that they had met their match. Livery and maintenance, and with it violence, began to die out. But the star chamber's work did not lessen. It had become popular because it was quicker, cheaper, and more efficient than the common law-courts. It did not enforce its own code of laws, but made sure that the law of the land was obeyed by all.

The court of requests, which had existed in Richard III's reign, was also revived by Henry. Its task was to deal with the complaints of royal servants and poor men. Some of the king's councillors sat as judges and gave decisions which were based on fairness (equity). It became very popular, because, like star chamber, it offered justice quickly, cheaply, and without favour to the rich man.

The north of England and Welsh Marches (borderlands) had always been turbulent and violent. To bring order to these regions Henry simply followed the policy of the Yorkist kings. The earl of Surrey, helped by a council, was given the difficult task of subduing the north, whilst the council of the prince of Wales, the infant Arthur, governed the Welsh Marches. These councils, which were staffed with the king's supporters, readily obeyed his commands. Progress was slow, especially in the north of England where the influence of old feudal families was greater than that of the king. But at least a start was made.

LOCAL GOVERNMENT

To maintain peace in the counties Henry used the system of local government which he found in existence. It was based on the justices of the peace (J.P.s), who were local unpaid gentlemen, chosen by the king. They dealt with petty crimes and called out the local militia to put down rebellions or riots. Henry extended their powers considerably and, under the Tudors, they became not only peace officers but also local civil servants. Fixing wages, prices, and working hours, keeping the highways in repair, and looking after the poor were just a few of the tasks imposed upon them. The system had its disadvantages: the J.P.s were amateurs, and they were unwilling to enforce laws which would harm themselves or the gentry as a class. But the king had a great degree of control over them. He appointed them and the council closely supervised their work. They were reappointed annually, and so a lazy or dishonest J.P. would not hold the office for long. The office of J.P. gave a gentleman great social distinction in his county, and its loss was a great blow to his prestige. So most J.P.s carried out their duties loyally rather than risk dismissal. This enabled Henry to place great trust in them and to use them to enforce his will in the countryside.

PARLIAMENT

Parliament consisted of the three estates of king, lords[1] and commons. Its existence depended upon the king who alone had the power to summon, prorogue (suspend), or dissolve it. This did not mean that it was insignificant: parliament alone could make laws and impose taxes; whilst its duty to discuss matters of policy placed before it by the king was a less obvious but equally important function. Yet Henry only called parliament six times during his reign and it remained, as it always had been, the least important part of the government.

TUDOR DESPOTISM

The strong monarchy which Henry VII established has often been called, incorrectly, the Tudor despotism. A despot was a

[1] The lords included all the lay peers, the bishops and some abbots; the commons consisted of 'knights of the shire' (two from each county, elected by freeholders whose property was worth 40s. or more a year) and burgesses (two from each of a number of cities and towns, where the franchise was usually limited to the propertied classes).

ruler who was above the law and able to force his will on the people at all times. The English had always regarded their king as being limited by the law, and the Tudors did not try to change this idea. In any case Henry VII did not have the means to enforce an unpopular policy, even if he had wished to do so. He had no standing army and had to rely upon militia raised by loyal nobles and J.P.s. Instead of police, he had to use informers to detect crime. Furthermore his rule was not very effective in the north and west of England, because the bad roads prevented news or troops from travelling quickly. Indeed the real strength of the Tudors came, not from military force, but from the support of people of all classes.

Henry's support came particularly from the middle class. The merchants, the large number of gentry who made up most of this class, and the craftsmen, were the people who benefited most by Henry's rule. They could now trade, farm, and produce goods in peace. Yet Henry did not rule for the benefit of the middle class alone. His aim was to make his throne secure and he could only achieve this by restoring law and order. His aim coincided with the nation's wish. When he died in 1509, both had been achieved: the country was at peace and Henry was able to pass on to his son, without challenge, a secure strong crown, a full treasury, and a loyal nation. This was Henry VII's achievement.

HENRY VII AND SCOTLAND

Scotland was primitive and economically poor, supporting only a small population. It was also a land where lawlessness was rife. Government was too weak to do anything about it: the Church was corrupt, the parliament was feeble; even the Scottish kings, though growing in strength, were not yet powerful enough to maintain order.

Scotland was a union of three regions, each very different in its way of life and economic activities:

(*1*) *The southern borderlands.* Here, where Scotland and England met, lived a rough turbulent mixture of hill farmers and herders, thieves and outlaws. Many of them were also raiders (known as 'mosstroopers'), who crossed the border into England to burn, rob, and kill. They lived in a constant state of war, fighting amongst themselves and with the English, raiding and being raided; occasionally an invading English army would devastate the entire region. Scottish kings made no attempt to bring law and order. So robbers and cattle thieves went undisturbed, and dwellings were fortified and provisioned as if for a siege. It was a state of affairs which was to last for many more years.

SCOTLAND IN THE 16TH AND 17TH CENTURIES

(2) *The central lowlands*, which run from east to west where Scotland is narrowest, were the most densely populated part of the country and in it were to be found the biggest towns. Of these the most important was Edinburgh, home of the law-courts and parliament, and famous for its castle and palace (Holyrood House). The lowlands were more settled and advanced than the rest of Scotland; some of the people farmed, but others were engaged in trade or industry.

(3) The highlands of the north, much of which was desolate and barren. Amidst the mountains and glens lived the clans— Macdonalds, Douglases and Frazers, Campbells and Mackenzies. The clan chieftains were like petty kings: they owned all the land, held their own law-courts, and had the power of life and death over their kinsmen. Frequently they led their clans to fight rivals, sometimes to steal from the lowlands. With their claymores and targets (shields), their plaids and kilts, the clansmen were impressive figures and the subject of many romantic poems. But they were also cruel, destructive, and an obstacle to progress.

Scotland's kings, members of the Stuart family, had a formidable task. With meagre resources they had to face a constant threat from their powerful neighbour, England. Throughout the Middle Ages, English kings had made attempts to conquer Scotland, or at least to become suzerains (overlords). But the Scots were tough, proud, and determined to remain free. In the twelfth century they had formed an alliance with France, in order to safeguard their independence. It proved to be of great advantage to both countries: whenever their freedom was threatened, the Scots could depend upon French help; and if France found herself at war with the English, the Scots would launch an invasion across England's northern border. The 'auld alliance', as it came to be known, lasted for nearly four hundred years.

The Stuarts also had their hands full at home. They ruled a wild and turbulent people – and none were more unruly than the Scottish nobles. They were greedy and quarrelsome, and they saw it as their right to settle their feuds by force. Sometimes they fought each other, sometimes they combined to fight the king. So Scotland suffered from murders, private wars, and frequent upsets. In one such upheaval, in 1488, James III was murdered. His fifteen year old son succeeded him as James IV.

Although he was young, James IV proved to be a strong king. He quelled disorder at home for the time being. Then he turned his attention to England. James was ambitious, and anxious for glory in war against the English, whom he hated. He stirred up trouble on the border—not a difficult task—but Henry was busily making secure his newly-won throne and had no time for useless wars aginst the Scots. During Henry's brief war with the French (1489–92) James renewed the 'auld alliance', but England and France soon settled their differences at Etaples (1492).

In 1495 a real chance to embarrass Henry VII occurred. James IV recognised Perkin Warbeck as King Richard IV of England. He welcomed the pretender to Scotland, gave him a pension and married him to one of his relatives. In 1496 James and Warbeck invaded England, but the English would not rise in support of 'Richard IV'. James swept the countryside with fire and sword and then withdrew. A second invasion, after the pretender's departure from Scotland, was equally unsuccessful. Henry VII refused to be roused. He hoped to avoid war, which was a costly business, and instead bring peace to the border by signing a treaty with Scotland. After two expensive failures James was now willing to come to terms. The result was a truce (1499), followed by a peace treaty (1502), and James IV's marriage to Henry VII's elder daughter Margaret (1503). This was to have momentous consequences. It established peace for the rest of Henry VII's reign. But, far more important, a century later it led to the union of England and Scotland under James VI, the great grandson of James IV and Margaret Tudor.

HENRY VII AND IRELAND

To Englishmen who visited Ireland it was a strange backward country: industry was hardly known and farming was primitive; communications were difficult; piracy flourished, whilst trade was confined to Dublin and a few southern towns. They believed that it could be turned into a rich contented land; but they reckoned without its turbulent population and the problems, feuds, and rivalries that divided it.

Tudor Ireland was peopled by three distinct groups:

(*1*) The Irish were the original natives of the country, a primitive lawless people. They lived in clans or septs (tribes), ruled by powerful chieftains who dispensed justice and controlled the lands of their tribes. They showed no respect for the authority of the English king, and spent much of their time making war on each other. Murders, skirmishes, and the theft of cattle were all part of the normal scene. National unity had not even begun to appear.

(*2*) In the twelfth century, English settlers had colonised the east coast around Dublin. They intermarried with the Irish, adopted native customs, and even their language; by the sixteenth century they differed little from the Irish. Many of these Anglo-Irish families were very rich and powerful. They recognised the king's authority, but ignored it whenever it suited them. The greatest of them were the Geraldines (or Fitzgeralds) and the Butlers. There were two branches of the Fitzgerald family, headed by the earl of Kildare in Leinster and the earl of Desmond in Munster. Between their estates lay the territory of the Butlers, their enemies and rivals for supremacy in Ireland. So they naturally supported different sides in the Wars of the Roses: the Geraldines supported York, whilst the Butlers were for Lancaster.

(3) Finally there were the English, either new settlers, merchants, soldiers, or government officials with their families. Most of them were confined to the coastal strip around Dublin and Dundalk (known as the Pale), where parliament met and the king's deputy lived. Only here was the royal authority effective; yet even the Pale was not immune from attack by the surrounding tribes.

Ireland was a threat to the new Lancastrian king, Henry VII. Irish sympathies were with the house of York, and both Simnel and Warbeck were helped by the Geraldines. It was a threat which Henry could not ignore: the Irish Yorkists had to be destroyed or weaned from their support of the White Rose, and Ireland brought under royal control.

The Tudors normally governed Ireland indirectly. The king appointed a lord lieutenant to represent him, but a deputy did the actual work of governing. At first Henry VII hoped to govern Ireland peacefully, with the aid of the Geraldines, so he made Kildare his deputy. This was typical of Henry's cunning. After all, the powerful earl was virtually the ruler of Ireland. Now he would rule it for the king—and at his own expense. But Kildare let Henry down by supporting Lambert Simnel, so in 1492 he was dismissed. Instead the king made his own son, Henry, lord lieutenant, whilst Sir Edward Poynings, an able and trusted councillor, became his deputy.

Poynings removed the Yorkist danger: Kildare was charged with treason and sent packing to the Tower. By a series of laws (known as Poynings' Laws) the deputy also destroyed the independence of the Irish parliament: only the king could summon it, and he could veto any of its bills and decide the topics which it could discuss. Laws passed by the English parliament were to apply to Ireland as well.

Poynings' success was short-lived. Henry VII decided that a policy of subduing the Irish was too expensive; so in 1496 he recalled Poynings and restored Kildare, who thereafter ruled Ireland, king in all but name. The first Tudor attempt to exercise real royal control had failed, and Henry left it to its own devices for the rest of his reign. Ireland relapsed into its old turbulent ways: the Geraldines under Kildare continued their old feud with the Butlers, and clan chieftains fought each other for power and prestige. The power of the English government dwindled until once again it was restricted to the Pale.

III

HENRY VII AND EUROPE

HENRY VII became king when the Middle Ages were waning. New economic developments, the Renaissance, changes in the form and powers of government, the decline of international institutions, and the rise of nation-states: together they marked a departure from the medieval way of life.

THE HOLY ROMAN EMPIRE AND THE PAPACY

The most important institutions in medieval Europe were international: the Holy Roman Empire and the papacy. The former, created in 962, sprang out of men's reverence for the ancient Roman empire, and its head the emperor was deemed superior in rank to all other rulers in western Europe; the latter was the head of the 'universal' Roman catholic Church. In theory they co-operated in the rule of Christendom; in practice they had engaged in a centuries long struggle for supremacy which had exhausted the Empire and caused the moral decay of the papacy.

Imperial territory had dwindled until, by the end of the fifteenth century, it embraced little more than Germany. It was a mosaic

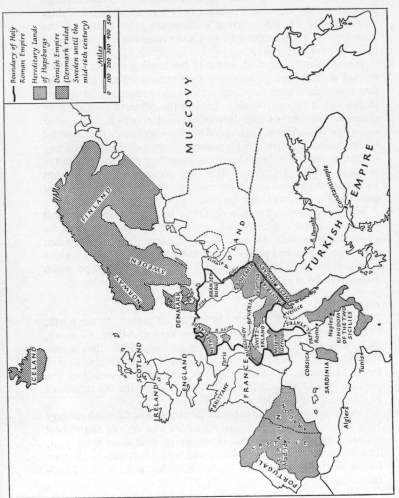

EUROPE IN CHARLES V'S TIME

of over three hundred states ruled by petty princes and bishops over whom the emperor exercised only a nominal overlordship. Occasionally, at the emperor's summons, the heads of the States met in a diet (assembly) to discuss common interests. But there was no real unity.

When an emperor died, seven of the leading princes met and elected a successor. Frequently they nominated the son of the late emperor. Thus for long periods the crown would remain in the hands of one family. During the fifteenth century they chose a member of the Hapsburg family, which ruled over extensive lands in and around Austria. Although the imperial title remained elective, the Hapsburgs made it virtually hereditary in their family. In the sixteenth century they were to become the greatest power in Europe. But that power would stem from their enormous hereditary possessions, not from their nominal control of a disintegrating empire.

The papacy as well was in decline. In the fifteenth century it had suppressed criticism and resisted attempts to reform its abuses and reduce its authority. It continued to pay more attention to political power and to the collection of taxes than to spiritual life. Respect for it had sunk low in Europe when Henry VII became king.

ITALY

Italy resembled the Empire in its lack of unity. In the north, several great commercial city-states—Venice, Milan, Florence, and Genoa—quarrelled and fought amongst themselves. Central Italy, which was conquered by Cesare Borgia, son of Pope Alexander VI (1492–1503), passed into the hands of the papacy after his death. To the south were the Kingdom of Naples and the Spanish colony of Sicily.

Despite constant strife between the city-states, fifteenth century Italy was the cradle of the Renaissance and one of the richest trading centres in Europe. However its best days were past. The discovery of the New World and new sea-routes to the east meant that the best trade routes now lay outside the Mediterranean.

THE 'NEW' NATIONS

Germany and Italy lacked unity or national feeling. In the west, however, nation-states were being created by strong kings.

In the fifteenth century the Iberian peninsula was divided into four Christian States (Portugal, Aragon, Castile, and Navarre) and a Moslem kingdom of Granada. Portugal remained an independent kingdom and became the owner of a great colonial empire. But Castile and Aragon were united by the marriage of their rulers, Isabella and Ferdinand. In 1492 Granada was conquered; and in 1515 Ferdinand seized a large part of Navarre. Thus a new kingdom, Spain, appeared on the European scene. Already it was expanding. It had colonies in the Mediterranean, to which Ferdinand added Naples despite French opposition (1504). In 1494 Columbus reached the Bahamas, and Spaniards followed him to found an empire in the New World.

In France too unity was being achieved. By the end of the Hundred Years' War the English had been expelled from all but Calais. The duke of Burgundy, the French king's vassal, acted as if he was an independent ruler; but in 1477 the last duke, Charles, was killed. The French parts of the 'Burgundian inheritance' were claimed by Louis XI. However, Duke Charles' daughter Mary had married the Hapsburg Maximilian, who claimed the whole inheritance through his wife. Maximilian got the lion's share: the county of Burgundy (Franche Comté), the Netherlands (including Flanders), and Luxembourg. Nevertheless France managed to obtain Burgundy and Picardy. And when Charles VIII (1483–98) married Anne, the ruling duchess of Brittany, the last semi-independent duchy was absorbed into France. At the same time, a number of capable French kings of the Valois family made the crown strong and increased royal control over the Church. So England's traditional enemy was united under a new strong monarchy.

THE REST OF EUROPE

The other European countries lay outside the mainstream of European affairs: Denmark, with its Scandinavian empire; Poland, with its weak elected kings; and Russia, still in a semi-barbarous state.

There was also the empire of the Turkish sultan. Although Poland and Russia were very backward, they were at least Christian (belonging to the Greek orthodox, not the Roman catholic faith). But the Ottoman Turks were of the Moslem faith. They were also very warlike. Until the fifteenth century they had been held in check by the Byzantine Empire[1] with its capital at Constantinople. But it had long been in decay; and when Sultan Mohammed II seized Constantinople in 1453, its long history was at an end. The Turks went on to conquer most of the Balkans, and by 1500 they were poised on the edge of Austria and the independent kingdom of Hungary. As non-Christians they constituted a major threat to the Roman catholic Church and the western way of life in Europe.

It should be remembered that England and Scotland too were not in the centre of affairs. England's failure in the Hundred Years' War, followed by the Wars of the Roses, had robbed her of her important position in European politics. She was an economic 'backwater', having nothing to offer but cloth and wool, whilst in culture, manners, and living standards, she lagged far behind the continent. Scotland was even more insignificant; but for the 'auld alliance' the Scots might well have lost their independence.

THE 'NEW' MONARCHIES

The 'new' strong monarchies of France and Spain had many novel features: more money, siege trains of cannon, standing armies, and law-courts which paid more attention to the power of the crown than to the political rights of the people. They were moving towards absolutism. England's king was certainly not absolute. His power was limited, for he was under the law, but he too was strong. The strength of these monarchies was based upon the growth of national feeling. National pride replaced the medieval reverence for the 'universal' empire of ancient Rome; in time it was bound to challenge the international authority of the pope.

Politics were dynastic; that is to say wars were fought and diplomacy conducted in the interest of the rulers and their families. This is especially true of the kings of France and Spain. Thus Charles VIII of France was ambitious to use his new found power, and anxiously sought fame and glory. In 1494 he launched an army across the Alps and with great ease occupied north Italy and Naples. However his success had aroused fears in the hearts of many: Maximilian had for long had his eye on Milan; Ferdinand was anxious to add Naples to

---

[1] This was the eastern portion of the ancient Roman empire which had survived when the western half had been overrun by barbarian hordes.

his empire; whilst the pope feared that French control of Italy would make him a virtual prisoner of Charles VIII. They took steps to resist him. Thus began the Italian Wars which lasted well into the sixteenth century. They provided a golden opportunity for England to play an active part in European politics again.

ECONOMIC LIFE IN EUROPE

Europe was still mainly rural and feudal; most of the continent was covered with farms and villages (and much wasteland and forest). Yet there were one or two areas, such as northern Italy and Flanders, where town-life flourished. In addition there were some north German trading cities, which were bound together in the Hanseatic League (or Hansa). It was a powerful organisation, able to wrest privileges from kings and to monopolise trade in the Baltic. However, the greatest commercial cities, those in northern Italy, were doomed to decline, and the discovery of the New World marked the rise of the newly united states on the Atlantic coast. The city-state gave way to the nation-state.

THE RENAISSANCE

Medieval man did not readily disobey authority or criticise its pronouncements. When he was told that the pope was head of the Church, or that the earth was the centre of the universe, he accepted it without question, so his ideas remained fixed and unchanging. Then in the fifteenth and sixteenth centuries the Renaissance produced a remarkable change in his attitude.

The Renaissance, as its name suggests, began simply as a renewed interest in the ancient world of the Greeks and Romans. Not that medieval man had no knowledge of such matters: the Greek thinker Aristotle had a large following; Latin was the language of the Church, government, law-courts, and diplomacy; and of the Vulgate, the official version of the Bible. But in the fifteenth century European scholars became enthusiastic about the playwrights, thinkers, and poets of Athens and Rome. They searched for old manuscripts, translated ancient writers into Italian, and studied classical statues and buildings.

Italy was the natural birth-place of this 'new learning'. The monuments of ancient Rome excited the imagination; Italian merchants, trading at Byzantium, also acquired a knowledge of the classics. As interest grew, Italian scholars were patronised by the rich merchants and old noble families who together ruled Florence, Venice, Genoa, and the other city states. In this way the scholars gained money and leisure to delve into the mysteries of the ancient world.

The Italian Renaissance owed its inspiration to the classics. Writers, painters, and sculptors (men like Fra Angelico, Leonardo da Vinci, Michaelangelo, and Raphael) tried to emulate them. But it also taught men to think for themselves, and they experimented with new ideas and methods. It produced new and exciting literature and art. Great Italian artists and writers adapted classical models and were inspired by them, but they did not merely copy them. Meanwhile the Church watched over them with a fatherly eye. Indeed the popes were among their leading patrons: one founded the Vatican library; another built St. Peter's, which Michaelangelo adorned with paintings of great beauty. It was only when the scholars of the 'new learning' began to criticise the Church that religion and Renaissance became opposed to each other.

The Renaissance was not confined to Italy. It spread northwards over the Alps, into the towns of Germany, the Netherlands, and England. Everywhere it produced the same effects: a renewed interest in the language, literature, ideas, and opinions of the ancient world; new artistic achievements; a desire to enquire after the truth. So, in Germany, Cardinal Nicholas of Cusa discovered some Roman plays and published them, and Albert Dürer produced engravings which were rich in beauty and feeling. Above all the Germans developed the art of printing. John Gutenberg, the 'father' of printing, set up the first press in 1454. By the end of the century many German towns had presses, and German printers had carried the art to Italy (1465), Paris, and Spain. One of them taught the art to William Caxton, who in 1476 set up his press at Westminster. The invention of printing was of momentous importance: without it literature would have remained a pleasure of the rich few who could afford costly manuscripts; it made universal education possible; and it carried the ideas of Renaissance thinkers to a much wider public. Meanwhile the burghers of the Flemish and Dutch towns were patronising painters, and in England Greek and

Latin were being studied and taught. The Renaissance was truly an international movement.

As we have seen, the classics encouraged a spirit of enquiry. Scholars ceased to accept old beliefs at their face value. They became curious and critical; they cast doubts on old notions and questioned the authority of medieval institutions. So men began to reinterpret old ideas in thought, the arts, and sciences—and finally in religion. Renaissance thinkers showed a great interest in Man. They had a profound belief in his ability to improve things or put them right, so naturally they were full of hope for the future. This was particularly true of the humanists, who were less interested in the Church and religion than they were in the individual. Philosophers, geographers, scientists, and theologians studied Man and the environments, some man-made and some natural, in which he found himself:

(*1*) *Man in Society*. In the feudal system of the countryside everyone had his appointed place in society, above which he ought not to rise; but the growth of trade and town-life gave the individual greater opportunity. This was not always a good thing. There were fewer restraints on the rich who often exploited their workers. And the wage-earner had much less security than the peasant with his plot of land. Some humanists disapproved of this new spirit of greed. Sir Thomas More condemned those merchants—and landlords too—who worked for profit regardless of the suffering they caused.

(*2*) *Man and the State*. Renaissance princes were guided less in their behaviour by religion or morals. They did not try to do what was right; they did what was good for their people, their families, or themselves. This was not an altogether new spirit. Niccolo Machiavelli was an Italian who had worked for the government of Florence. His book, *The Prince*, explained the methods which a prince should use in order to govern his realm successfully. His government ought not to be guided by a desire to do what was morally right; instead it must act with cunning, deceit, and ruthlessness—only success was right in politics. However Machiavelli was putting forward no new ideas. He was simply writing down what had been practised by kings for a long time.

(*3*) *Man and his World*. In the Middle Ages Europeans had thought that the Mediterranean Sea was the heart of the world. The discovery of the New World broadened their horizons and

2

sparked their imaginations. Old notions about the shape of the world[1] and the number of continents were thrown aside.

(4) *Man and the Universe.* The enquiring minds of Renaissance men turned to astronomy too. It was an accepted belief that the earth was the centre of the universe, and that the sun and other stars revolved around it. A Polish clergyman, Copernicus, proved that the earth moved round the sun. So yet another medieval belief was overthrown.

(5) *Man and God.* It was inevitable that sooner or later the scholars of the Renaissance should adopt a critical attitude to the Church. When they read the Latin Vulgate they could not find anything to justify the pope's supremacy. And when they looked at the Church they found much to criticise: lax clerics, ignorance, and superstition. Erasmus, a Flemish monk, took the lead in the attack on abuses. He was a humanist; he was also an international figure who travelled widely. Erasmus found plenty to attack: Pope Julius II, clad in armour, going off to war at the head of his army; the luxury of popes and corruption amongst the clergy. He despised the monks. And he mocked at the practice of many monasteries in keeping sacred relics, which pilgrims could see on payment of a fee. Erasmus, in common with the other humanists, wanted to reform not split the Church. But by publishing translations of the Bible he paved the way for the protestants.

THE EFFECTS OF THE RENAISSANCE

(*1*) It produced new ideas on education. New teaching methods were used. More important, thanks to the printing press, fresh ideas were carried to the entire reading public.

(*2*) Roman law came back to Italy from Byzantium. Based on the laws of ancient Rome, it tended to place all authority in the hands of the father (in the family) and of the king (in the State). It exercised great influence on men in the sixteenth century and encouraged the growth of absolutism.

(*3*) It led on to the reform and schism of the Church. The humanists' criticism of the Church provided ample ammunition for others who believed that the only solution was to break away and establish their own Church. The men of the Renais-

---

[1] Few people, even in the Middle Ages, believed that the world was flat. But it was not until Magellan sailed round the globe that its real shape was finally proved.

sance did not mean this to happen. It was unintentional, but they made it inevitable.

(*4*) In the Middle Ages religion was of paramount importance. The Renaissance challenged its supremacy by encouraging men to think more of life in this world.

HENRY VII AND EUROPE

Although Henry Tudor became king at a time when Europe was undergoing many changes, one thing remained constant: France was still the traditional enemy of England. However, during the Wars of the Roses, the French king had favoured the Lancastrians, Henry Tudor's party. On the other hand Burgundy, England's ally during the Hundred Years' War, had supported the Yorkists, and after Bosworth the duchess of Burgundy assisted the Yorkist pretenders and sheltered their followers. Therefore it might appear that Henry's natural ally was France, and his obvious enemy Burgundy. Such a policy would also remove the constant threat of a Scottish invasion. However the nation had a deep and abiding enmity towards France; whilst the sheepfarmers, clothworkers, clothiers, and merchants depended for their livelihood on the Flemish cloth trade. If Henry VII wanted to retain his newly-won crown, he had to avoid foolish acts which might turn his subjects against him.

Thus Henry's foreign policy was determined by his immediate personal needs:

(*1*) to make his rather shaky position more secure by discouraging foreign powers from helping the Yorkists, and by gaining recognition from the more important European rulers.

(*2*) to foster trade. This would make him popular, and at the same time increase his income from customs dues.

(*3*) to marry his sons, Arthur and Henry, to European princesses, so as to ensure the continuance of the Tudor dynasty.

(*4*) to avoid expensive wars if possible, for heavy taxes would only make him unpopular.

In view of the national feeling against France, Henry was not in a position to make a friend of the French king. Neither could he ally with France's old enemy, Burgundy. Margaret, the duchess, was filled with an unquenchable hatred of the Lancastrians, and remained a constant threat to Henry's throne.

It was not until 1491 that England found an ally. Ferdinand

of Aragon feared the growing strength of the French king.
Henry took advantage of this to negotiate the Treaty of Medina
del Campo with him. It clearly reveals the main objects of
Henry's foreign policy. Catherine, the younger daughter of
Ferdinand and Isabella, was to wed his eldest son, Arthur.
Furthermore Spain gave important trading privileges to English
merchants. In return Henry bound himself to support
Ferdinand in a war against France. He had no appetite for
costly wars; he was simply fulfilling his part of a valuable
bargain.

Henry's subjects were always willing to strike a blow against
France. When he declared that he meant to revive the old
claim to the French crown, parliament voted him £100,000. He
used it to raise an army which he led in person across the Channel
in 1492. Charles VIII was sufficiently impressed to buy his
neutrality. By the Treaty of Etaples he promised to pay Henry
a sizeable pension. He also agreed to expel Perkin Warbeck
from France, an action which implied that he recognised Henry
as rightful king of England.

Two years later the Italian Wars began. Henry wisely refused
to get involved. In any case he had his hands full with plots at
home and the threat of Perkin Warbeck abroad. The Yorkist
pretender secured the support of Margaret of Burgundy,
Emperor Maximilian, Scotland, and parts of Ireland. Henry
retaliated. He placed an embargo on trade with the Netherlands, Maximilian's richest possession. The embargo inflicted
hardship on the English merchants who sold most of their raw
wool and unfinished cloth to the Flemish cloth towns. However,
it was even worse for the Flemings who could not survive without
these raw materials. By 1496 Philip who ruled the Netherlands
for Maximilian, his father, was ready to come to terms. He
signed the Magnus Intercursus. It ended the embargo and
permitted free trade between England and Flanders.

By 1497 Warbeck was in Henry's hands and he could breathe
easily. For the rest of his reign he continued his sound but
unadventurous foreign policy. He sought better trade terms for
his merchants. In 1506 the Malus Intercursus gave the English
more favourable trading rights in Flanders than the Flemings
themselves. This aroused the Flemish merchants to bitter
opposition and was soon abandoned. He was more successful
in his policy of marrying his children into the royal houses of

Europe. As we have seen, Ferdinand of Aragon had agreed to marry his daughter, Catherine, to Henry's son, Arthur. Even so it was only after the execution of Warwick and Warbeck that Ferdinand would allow his daughter to come to England. In 1501 she married Arthur, but he died in the following year. Henry VII did not wish to lose the Spanish alliance or Catherine's dowry, so he compelled Ferdinand to agree that she should marry Arthur's younger brother, Henry. Although the Church forbade a man to marry his brother's widow, Pope Julius II was persuaded to grant a dispensation which would permit Henry to do so. In 1503 he was betrothed to Catherine, who remained in England until they were married in 1509, soon after Henry's death.

Suitable marriages were arranged for Henry's other children: Margaret became the wife of James IV of Scotland; and Mary, after her father's death, married Louis XII of France. Europe's kings clearly regarded the Tudors as the ruling house of England.

In his last years Henry became more daring. He took part in the confusing diplomatic manoeuvres of the time—he even proposed to marry Joanna, Ferdinand's insane daughter. However he would not become involved in wars, and when he died in 1509 he had achieved all that he had set out to do. His foreign policy had been cautious and lacked splendour, but it had served England well.

IV

CARDINAL WOLSEY

THE EARLY YEARS OF HENRY VIII

HENRY VIII was very different from his cautious painstaking father. He was all that men expected a Renaissance king to be. He was tall and robust, a keen sportsman, and reputed to be the handsomest prince in Christendom. In addition he studied theology, played the lute and harpsichord, and patronised artists and scholars. The humanists crowded to his court; Erasmus wrote, 'That king of yours may bring back the golden age.' Never was a king more popular, and never did a nation have such high hopes of its ruler.

Yet beneath the bluff, hearty exterior Henry was ambitious and ruthless. Once he dined at Sir Thomas More's home and afterwards walked in the garden, his arm around his host's shoulders. More was not deceived by this mark of friendship: 'If my head could win him a castle in France, it should not fail to go.' One of Henry's first actions as king revealed his ruthlessness. He wanted to make himself popular; and what better way than to punish his father's hated advisers, Richard Empson and Edmund Dudley. These unfortunate men paid the penalty for loyal service to a Tudor king. They were tried on a trumped-up charge of treason and sent to the block.

Henry VIII was heir to the claims of both Lancaster and York. As his throne was secure, he could turn his attention to matters of foreign policy. He was eager for prestige and anxious to display his talents in war. Certainly European politics gave him the opportunity to do so. France and Spain were grappling for the control of Italy. Pope Julius II saw with alarm that Italy, and with it the papacy, was in danger of falling into French hands. Henry was only too willing to help him: he could revive his claim to the French crown and so strike a blow at England's traditional enemy. In 1512 he launched himself into European politics.

Henry VIII's first war was successful. In 1513 he led his army to victory over the French in the 'Battle of the Spurs'.[1] As a result he captured Therouanne and Tournai. Meanwhile danger threatened nearer home. James IV of Scotland revived the 'auld alliance' with France. In August 1513 he invaded England with a large force, but was routed at Flodden by the old earl of Surrey. James IV and a number of Scottish nobles were among the many thousands slaughtered. Surrey had ended the Scottish threat for many years to come: the new king, James V, was a child and his mother, Henry VIII's sister Margaret, acted as regent.

In 1514 Henry made peace with Louis XII: he received Tournai and a large pension; and the treaty was sealed with the marriage of his younger sister, Mary, to the French king. Henry

[1] So named because of the rapid flight of the French from the battlefield.

was well satisfied. He had tasted success and glory, and for the time being it was enough.

Within three years the European scene underwent a startling change. In 1514 Louis XII died; and Ferdinand in 1516. They were succeeded by young rulers who were full of ambition: Francis I became king of France, and Ferdinand's grandson, Charles, inherited Spain. Francis I invaded Italy, won a crushing victory at Marignano, and seized Milan. Once again France threatened to dominate Italy. However, this time Henry took no heed. He was too busy gambolling with his players, wrestlers, musicians, and fellow hunters. Furthermore the dull routine of governing England bored him. But by then Henry had found in Thomas Wolsey the man who would shoulder the burden of government for him.

WOLSEY'S RISE TO POWER

Thomas Wolsey, the son of a cattle-dealer, was born in Ipswich in 1473. He was educated at Oxford and then entered the Church; as a man of consuming ambition he knew that the Church offered the one path to promotion for men of humble birth. He began his career as a chaplain to the archbishop of Canterbury, but in 1507 he entered royal service when Bishop Fox of Winchester introduced him into the court of Henry VII. Later, Henry VIII was quick to recognise the ability of Wolsey, who became almoner, dean of Lincoln, and a member of the king's council. In 1513 he organised and supplied Henry VIII's army in Flanders; for this service he was rewarded with the bishoprics of Tournai and Lincoln; in 1514 he was raised to the archbishopric of York; and in the following year Henry made him lord chancellor. By hard work and ability Wolsey had gained Henry's complete confidence and ousted the other councillors. He continued to acquire power and wealth: Pope Leo X made him a cardinal (1515) and Henry VIII made him bishop of Bath and Wells (1518), which he exchanged for Durham (1524) and finally Winchester, the richest bishopric in England. He also became abbot of Saint Albans from which he drew a large income. Yet no matter how rich and powerful he became, Wolsey always sought more. As lord chancellor he stood next to the king and could go no higher, but in the Church his ambitious eyes turned towards the papacy. When he was appointed papal legate in 1518 he took a step towards the fulfilment of his lifelong ambition to become pope. A legate was appointed by the pope to exercise some of his powers in a particular country. There were two kinds: the native-born legate who held the office for life, and the *legatus a latere* who was sent from Rome with special papal powers in order to solve some urgent problem—his appointment was temporary, but during that time his ecclesiastical authority was supreme in the country to which he was sent. Wolsey became *legatus a latere*, although he had not been sent from the papacy. Furthermore he was appointed for life. So he acquired a position superior to that of even the aged Archbishop Warham of Canterbury. As lord chancellor and permanent legate, Wolsey dominated State and Church in England until his fall in 1529.

WOLSEY'S DOMESTIC POLICY

Wolsey was vain, ostentatious, and extravagant; he even built two palaces, York House in Westminster and Hampton Court near Kingston, where he lived in great state. He has often been severely criticised because with this accumulation of wealth and power he carried out few reforms in government. Naturally he has suffered by comparison with his successor, Thomas Cromwell, who was responsible for many of the profound changes in the 1530's. But it must be remembered that Cromwell and his king were carrying through a revolution. This had become necessary because Wolsey had failed to find a less drastic way to annul Henry VIII's marriage to Catherine of Aragon. However, a revolution was not needed, or desired, during Wolsey's term of office. In fact the cardinal was simply the chief minister of a medieval government whose essential functions were few: to ensure justice, maintain law and order, protect the kingdom from attack, and defend the Church. Foreign affairs were also the king's concern; his policy was guided by his personal interests or those of his family, and usually did not affect the nation unless it harmed trade or required fresh taxes. A medieval minister was not expected to carry out reforms in government. Indeed if he had done so, he would probably have been treated with suspicion and mistrust. So, like many a minister before him, Wolsey contented himself with carrying out the normal functions of government.

Many of the nobles and gentry detested Wolsey as an upstart of low birth, who kept all power in his own hands and deprived them of their rightful share in the government of the country. But so long as Wolsey retained the king's trust his opponents could not remove him. Indeed, though he was the effective ruler of England for fifteen years, his great authority rested entirely on Henry VIII's confidence in him—when that disappeared, so did his power.

Wolsey was hostile to any person or institution which might reduce his power. Thus he preferred to manage without parliament. Although it met four times between 1509 and 1515, it was only summoned once under Wolsey—in 1523. And even then it was only summoned because the government needed money. Wolsey was a very bad financier. His foreign policy cost more than the king could afford. By 1522, when war with France broke out, Wolsey was desperate for money. A forced loan did not provide enough and, in 1523, parliament had to be called. However, it refused to meet his exorbitant demands and offered only half the sum which he wanted. So in 1524 Wolsey was compelled to introduce another forced loan. He called it the 'Amicable Grant'; this was intended to suggest that men should lend money to the king out of love for him. But everyone knew that the money would go to finance the cardinal's ambitious foreign policies. Discontent spread rapidly. Many resisted the tax-collectors with violence. Further trouble was prevented by Henry, who personally intervened to cancel the Amicable Grant. Wolsey had obtained no money; he had simply made himself even more unpopular.

It was in the field of law that Wolsey had most success. As lord chancellor he had wide judicial powers, especially in the prerogative courts of chancery, of star chamber, and of requests. Chancery was a civil court concerned with disputes over property, wills, and contracts; its decisions were based on equity (fairness). Wolsey overhauled it, making it work more rapidly and efficiently. His work in star chamber was even more impressive: he turned it into a cheap court for all subjects, whether rich or poor. He often sat as a judge himself, meted out justice impartially, and tried to make everyone obey the king's laws. Likewise, he revived and increased the activity of the poor men's court of requests. As a result Wolsey was popular with the common people. But he made many enemies amongst the nobles and gentry by his readiness to punish them for breaches of the law.

2*

WOLSEY AND THE CHURCH IN ENGLAND

It is in the affairs of the Church that Wolsey is most deserving of criticism. He was well aware that there were glaring weaknesses in the Church and he claimed that he intended to reform them. Yet he did nothing more than dissolve a few small and decayed monasteries and use the proceeds to found two colleges: one at Ipswich and the other, Cardinal College, at Oxford (1525).

That Wolsey went no further with reform was partly due to his time-consuming commitments in foreign affairs and the law-courts. Above all, he could hardly carry out a drastic reform of abuses when he was guilty of so many of them himself. He neglected the spiritual duties of his various offices, and bribes were taken and offices were sold. And although he was a priest he had several daughters and a son, Thomas Winter, whom he placed in the Church. Indeed the purpose of his various offices was to give him riches and authority, rather than the means to reform.

WOLSEY'S FOREIGN POLICY

The apparent purpose of Wolsey's foreign policy was to raise England's prestige in Europe. But he was in fact more concerned with the papacy and its position in Italy. The pope was caught up in the long conflict between the Hapsburgs and Valois for the possession of Milan. There was a danger that Italy, and with it the pope, would be dominated by the victor of this struggle. So Wolsey intervened in the Italian Wars to guarantee the pope's freedom of action. He was not simply concerned with being loyal to the papacy. If ever he fulfilled his ambition to become pope, he would not want to find himself a mere puppet in the hands of the emperor or the French king. In the same way his ambitions led him to choose the Hapsburg emperor as his ally. He supported Maximilian until his death in 1519, and then Charles V, who could give him the support of Spanish, German, and Italian cardinals in the next papal election. The English merchants also favoured the alliance for the emperor ruled Flanders which was the major market for English wool.

In 1518 came Wolsey's moment of triumph. After long talks in London, he successfully concluded a peace treaty between England, France, Spain, the Holy Roman Empire, and the pope.

Furthermore, they agreed to join together in a common defence against the Turks, whose armies threatened Hungary and whose ships controlled the Mediterranean. Wolsey's desire for a crusade against the Turks revealed how medieval he was, for the age of crusades had long since passed. But he had done something new: he had made England appear an important power in European politics. He was praised on all sides for his achievement. Yet when Emperor Maximilian died in 1519 the new alliance was soon forgotten. Charles, the only grandson of both Ferdinand of Aragon and Maximilian, had already inherited Spain on Ferdinand's death in 1516; now he inherited Austria and was elected Emperor Charles V. He regarded Milan, at present in French hands, as the essential link between Germany and Spain. Charles and Francis I prepared for war and both sought England's help.

Francis was the first to offer an alliance. Henry VIII agreed to discuss terms and in 1520 the two kings met in France, not far from Calais. A city of gaily coloured tents and marquees was erected for the occasion. Henry VIII and Francis I arrived, each escorted by a vast following of gorgeously-attired nobles, soldiers, and officials. Talks were held in intervals between the many banquets, tournaments, and entertainments. But nothing came of it all. And the festivities did nothing to reduce the mutual suspicions of the two kings. The result of this meeting, the famous 'Field of Cloth of Gold', was not an alliance but only a considerable expense; in 1521 Wolsey joined Charles V and the pope in a treaty aimed against France.

Although Wolsey had remained true to his imperial alliance, England gained no advantage from it. By 1525 even Wolsey doubted its value. It was then that Charles V defeated the French army and captured Francis I at Pavia. The whole of Italy, including the papacy, passed under the emperor's sway. So in 1526 Wolsey decided to change sides, and England and France joined forces against Charles in the League of Cognac.

Wolsey was not trying to maintain a 'balance of power' in Europe, by siding with the weaker country against the stronger. It has sometimes been suggested that he even invented this idea— but it was practised long before his time. In any case such an idea did not interest him. Since 1519 Charles V had appeared to bestride the world like a colossus: he was ruler of Germany, Spain, Naples, the Netherlands, and much of the New World, and his lands encircled France. Yet England had loyally supported him against Francis. When Wolsey finally changed sides after Pavia, he did so for personal reasons: in 1522 and again in 1523 Charles V had failed to support the cardinal as a candidate in the papal election. And now the pope's freedom was threatened by Charles' victory at Pavia. Wolsey hoped that an Anglo-French force would drive Charles from Italy, and that a grateful Francis would back him at the next papal election. The French alliance proved to be a disappointment—and it was fatal to Wolsey. He ignored the traditional English hatred of France, and the harm which might be done to the cloth trade with Flanders. Most important of all, soon after Wolsey had deserted Charles V, Henry decided to end his marriage to Catherine of Aragon.

Henry married his brother's widow in 1509, and for some years they were happy together. But now Henry wanted a divorce. The real reason for this has long been a matter for dispute. Henry himself claimed that doubts had arisen in his mind about the validity of his marriage; in particular he had come to believe that Julius II had exceeded his powers when he granted the dispensation.[1] Except for Princess Mary, all his children had died when very young. This strengthened his belief that he had incurred God's anger by marrying his sister-in-law. There seems little reason to doubt Henry's explanation of his desire for a divorce. But it was not the only reason.

Henry desperately needed a male heir to succeed him as king. True, he had a daughter Mary, but no woman had ruled since Matilda in the twelfth century. It was doubtful whether the nation would accept a queen. And even if it did, the surviving Yorkists might rekindle the Wars of the Roses. Henry VIII always dreaded this. He had to have a son, in order to remove the danger of a disputed succession—and Catherine had failed to give him one.

By 1527 Henry had found a suitable second wife: Anne Boleyn, daughter of one of his courtiers. His desire to marry her finally prompted him to seek a divorce from Catherine. Wolsey was well aware that his position depended upon his ability to get the king what he wanted. So he asked Pope Clement VII to declare Julius II's dispensation null and void.

[1] See page 29.

In the normal course of events Clement would have been unwilling to offend Henry, who was a loyal and orthodox catholic. But in 1527 the war in Italy complicated the situation. Charles V's army, unpaid and mutinous, marched on Rome, sacked it, and took Clement prisoner. And even when the emperor restored order in his army, the pope remained a captive. Clement was now in a difficult position. Charles was Catherine's nephew and he would not allow her marriage to be annulled, partly because Wolsey had deserted him for Francis. Although he released the pope from captivity in 1528 he kept a close watch on him. Clement was afraid to offend either the emperor or the English king, so he simply played for time.

Wolsey was desperate. If he failed to get Henry his divorce he was finished. He continued to press the pope for a decision. Finally in April 1528 Clement appointed a commission to consider the case. When the two commissioners were named, Wolsey was one of them. Henry's hopes of a favourable decision rose. But Clement secretly instructed the other commissioner, Campeggio, the Italian absentee bishop of Salisbury, to delay the hearing for as long as possible. Although Campeggio arrived in England in October 1528, he managed to postpone the opening of the commissioners' court at Blackfriars until March 1529. The proceedings dragged on, but by July Henry was confident of a favourable verdict. And it was then that Charles V forced the pope to recall the case to Rome. Wolsey had failed.

Worse was to follow. In August, Francis I and Charles V signed the Treaty of Cambrai. Charles was left supreme in Italy, with the pope a puppet in his hands. To add insult to injury the two combatants made peace without consulting England. No longer could Wolsey hope to defeat Charles by an alliance with Francis. Indeed his foreign policy had produced nothing of value at all—and, fatal for the cardinal, it had not given Henry his divorce. The penalty for failure was dismissal. In October 1529 he was forced to give up the chancellorship, and he retired to York to administer his archbishopric. Yet he could not resist the temptation to dabble in politics. In 1530 Henry accused him of intriguing with France and summoned him to London to answer the charge. But Wolsey's trial was not to be. He was a sick man, and at Leicester, on his leisurely way southwards, he died (24 November 1530).

WOLSEY'S ACHIEVEMENT

Wolsey can be criticised for many things which he did not do or did badly: he mismanaged the king's finances; his foreign policy, though spectacular, achieved nothing in the long run; and he ignored his splendid opportunity to reform the Church. Yet he rendered a great service to order and justice. Sir Thomas Smith, one of Queen Elizabeth's advisers, wrote of star chamber: 'This court began long before, but took great authority at that time that Cardinal Wolsey, archbishop of York, was chancellor of England, who of some was thought to have first devised the court because that he augmented the authority of it, which was at that time marvellous necessary.' At least this was to Wolsey's credit.

THE REFORMATION
1529–1559

V

THE CONDITION OF THE CHURCH

INTRODUCTION

In England the Church was divided into two archbishoprics of Canterbury and York. The archbishop of Canterbury was the 'Primate of All England'. Bishops controlled the dioceses, into which the archbishoprics were divided. Their task was to supervise the spiritual life of their dioceses, suppress heresy, and discipline the clergy under their control. These were the secular clergy (parish priests). Some were appointed by the bishops or by the king, but many were chosen by private patrons who owned churches.

The bishops had little control over the regular clergy, those men who had dedicated their lives completely to God and had taken the vows of poverty, chastity, and obedience. The regular clergy were of two kinds: monks (and nuns) and the friars. Apart from the world, the monks were intended to lead a life of meditation, study, and prayer. They lived under their abbots in monasteries, many of which were situated in bleak and isolated places. Yet they had some contact with the world outside: providing education, charity, and food and shelter for travellers were amongst their most important responsibilities. They also farmed or rented out their great estates.

The friars' task was different: they had to go out into the world and preach. Like the monks, they could own no property. Though some of the friaries were very rich their wealth was meant to be used for religious and social purposes.

39

In addition there was a host of minor clerks.   They were not priests, but men employed by the Church to help in the administration of its lands and courts.

THE CONDITION OF THE ENGLISH CHURCH IN 1529

In the early sixteenth century the English Church was unpopular and often criticised.   Much of this criticism was justified.   The parish priests were uneducated and poor.   They envied the upper clergy who were wealthy and ostentatious. Little attention was paid to spiritual affairs by the leaders of the Church: the bishops interested themselves in politics, whilst the abbots farmed their estates.   Many of them were guilty of simony (the sale of offices in the Church), nepotism (the grant of offices to relatives), and pluralism (holding more than one benefice; a pluralist took the income but failed to carry out the duties of his benefices).   There were even cases of immorality among the clergy.

The 800 monasteries in England were in decline.   Few had more than twenty monks and the 600 smaller monasteries had a total of less than 3,000 monks.   It was popularly believed that there was much immorality and laxity in the monasteries.   This was an exaggeration of the truth.   In some houses the number of monks was increasing, standards were high, and discipline strict.   But it is what the public thought that mattered.   They felt that, as the Church seemed to have lost its spiritual purpose, it should be made to part with some of its wealth.   Actually the worst feature of the monasteries was not immorality but worldliness.   Charity for the poor and lodging for travellers were less important than hospitality for the gentry and nobles, who came to dine and hunt with the monks.

The friars were as unpopular as the monks.   Originally they had observed the vow of poverty and all the money which they had obtained by begging had been handed over to their friaries. But now they had become greedy money-grubbers.

The wealth of the Church was an object of envy to Englishmen. During the Middle Ages the Church had received many gifts of land from laymen, who wished to show their respect and devotion.   In particular the monasteries had become wealthy in this way.   By the sixteenth century the Church owned nearly one third of the land in England.   Some of the bishops and abbots were richer than any of the nobles.   However, the Church and clergy had lost the respect and devotion which had led to the gifts of land. Indeed many thought that the Church had too much wealth. They wanted to obtain its lands, many of which were badly managed. As landlords, many of the clergy were as harsh as any of the nobles and gentry.

The Church's taxes were disliked, especially the tithes for the upkeep of individual churches. But the most hated payment was the mortuary fee which had to be paid before a body could be buried in a church cemetery. Its courts were even more unpopular. They existed alongside the king's courts and dealt with all cases concerning the clergy. They also had control over laymen in all matters concerning marriage, divorce, wills, moral offences, and heresy. These courts now failed to serve a useful purpose and were often misused, especially when they enforced the payment of Church taxes.

Not only the laity but also the king was affected by the privileges of the Church. Benefit of clergy protected any man in holy orders against punishment for his first crime. This privilege extended even to minor clerks, who were not priests. The ability to read and write qualified a man to become a minor clerk. Many rogues did so to avoid punishment for their crimes. Furthermore the clergy were tried, not in the king's courts, but in the Church courts where punishments were lighter. Criminals who were not clerks could escape from the king's justice as well: many churches with their graveyards were sanctuaries, in which a criminal could take refuge from the law. Once there he could not be seized; he was then given the choice of surrendering to the king's justice or leaving the kingdom. There were several very large sanctuaries, such as the Palatine County of Durham, in which the bishop's courts replaced the king's law.

This was a situation of which no king could approve. It meant that some of his kingdom and many of his subjects were outside the control of his courts. Behind all this lay the real problem of the dual loyalty of the clergy: as the king's subjects they owed obedience to him, but they were also loyal to the pope as the supreme head of the Church. In the past the English clergy, more often than not, had supported the pope in his struggle with the king for control of the Church. The pope's power to interfere did not stop there: he could tax the clergy; he chose priests, often Italians, for offices in the English Church;

cases in the Church courts could be transferred from England to Rome, at the pope's command.

Such a situation was becoming intolerable to the independent spirit of England. Steps had already been taken to remedy this state of affairs. In the fourteenth century a number of statutes known as Praemunire had been passed to limit the pope's power in the Church. In 1512 an act of parliament took away benefit of clergy from minor clerks; other acts limited the right of sanctuary. But this did little to alter the fact that the king was not master in his own house.

The Church had one last chance to save itself when Wolsey was papal legate. But Wolsey's failure to reform showed that the Church was not prepared to set its house in order. Therefore it would have to be done by the king. After Wolsey's downfall the clergy were not even in a position to unite against Henry VIII's attack. Wolsey had exercised the pope's power. His overbearing manner had made that power hateful to the clergy, and they were unwilling to defend the pope's rights. In any case many of the bishops had received their offices as rewards for faithful service to the king. They were not prepared to turn against him now.

THE DECLINE IN THE PRESTIGE OF THE PAPACY

Much of the hostility towards the Church was due to the fact that the papacy itself no longer commanded respect. The papal court at Rome was more extravagant and corrupt than any other in Europe, and popes were more interested in politics than religion. Cesare Borgia, the son of Pope Alexander VI (1492–1503), conquered central Italy, which was then attached to the papacy. As a political rival to the kings and princes of western Europe, the pope could hardly be the impartial ruler of Christendom. Englishmen, who had disliked the interference of the head of the Universal Church, resented far more deeply the power of an Italian prince.

THE LUTHERAN REFORMATION

The English Church was influenced by two movements on the continent. The first of these was the Reformation. This began as a movement for the reform of the Roman catholic Church and ended in the establishment of new rival Churches. There was indeed a great need for reform. The many abuses which weakened the English Church were also to be found on the continent. Many people disliked the pomp and ceremony of the Church and wanted a simple form of Christianity. This desire for reform was supported by the German princes, but for a very different reason. Government was becoming more expensive and the princes wanted to increase their income by seizing the lands of the Church.

Martin Luther, the first man to found a rival religion, was less concerned with the many abuses in the Church. Of peasant stock, he was born in Saxony in the empire in 1483. He became an Augustinian monk and in 1509 he was appointed professor in the university of Wittenburg, newly created by the elector of Saxony. Luther was dissatisfied with the doctrines of the Church. Gradually, through constant study of the Bible, he came to hold new and heretical opinions: pilgrimages, charity, Indulgences and other 'good works' did not help a man to find salvation; the Bible was the source of all truth, and each man should be allowed to read it and discover the truth for himself (the Church insisted that it alone could interpret the Bible—it was not for mere men to do this).

Luther did not express his heretical views publicly until 1517. In that year Pope Leo X sent out friars to sell Indulgences, because he needed money to continue the building of St. Peter's at Rome. Sinners were normally required to confess their sins and to do penance to show that they had truly repented. But there had developed the practice of Indulgences, which sinners could buy instead of doing penance. Recent popes had made more extravagant claims: Julius II declared that Indulgences could replace both confession and penance. Now Leo X promised entry to heaven for the souls of all who bought them. This was too much for Luther. When the Dominican friar John Tetzel toured Saxony, selling Indulgences, Luther drew up 95 theses. These were written arguments intended to show that the sale of Indulgences was a fraud. He pinned these theses on the door of the castle church of Wittenburg on 31 October 1517.

Luther became famous overnight, because he represented German public feeling. He did not stop there. He publicly condemned the pictures, pilgrimages, confession, candles, and elaborate ceremonies of the Church. He went on to deny many of its principal doctrines. The Bible made no mention of the papacy, so in 1520 he condemned the office of pope, whom he called 'anti-Christ'. At the same time he called upon the German nobility to reform the Church. The pope could not allow Luther's challenge to go unanswered. Leo X issued a bull excommunicating Luther. The German monk replied by publicly burning it (1520).

The young Emperor Charles V was a devout Roman catholic. At the pope's request, he summoned Luther to appear before the diet (assembly of German princes) at Worms. Charles ordered him to give up his views, but Luther boldly refused. Thereupon the diet issued the Edict of Worms, which condemned Luther as an outlaw.

Luther was saved from punishment by some of the German princes, especially Frederick the Wise, the elector of Saxony. This kindly, peace-loving, and pious ruler favoured Luther's views and allowed them to flourish in Saxony. From here Lutheran doctrines spread far and wide through Germany.

Luther was very popular with all classes in Germany, especially with his own class, the peasantry. In 1523 the German peasants, suffering from the harsh rule of the nobles, rose in revolt. They expected Luther's support, but he condemned them. He believed that God appointed everyone to a certain social position with a certain duty: the peasants to farm, the knights to fight, the nobles and princes to rule. The peasantry owed obedience to their lords, and Luther could not forgive them for trying to deny their duty. He supported the princes as upholders of law and order. To prevent chaos in Germany he also called upon the princes to control the Church. Many of them answered his call; they adopted Lutheranism and made themselves masters of the Church in their lands, in order to seize monastic estates and increase their wealth.

So the Lutheran Church became firmly established in Germany. Its doctrines spread and even reached England, where they influenced a group of reformers in the university of Cambridge. It also set an example for those men in England who, like Thomas Cromwell, wished the king to control the Church.

HUMANISM

The second movement to influence the Church in England was Humanism, which was a product of the Renaissance. Humanism meant two things: a study of Greek and Latin classics, and a concern with human affairs rather than with religion. The continental humanists studied the classics and paid little attention to religion. However, the English humanists, with the exception of Thomas Linacre the famous physician and student of Greek, were not only classical scholars, but also devout and orthodox Roman catholics. The leading figure, Erasmus, was Dutch, but he often visited England. He issued the New Testament in the original Greek and a paraphrase in English. He also produced a Latin version which showed the errors of the Vulgate (the official Roman catholic version of the Bible).

The English humanists were patronised by Henry VIII and formed a brilliant group at his court. Dr John Colet, dean of St Paul's, was famed for his lectures on St Paul's Epistles. William Grocyn was a Greek scholar and teacher. His pupils included the greatest English humanist Sir Thomas More. More was an industrious worker with a very rapid brain and many interests: he wrote plays, studied Law, and learnt Greek. He was deeply religious, wore a hair shirt, and spent much time in prayer with the Carthusian monks at Charterhouse. His finest achievement was *Utopia*. It is in the form of a conversation between More and a traveller, Raphael Hythloday, who has returned from the imaginary land of Utopia in the New World. Raphael describes the way of life of the Utopians: how they work for only six hours a day; how they despise money and shun war. More was not concerned to portray a society which was godly and righteous. His book was a biting satire on the wickedness and sin of his own time; he was not expressing a liking for Utopia so much as disgust for much that he saw around him. Thus, whilst the Utopians loved peace and so were happy, Europeans preferred war with all the misery it caused. In fact, More was showing how much better was a society based on fairness and sound morals, than one based on war, love of power and riches.

The humanists were anxious to apply this 'new learning' to the reform of the Church. But they hoped to avoid a clash with the pope. As they were to find out, Henry VIII and his advisers were not of the same opinion.

VI

THE TUDOR REVOLUTION

THE REFORMATION PARLIAMENT

WOLSEY had failed to obtain Henry VIII's divorce with the help of the papacy. The king now turned to 'political blackmail': he threatened the pope with the direst consequences if he refused to do Henry's bidding. However, he had to be sure of the nation's support if he was going to bully the pope. And this could best be obtained by co-operating with members of the ruling class in parliament. So the king summoned parliament, which met in November 1529. It was to sit for 7 years, carry through momentous changes, and become famous as the 'Reformation Parliament'.

During the first months in session parliament was encouraged to reform abuses in the Church. Their dislike of priests and popes and their greed for Church lands made the commons willing accomplices of the king. In the house of lords some of the bishops and abbots remained loyal to the pope, but they were usually outvoted. As a result some important reforms were passed: pluralism and absenteeism were forbidden, and a scale of mortuary fees (charged for Christian burials) was laid down. Henry hinted to the pope that more drastic reforms might be made, curtailing his powers in the English Church, if he did not give the king his divorce.

Whilst the commons attacked abuses, Henry was listening to the advice of Thomas Cranmer, a Cambridge clerk, to seek the opinion of Europe's universities on his marriage. In 1530 this suggestion was adopted. Universities in France, Spain, Germany, and Italy, as well as Oxford and Cambridge, were consulted: some favoured Henry, others supported Pope Clement VII. Nothing of value was achieved, except to bring Cranmer to the notice of the king.

THE CLERGY SUBMIT TO THE KING: 1531

Although parliament supported Henry, there was a danger that the clergy might oppose him. He decided to bully them into obedience by using the famous Statute of Praemunire.[1]

[1] Enacted in 1393.

This protected the king's rights from encroachment by Church courts particularly those at Rome. Offenders were liable to forfeit their property. Henry argued that Wolsey had broken the law of praemunire, and as the clergy had not protested against his action they must share in his guilt. He threatened to deprive them of their lands and money and demanded that they should recognise him as Supreme Head of the Church. The clergy, meeting in convocation, surrendered. But their surrender was expressed vaguely, for they agreed to recognise him as Supreme Head only in so far as 'the law of Christ allows it'. The pope's supporters would certainly say that it did not. More definite was the £118,000 which the clergy had to pay Henry in order to obtain a royal pardon.

THE RISE OF THOMAS CROMWELL

In a crude fashion Henry had made sure that the clergy would not, or rather dare not, oppose him. But his divorce was no nearer. He needed a stronger policy and a strong minister to carry it through. The rise of Thomas Cromwell solved this problem. Cromwell was born in Putney in 1485, the son of a local smith. Little is known of his earlier years, but he seems to have travelled a good deal in Europe and studied Law. In 1520 he entered Wolsey's service, and when the cardinal decided to dissolve some monasteries to endow his new colleges, Cromwell was entrusted with the task. His career was endangered by the fall of his patron. However, he entered parliament in 1529 and distinguished himself by attacking the clergy. The king valued such supporters, and in 1530 he appointed Cromwell to his council. Within a year the new councillor had become one of Henry's closest advisers.

Cromwell made his fortune by offering to solve all of Henry's problems. His advice was simple: that the king should destroy the papal power in England. The pope's authority over the English Church was fourfold: he alone could approve or reject laws made by convocation (the Church's parliament); he consecrated bishops; he taxed the clergy; he was the supreme judge in matters of law, hearing cases referred to him if the Church courts in England were unable to solve them. Such authority was enforced by an oath which the clergy took, promising to remain loyal to the pope; and disobedient priests could be punished by excommunication. Cromwell intended to rob the pope of these powers and transfer them to the king. As master of his own Church Henry could require his archbishop to grant him a divorce. Furthermore he would control the enormous wealth of the Church. Cromwell's advice was simple. But put into force, its effects were profound and far-reaching.

DIVORCE AND REVOLUTION

In 1532 the attack on the pope's authority began. The house of commons was encouraged by Cromwell to present a petition, known as the 'Supplication against the Ordinaries', to Henry VIII. It complained that the laws of the Church, which were made by convocation, did not require the king's assent; and it asked that this might be changed. After a brief resistance convocation (in a document entitled 'The Submission of the Clergy') recognised the king instead of the pope as the supreme lawmaker of the Church.

At the same time the first Act of Annates was passed. This abolished annates, a tax paid by newly appointed bishops to the pope, and arranged for the archbishop of Canterbury to consecrate (dedicate and bless) new bishops. However Henry was still hoping to obtain his divorce without a complete breach. Therefore he insisted that the act should not take effect until he had held further talks with the pope.

In 1532 Archbishop Warham of Canterbury died. Henry decided to appoint Thomas Cranmer as his successor. However, few men would recognise Cranmer as archbishop unless the pope consecrated him, so in January 1533 Henry forced Clement VII to do so, by threatening to enforce the Act of Annates. But on the question of the divorce the pope would not give way. Henry was driven at last to make a complete break. Indeed he was willing to do so now, because he had an archbishop who would do his bidding. On 25 January 1553 Henry secretly married Anne Boleyn. In March, parliament passed the Act 'in restraint of appeals', which placed the Church's courts under the king's control and forbade appeals from them to Rome. This meant that Cranmer could pass judgement on Henry's marriage to Catherine, and it made any appeal by the queen to the pope illegal. In May Henry permitted the archbishop to open his court at Dunstable. Catherine refused to appear and so Cranmer declared her marriage to the king null and void. A week later Anne Boleyn was crowned queen in Westminster Abbey.

The king and his minister had triumphed. Henry had got his divorce at last, and he was master of the Church into the bargain. But his hopes of obtaining a male heir were doomed to disappointment: in September 1533 Anne Boleyn gave birth to a daughter, Elizabeth. Furthermore the pope had not allowed Henry's actions to pass unchallenged. He excommunicated the king in July. Henry's answer was to enforce the suspended Act of Annates.

Further acts of parliament in 1543 completed the Tudor Revolution. A second Act of Annates confirmed the abolition of all taxes formerly paid to Rome. It also laid down the procedure for electing bishops: the king was to choose and the clergy to confirm his choice. An Act 'for the submission of the clergy' confirmed convocation's surrender in 1532 and allowed appeals from the archbishop's court to the king. The old papal taxes were transferred to the king. Finally the Act of Supremacy recognised the position which Henry had acquired: that he 'justly and rightfully is Supreme Head of the Church of England'. It was his right to discipline the clergy, suppress heresy and punish abuses. He could appoint a vicar-general to take charge of convocation and visitors to inspect dioceses and monasteries. He not only controlled the law-making, courts and administration of the Church, but also its doctrines. Clearly the pope's power in England had been extinguished. Now the English Church was not a part of an international organisation, but a separate body. No longer was it the Church in England; now it was the Church of England. It was equally clear that the Church had been freed from papal control only to become the servant of the State. And the State, in the shape of Henry VIII, was to prove a harsher taskmaster than the popes had ever been.

Henry was still anxious about the succession to the throne. His divorce and remarriage had not been universally popular. Some men suggested that, unless Anne gave birth to a son in the future, Mary and not Elizabeth should succeed Henry. The king turned to parliament again. The Act of Succession (1534) acknowledged Henry's marriage to Anne and restricted the succession to their children. It was made a treasonable offence to oppose or deny Henry's second marriage. Furthermore, the king was empowered to make anyone take an oath to obey and accept the succession. Henry was still not satisfied. A Treason Act was enacted by parliament in 1534. It listed some old treasons, but included a new one: writing or saying that the king was a heretic, tyrant, schismatic or usurper. Such an act placed enormous power in the hands of Henry and Cromwell. And they were not afraid to use it.

Henry's revolution depended upon the support and consent of parliament. The nobles and gentry were anticlerical and greedy for church lands. Therefore they were willing to go along with Henry. This is not to say that there was no opposition: some M.P.s criticised the divorce; many wished to see the papacy reformed but not thrown out. However, the Treason Act was effective in silencing this opposition from all except a very few—and to this minority loyalty to the pope was more precious than life itself. It included some of the leading men of the day, especially Sir Thomas More, but they were very few in number.

Active opposition first appeared with the prophecies of the 'holy maid' or 'nun' of Kent. Elizabeth Barton was a poor serving maid who suffered from epilepsy. During attacks of this disease she had made prophecies, some of which came true. Her predictions were harmless enough until she came under the sway of a monk, Dr Edward Bocking, who used her to attack Henry. She foretold that Henry would lose his throne and die within six months if he obtained a divorce. The government realised that she was too dangerous to remain at large. So the nun and her confederates were arrested. Parliament passed a bill of attainder (this removed the need for a trial, for a bill of attainder simply declared that they were guilty; once passed it became law, and all that remained was to punish them for treason by execution). In April 1534 they were put to death at Tyburn.

The death of the holy maid of Kent did not end all active opposition. Sir Thomas More had had a long and honourable career in the king's service: as M.P. in 1504, speaker of the house of commons in 1523, and finally lord chancellor in 1529. As chancellor he had carried on the good work of Wolsey in star chamber. But troubled by the divorce, with which he could not agree, he felt bound to resign in 1532.

Henry VIII was a vindictive man. He wanted to punish More for deserting him. Consequently More was soon in serious trouble. Neither he nor Bishop Fisher of Rochester had approved of the divorce, whilst as good Roman catholics they were positively hostile to the royal supremacy. When in April 1534 they were required to take the oath, as laid down in the Act of Succession, they refused to condemn Henry's first marriage or to deny papal supremacy. The king imprisoned them in the Tower, until the new Treason Act of 1534 encouraged him to bring them to trial. Although More defended himself skilfully—he was after all a lawyer—he was defeated by a lie: Sir Richard Rich, the king's solicitor-general, claimed falsely that More had confided treasonable opinions to him. More was found guilty, so was Fisher. In the summer of 1535 they were executed.

There was little resistance elsewhere to the momentous changes of the years 1529–35. A few of the parish clergy were turned out of their livings, and one or two unfortunates were executed, but most of the clergy took the full oath as willingly as laymen. Even most of the monks did so. However, a few resisted: eight monks were put to death, others were subjected to a long imprisonment. Despite barbarous tortures and foul prison conditions, they all bore their hardship without breaking down. Yet the resistance of these opponents was in vain, for the royal supremacy was a fact.

THE DISSOLUTION OF THE MONASTERIES: FIRST STAGE

Henry and Cromwell now turned their attention to the monasteries. Unlike the parish clergy, the monks and friars were not subject to the regular discipline of bishops. Abbots were directly responsible to the pope for the standards in their houses. As they were obedient to the papacy, the monasteries remained a potential centre of opposition to Henry VIII. Therefore Henry meant to suppress them.

There was another reason: money. In an age of rising prices, the king's income was not enough for his needs. No wonder the government looked longingly upon the wealth of the Church. This wealth was enormous, comprising as it did nearly one-third of all the land in England, as well as tithes,[1] gold and silver plate and other valuables. The greater part of it was owned by the monasteries, and it was this which Henry aimed to seize. He was not being merely greedy. The monasteries did not need the huge income which they got from their property, whereas Henry could use it to carry out his duties as king more effectively.

---

[1] Tithes were payments made by all landowners. Some went to the vicar; the rest to the man who held the advowson (i.e. who had the right to appoint the vicar). Payments were in kind, e.g., meat, eggs, corn, etc.

In 1535 Cromwell was appointed vicar-general with the power to inspect monasteries. He sent out commissioners to assess the value of all ecclesiastical property, and their findings were recorded in a book called the *Valor Ecclesiasticus* ('the value of Church property'). Cromwell now had detailed knowledge of the wealth of the monasteries: a total income of over £110,000 a year from land and £25,000 more from other sources. In July 1535, he sent 'visitors' to inspect the religious houses. Their task was not to suppress abuses, but to show that the monasteries were in such a corrupt, worldly, and decayed condition that they were not fit to continue—in short to provide an excuse to dissolve them. They were ruthless and thorough; with great speed they hurried from one monastery to another, asking awkward questions and ferreting out scandals. Their reports to Cromwell showed that many of the houses were in a sorry state, but as this was what they had set out to prove, we cannot place too much trust in them.

In March 1536 Cromwell acted. He introduced into the commons a bill, whereby all religious houses with an income of less than £200 a year were dissolved. The larger monasteries survived for the time being. Cromwell had divided the monasteries into two groups for a practical purpose: the Tudor civil service was too small and antiquated to deal with the dissolution of them all at once. The commons passed the bill readily enough. Even the upper house did not resist—most of the bishops were king's men and the abbots had been bribed with the promise of fat pensions.

The act was straightway carried out. Royal officers visited the monasteries and seized their land and livestock, gold plate and jewels. They even stripped the valuable lead from the roofs. Cromwell set up a new government department (the court of augmentations) to handle these new revenues. It kept a record of the king's new gains, and on his instructions sold lands to nobles, gentlemen, and merchants. The whole operation was carried through with great efficiency and ruthlessness. So life in over half the English monasteries came to an end.

THE PILGRIMAGE OF GRACE: 1536

The northern counties of England were very different from the south and east. Far from the king at Westminster, they had an independent temper and a deep mistrust of the government. The north was also backward. Large areas were given up to forest and moor. It had few industries and its farm-lands were poor, supporting a much smaller population than the south. In addition it was still feudal, and the king's command counted for less than the word of a Percy or a Neville, great nobles who owned vast tracts of land. It was not worth the king's while to deprive them of their great authority. The age-old hostility between England and Scotland frequently showed itself in border-raids. However, the cost of keeping a permanent army in the north was too great for any king to bear. So the Percies and Nevilles and other great families were given authority to protect the border counties. But it was a dangerous practice. These families were ambitious. During the fifteenth century they had even challenged the might of the crown. Richard III and the first two Tudors tried, by means of a royal council at York, to bring peace and the king's authority to the north. Yet it was ineffective so long as the north was dominated by great nobles and gentlemen, who only obeyed the king when it suited them.

So the north remained as independent and mistrustful as ever. The nobles and gentry detested the powerful upstart, Cromwell. And now Henry VIII's religious changes added fuel to the fire. The north was devoted to the pope and hostile to the royal supremacy. As Cromwell's agents set about closing down monasteries in Lincolnshire revolt broke out. The rebels insisted that they were loyal subjects. Nonetheless they demanded Cromwell's dismissal and an end to the closing of religious houses. Henry easily put down the revolt, but another. outbreak, this time in Yorkshire, proved to be more serious. The rebels there were led by Robert Aske, a lawyer and land-owner. Aske regarded the movement as a religious one. He called it the 'Pilgrimage of Grace' and adopted a banner which displayed the Five Wounds of Christ. The rebellion rapidly grew and soon Aske had an army of thirty thousand. Henry lacked a standing army, so he played for time whilst forces were raised. He sent the duke of Norfolk to parley with the rebels, who submitted their demands: they too wanted the monasteries to stay and Cromwell to go. Henry ordered Norfolk to promise the rebels that he would pardon them and consider carefully their demands. Aske trusted the king and dismissed his

followers. But Henry had no intention of keeping his word.
When enough troops had been raised, they were used to execute
Aske and hundreds of his followers. The north was cowed by
this dreadful punishment.

Henry made up his mind to bring the northern counties firmly
under his control. So he created a new council to govern the
north. It was staffed by Tudor civil servants and judges, who
owed their power and wealth to the king alone, and so were not
likely to disobey him. Although it was given great power, it
took its orders from the privy council[1] at Westminster. The
creation of the 'council of the north' marked the beginning of the
end of the north's independence.

THE DISSOLUTION OF THE MONASTERIES: SECOND STAGE

Many monks from the larger monasteries had joined the
Pilgrimage of Grace and afterwards four abbots were executed
for their part in it. The larger abbeys and priories, excluded
from the act of 1536, were now doomed. Cromwell's agents
visited them and persuaded the inmates to surrender their
property. Some did so willingly, others had to be threatened.
The abbots of Woburn, Glastonbury, Colchester, and Reading
resisted and were hanged before the gates of their abbeys, as a
warning to others. In 1539 parliament passed an act which
confirmed the recent confiscations. It claimed that the abbots
and priors had given their monasteries, 'of their own free and
voluntary minds, without constraint or compulsion, to our said
sovereign lord, his heirs and successors, for ever'.

THE EFFECTS OF THE DISSOLUTION

(*1*) Cromwell ruthlessly removed any monk who opposed the
dissolution. However the obedient monks—the overwhelming
majority—were well treated. Some became parish priests.
Others, especially the abbots and priors, received pensions; as
late as 1551, the government was still paying out over £44,000
annually in pensions to the monks. Nonetheless some were
bound to suffer hardship. The monks' servants lost their jobs.

[1] The king ruled with the aid of advisers who formed the king's council.
But he placed special trust in a few who did the real work of government.
They formed the privy council which had two functions: (*1*) to advise the
king; (*2*) to look after day-to-day problems in government. In addition
some privy councillors sat as judges in star chamber.

Many of the monasteries had not bothered to care for the poor, but the plight of those people who had received charity now became desperate. In the towns the monks' hospitals were closed; a few were later re-opened, but most of them had gone, never to reappear.

(2) A quarter of the land in England fell into the king's hands. It would have solved his financial problems if he had kept it. But he needed ready cash for wars against Scotland and France. Thus, whilst some lands were given as rewards to Henry's faithful supporters, much more was sold to nobles, gentlemen and yeomen, merchants, and lawyers.[1] Whilst Henry squandered the wealth of the monasteries on useless wars, the men who bought lands from him farmed them and grew rich.

THE IMPORTANCE OF HENRY VIII'S REVOLUTION

(1) How the king became master in his own house

Henry VIII and Thomas Cromwell destroyed the pope's power in England, and so made England a 'sovereign nation state' (i.e. a State which owed no allegiance to any foreign authority). But they did much more than this. They brought the whole of England and Wales under royal control. In the Middle Ages, English kings had been very limited in their power. The clergy and Church lands were subject to the pope. There were also many franchises (lands over which the king had no control). Many were small but some were large. The greatest was the County Palatine of Durham. It was ruled by the bishop of Durham, who enforced his laws in his own courts. There were no royal courts here and royal officials could only enter the county with the bishop's consent. It was a source of annoyance to English kings, because criminals could hide there and be safe from the king's officers. Elsewhere in the north, as we have seen, the king was less important than the Percies and Nevilles. In the west the position was very much the same. Wales had been conquered by Edward I (1272–1307), but the real rulers were the marcher lords. They owned vast estates both in the Welsh Marches (borderlands) and in Wales itself. Their task was to maintain law and order, but more often than not they fought amongst themselves and ignored the king's commands.

---

[1] This ensured the permanence of the recent changes, for any future attempt to restore papal supremacy would threaten their right to monastic lands.

Indeed effective royal control was limited to the Midlands and south-eastern England.

Henry VIII set about making his will and laws effective everywhere. He had already become master of the Church. In

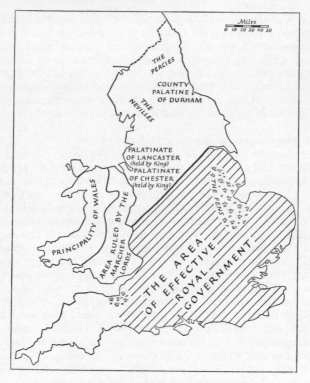

**THE LIMITS OF EFFECTIVE GOVERNMENT
IN ENGLAND IN 1529**

1536 Parliament abolished all the franchises, including Durham. The council of the north was set up in 1537. In the west another council, the council in the Marches, forced the marcher lords to obey the king. An act of 1536 remodelled the government of Wales and its borderlands on English lines: Wales was divided into counties; English laws, courts, and justices of the peace were introduced; for the first time Wales sent M.P.s to parliament. Whereas, in the past, political authority had been shared among kings, pope, marcher lords, and many others, it was now in the hands of one political head, the king. His laws were enforced everywhere in England and Wales. And all, whether laymen or priest, owed loyalty and obedience to him.

(2) *Why Henry VIII did not become an absolute king*

The revolutionary changes of the 1530's did not make Henry an absolute king. During the sixteenth century, absolute monarchies were created in France, Spain, Austria, and other parts of Germany: these kings and princes had the power to make laws and impose taxes. Not so with Henry VIII, who was 'under the law' and could do neither of these things without parliament. He achieved his aims not by force, but by statute (act of parliament). Without a police force or a standing army, he could not have imposed on the people any changes which they detested. His policy had to be carried through with the help of the ruling classes in parliament. And he only succeeded because they too welcomed the changes.

(3) *How 'king-in-parliament' became supreme in England*

English law in the Middle Ages was made up of customs and old practices handed down 'from time immemorial'. These laws were thought to have been inspired by God and so were better than any which might be made by men. Statute was not used to cancel old laws or make new ones, but simply to alter existing laws in order to fit new conditions. Thus acts of parliament were very limited in what they could do. But Henry VIII's revolution turned the Englishman's world upside-down: the age-old supremacy of the pope had gone, rich monasteries and wandering friars were no longer to be seen, the Bible could actually be read in English.

If statute could do all this, surely it could do anything. Though Englishmen did not realise it at once, this was indeed the case. King and parliament together had the power to make and unmake anything by act of parliament. As yet the king was the dominant partner and parliament usually did his bidding. This meant a great increase in the king's power. When Henry's terrifying personality was added to this, he must have looked all-powerful to his contemporaries. Books and pamphlets encouraged this view. Bishop Gardiner of Winchester wrote, in 1535, that 'princes ought to be obeyed by the commandment

3

of God; yea, and to be obeyed without exception'. Even his most wicked actions must not be resisted, for he answered only to God. Despite this, the king's authority was in fact limited. The right to make laws, the essential of an absolute king, was not Henry's alone; he shared it with the commons and lords. The king's personal powers were great, but they were by no means as great as those of the king-in-parliament. So it is that we say the supreme authority (the sovereign) in England after the 1530's was not the king alone, but the king-in-parliament.

(4) The Tudor Revolution

The changes wrought by Henry VIII and his minister amounted to a revolution—a major change in the powers and forms of government. The revolution was parliamentary, that is to say it was carried out by acts of parliament. However Cromwell carefully worded the statutes to make it appear that parliament did not make the changes, but only confirmed changes which Henry had already made: the Act of Supremacy simply stated that the king 'is Supreme Head of the Church', not that parliament had given him that authority. In later years parliament could not demand that, as it had made the original changes, so it had the right to criticise or cancel them.

(5) Why there was no religious reformation in Henry VIII's reign

Whilst the changes of the 1530's may be termed a revolution, there was no religious reformation (unless we count the end of the pope's supremacy as such). Henry VIII had always been a staunch catholic in matters of doctrine. In 1521 he wrote a defence of his beliefs in answer to Luther's attacks. The pope rewarded him with the title of *Fidei Defensor* ('Defender of the Faith'). Even when Henry became Supreme Head of the Church, he remained unswervingly loyal to the old catholic faith, in everything except papal supremacy. And he was equally merciless to papal supporters (i.e. Roman catholics or 'papists') and Lutheran heretics (protestants). The number of protestants was growing, but so long as the awesome Henry VIII sat on the throne, no change in religion was possible.

HENRY VIII'S RELIGIOUS POLICY: THE SIX ARTICLES AND THE ENGLISH BIBLE

Henry wanted 'above all things that diversities of religious opinions should be entirely rooted out and destroyed with all dispatch from his dominions'. His orthodoxy was revealed in the Act of Six Articles, passed by parliament in 1539. It commanded all men to accept (*1*) the doctrine of transubstantiation,[1] (*2*) communion in one kind, (*3*) celibacy of the clergy, (*4*) the need to observe vows of chastity, (*5*) and (*6*) the continuance of private masses and confessions. Anyone who denied transubstantiation was to be burnt for heresy. Infringement of the other articles was punishable by imprisonment for the first offence, death for the second. These savage penalties clearly showed that Henry meant to maintain the old catholic faith.

The reformers scored one success. Roman catholics held that the Church, not individual men, should interpret the Bible. So they used the Greek version, which few, other than the priests, could read. On the other hand the protestants believed that it should be available for all men to read, so that they could resolve problems by using their own judgement. The first English translation was the work of a protestant, William Tyndale, who fled abroad to escape punishment for heresy only to be caught and burnt alive in Germany (1536). In the following years Miles Coverdale and John Rogers published new translations. The latter became the official version in 1539, when Cromwell persuaded Henry that a copy should be placed in every parish church.

However, the king was not really happy about making the Bible available to all. In 1543 he restricted the right to read even the official version. It was to be read in churches only by those of whom the king or bishop approved. Only nobles and gentlemen, merchants and gentlewomen could own private copies, and 'husbandmen, workmen, and women except gentlewomen' were forbidden either to own or read the Bible. Clearly the reformers could hope for little from their conservative king.

HENRY VIII'S WIVES AND THE SUCCESSION PROBLEM

By 1536 Henry had decided to end his marriage. Anne had failed to give him a male heir. She was unpopular and many did not look upon her as Henry's legitimate wife, as he had married her whilst his first wife was still alive. But Catherine of Aragon had since died. If Henry could get rid of Anne and remarry, everyone would regard the third marriage as legitimate.

---

[1] Transubstantiation was the doctrine that, in the mass, the bread and wine turned to the flesh and blood of Christ. Luther rejected this, but accepted that Christ was present in the spirit. Calvin rejected even this; communion simply commemorated the Last Supper.

When Anne's second child was stillborn, in January 1536, he transferred his affections to Jane Seymour, one of his wife's ladies-in-waiting. Anne was easily removed from the scene. Her pride and arrogance had made her many enemies, and when she was charged with unfaithfulness to Henry they were ready to give evidence that this was so. Henry chose to regard her infidelity as treason; it suited his own ends and satisfied his conceit. She was put on trial and found guilty. On 19 May 1536 she went to the block, and a fortnight later Henry married Jane Seymour.

The new queen learned from her predecessor's mistakes. She was modest, made herself popular, and did not interfere in politics. Consequently she kept Henry's affection and the fortunes of the Seymour family were made: her brother Edward became earl of Hertford and other relations were given offices at court. Then, in 1537, Jane was delivered of a son, Edward. But she died in child-birth. At last Henry had the male heir for which he had waited so long. Now he sought a new queen.

The search for a fourth wife became mixed up with religious problems. It was also the cause of Cromwell's downfall. Although Henry remained a catholic, Lutheranism gained converts in England. It had many sympathisers, even among the bishops and the king's advisers. Cranmer and Cromwell were their leaders. They were opposed by a party of conservative catholics, led by Bishop Gardiner and the duke of Norfolk. Naturally, in religious matters, Henry sided with the conservatives. However, Cromwell's opportunity came with a fresh turn of events in Europe. His constant fear had always been that the Valois and Hapsburgs, Roman catholics both, might unite in a crusade against England. Their rivalry over Italy made this unlikely. But in 1537 Francis I and Charles V drew closer together and the following year they made peace. The threat of a Franco-Spanish crusade grew. Cromwell tried to commit the king to an alliance with the German Lutheran princes against their emperor. To this end he proposed that Henry should marry Anne, daughter of the powerful Lutheran duke of Cleves—no doubt he was hoping that a protestant queen might persuade Henry to accept religious reform. In view of the danger to his kingdom Henry agreed and the wedding took place in January 1540.

Three factors now combined to destroy Cromwell:

(*1*) Holbein, the court-painter, had been commissioned to go to Cleves and paint a portrait of Henry's bride-to-be. The painting obviously flattered Anne. When the king met her, he was appalled to find that she was much older and less attractive than he had been led to believe—and bad mannered into the bargain. He had been tricked.

(*2*) Nonetheless Henry married her in order to strengthen England against a probably attack. But no attack took place. Indeed it became obvious that France and Spain would soon fall out again. Henry realised that he had made a disastrous marriage for nothing.

(*3*) Norfolk had placed his niece, the beautiful Catherine Howard, at court, where she attracted the king's attention. Henry determined to annul his marriage with Anne in order to marry Catherine. Norfolk was now high in the king's favour. He was able to persuade Henry that Cromwell was sympathising with the heretics and mismanaging his affairs.

Although Cromwell was made earl of Essex in April, his fall was now certain. In June he was arrested on charges of heresy and treason. Parliament passed a bill of attainder against him, and he went to his death on 23 July 1540.

THE ACHIEVEMENTS OF THOMAS CROMWELL

(*1*) It was Cromwell who first proposed the breach with the papacy. He planned it with Henry's approval, supervised the careful wording of the statutes by which it was achieved, and made sure that they were passed by his management of parliament. To him must go most of the credit for making Henry VIII Supreme Head of the Church.

(*2*) It was Cromwell who proposed that the king should dissolve the monasteries and confiscate their property (though Henry probably did not need advice on this matter). As vicar-general he supervised the whole operation very efficiently.

(*3*) Not content with extinguishing the pope's power he removed the franchises, marcher lordships, and all other obstacles to the king's authority in England and Wales.

(*4*) The Tudor civil service was adequate to handle the smaller income and fewer duties of a medieval king. Cromwell realised, however, that it was not competent to manage the vast new sums of money which the king received as Supreme Head. He created several new departments, each of which was to deal with one kind of income: customs dues, crown lands, the monasteries, first fruits and tenths, and feudal dues. This new organisation was able to cope with all the demands placed upon it. Cromwell had indeed given the king a civil service worthy of his new status and duties.

(5) Cromwell served his master faithfully, and in doing so made him probably the most powerful king ever to sit on the English throne. But he had made the mistake of trying to lead the king to protestantism. Henry was old fashioned and set in his ways and he would have none of it. So Cromwell fell. Henry felt no gratitude for his past services. He was only too willing to sacrifice an unpopular minister once he had served his purpose.

THE CLOSING YEARS OF HENRY VIII'S REIGN: 1540–47

After Cromwell's fall, no-one took his place as the king's chief adviser. Henry preferred to rely on his own judgement. There was no new policy either. In religion Henry remained an orthodox catholic, although he kept Cranmer and other reformers in his council.

The king's distasteful marriage to Anne of Cleves was quickly ended: she gave Henry his divorce and in return he granted her a royal palace and estates. Then he married Catherine Howard in August 1540. At last he thought he had found happiness with his young and beautiful queen. But little more than a year later the privy council discovered that she was continuing a secret love affair, which had begun long before she married the king. When Henry learned of her unfaithfulness, he was stricken with grief. His brief spell of happiness had come to a pathetic end. Catherine paid the full penalty: she was attainted and executed in February 1542. When Henry married for the sixth time, in 1543, it was to a widow, Catherine Parr. She was a woman of common-sense and moderation. Her religious sympathies were protestant, but she kept her views to herself and showed no interest in politics.

In foreign affairs Henry returned to the bolder policy of his youth. He wanted to conquer Scotland and gain glory at France's expense. There was some sense in the former aim: the conquest of Scotland would increase Henry's power, secure England's northern frontier, and end the 'auld alliance'. In 1542 an English army invaded Scotland. The Scottish king,

James V, counter-attacked, but his forces were routed at Solway Moss. Things went from bad to worse for the Scots. Their king died, leaving his infant daughter Mary to succeed him. Henry forced the Scottish nobles captured at Solway Moss to sign the Treaty of Greenwich (1543). It ended the war and arranged that Mary Stuart should marry Prince Edward. This marriage would unite the two realms. But the Scots feared that it would also subject them to English rule. Henry's bullying roused them to resist the treaty. Lord Hertford invaded Scotland in order to make them change their minds. He laid waste the countryside, but this only made matters worse. The Scots refused to give way, and Henry was forced to abandon his scheme for a union.

Henry, still thirsting for conquests, also joined Spain in a fruitless war with France (1543). Three years of aimless campaigning ended with a peace treaty, from which England gained nothing. The war had been not only valueless, but expensive. It had cost the king over two million pounds. To raise the money he had to resort to all manner of means, including the sale of more monastic lands. Rapidly his newly-gained riches were squandered on his futile wars. Thus the crown lost its last chance to be financially independent.

In religious matters Henry VIII had continued to tread the middle path between Roman catholics and protestants. But in his last years a change was apparent. He allowed Prince Edward to be educated by two reformers, John Cheke and Roger Ascham. The earl of Hertford, John Dudley (now Viscount Lisle), and Cranmer had protestant leanings, yet were Henry's most trusted advisers. The catholic councillors were out of favour. Indeed in 1545 their leader, Norfolk, and his son the earl of Surrey were condemned to death for treason. Surrey was executed, and Norfolk was only saved by the king's death. The protestant party had triumphed. The reason for this is clear. Henry had not changed his religious opinions. He simply realised that the protestants were less likely than the catholics to restore papal supremacy. Perhaps he realised that change was inevitable, although he himself was too old and set in his ways to alter his opinions.

Henry also settled the succession in favour of the protestants. The Succession Act of 1543 had recognised his heirs as Edward, Mary, and Elizabeth, in that order. The king's will stated that if none of them had children, the crown would pass to the protestant descendants of his younger sister, Mary; this meant setting aside the claims of his other sister Margaret's catholic Stuart heirs. Finally, he made arrangements for the government of England by the privy council during his son's minority. It was to consist mainly of protestants under Hertford and Lisle. Henry's work was done. On 27 January 1547 he died.

THE GREATNESS OF HENRY VIII

Henry was a great king. The most important achievements of his reign were really the work of his ministers, but it is a sign of Henry's own ability that he recognised greatness in such men as Wolsey and Cromwell. He raised them up and gave them the power to get on with the job. Yet he never let go the reins of government, although he allowed them great scope. Both Wolsey and Cromwell learned the painful lesson that power was always finally in the king's hands. He raised them up, but he also dashed them down.

The king was a harsh taskmaster. Ministers who failed him were not only dismissed but also punished. He could be cruel and vindictive, and he was always selfish and egoistical. He pursued his political aims and his pleasures with equal ruthlessness, and all who opposed him were destroyed. However his despotic temper touched few of his subjects—only his courtiers, who were in personal contact with him, and a handful of heretics and papists. To the people at large he was the symbol of the new national spirit: hearty and strong, independent and self-willed. The people viewed him with affection mingled with awe and some dread. He was 'Bluff King Hal'.

In his last years Henry deteriorated. Swollen with power and embittered by ill-health, he terrified his court—and to a lesser extent his country—into obeying his whims. The misgovernment of these years undid much of Cromwell's patient work. The monastic wealth was frittered away and England's energy spent in pointless wars. But the essentials were unharmed: the new nation-state and the royal supremacy remained intact. And Henry was able to hand them on to his undisputed successor, Edward VI.

VII

THE EDWARDIAN REFORMATION

CALVINISM

THE revolt which Martin Luther had begun against the Roman
catholic Church soon spread beyond Germany. In Switzerland
the reformers were led by Ulrich Zwingli, whose protestantism
was more extreme than that of Luther. He established protestantism in some of the Swiss cantons, but, when he tried to impose
his beliefs on the rest by military force, he was defeated and
killed at the battle of Cappel (1531).

That the protestant cause in Switzerland was not lost was due
to the arrival of John Calvin in Geneva. Born at Noyon in the
north of France in 1509, Calvin had studied theology and Law in
Paris, Orleans, and Bourges. Whilst a student he had warmly
accepted Lutheran teachings, and so had been forced to flee from
France when Francis I began a persecution of protestants.
When he visited Geneva in 1536, he had already published a book
called the *Institutes* in which he expressed extreme protestant
views on the Christian Church. He was invited by leading
protestants to stay in Geneva as a minister, and apart from a short
spell in exile (1538–41) he remained there until his death in 1564.
During this time he created in Geneva a strict and intolerant
protestant Church.

Calvin believed in predestination, that some were destined to
be saved and others damned, regardless of their actions. If a
man was predestined to damnation, a blameless life would not
save him. On the other hand, a member of the elect, those who
were destined for salvation, would not be damned because of a
sinful life. Such a belief might encourage a life of sin and ease,
and so Calvin kept a close watch on moral life. Dancers, card-
players, blasphemers, and other sinners were punished, and
heretics were put to death. Indeed Calvinism proved to be no
more tolerant than the Roman catholic Church which it
challenged.

Most of Calvin's ideas were directly opposed to those of
Rome. Catholics attached great importance to the mass
(communion), transubstantiation, vestments, ceremonies, and the

3*

pope's pronouncements on matters of doctrine. Calvin claimed that communion had no spiritual importance and was merely commemorative, and he insisted on communion in both kinds. In the catholic Church the congregation partook of the bread; only the priests received the wine as well. Calvin insisted that laymen as well should partake of both. He forbade pictures, images, incense, and vestments, and insisted upon plainness in worship. In particular he rejected the catholic claim that the pope could lay down doctrines for the Church. Instead Calvin, like Luther, turned to the Bible as the source of all truth and the only guide of conduct. It could be interpreted by individuals without the guidance of priest or pope.

Despite points of similarity, Calvin's ideas became more extreme than those of Luther, for he moved much further away from Rome. In economic and social matters too he did not agree with Luther. Luther was very conservative. He upheld feudalism, and condemned money-lending and the new commercial spirit of the towns. Calvin disliked the new commercial spirit, but he accepted the growth of town life, industry, and trade; and when Calvinism spread its keenest supporters were to be found in the cities and ports of western Europe. The Calvinists regarded wealth as a sign of virtue, whilst poverty was the result of sin. This appealed to merchants and manufacturers who could point to their wealth as the result, not of greed and ruthlessness, but of a virtuous life.

In the sixteenth century the rulers of western Europe were gaining control of the Church. Henry VIII became Supreme Head of the Church in England, and the Lutheran princes of the Empire gained a mastery over the Church in their states. This process was also occurring in great kingdoms which continued to recognise the spiritual headship of the pope. In 1516 Francis I and Pope Leo X signed the Concordat of Bologna, by which the French king gained an increased share in the control of the Church in France. Even the Spanish kings, the most catholic rulers in Europe, nominated their bishops, taxed their clergy, and forbade the publication of papal bulls (decrees) in Spain without their consent. Calvin's ideas were directly opposed to this development. He believed that the Church and State should be independent of each other, but that the State should co-operate with the Church by punishing sinners and heretics. Between 1541 and 1564 he put this idea into practice in Geneva. The city was ruled by a number of elected councils of citizens; the Church was governed and the citizens' morals were supervised by the consistory, a council of clergy and of 'elders' who were simply the more fervent members of church congregations. The Calvinist Church itself was elective in character: the congregations chose their ministers, and the Church was governed by elected assemblies. Calvin did not condemn the rule of kings and princes in western Europe, but he claimed that a nation could depose a ruler who was tyrannical or in any other way unfit to rule.

Calvin's political ideas were naturally not popular with the kings of western Europe, but he would not have come into conflict with them, if his influence had been limited to Geneva. However, it was more widespread than that of Luther, whose doctrines were only accepted in parts of the Holy Roman Empire and Scandinavia. Calvinism became international: it spread along the trade routes down the Rhine to the Spanish Netherlands, the lowlands of Scotland, and the ports of England and France. The French Huguenots, the Scottish presbyterians, and the English puritans all followed the teachings of Calvin.

In England, the heretics whom Henry VIII persecuted were all Lutherans, and it was not until Edward VI's reign that the Calvinists arrived. Yet, as we shall see, it was Calvin's protestantism, not Luther's, which triumphed in England.

Edward, a nine year old boy, was now king of England. Since his birth he had been schooled for this position. Indeed from the age of four the young prince received the most up-to-date education that a Renaissance prince could have. In spite of this, he was to count for nothing. During his brief reign Edward played at being king, but political power was exercised, first by a Seymour, then by a Dudley.

THE PROTECTORATE ESTABLISHED

Henry VIII had arranged for the kingdom to be governed by the privy council until Edward came of age. Gardiner and most of the other catholics were excluded. Instead, Henry had staffed the council with protestants and their sympathisers. The most important were the earl of Hertford, Archbishop Cranmer, and Viscount Lisle. To prevent any one man from seizing all power for himself, Henry ruled that each councillor was to have equal power. It proved to be a useless safeguard.

No sooner had Henry died than Hertford persuaded the council to appoint him lord protector.   To prevent any opposition there was a general distribution of honours: Hertford himself became duke of Somerset and his most dangerous rival, Lisle, received the earldom of Warwick.   So the new reign was launched with Somerset at the helm.   Although he was greedy and ambitious like the rest of his contemporaries, his fine ideals set him apart from them.   It remained to see what success he would make of the job of governing.

SOMERSET AND SCOTLAND

Somerset wanted to bring Scotland into union with England. Such a union was urgently needed.   Mary Queen of Scots was a minor, whose kingdom was ruled for her by James V's widow, Mary of Guise.   She was catholic and French, and she favoured a Franco-Scottish alliance directed against England.   So he revived Henry VIII's plan to marry Mary Stuart to Edward VI. But still the Scots would have none of it.   They were not ready to surrender their independence to the more powerful southern kingdom.   Like Henry VIII, Somerset thought that he could use force to make them see reason.   In September 1547 he invaded Scotland and gained an overwhelming victory at Pinkie.   His generalship was better than his common sense.   When, after Pinkie, he laid waste the Scottish countryside he stiffened the Scots' determination not to submit.   Hastily they sent Mary to safety in Paris, where she later married the French dauphin,[1] Francis.   Somerset gave up and returned to England.   His policy of force had not only failed to achieve the desired union. It had revived the old alliance of Scotland and France.   What Englishmen dreaded might soon come to pass: a French army in Scotland, ready to strike across the border.

SOMERSET AND THE PROTESTANT REFORMATION

When the heavy hand of Henry VIII was removed, the protestants came out into the open.   Somerset, who was one of them, stopped the enforcement of all laws against heresy. Leading reformers, like Martin Bucer, a German Calvinist, now came to England to spread the new gospel.   They preached against the catholic ceremonies and beliefs which the old king had kept.   As a result violence broke out, there were disturbances

[1] The heir to the French throne.

during catholic services, images were smashed, and stained-glass broken. It was Somerset's duty, as protector, to maintain law and order. Instead he persuaded parliament to repeal Henry VIII's treason and heresy laws, together with the Six Articles. Thus he removed the restraints on the reformers' lawlessness. In so doing he sacrificed peace and security for the sake of tolerance.

Somerset went even further. Assuming the leadership of the reformers, he commissioned Cranmer to draw up a prayer-book in English instead of Latin. This was approved by parliament in 1549, along with an Act of Uniformity, which laid down penalties for opposition to it. It gave little comfort to the extreme protestants, for it contained few differences from the catholic faith. But in it Cranmer gave us some of the finest prose in the English language.

Moderate though the Prayer-Book was, it caused much discontent and, in 1549, a rebellion. The catholic peasants of Devon and Cornwall rushed to arms, demanding that the mass, the Six Articles, and the monasteries be restored. As for the Prayer-Book, they said 'we will not receive the new service because it is but like a Christmas game'. The situation looked ugly for the privy council. Thousands were in arms under Sir Thomas Arundell and John Winslade. Local priests exhorted them and celebrated mass in the parish churches. The rebel army advanced to Exeter and besieged it. However, an army of foreign mercenaries under Lord Russell raised the siege. The rebels made a last-ditch stand at Sampford Courtenay, but were crushed. The ringleaders were hanged and their followers heavily fined. Thereafter, much as they disliked it, the men of Devon and Cornwall were forced to accept Cranmer's 'Christmas game'.

Many men had become protestants in the hope of plundering the Church. In this respect Somerset was no different from the rest. Henry VIII had planned but not carried through the dissolution of the chantries.[1] Somerset now took it upon himself to do so. In 1547 parliament dissolved the chantries, on the grounds that they bred superstition. Their property went to the crown. Many of them had contained small schools and

---

[1] A chantry was a small house of monks whose most important task was to pray for the souls of the dead. Wealthy people left money to the chantries in return for their prayers; so they waxed rich.

their loss was a serious blow to education in England. A few of
them were re-founded as Edward VI Grammar Schools, and
they were endowed with confiscated lands. But the property
used in this way was only a fraction of the total seized. The rest
went to replenish the royal treasury, but not for long. Lands
were granted or sold to privy councillors, their friends and
followers. The protector benefited more than anyone. From
his share of the spoils he built Somerset House on Thameside.
The greed of Somerset, and later of Northumberland, caused
many to regard the protestants as grasping men, who were
anxious only to despoil the Church.

SOMERSET'S ECONOMIC POLICY

The mid sixteenth century was a period of great economic
upheaval.[1] The price rise and the booming wool trade
encouraged rack-renting, enclosures, and eviction of tenants
which caused a good deal of discontent and hardship amongst
the small farmers and peasants. Such practices were also quite
contrary to the medieval attitude upheld by the Church, that
economic life should be conducted in accordance with a moral
code: usury (moneylending at rates of interest) was condemned;
articles should be sold at a just price (sufficient to cover the
costs, with a surplus which allowed the merchant to maintain
his social position and no more). Not that these ideals were
frequently observed in the Middle Ages, but people did at least
pay lip-service to them. But with the chance or need to make
more money in the sixteenth century many rejected these old ideas.

In the 1540's matters came to a head. Prices soared, enclosures
and rack-renting increased. However, a number of men were
prepared to take active steps to oppose these practices. In
Edward VI's reign they became known as the commonwealth
party ('commonwealth' meant the 'common good' or 'general
welfare of the community'). Their leader was a layman, John
Hales, but churchmen too were prominent, among them Hugh
Latimer and Thomas Lever. Latimer attracted large crowds by
his fiery preaching. He condemned greedy enclosers and those
who squeezed their tenants for more money, which they spent on
idle living.

By pamphlets, letters, and speeches in parliament, the commonwealth men attacked grasping landowners, and they convinced

[1] See Book 4, Chapter XVII: 'The Price Rise'.

Somerset that they were right. He wished to help the poor, the unemployed, the evicted. This, he thought, could only be done if he put an end to enclosures. It was a dangerous policy. If Somerset was to govern successfully, he needed the support of parliament at the centre and the J.P.s in the counties. But the justices and many members of parliament were themselves enclosers. To upset these men might prove fatal to him. Somerset went ahead regardless. He supported John Hales' bill against enclosure in the 1547 parliament. But the many gentlemen there combined to reject it.

Thwarted in parliament, Somerset sent commissioners into the Midlands where they destroyed recent enclosures, including the earl of Warwick's park. Unfortunately this encouraged men to take matters into their own hands. Hedges were uprooted, fences pulled down. When the protector condemned this lawlessness, no-one took any notice. And he hesitated to use force against the very people he was trying to help.

Power was slipping from Somerset's control. He had thrown his weight on the side of the peasants. But he had made no attempt to conciliate the powerful body of landowners, who felt that Somerset had betrayed his own class. And now he had lost control of the movement he set in motion. In 1549 lawlessness spread. The Prayer-Book Rebellion began in June. Before it was finally suppressed, there was a more serious rising in Norfolk. Although enclosures were not widespread in East Anglia, the rebellion was economic in origin. Here the main grievance was that the lords of the manor had infringed the tenants' grazing rights. On most manors it was the right of lord and tenants to graze a number of sheep and cattle on the common lands. The number or 'stint' permitted to the lord and each tenant was fixed by custom, but varied from manor to manor. However, the manorial lords of Norfolk had been grazing more than their customary number of livestock on the common lands. As pasture was limited, this harmed the tenants' grazing rights. It was also a serious blow to their livelihood, for they depended upon their livestock to eke out the food obtained from their arable land. Rising prices and rack-renting also contributed to the social discontent which culminated in Ket's Rebellion.

The rebels were no mere disorganised rabble. They were led by Robert Ket, a prosperous landowner who sympathised with the tenants' complaints. He gathered about him some fifteen thousand armed men on Mousehold Heath outside Norwich. During July and August he 'held court' there, governing Norwich and the surrounding countryside and enforcing discipline amongst his followers. But Ket was only concerned with local grievances. He did not strike for London. Neither did he join forces with the Roman catholic Mary Tudor, who was living nearby, for the rebels were not hostile to the recent changes in religion. So Ket sat tight, whilst Somerset dithered in London. It was left to the other councillors to take action. In August, Warwick, a man of altogether more ruthless stamp, was sent to Norfolk with an army. Ket's forces were routed, more than three thousand being put to the sword. In December Robert Ket was executed for treason. Order returned to Norfolk, and with it the gentlemen who had fled during the rebellion. Overstocking, rack-renting, and rising prices went on as before.

THE FALL OF SOMERSET

In politics the main result of Ket's Rebellion was the downfall of the protector. He had alienated the landed classes by his support of the tenants, whereas Warwick had emerged as their defender and the champion of order. But even before the rebellion he had undermined his own position by his actions and politics:

(*1*) His brother Thomas Seymour, the lord admiral, was greedy for power and jealous of Somerset's success. Seymour used every means to undermine the protector's authority. He gained the young king's sympathy by flattering him and sending him pocket money; he married Henry VIII's widow, Catherine Parr, in 1546, and when she died two years later he unsuccessfully proposed marriage to Princess Elizabeth, who was second in line of succession to the throne. For a long time Somerset ignored his brother's obvious attempts to remove him. But at last he was forced to act: Seymour was arrested and attainted and on 20 March 1549 he was executed. The protector had ignored his brother's activities for two years—for this he was accused of weakness. When at last he acted, he had Seymour condemned without a trial—so he was blamed for his callousness.

(*2*) Even Somerset's virtues were a disadvantage. He was easy-going, with fine ideals; he disliked the cruel punishment inflicted on heretics and traitors, and he was tolerant. But his enemies saw his leniency and kindness as weakness. And a weak ruler was unfit to govern in the rough-and-tumble of Tudor politics.

(3) The protector's haughtiness made the council hostile to him. He kept all power in his own hands, often acted without discussing matters with the council first, and even began to act as if he were king. It was easy for Somerset's dangerous rival, Warwick, to win the other councillors over to his side.

After Ket's Rebellion Warwick schemed Somerset's downfall. Although Somerset got wind of the plan and fled from London with the king, the other councillors joined Warwick (October 1549). They demanded that he give himself up. Somerset was a beaten man. He allowed himself to be arrested and imprisoned in the Tower, on condition that his life was spared. Warwick had come to power.

Somerset was deprived of his office of lord protector. However, he was released in February 1550. He was even allowed to rejoin the privy council. Warwick remained in control, but he felt insecure so long as his old rival was alive. So in 1551 Somerset was arrested on a charge of treason. He was attainted and, in February 1552, went to the block, much to the sorrow of the common people of England.

NORTHUMBERLAND'S RULE: 1549–53

Warwick did not adopt Somerset's title of lord protector; but he became instead the duke of Northumberland. He was the complete opposite of his predecessor: where Somerset was incompetent, he was efficient; where Somerset was weak and lenient, he was strong and ruthless; where Somerset had high ideals, he had only greed and ambition. Yet Northumberland was certainly capable. He found the treasury empty, a debased coinage, and the civil service decaying through neglect. During his brief spell in power, he did something to reform the finances, improve the coinage, and revive the Tudor civil service. But all his reforms were marred by his own greed, for he made a large fortune at the king's expense.

In religion, Northumberland led the way towards extreme protestantism (of the Calvinist type). This was not due to any religious conviction on his part, but rather because he hoped for further plunder from the Church. The catholic bishops, such as Bonner and Gardiner, were replaced by protestants. The extreme reformers had criticised Cranmer's Prayer-Book; it was too catholic for them, so in 1552 Northumberland encouraged the archbishop to produce a revised version. This second Prayer-Book was decidedly protestant: transubstantiation was rejected, popish vestments were dropped, services made simpler, and cherished ceremonies forbidden. A second Act of Uniformity laid down penalties for non observance. In the same year, the privy council ordered all 'superfluous' ornaments to be removed from churches. Commissioners visited parish churches. They destroyed images, seized gold and silver ornaments and even some of the bells for the king's use. Altars were replaced by communion tables and gaily decorated walls were white-washed. Each church was left with just a chalice (to hold the communion wine) and one or two bells. The protestants' love of plainness and the government's need for money left the churches quite bare.

THE 'DEVICE FOR THE SUCCESSION'

Edward VI was completely under the sway of Northumberland. He was passionately interested in theology. And as one of the most ardent protestants in England, he approved of Northumberland's religious reforms. Indeed the duke's position was quite secure, so long as Edward lived. But early in 1533 the king became consumptive. As he weakened, it became clear that he would not live long. His successor was Mary, a devout Roman catholic. She hated Northumberland for his protestantism and greed; and he knew that Mary would not forgive him for trying (unsuccessfully) to prevent her from attending mass in her own home. In desperation, he planned to alter the succession.

Northumberland persuaded Edward to draw up the 'Device for the Succession'. Mary and Elizabeth were to be passed over in favour of Lady Jane Grey. This sixteen year old girl was a grand-daughter of Henry VIII's younger sister Mary. She was a protestant; and she was married to Northumberland's own son, Guildford Dudley. In this way the duke hoped to maintain both the new religion and his own power. The other privy councillors were reluctant to accept the alteration of Henry VIII's will. However, Northumberland and the dying Edward bullied them into obedience. On 6 July 1553 the king died, happy in the knowledge that the protestant faith would continue.

Four days later, Jane was proclaimed queen in London. The

citizens greeted the proclamation with an ominous silence. In fact Northumberland had entirely mistaken the true feeling of the nation. Most people were still catholic. Even protestant sympathisers had been sickened by the greed of the duke and his councillors. In any case loyalty to the Tudors was stronger than any religious feeling. The people preferred to regard Mary as their rightful ruler. Northumberland's cause suffered a fatal blow when he failed to seize her. She had herself proclaimed queen in Norfolk, where nobles and gentry flocked to her aid. Northumberland set out to defeat her supporters, but his own soldiers did not have the stomach for the task, and they deserted in large numbers. Behind his back the other councillors deserted him and proclaimed Mary queen in London. When he reached Cambridge, the duke realised that he had failed. In a frantic attempt to save himself he led the cries of 'God save Queen Mary' in the market-place. But all to no avail. He was arrested and imprisoned in the Tower, along with his supporters and the luckless Lady Jane Grey. Mary rode triumphantly into London, where she was greeted by a joyous welcome from thousands of her loyal subjects. So began the reign of England's first queen for four hundred years.

VIII

MARY TUDOR AND THE COUNTER-REFORMATION

MARY'S CHARACTER AND POLICY

THE failure of Mary's reign was due to her past: her mother had been divorced, Mary herself had been declared illegitimate and her claim to the throne temporarily put aside; she had been exiled from her father's court and held almost as a prisoner for a long period. It would not be surprising if her past had soured her. Nevertheless she remained an attractive personality, gentle, kind, and merciful, except when faced with heresy. Yet this does not alter the fact that her policy was unwise and bound to be unpopular. Mary's policy was determined by her earlier experiences. Her devotion to Roman catholicism and her pride in her Spanish ancestry were the only things which had been left to her. It was this attachment to Spain and her religion which guided her policy when she became queen.

THE BEGINNING OF THE REIGN

Mary succeeded to the throne in a blaze of popularity. The protestant rulers of England had been unpopular. In any case England had no fear of a catholic sovereign for Henry VIII had remained a catholic until the end of his life. Above all, in that age of king-worship, Mary received the loyalty of the mass of Englishmen. She would have kept that loyalty and popularity if she had been content to restore the catholicism of her father's reign. Unfortunately she wanted to undo the work not only of Edward VI but also of Henry VIII.

Northumberland's attempt to ensure a protestant succession had failed. The innocent Jane Grey and her husband were imprisoned in the Tower, whilst Northumberland himself was sentenced to death on a charge of treason. Although he declared his conversion to catholicism in a desperate attempt to save himself, he was executed. Mary was now free to try and fulfil her greatest ambition: to bring England back into the Roman catholic Church.

Her first step was to remove the protestant councillors, and imprison the leading bishops, Cranmer, Latimer, and Ridley. She replaced them by faithful catholics, including Gardiner and Bonner whom she had released from prison. However Mary could go no further without the co-operation and consent of parliament. As the religious changes of Edward VI's reign had been carried out by statutes, only parliament could reverse them. So in 1553 Mary summoned her first parliament. It was prepared to repeal the statutes which had established Edwardian protestantism. So the Latin mass returned and the Prayer-Book began to disappear.

To restore the mass was one thing, but to restore the pope was quite a different matter. The nobles in the house of lords and the gentry in the commons were hotly opposed to Mary's wish to restore the monastic lands to the Church. Henry VIII had done his work well, for the nobles and gentry who had received these lands would on no account give them up. Mary was reluctantly forced to accept this; she was afraid that, if she persisted, parliament would not repeal Henry VIII's Act of Supremacy. Nevertheless she did restore those monastic lands which the crown still held. The result was that the crown's financial position was weakened.

OPPOSITION TO THE SPANISH MARRIAGE

Opposition to Mary was not limited to her religious policy: both parliament and the nation were hostile to Mary's proposed marriage to a Spaniard. At her accession, she was 36. This was middle-aged by sixteenth century standards. The possibility of having a child was remote, and perhaps it would have been better if she had not married at all. Yet Mary wanted an heir to succeed her and she would accept no one but a Spaniard as her husband. Her decision to marry her cousin, Philip of Spain, was very unpopular. Philip was the son of Emperor Charles V, and heir to the Spanish empire. A son born from such a match would probably inherit Spain and its empire, and would place Spanish interests before those of England.

Despite the opposition from her council, parliament, and the nation, Mary went ahead with the marriage negotiations. These were completed in January 1554. By the terms of the marriage treaty Philip's power was strictly limited. He was to be called 'King', and was to assist his wife in the government. But offices in the Church and government were to be filled by Englishmen only. The treaty was not to involve England in war in the interest of Spain. Nevertheless the treaty was unpopular, and Mary found herself facing a series of risings. They all misfired except the rising in Kent; this was serious because it was so near the capital and seat of government. Its leader, Sir Thomas Wyatt, was concerned less about the restoration of catholicism than with the Spanish marriage. For a time it seemed as though Wyatt and his four thousand followers might succeed. The Tudors had no regular army, and the duke of Norfolk's hastily-raised troops deserted to the rebels. But Mary showed her Tudor courage, and London continued its traditional support of the Tudor dynasty. The advancing rebels were halted outside the City wall at Ludgate. Trapped between the wall and government troops, Wyatt was forced to surrender.

The first to suffer for Wyatt's rebellion were two people who had not been involved in it: Lady Jane Grey and her husband were executed, innocent victims of Northumberland's ambition and Wyatt's revolt.   They were soon followed by Thomas Grey, Jane's uncle, and Wyatt himself, whilst nearly one hundred rebels were hung in London and Kent.   Even Princess Elizabeth, suspected of implication in Wyatt's rebellion, was imprisoned in the Tower.   The punishment meted out after the rebellion was not uncommonly severe for the sixteenth century: the Pilgrimage of Grace in 1536 was followed by two hundred executions, whilst eight hundred men died for their part in the Northern Rebellion of 1569.

MARY'S SUCCESSES IN 1554

Mary had survived a serious crisis, and there was no further opposition to the Spanish marriage.   But she was still no nearer a reunion with Rome.   Her second parliament, summoned in 1554, proved even more troublesome than the first.   It failed to revive the old laws against heresy, and refused to give Philip the powers of a king.   Nevertheless 1554 marks the peak of Mary's success.   Soon after Wyatt's rebellion, Mary and Philip were married by proxy.   In July Philip arrived in England, and the marriage was celebrated with great pomp and ceremony in Winchester Cathedral.   Four months later a third parliament was summoned.   Mary's councillors had influenced the elections, and this parliament proved to be more willing to co-operate.   It passed the heresy laws, which gave the government power to bring heretics to trial and to punish them.   Most important of all, it repealed all the laws which had been passed against the pope and Church since 1529;   the only exceptions were the statutes which registered the dissolution of the monasteries.   In the same month the English cardinal, Reginald Pole, chosen by the pope as archbishop of Canterbury and papal legate, arrived in London.   He accepted the submission of England from Philip and Mary, and welcomed the nation back into the Roman catholic Church.   The pope was once again the head of the Church in England.

THE PERSECUTION OF PROTESTANTISM

With a Spanish husband and with the pope's supremacy restored Mary had reason to feel that she was successful.   But, although she could destroy Henry VIII's anti-papal laws, she could not destroy the anti-papal feeling which her father had done so much to increase. England was very anti-clerical and anti-papal, even if it was not yet really protestant. Yet protestantism had spread especially in London and south-east England, which was in close touch with the new ideas on the continent. Mary, encouraged by Cardinal Pole, determined to save the souls of her heretic subjects from damnation, as she believed. This was to be done either by forcing them to renounce protestantism or, if this failed, by destroying their bodies. When Mary's third parliament passed the heresy laws, it gave her the power to burn heretics alive. Armed with this authority she began the task of persecution.

Amongst the first to suffer were the protestant leaders, Cranmer, Hooper, Ridley, and Latimer. They displayed great courage. Before Latimer was burnt at Oxford, he said to his companion: 'Play the man, Master Ridley; and we shall this day light such a candle by God's grace in England as I trust shall never be put out.' Cranmer wavered and actually recanted, but at the end he withdrew his recantation and went serenely to his death. As flames leapt up around him he thrust the hand which had signed the recantation into the flames, as if to punish it.

These leaders were followed by many humble people. Between January 1555 and the end of the reign some three hundred people were burnt to death; of these a hundred came from the clergy and 80 were women. Instead of destroying protestantism, Mary's persecution served only to strengthen it. Northumberland's leadership had made protestantism the mere tool of the greedy and ambitious politicians. Now, as the people in London and south-east England watched shopkeepers and craftsmen die, they realised that it was a faith for which men and women were ready to face an awful death. Not only did Mary turn many away from her religion. Her persecution, mistakenly believed to have been encouraged by the Spaniard Philip, associated the protestant religion with nationalism; at the same time it created a permanent hatred of the pope.

MARY'S FAILURE

After Mary's successes in 1554, everything seemed to go wrong. In 1555 Philip left England to become king of Spain. Mary was left, pathetically and vainly hoping for an heir. There was considerable opposition to her religious policy in her next parliament, which met in October 1555. In November her trusted councillor, Gardiner, died.

The following year saw matters go from bad to worse. Philip quarrelled with the pope, Paul IV, who excommunicated him and deprived Pole of his legateship. Mary, devoted to her Church, was forced into a position of hostility towards its head. In his quarrel with Philip, the pope obtained the help of France. Philip made a brief visit to England to request Mary's help. She agreed, and England entered into war against France. It justified the nation's earlier fears about the Spanish marriage, for it was a war fought only in the interest of Spain. It was expensive, unpopular, and badly-managed. Above all it was disastrous, for in January 1558 the French conquered Calais, the last English possession in France. This was a blessing in disguise. Calais was of no value and was expensive to maintain. But it was a humiliating blow to the nation's pride.

The loss of Calais was also a blow to Mary's spirit. She died a few months later in the knowledge that her policy was a failure. It had turned England against Spain and her religion. She had not produced an heir to carry on her work, and as she died, in November 1558, the nation was already welcoming her successor, Elizabeth.

IX

THE ELIZABETHAN SETTLEMENT

THE NEW QUEEN

ALTHOUGH Elizabeth became queen when she was only 25, she had already learned to tread warily in the harsh uncertain world of Tudor politics. She remained cautious and secretive, hiding her thoughts, speaking in riddles and giving evasive answers. As she grew older, her caution grew stronger. She would hesitate for a long time before making up her mind, and important decisions would be delayed until her councillors despaired. Certainly she could not be accused of being impetuous.

The queen was a typical Tudor and a true daughter of Bluff King Hal. She could be outspoken and blunt when the occasion required it, and her outbursts of anger cowed her courtiers. She had her father's pride, his love of power, and his sense of responsibility. She was a great queen, as he had been a greater king. Her character was not without its unpleasant features: she was selfish and coarse; a poor monarch, she had to be thrifty but was capable of real miserliness; unmarried herself, she was spiteful to courtiers who married without her permission. But Elizabeth's virtues were stronger than her vices: she had wisdom, tolerance, and a genius for politics, especially in her dealings with foreign powers. Above all she knew how to command men's loyalty. A born actress, Elizabeth used every trick she knew to gain the love and respect of her subjects, touching gestures, acts of generosity, and stirring speeches. She succeeded. But as yet all that was in the future. In 1558 she was an unknown quantity; only time would reveal her political genius.

ELIZABETH'S DIFFICULTIES

Elizabeth's first task as queen was to choose her privy councillors. Most of Mary's catholic advisers were replaced by protestants, amongst them William Cecil.[1] He had previously served Somerset and Northumberland. At heart a protestant, he had conformed under Mary. Now Elizabeth chose him as her chief adviser and he was to remain so for 40 years. No monarch ever had a better servant. He was honest, tireless, clever, and utterly devoted to her. She had great need of him for the problems she faced in 1558 were formidable:

(*1*) England had just experienced rule by a woman for the first time since the twelfth century; and Mary Tudor's failure made many dislike the idea of yet another woman on the throne. This feeling was expressed by the Scottish presbyterian John Knox in his book *First Blast of the Trumpet against the Monstrous Regiment* (meaning 'government') *of Women*. It was aimed at three catholics: Mary of Guise (regent in Scotland), Mary Tudor, and Mary Stuart. But it deeply offended Elizabeth, who regarded it as a slight upon her sex. She would not even allow Knox to pass through England on his way home to Scotland.

[1] He was created Lord Burghley in 1571.

No doubt Elizabeth was well aware of the difficulties for a queen in an age when women kept house, reared children, and left politics to the men. She would have all her time cut out to control the passionate tumultuous men who surrounded her in her court and parliament. Knox and his kind only made things worse.

(2) Fifteen years of misrule had left government and country in a sorry state. The treasury was empty, and saddled with a debt of over £250,000; local government was breaking down. Everywhere there was economic confusion, resulting from rising prices and a bad coinage. Enclosures, rack-renting, and eviction caused widespread discontent.

(3) England was still involved in a dangerous and useless war with France on Spain's behalf.

(4) However, the most pressing need was for a settlement of religion. England had seen many changes since 1529. Henry VIII had rejected the authority of the pope; Edward VI's reign had seen the creation of a protestant Church; while Mary had put the clock back and restored Roman catholicism. Mary's persecution had strengthened the protestants and embittered their feelings towards the Roman catholics. Elizabeth was faced with the prospect of continued religious strife. This she hoped to avoid by establishing a Church which would satisfy the majority of Englishmen.

THE PROBLEM OF RELIGION

There were 3 courses of action open to Elizabeth:

(*a*) She could keep her sister's Church in being. Yet to do so would be against her own interests because she would exercise no control over the Church. It would also be folly, for Mary's reign had strengthened the anti-papal feeling of Englishmen. Roman catholicism was associated in their minds with Spanish rule, and the fires at Smithfield made it appear a harsh intolerant religion (as indeed all religions were in the sixteenth century). In particular the gentry (who served as justices of the peace, members of parliament, and army officers, and were essential to Elizabeth) felt their property threatened by a Roman catholic regime. Mary had already tried to restore the monastic lands to the Church.

(*b*) Elizabeth could return to the catholicism of Henry VIII. It would alienate the pope as surely as if Elizabeth established a protestant Church, for both involved a rejection of his authority. In England it would dissatisfy the powerful, growing, protestant party. This policy offered one advantage however: the Roman catholics might come to accept royal supremacy if they were left free to worship in their own way.

(c) She could adopt protestantism. The Marian persecution proved to be the best possible advertisement for a national protestant Church. Mary's death was followed by the return of the protestants who had fled abroad to Geneva or Frankfort. They came back, burning to destroy not only papal supremacy, but all popish remnants too: vestments, images, altars, incense, and the mass. These 'puritans',[1] some moderate and some extreme, were determined about one thing: that there should be no return either to Mary's religion or to the catholicism of her father. And many of Elizabeth's subjects sympathised with them.

What would the queen do? The key lies in Elizabeth's own character. She was not pious. And she was certainly not dogmatic—she disliked theological hair splitting. She was in fact quite worldly and she put a united and prosperous England before the establishment of 'pure religion'. Elizabeth felt that her mission was to unite England again after the rebellions, scrambles for power, and religious strife of the past decade. Because of this she was tolerant. She would neither 'make windows into men's souls', nor punish them for their religious opinions. It would only cause further disunity.

No one knew—or has since discovered—exactly what her own religious views were. Naturally she rejected the pope's authority in favour of royal supremacy. She also disliked the mass. In 1558 she stalked out of a service in the royal chapel when the bishop of Carlisle insisted on using the catholic ritual. On the other hand, she liked ornaments and vestments, the pomp and ceremony of catholic services. And she did not approve of the clergy marrying. On matters of doctrine, however, she expressed no opinion.

Whatever Elizabeth's opinions were, they sat lightly upon her. When she fell in with the protestants, it was for political reasons:

(*1*) When the Marian bishops realised that she meant to break with Rome again, all but one of them resigned. The only suitable men to fill their places were the returned protestant

[1] See page 146.

exiles. So Elizabeth had to staff her Church with puritans, albeit moderate ones. Such men would only serve in a protestant Church.

(2) To become a national leader Elizabeth would have to adopt protestantism, because it was identified with the opposition to Mary Tudor's foreign allies, Philip of Spain and the pope.

(3) All the religious changes since 1529 had been confirmed or made by statute. Thus the only way to end papal supremacy and to make a new religious settlement was by summoning parliament. When it met in 1559 it contained a large number of the Marian exiles, their friends and supporters. Elizabeth could not hope to prevent her Church from becoming protestant even if she had wanted to.

But at least she wished to proceed slowly and cautiously. There were grave dangers in rushing into a protestant settlement. Elizabeth was at that moment conducting peace negotiations with France by which she hoped to regain Calais. A false move would dash her hopes. It might even cause her ally, Philip of Spain, to combine with France in a mighty catholic crusade against the heretic queen, and as yet she had no money for defences. In the north too there was danger. Scotland was still ruled by Mary of Guise, and its queen was married to the French dauphin. In the face of such dangers national unity was essential. Therefore it would be folly to alienate her catholic subjects by a sudden and immediate reformation. Instead Elizabeth hoped to make slow and moderate changes, carrying the catholics along with her.

PARLIAMENT AND THE REFORMATION SETTLEMENT: 1559

By the time Elizabeth's first parliament met, in January 1559, she had already indicated which side she favoured. She had surrounded herself with councillors, most of whom were protestants. A proclamation permitted the Gospel and the Epistle, the Lord's Prayer and the Ten Commandments to be recited in English in Church services. As she was on her way to the house of lords to open parliament, she was greeted by the abbot and monks of Westminster. Seeing that they carried lighted tapers, a catholic practice, she cried, "Away with these torches, for we see very well'. By such actions she made clear her protestant sympathies.

The protestants took these signs to mean that Elizabeth was going to lead a thorough-going reformation. But they were in for a shock when her councillors in the commons introduced her bill of supremacy. Its contents can be summarised as follows:

(*a*) Mary's act of 1554 was to be repealed. This would end papal supremacy and restore the ecclesiastical statutes of Henry VIII. Thus the queen was to be Supreme Head.

(*b*) Royal supremacy was to be enforced by an oath to be taken by the clergy.

(*c*) No mention was made of bishops, vestments, ceremonies, and catholic doctrines all of which were to remain unchanged, at least for the time being. The only innovation was communion in both kinds.

This bill would have marked a return to the Church as it was in the first year of Edward VI's reign. No further did the queen mean to go for the time being. Spain and France had not yet recognised her as queen, and there was a danger that, if she embraced protestantism, they would attack her.

The exiles were horrified at such mild proposals. They were backed by an overwhelmingly protestant house of commons. So a tug-of-war ensued, with the queen unwilling to make further concessions and the commons fighting for an out-and-out protestant Church. Neither side would yield an inch and parliament was adjourned for Easter without the matter being settled. Then Elizabeth decided to give way. England, France, and Spain had made peace at Cateau-Cambrésis. By signing the treaty with Elizabeth, France and Spain had acknowledged her as queen with the authority to make peace—Elizabeth need no longer fear an attack on England. So when parliament reassembled after Easter, she was willing to make further concessions. But even these were not enough for the protestants. Step by step she was forced to give way and accept drastic changes. The final settlement was hammered out in parliament and became law in May 1559. It consisted of two acts:

(*1*) An Act of Supremacy, which repealed Mary's ecclesiastical laws and so revived the royal supremacy. The general hostility to a woman as Supreme Head of the Church, however, had made Elizabeth change her title to 'Supreme Governor as well in all spiritual or ecclesiastical things or causes as temporal'. All judges, members of the government, justices of the peace, and mayors were required to take an oath accepting the royal supremacy. The penalty for refusing to do so was imprisonment and, for the third offence, death.

(*2*) An Act of Uniformity, which introduced a Prayer-Book similar to the second and more protestant one of Edward VI's reign. Its use was to be imposed on the clergy by an oath. Vestments were to be worn and ornaments allowed in the churches, as permitted by parliament in 1548. Laymen who failed to attend the protestant Church were to be fined a shilling for each offence.

Elizabeth had obviously made great concessions. She had wanted gradual change, probably arriving at a Church midway between catholicism and a mild protestantism. But the 'Elizabethan Settlement' was not a compromise in doctrine. It was decidedly protestant and even then it was not enough to satisfy the extreme puritans. It was certainly too protestant for Elizabeth's liking. She simply had to make the best of a bad job:

(*1*) Although her Church was protestant in doctrine, she made it catholic in appearance and government: she kept the heirarchy of bishops, deans and deacons; and vestments and ornaments were still used.

(*2*) The Act of Supremacy gave Elizabeth the right to govern the Church through her bishops. So she was careful to choose moderate men such as Matthew Parker whom she appointed archbishop of Canterbury. Parker was no fanatic and disliked the puritan hot-heads. He did not want the job of archbishop, preferring his life of study. But the queen needed him and meant to have him, so he became the first primate of the Anglican Church. With moderate men like Parker to do her bidding, she could be lenient with the Roman catholics. Thus they would not be driven into disloyalty. In any case the catholics found it easy to compromise with the vague doctrines of the new Anglican Church—it was not until 1571 that they were defined in detail by the Thirty-nine Articles.

The new Church displeased the more devout Roman catholics and puritans alike—none of them regarded it as a final settlement. But by her wisdom and tolerance Elizabeth made it acceptable to the majority of Englishmen, who were indifferent to theological quibbles and wanted only to worship God in peace and quiet.

X

THE REFORMATION
IN SCOTLAND AND IRELAND

SCOTLAND

THE weaknesses and abuses of the Scottish Church were similar
to those elsewhere in Europe, but here they were much more
pronounced. However, there was little hope of reform so long
as the Church was protected by the king, James V (1513–42),
who had close allies in the catholic king of France and the pope.
So the unreformed Church slumbered on.

THE REFORMATION TO 1547

The early demands for reform were made by devout catholics.
When they failed, some turned to Luther for inspiration. They
concluded that reform would only come if they rejected the pope
and established a new Church. The first protestants underwent
a harsh ordeal. James V condemned them, the Church persecuted them. In 1527 Patrick Hamilton began a preaching
campaign which led him to his execution at the stake. Others
were similarly burned, exiled, or forced through fear to
recant.

James V died in 1542, leaving the kingdom to his infant
daughter Mary. In the following year George Wishart returned
to his native land, after a long stay in Germany. He began to
spread Lutheran doctrines with great success in Dundee, Ayr,
and Leith. Now, it seemed, the protestants' opportunity had
come. But strong forces were marshalled against them.
Government was in the hands of the catholic and French queen-
mother, Mary of Guise, whilst the Church was controlled by the
intolerant Cardinal Beaton. Wishart was seized, tried, and
condemned to death. From the walls of St Andrews Castle,
Beaton watched his execution (March 1546). Three months
later Wishart's supporters, among them Leslie and Melville,
took their revenge by murdering Beaton in St Andrews and
hanging his body from a window. The catholics were roused to
a fury and besieged the castle, which the assassins had fortified.

Despite the protestants' stout resistance the arrival of some French galleys compelled the garrison to surrender (July 1547). Their ringleaders were taken to France where some were imprisoned and others, including John Knox who was the garrison's chaplain, were sent to the galleys.

The protestants had been defeated in war. They were also discredited by their close links with the English king. Although a catholic, Henry VIII had not scrupled to use them to stir up trouble in Scotland, and he certainly supported the plot to kill Cardinal Beaton. The reformers were playing with fire. The independent-minded Scots looked with suspicion on this alliance with their traditional enemy. So long as the Scottish protestants swam against the tide of national feeling they could not hope to succeed.

THE REFORMATION: 1547–53

Somerset's victory at Pinkie drove Scotland into the arms of France. A French army arrived to protect Scottish liberties and Mary Stuart was packed off to Paris to marry the dauphin, Francis. The catholic government of Mary of Guise, backed by France, now posed as the defender of Scottish independence. The protestants still appeared as allies of the old oppressor, England. Some of them sought refuge at the English court, where they were protected and well-treated, and it was at Edward VI's request that John Knox was released from the galleys in 1549 to become chaplain to the young king.

THE REFORMATION: 1553–58

When Mary Tudor became queen, Knox and the other Scottish exiles scattered to France, Geneva, and Strasbourg. In these centres of Calvinism they rejected Luther's milder reforms in favour of Calvin's extreme and intolerant Church. Meanwhile Mary Tudor's reign paved the way for the protestants' eventual triumph, not only in England but also in Scotland. In both kingdoms the catholic Church became the oppressor and persecutor. Scottish and English protestants were fighting for the same cause and in desperation drew closer together.

In the northern kingdom government was still in the hands of the regent, Mary of Guise, backed by the Church and French troops. The marriage of Mary Stuart to Francis, in April 1558, emphasised the regent's dependence on French support. People feared that Scotland was becoming a mere province of France.

So national feeling began to turn against the old ally. Nowhere was resentment more deeply felt than amongst the nobles. Some were genuine protestants; others were angry because they were excluded from the government; most of them looked longingly at the Church's wealth. In 1557 Glencairn, Argyle, Morton, Erskine, and other nobles pledged themselves to establish a protestant Church. 'We shall maintain them (the protestant preachers), nurse them and defend them, the whole congregation of Christ and every member thereof, at our whole powers and risk of our lives.' This marked an important change. These 'Lords of the Congregation' were opposing a catholic French government. Their protestant faith had become the symbol of Scottish independence.

THE REVOLT OF THE LORDS OF THE CONGREGATION: 1559

As the preachers moved from town to town, the protestants increased in strength and numbers. Events in 1558 and early 1559 buoyed up their hopes: Elizabeth became queen of England and her religious settlement established a protestant Church there. In May 1559 John Knox arrived in Edinburgh. He had returned to help the preachers and support the Lords of the Congregation against the regent. Instead he set in motion the complete destruction of the Roman catholic Church in Scotland. The signal for revolt was given by a sermon which he preached at Perth on 11 May. He delivered a furious attack on idolatry. It aroused the mob to sack the local churches and monasteries. Images were smashed, gold and silver ornaments were stolen, even the lead stripped from the roofs. Iconoclasm (image-breaking) spread throughout the country, to Edinburgh, Stirling, Linlithgow, St Andrews, and Dundee. Knox was delighted at his handiwork. 'Down with the nests,' he cried, 'and the rooks will fly away.'

The Lords of the Congregation knew full well that the regent would attempt to stop this violent reformation. They raised a force of six thousand and occupied Edinburgh. Soon the first flush of enthusiasm waned. There was not enough money to pay the troops who began to desert in large numbers. By July their forces had dwindled to one thousand five hundred and the rebel lords were glad to come to terms with the regent. She promised them religious freedom and the army of the Congregation withdrew from Edinburgh. But neither side was sincere.

4

Mary of Guise appealed for help to Francis, Mary Stuart's husband, who had just become king. He was naturally anxious to restore order in his wife's kingdom, and despatched troops with the promise of more to follow. When the Congregation learned that French troops had landed at Leith to help Mary they rose in arms again. In October they reoccupied Edinburgh where they publicly declared the regent deposed.

ELIZABETH'S INTERVENTION IN SCOTLAND

The Congregation appealed to England for help. However, Elizabeth believed that as princes were appointed by God their rights were sacred. Subjects should be loyal and obedient. If they rebelled against their prince they committed not only treason, but a sin as well. For Elizabeth to support rebels in another queen's realm was far worse. Furthermore she disliked the narrow-minded Calvinism of these rebels and she was not going to spend money just to help them establish a Church to their liking. In any case it was dangerous for Elizabeth to help the Congregation; the French might retaliate by assisting catholic rebels in England and they might even wage war against her. On the other hand there were sound reasons why she should intervene: if she could drive the French out of Scotland, she would remove the threat from her northern border and earn the gratitude of the Scots.

At first Elizabeth did not openly commit herself, for fear of offending France. She secretly sent the rebels money and munitions—and plenty of advice (which cost nothing). Cecil pressed her to send troops and a fleet, but she wanted to avoid the enormous expense which this would involve. However, Elizabeth was gradually forced to take more active steps. The raw, ill-equipped, rebel army was no match for the French veterans. In November 1559 its assault on Leith was repulsed with severe losses. The soldiers of the Congregation retreated. During the winter months the French occupied Stirling and prepared to advance on St Andrews.

Maitland of Lethington, the protestants' ablest politician, knew that their only hope was England. So he ignored the religious aims of the rebels. Instead he declared that they were fighting for the liberty of the Scots against France. This was more to Elizabeth's liking. As the French marched towards St Andrews, she dispatched a squadron of ships under Winter to the Firth of Forth. They blockaded Leith (December 1559) and prevented the arrival of further French reinforcements. On Christmas eve, an English army, under the duke of Norfolk and Lord Grey, was ordered to invade Scotland. In February 1560 Elizabeth's intervention was put on an official footing. She signed a treaty with the Lords of the Congregation whereby she became the protector of Scottish liberties. Her army and fleet would continue to assist the lords to safeguard Scotland's independence. However, she insisted that Mary Stuart's rights as queen were to be safeguarded.

Leith was besieged by the English and Scots. Their great assault was a dismal failure, but the French were starved into surrender (July). In the previous month Mary of Guise had died in Leith. By the Treaty of Edinburgh (July 1560) the French troops were to leave Scotland. The country was to be governed by a Scottish council of twelve on Mary's behalf. Elizabeth made no demands at all. She did not ask for money or suzerainty. Her restraint was a masterly stroke, because it earned her the gratitude and trust of the Scots. This, and the fact that both countries were fighting for a common cause, made them value her protection. Later it enabled her to execute their queen without destroying their friendship.

In August 1560 the Scottish parliament met and established a reformed Church. It adopted Edward VI's second Prayer-Book. Papal supremacy was abolished and heavy penalties were laid down for adhering to Roman catholicism. The Church was to be governed by a number of elected assemblies (presbyteries) as in Calvin's Geneva. At last Knox and his fellow-reformers had succeeded in erecting the intolerant presbyterian Church for which they had fought so long.

The success of the Scottish Reformation was due to four very different people: Knox, whose preaching and spiritual leadership inspired the Scots; Lethington and Cecil who between them brought Elizabeth to the rebels side; Elizabeth herself whose restraint in victory gained the loyalty of the Scots and avoided a clash with France. She had removed the French from Scotland, and though she disliked the presbyterians, at least a protestant Scotland gave her what she really sought—an ally, not an enemy on the northern border. In time the protestant faith was to become a common bond between the two kingdoms.

Finally it is important to recognise the form which reform of the Church took in Scotland. In England the religious changes were carried through by the government, using all the weapons of the State. The Scottish Reformation was a popular movement which succeeded in spite of the government. In the seventeenth century a similar religious movement in England was to lead to the execution of Charles I.

IRELAND

Wolsey neglected Irish affairs in favour of wars in Italy. The Geraldines were left to rule Ireland; and when Kildare died in 1513 his son succeeded him as earl and lord deputy. However, the breach with Rome made royal control of Ireland both urgent and essential. There was a danger that the pope might exploit discontent there as the Yorkist pretenders had done. As the Geraldines were the centre of unrest, Cromwell and Henry set to work to break their power. In 1533 Kildare was arrested as a result of complaints of his misbehaviour as the king's deputy. He was sent to the Tower where he died a year later. His son 'Silken Thomas' (so called because of the silken fringe on his helmet) believed that he had been executed. So he rose in revolt, supported by the rest of the Geraldines. Nevertheless, the new deputy, Lord Grey, was more than a match for them; the rebellion collapsed (1535-6) and Thomas Fitzgerald threw himself on the king's mercy. But Henry never showed pity to rebels and Thomas and his five uncles were executed. The power of the Geraldines was no more. Henceforth the Tudors put their trust in English deputies.

Lord Grey was given the task of imposing the acts of the 'Reformation Parliament' on Ireland. These changes caused little discontent. Many of the Irish, especially those in the more backward parts, were not Christians at all, and most of the Roman catholics felt little affection for a Church which had become so worldly and corrupt. No-one was executed for denying the royal supremacy. When the Irish monasteries were dissolved, the nobles and clan chiefs willingly joined in the share out of lands. Even the doctrinal changes of Edward VI's reign were accepted, and protestant preachers were well-received.

THE BEGINNING OF THE LAND PROBLEM

Nonetheless it was during the years of the Reformation in England (1529–1559) that the seeds of four hundred years'

IRELAND

bitterness and strife were sown. And the reason for this is not to be found in religion. The tribal chiefs and the Anglo-Irish families wanted to maintain their old independence, which gave them the right to plunder, kill, and make war on each other.

The king was determined to subject them to his will. Nonetheless he preferred to win their loyalty rather than use brute force 'lest by extreme demands they should revolt to their former beastliness'.

Henry VIII's grand dream was to unite the British Isles under one crown. He tried to wed Mary Stuart to his son; likewise he wanted to bring Ireland into closer union with England. To this end he changed his title from 'Lord' to 'King' of Ireland. He gave titles to some of the Irish chieftains: O'Neill became earl of Tyrone and O'Donnell earl of Tyrconnel. He persuaded them to surrender their tribal lands to him and receive them back from his hands as personal hereditary possessions. The meaning of this ceremony was clear: they were now the king's subjects, bound to serve him loyally. In return he would protect them and their right to own these lands.

Somerset and Northumberland neglected Irish affairs. But Mary Tudor tried to subdue Ireland by colonising it. When some Irish rebels were executed for treason in 1556, their lands were confiscated. Mary sold or granted them to English courtiers and gentlemen who were obliged to colonise them with English settlers. In return they were entitled to rents and other dues. Thus Mary created King's County (named after Philip) and Queen's County for this purpose. Elizabeth and the Stuarts were to carry on this policy, which was to prove so disastrous in Irish history. The actions of Henry VIII and his daughters showed a complete misunderstanding of Irish life and land law. In England all land was private property. But in Ireland it belonged to the clans. A chieftain had no right to part with it, because it was not his to give away. In English eyes Henry VIII's land transaction turned tribal lands into the private property of the chiefs, but when Mary (and Elizabeth) confiscated the property held by rebel chieftains, they were in fact harming the clans to whom the land really belonged.

THE FAILURE OF THE ELIZABETHAN CHURCH IN IRELAND: 1558–1603

In 1559 the Elizabethan Settlement established a protestant Church in England, and, by Poyning's Law, it applied to Ireland too. But here the Tudors failed. The Irish had accepted the frequent changes since 1529, yet the government had done nothing to arouse their enthusiasm for the new doctrines: no

Irish Bible or prayer-book, no schools or university. In this condition of apathy Ireland received the Jesuit missionaries. They came burning with a fiery zeal, ready to die for their faith. They aroused great enthusiasm; the faith of the old catholics was stiffened, and there were many converts. The protestants had lost their chance in Ireland—and by 1603 it was united in its loyalty to the pope.

THE AGE OF ELIZABETH I

XI

THE PEACEFUL YEARS : 1558–68

THE PROGRESS OF THE REFORMATION IN EUROPE

By 1558 the Church in western Europe had been split into three groups by the Reformation. Roman catholics, Lutherans, and Calvinists each believed that they alone had found the truth and tried to force their beliefs on the others. The protestants (who called themselves reformers, but whom the pope condemned as heretics) were still winning converts from the 'universal' catholic Church. However, the protestants themselves were not united, for the Lutherans and Calvinists disliked each other almost as much as they hated the Roman catholics. The Lutherans were now less important. Originally they had spread their influence far and wide, but, as the first enthusiasm faded, they became confined to north Germany and Scandinavia. Elsewhere— along the Rhine, in the Netherlands and France, in Scotland and England they were replaced by the Calvinists.

THE COUNTER-REFORMATION

The wiser catholics had long seen that there were grave abuses in their Church. Several problems urgently required a solution: the papacy's extravagance and worldliness; the confused and vague doctrines of the Church; pluralism, simony, and many other malpractices; the schism which had destroyed the unity of the universal catholic Church. We must now consider the instruments which the Church used to solve these problems:

(*a*) *The Council of Trent* (*1545–63*). In the mid-sixteenth century the popes were devout, pure, and intent on reform. One of them, Paul III (1534–49), summoned a Church council which met at Trent on imperial territory in 1545. Its object was reform.   The council consisted of cardinals and bishops from all the catholic countries of Europe, and during the following eighteen years it met three times.   It did not achieve everything it set out to do.   In particular it failed to reach a settlement with

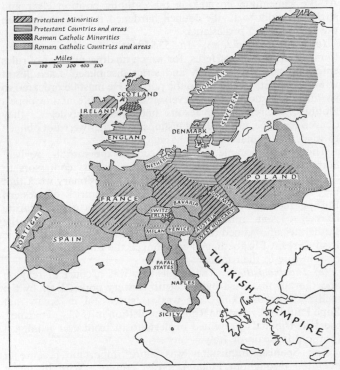

RELIGIONS IN EUROPE IN 1558

the Lutherans who showed no willingness to compromise, and no attempt was made to come to terms with the Calvinists.

Despite these setbacks the Council of Trent was a great success.   It clearly defined the doctrines of the Roman catholic Church; for example it ruled that, (*1*) both faith and good works are necessary for Salvation (Luther attached no importance to good works), and (*2*) the Bible ought to be interpreted in

4*

accordance with the traditions of the Church (both Lutherans and Calvinists insisted that the individual was free to interpret the Bible as he saw fit). When the catholics defended their faith they now had a set of defined doctrines to which they could refer. At the same time, in making the catholic position clear and sticking rigidly to it, the council hardened the breach between the catholics and protestants.

(*b*) *The Society of Jesus.* In 1534 Ignatius Loyola, a Spaniard, founded the Society of Jesus, for which he drew up a set of rules enforcing poverty, chastity, and strict discipline. Each Jesuit vowed complete obedience to the pope. He must be prepared to go anywhere, do anything, even give up his life at the pope's bidding. In return the Jesuits had special privileges: they obeyed the pope, not the local bishops; and they were not obliged to wear the normal monastic habit.

The Jesuits became the spearhead of the catholic revival. Some were trusted advisers of the pope, others confessors to catholic kings. But it was in teaching and missionary work that they excelled. In most of the catholic countries of western Europe they founded schools to train Jesuits or to educate laymen. Jesuit missionaries recaptured Poland from the Lutherans, and gained converts in Germany; they stirred up the Irish to resist Elizabeth, and encouraged the English catholics to remain true to their faith.

(*c*) *The Inquisition.* The Inquisition was a court of religion and morals, first used by thirteenth century popes, later by the medieval Spanish kings. It was so successful in Spain that Pope Paul III revived the Roman Inquisition in 1542. Together, the two tribunals prevented protestantism from ever gaining a foothold in Spain or Italy.

The Spanish Inquisition was more important because it operated throughout Philip II's vast empire. With its secret trials, its use of torture, and its horrible executions of obstinate heretics, the Inquisition was an object of fear. Yet its methods were by no means as dreadful as rumour and protestant propaganda suggested. In any case let us remember that in the sixteenth century every ruler executed heretics and every government used torture.

So in the second half of the sixteenth century the Church launched its great counter-attack. Its task was formidable.

The protestants had triumphed in England, Scotland, Denmark, Sweden, Switzerland and much of north Germany, and there were protestant minorities in France, the Netherlands, south Germany and Poland. Yet it was to achieve considerable success, and complete victory was only denied it by Elizabeth's England which emerged as the champion of protestantism.

POLITICAL CHANGES IN EUROPE

The 1550's marked the beginning of a new era in international politics. In the first place, a new set of rulers replaced the old. Charles V abdicated, after he had partitioned the Hapsburg empire. Austria went to his brother Ferdinand, who was in due course elected emperor. Ferdinand was weak, his empire disunited, and for the next fifty years the Austrian Hapsburgs were insignificant. To his son, who became Philip II of Spain, Charles bequeathed not only the Spanish possessions in Italy, the Mediterranean, and the New World, but also Franche Comté, Luxembourg and the Netherlands. Philip II's wife, Mary Tudor, died in 1558 and was succeeded by Elizabeth. In the following year Henry II of France was killed. For the next thirty years his sons reigned over France: Francis II, Mary Stuart's husband (1559–60), Charles IX (1560–74), and Henry III (1574–89). But the real ruler was Henry II's widow, Catherine de Medici.

Secondly the Treaty of Cateau-Cambrésis ended the long period of war between France and Spain. New problems held the attention of the new rulers: in France the rumblings of religious war; for Philip II all the questions arising from the management of his empire.

Finally, the 1550's were a decade of preparation for the great religious conflict to come. The Calvinists were still advancing: they helped to mould the Elizabethan Church, they were victorious in Scotland and they were making rapid headway in the Spanish Netherlands and France. The catholics, however, were preparing to launch their Counter-Reformation. The result was to confuse the normal issues of European politics. No longer was Europe dominated simply by the dynastic conflict between Valois and Hapsburg, with the rest of Europe siding with one or the other. New issues and new rulers meant new alliances.

SPAIN IN 1558

The size of the Spanish empire filled men with awe. Its ruler, Philip II, was hard-working, conscientious and concerned for the welfare of his empire. He was also a devout Roman catholic and believed that it was his special mission to restore the universal catholic Church. He showed no mercy to heretics in his own dominions, and was always willing to advance the catholic cause in other countries. However, Philip was no friend of the papacy: he meant to be master of the Spanish Church and would brook no papal interference, and he was the pope's political rival in Italy. Furthermore, he was an ardent patriot, anxious to promote Spanish interests. When his religion and his patriotism clashed as they sometimes did, the latter usually won. Nowhere was this more obvious than in his dealings with Elizabeth.

The English queen was a heretic and the pope urged Philip to depose her. As he was hailed by the catholics as leader of the Counter-Reformation, it was reasonable to assume that nothing would please Philip more. Quite the reverse. He was not going to let the pope rush him into an expensive and risky crusade against England, unless it would benefit Spain. Philip knew well enough that, even if he successfully invaded England and deposed Elizabeth, he could hardly prevent Mary Stuart from becoming queen—after all she was the strongest claimant and a staunch catholic. But she was also half-French. Her mother, Mary of Guise, ruled Scotland as regent, whilst the Guise family dominated the French court. A Spanish crusade might restore catholicism in England, but it would also create a French empire, embracing France, England, and Scotland. Philip preferred friendship with Elizabeth. Everything pointed to this as the most reasonable solution: England and Spain were traditional allies and their common enemy was France; both Philip and Elizabeth wanted the continuation of the Flanders trade.

The Netherlands were of prime importance to Philip on account of their wealth. However, communications were difficult. There was a land-route from Spanish-Milan, through the Alps by way of the Valtelline pass and across Germany, but the French obstructed this whenever they could. The alternative route was by sea up the English Channel. It was quicker, cheaper, and safer, although a hostile England could bar the way with her ships. As Philip's difficulties in the Netherlands increased, it became imperative to remain on good terms with Elizabeth.

At first Philip had hopes of marrying his dead wife's sister. When Elizabeth politely rejected his offer, Philip remained friendly. He tried to prevent any incident which might cause friction between England and Spain. To this end he urged the pope not to excommunicate Elizabeth and he stopped a papal ambassador from visiting her. Elizabeth had little to fear from Spain in the early years of her reign.

FRANCE IN 1558

The chief threat to the queen's security came from France, still England's traditional enemy. Mary Stuart's claim to be Elizabeth's successor was backed by her husband, who became king in 1559, and by the Guise family who dominated France and Scotland. To this political rivalry was added the religious conflict. France was catholic, so were her kings. The duke of Guise and his brother, the cardinal of Lorraine, were prominent amongst the leaders of the Counter-Reformation. Clearly Elizabeth had much to fear from France.

ELIZABETH'S FOREIGN POLICY

When Elizabeth became queen, she had two aims: to restore national unity and to preserve the independence of England, especially its freedom from papal control. In 1559 she added to these her desire to preserve the Elizabethan Settlement— although it was too protestant for her liking, it was at least a national Church. She never wavered in her pursuit of these objectives. To achieve them she used everything that came to hand: religion, the encouragement of rebels against her rivals, and the fact that she had yet to choose a husband. Her policies were endangered by France, Spain, and the Counter-Reformation. Her reign is the story of how she averted these dangers and, to a remarkable degree, achieved what she set out to do— though at the cost of fatally weakening the crown.

MARRIAGE AND SUCCESSION

The catholics persisted in the hope that England could be rescued from heresy. Elizabeth might marry a Roman catholic, preferably the devout Philip II or another Hapsburg. If the queen remained single, or chose to marry a protestant, she could be assassinated. Her rightful successor, Mary Stuart, could then claim the throne. If all other means failed, England could be invaded and Elizabeth deposed. All these proposals assumed that it only required the removal of the queen to bring England back to the fold. They ignored the fact that, after the experience of Mary Tudor, Roman catholicism and foreign rulers were anathema to most Englishmen. So Philip II and Mary Stuart, with her French connections, were equally objectionable.

It is hardly surprising, therefore, that Elizabeth's choice of a husband and the succession to the throne became matters of national concern. Until she married or named a protestant successor, she was the only safeguard against foreign domination and the return of the pope. No wonder the house of commons pestered her to do one or the other. In 1559 it made 'request to her Highness for marriage'; in 1563 it debated the succession and petitioned her to marry. But all to no avail. In the parliaments of 1566 and 1571 the result was the same. Elizabeth simply would not explain what she intended to do. She drove her faithful commons, her councillors, even loyal Cecil to despair.

Elizabeth's behaviour was exasperating, but wise. If she married an Englishman, it was bound to cause jealousy and strife amongst her courtiers and nobles. She could marry a foreigner, but the only eligible suitors were Roman catholics. Marriage would indeed cause more problems than it solved. In any case Elizabeth loved her power too much to share it with anyone. But she was equally aware of the value of marriage as a diplomatic weapon, for no king would jeopardise his chances of marrying her by committing hostile acts. The royal suitors queued to woo her: Philip II, Eric of Sweden (in 1561), Archduke Charles, son of the Emperor Ferdinand (until 1567), and the duke of Alençon (1573 and 1579–81). So Elizabeth dangled the bait of marriage before the princes of Europe, whilst she allayed the house of commons' fears with honeyed words and evasive answers. But she probably had no intention of marrying anyone.

There remained the question of her successor. If Elizabeth remained single, and therefore childless, the strongest claimant would be Mary Stuart. Her religion and her French connections would make her an unpopular choice, yet Elizabeth was unwilling to pass over the rights of another queen. Catherine Grey was the second claimant. She was the grand-daughter of Henry VIII's youngest sister Mary. Although she had her English birth and her protestantism to recommend her, she spoilt her chances when she married the earl of Hertford, son of the duke of Somerset (1561). Her husband was Jane Seymour's nephew and so had close ties with the crown. He was also the enemy of the queen's favourite, Robert Dudley. When Elizabeth learned of the marriage she was furious and thereafter refused to consider Catherine as her heir. If she died suddenly without having named her successor, the result might be a disputed succession and all the horrors of a civil war. But this too she refused to do. It would make the successor a centre of intrigue and opposition to her, especially as Mary Stuart was the strongest claimant. Elizabeth knew who the rightful heirs were, but they did not suit the needs of the country. So she refused to commit herself. Perhaps she hoped that if she waited time would solve the problem for her. It did.

ROBERT DUDLEY

To Elizabeth, marriage was normally a weapon of diplomacy and her courtships were with foreign suitors. On one occasion, however, her name was linked with an Englishman. He was the young, handsome, and ambitious Robert Dudley, son of the notorious duke of Northumberland and grandson of Henry VII's equally notorious minister. In 1560 the romance between the queen and her new favourite became the talk of England. Dudley certainly had ideas about becoming Elizabeth's husband. But there was one obstacle: he had a wife, Amy Robsart. In 1561 the romance became a major scandal when Dudley's wife was found dead with a broken neck, at the foot of a flight of stairs in her Oxfordshire home. At the inquest the jury returned a verdict of accidental death. Cruelly deserted by her husband she probably killed herself. However, rumour and gossip accused Dudley of murder. Some thought that Elizabeth herself was involved. If she had married Dudley she might even have lost her throne, but she was too level-headed to do anything so foolish. She made Dudley earl of Leicester, and showered him with gifts. But his hopes of a crown were gone forever.

ELIZABETH AND FRANCE: 1559–68

Elizabeth failed to recover Calais. By the Treaty of Cateau-Cambrésis (April 1559), France was to keep England's last outpost on French soil. However, Elizabeth's government could not afford to ignore developments in France, especially when the French Wars of Religion began. These were to cripple France until Henry IV brought them to an end in 1598. To refer to them as wars of religion is misleading. They were the result not only of religious intolerance, but of political ambitions, greed, weak kings, and court intrigues. At first religion was the most important factor. From Geneva Calvinist teaching spread rapidly through France. Amongst the converts were a number of nobles, who hoped to turn the religious movement into a rebellion against the king and so regain some of the power which they had lost in recent years. Some of the greatest nobles in the land, such as the Condés, Coligny, and the Bourbon kings of Navarre, became Huguenots (Calvinists). But the majority of Frenchmen remained catholic. They were led by the powerful and bigoted Guise family.

The growth of the religious problem coincided with a period of weak government. Francis II was a sickly youth of fifteen who reigned for only a year (1559–60). His younger brother, Charles IX, who succeeded him, was a minor and France was really ruled by his mother Catherine de Medici. The Guises controlled Francis II, and they struggled with Catherine and the Condés for control of Charles IX. The crown became the plaything of power-hungry nobles, and it was in no fit state to check the growth of protestantism.

When family rivalries and religious strife flared up into civil war, Elizabeth was quick to seize her opportunity. France, or rather the Guises, remained the gravest threat to her security. So she sent an army to help the Huguenots. In 1563, however, the catholics and Huguenots made peace and then joined forces to expel Elizabeth's soldiers from French soil. It is clear that at this point the national pride of the Huguenots was stronger than their friendship with the English protestants. Elizabeth had blundered; the only thing she could do was to make peace. The Treaty of Troyes was a landmark in Elizabeth's reign (1563). It confirmed the French in their possession of Calais, and so removed a major obstacle to a better understanding between the two countries. England turned away forever from the idea of conquests on the continent. Instead she sought new successes in the Americas—a policy which was bound to cause a conflict with Spain.

By 1568 the danger from France had diminished. The Guises' stranglehold on Scotland ended with the death of Mary of Guise and Francis II; French military occupation came to an end with the Treaty of Edinburgh; the 'auld alliance' was broken by the Scottish Reformation. As France became engrossed in her religious wars her power was neutralised. Elizabeth continued to fear the Guises who were still a power to be reckoned with. After the Treaty of Troyes her policy was to befriend their opponents, especially Catherine de Medici, who was not concerned to conduct religious wars against England but only to safeguard her sons' right to the French crown. England had begun to shift from the old alliance with Spain to a new friendship with France.

ELIZABETH'S POSITION IN 1568

Elizabeth had good reason to feel satisfied with the first ten years of her reign. At home the economic chaos had been taken in hand and religious strife had been allayed. Her spirit of tolerance towards the English catholics had reaped its reward: many had entered the Church of England and the remainder were nonetheless loyal to the government.

The government's finances were in a healthier state. In 1558 Elizabeth had had no money but large debts. She was a poor[1] queen but she disliked calling parliament to obtain extra money —taxes were unpopular and parliament was becoming too bold in matters of religion, marriage, and the succession. She preferred to manage on her income, although to do so she had to economise and curb her love of display. By careful management Mary Tudor's debts were paid and by 1568 Cecil was beginning to lay by a reserve of treasure for emergencies.

Abroad Elizabeth had averted the immediate danger of a catholic attack on England. She had scotched the Guise dreams of empire for the time being. France was embroiled in religious conflict, whilst Philip II was becoming absorbed in his efforts to suppress heresy in the Netherlands. The power of the leading Roman catholic States was being neutralised. Elizabeth's closer relations with Catherine de Medici, the tolerant

[1] For a full explanation of her financial difficulties see pages 163-164.

spirit of her government, and her marriage policy had all combined to blunt the forces of the Counter-Reformation. Things were going well. Then the arrival of Mary Stuart precipitated the first great crisis of Elizabeth's reign.

XII

THE YEARS OF CRISIS : 1568–72

THE DOWNFALL OF MARY STUART

After the death of her husband, Francis II, Mary returned to rule Scotland (1561). She was cultured and self-willed, half-French and Roman catholic. But she came to a backward, even barbarous land, where a turbulent nobility and a presbyterian Church held sway. There was little doubt that the going would not be smooth for Mary. At first, however, she acted quite reasonably. Although she insisted on attending her own private mass, she promised to leave the kirk in power. She chose two protestants, Maitland of Lethington and Lord James Stuart (later the earl of Murray), to be her leading councillors. Mary did all in her power to make herself popular. But preachers like Knox mistrusted her, hated her religion and insulted her in every possible way. When she met Knox his manner was that of the schoolmaster scolding his pupil. She asked him, 'Think you that subjects may resist their princes?' Knox replied, 'If princes exceed their bounds, madam, no doubt they may be resisted.'

'If there is not in her a proud mind, a crafty wit, my judgement faileth me.' So Knox wrote after his meeting with Mary. He was not wrong. Outwardly Mary remained reasonable, patient, and charming despite the insults heaped upon her. If she had continued to behave with tact and care she might have triumphed over the protestants and had a long and successful reign. But the folly of her actions in the following years swept her from her throne.

She took the first fatal step when she decided to marry again.

She might marry someone of Tudor blood, thus strengthening her right to succeed Elizabeth. She might acquire a powerful husband who would force the English queen to name Mary as her successor. Elizabeth was well aware of Mary's ambitions. She took alarm when she heard that the queen of Scots was seeking a husband. She even offered her favourite, the earl of Leicester, as a suitor. Instead, in 1564, Mary married her own cousin Henry, Lord Darnley. Both Mary and Darnley were grandchildren of Margaret Tudor and their marriage greatly strengthened the queen of Scots' claim. The alarming prospect of a catholic queen on the English throne had come one step nearer.

Although Darnley was dashing and handsome, he was also vicious, with loose morals and without intelligence. When she realised his true nature Mary refused to share with him her right to govern. Instead she confided in her Italian secretary, David Rizzio. It was rumoured that they were lovers. This was probably untrue, but many believed it. Worse still, she became obstinate and ceased to co-operate with the protestants. Darnley joined forces with some of the discontented lords. In March 1566 they acted. Mary and Rizzio were at supper one night when Darnley burst in, followed by Morton and other armed men. Begging for mercy Rizzio was dragged from Mary's side into an adjoining bedroom, and there stabbed to death. The lords took over the palace and the queen became their prisoner.

When all seemed lost Mary turned the tables on her opponents. She exerted her great charm to win over her husband who helped her to escape to Dunbar. Public opinion, disgusted by Rizzio's murder, was on her side and she easily gathered an armed force. The murderers fled from Edinburgh, whilst Mary returned in triumph to Holyrood Palace. If she swore to avenge Rizzio's death she gave no outward sign of it. In June 1566 she gave birth to a son, James. She pretended a reconciliation with Darnley and pardoned the other murderers. All seemed forgiven and forgotten.

When Darnley caught smallpox at the end of the year, Mary showed great concern. She took him to convalesce at Kirk o'Field, a house just outside Edinburgh. One night in February 1567, while Mary was at a masque in Holyrood Palace, an explosion demolished the house. Darnley's body was found in the garden. An examination showed that he had not been killed in the explosion; he had been strangled. Public opinion held Mary responsible. She certainly had a motive and she was conveniently out of the way at the time of the explosion. The truth will probably never be known, but one thing is certain: the Scottish people had made up their minds that the earl of Bothwell was the actual murderer.

Mary foolishly ignored public opinion. When Bothwell was brought to trial, she had him acquitted by a packed jury. Not content with this, she made him duke of Orkney—was this a reward for getting rid of Darnley? The truth of the matter is that Mary had fallen in love with Bothwell, whether before or after her husband's murder is not known. In April 1567 she allowed him to seize her and carry her off to Dunbar. Next month, twelve days after Bothwell had divorced his wife, they were married in a protestant church.

The Scots could stomach no more. Their queen had married a murderer, even if she herself was not one. In June they rose in revolt. Mary had little hope of finding support. She was even deserted by her husband who fled abroad. At Carberry Hill she surrendered to the rebels, who imprisoned her at Loch Leven. She was compelled to abdicate in favour of her son, and to hand over the reins of government to a regent, Murray.

Mary was not beaten yet. She exerted her remarkable influence on her gaoler, who allowed her to escape (May 1568). She tried to raise an army, but only the ever-faithful Hamiltons hurried to join her; the rest of Scotland remained hostile. Once again the protestant lords took the field and the Hamiltons were routed at Langside. Mary could not fly to France or Spain, where catholic opinion was outraged by her recent behaviour. So she crossed the border into England and threw herself on Elizabeth's mercy.

ELIZABETH'S DILEMMA

Mary's arrival presented Elizabeth with a serious problem. On the one hand Elizabeth felt bound to respect Mary's rights as queen, and she denied that the Scots could depose her. Yet if she compelled them to accept Mary back as their queen, she would make enemies of them once again. There were several courses of action open to Elizabeth, but all of them involved risks. She could send Mary back to Scotland, where she would probably be tried and possibly executed. Elizabeth's belief in the sanctity of princes forbade this. If she sent her to France it would revive the old Franco-Scottish connection, which Elizabeth had worked so hard to sever. It might even lead the Guises to intervene in Scotland. The only other solution was for Mary to remain in England.

Elizabeth pondered the problem. Finally she decided to hear both sides of the case. In October 1568, representatives of Mary and the Scottish lords were summoned to meet Elizabeth's commissioners at York (and later at Westminster). There the Scottish queen accused her subjects of rebellion, and they accused her of murder. The case of the Scottish lords rested partly on Mary's known actions, but also on the notorious 'Casket Letters'. The lords claimed that these letters had been written by Mary to Bothwell, and showed conclusively that she had been a party to Darnley's murder. Whether or not they were genuine or forged, they did much to persuade both the queen and her commissioners of Mary's guilt. In any case it was in Elizabeth's interest to establish this. She would not then be in honour bound to restore Mary, and Scotland would remain under the rule of her allies, the protestant lords. On 10 January 1569 Elizabeth gave her verdict: nothing had been proved against Murray and the other lords, whilst the evidence against Mary was insufficient. Murray was permitted to return to Scotland to act as regent for the young king, James VI. Mary remained in England as Elizabeth's prisoner.

So began her long imprisonment which was to last eighteen years. During that time she presented a constant threat to Elizabeth. She became the hope of Roman catholics and the rallying point of all resistance to the English queen. Until her execution in 1587 she was connected with catholic plots to assassinate Elizabeth, who went in peril of her life. For the English queen to take such a risk may seem foolish. The privy council, parliament, and public opinion set up an increasing clamour for Mary's death. Yet Elizabeth knew best. To execute Mary would be to call down upon her head the wrath of catholic Europe. Instead Elizabeth used her as a hostage to guarantee France's good behaviour; while Philip II was unlikely to make any serious attempt to dethrone the English queen, for it would only benefit Mary and therefore France. Although Elizabeth's decision to keep Mary in England was fraught with dangers, it was also merciful, wise, and courageous.

ANGLO-SPANISH RELATIONS

Mary's arrival in England coincided with an important point in the deteriorating relations between Philip II and Elizabeth. It has been seen that Philip was not prepared to oppose Elizabeth's protestant regime unless she gave him serious political reasons for doing so. In the sixteenth century, however, politics and religion were not easily separated. The Calvinists represented a threat to Philip's power: they encouraged national feelings, upheld economic freedom, and wanted a Church free from royal control. The merchants of other countries, most of them protestants, would not acknowledge Spain's monopoly in the New World. So the advance of Philip's power depended upon the success of the Counter-Reformation. Elizabeth was clearly becoming the greatest obstacle to the success of both Spain and the Roman catholic Church. It was therefore only natural that the old allies, England and Spain, drifted into opposite camps.

THE REVOLT OF THE SPANISH NETHERLANDS

Elizabeth fully realised that England's safety depended upon the survival of the protestant faith in Europe. So long as the catholic princes were busy dealing with heresy amongst their own subjects, England was safe. To this end Elizabeth had helped the Huguenots in 1562. She acted in the same way in the Netherlands.

With their rich cities and wealthy merchants, the seventeen provinces of the Netherlands were Philip's most precious possession. They were also a source of trouble. There was no real unity. The provinces were jealous of their rights and privileges and constantly squabbled with each other. The spread of the Reformation produced another division, that between Lutherans and catholics. Charles V had been faced with the same problems, but at least he was a popular ruler, born and bred in Flanders. With Philip II it was different. The people saw him as a stiff-necked Spaniard, who ruled his vast empire from Madrid in the interests of Spain. He did not bother to consult them in matters of government, but simply sent his orders which were carried out by a regent, Margaret of Parma.

The Reformation increased Philip's difficulties. Calvin's doctrines replaced the milder beliefs of Luther, especially in the cities. Although Philip harshly persecuted the Calvinists, he was wise enough to see that persecution alone was not enough. Calvinism would continue to spread, unless the Church was reformed. Yet even his plans to do this were not welcomed, for he intended to stop the nobles from using the Church to provide money and livings for their relatives.

Much that Philip set out to do was wise in itself, but he paid no attention to the feelings and traditions of his subjects. They feared that he wished to deprive them of their ancient liberties, and they suspected that, sooner or later, they would be required to contribute to the costs of Philip's expensive and ambitious foreign policy. They sympathised with the persecuted Calvinists as defenders of their freedom against Philip's harsh rule, and many people became protestants for this reason. In 1566 Calvinist preachers in the towns aroused their audiences to ransack the churches. Philip sent the duke of Alva with a Spanish army to restore order and punish the trouble-makers. Alva's ruthless iron-fisted rule and his imposition of new taxes on trade made armed rebellion a certainty. In 1572 some Dutch pirates, known as the Sea-Beggars, seized the port of Brill and raised the flag of revolt. Many other towns followed suit and Alva was faced with a national rebellion.[1]

Elizabeth had already done what she could to assist the Netherlands in their fight against Philip. She welcomed to England refugees from Alva's persecution, and allowed Dutch pirates to shelter in English ports. In 1568 Spanish ships, carrying money to pay Alva's troops, were driven by Huguenot pirates into English ports. Elizabeth took the money, which Genoese bankers had lent Philip, and borrowed it from them herself. She was not prepared to help the rebels openly, for that would mean risking war with Spain. But she was making sure that Philip was kept too busy in the Netherlands to worry about England.

ECONOMIC RIVALRY

Spain and England were becoming economic rivals. Previously their alliance had rested on the sale of English wool and unfinished cloth to the Flemish cloth towns. But this was becoming less important: the English cloth industry was

---

[1] The rebels found a magnificent leader in the wealthy German-born noble, William of Orange. At first loyal to Philip, his devotion to his adopted country drove him to resist Spanish rule.

growing and merchants no longer depended on the Flemish markets alone.

Meanwhile there was growing conflict in the New World. English merchants refused to recognise the monopoly claimed by Spain and Portugal in the Americas. They wanted to share in its enormous wealth, and at first they were anxious to trade in a peaceful manner. The Spanish settlers were willing to let them in although Philip forbade it. They needed slaves to work on their plantations and in their mines and at least one English seaman was ready to provide them. In 1562 John Hawkins sailed to West Africa and bought slaves from the local chieftains. He sold them to Spanish colonists in the West Indies and returned home with a handsome profit. Elizabeth became interested and lent him a ship for his second voyage in 1564. Elizabeth's action meant that the English government thought as Hawkins did: that Philip had no right to claim a monopoly in the New World. This second venture was even more profitable than the first—and the queen shared in the profits.

In 1567 Hawkins followed the same route again with a bigger fleet. All went well until a severe storm caused him to put into the Mexican port of San Juan de Ulua to refit. Before his ships were ready for sea again a fleet appeared outside the harbour. It was bringing Philip II's new viceroy (governor) to the New World. Hawkins permitted the Spanish galleons to enter. In return he was promised that he would be allowed to complete his repairs. The viceroy broke his word, however, and treacherously attacked the English ships. Only two escaped: Hawkins' own 'Minion' and Francis Drake's 'Judith'. They returned home, thirsting for vengeance. If they could not earn some of the New World's wealth by peaceful trading, in future they would take it by force. As English seamen attacked Philip's colonies, plundered his merchant ships, and threatened his treasure fleets, it is small wonder that the Spanish king's relations with England became strained.

Thus Mary Stuart arrived in England when the Anglo-Spanish alliance was breaking down. Devoted catholics plotted to put Mary on the throne. Philip was not yet willing to see this happen, nor was he ready to risk war. However, he was prepared to stir up discontent against Elizabeth and weaken her position—in fact to pursue the very same policy which she adopted in the Netherlands.

THE NORTHERN REBELLION: 1569

The first challenge to Elizabeth's rule came in 1569. Through Roberto Ridolfi, a Florentine banker, the Spanish ambassador, Guerau de Spes, brought together those who were discontented with things the way they were: proud nobles, like the earls of Northumberland (a Percy) and Westmorland (a Neville) who regarded Cecil as an upstart, discontented catholics, and many others who wanted a return to the old known ways. The most important conspirator was the duke of Norfolk, a vain man with great ambitions and little courage. The plotters' plan was simple: Norfolk was to marry Mary Stuart; the catholics would rise in revolt and Alva would invade England with a Spanish army; Cecil would be dismissed, the catholic religion restored, and Mary proclaimed heir to the throne. But Cecil learned of the plot and nipped it in the bud. When Norfolk was summoned to court he meekly obeyed. He was imprisoned in the Tower, though released in 1570.

Northumberland and Westmorland feared that their arrest would follow. They became desperate and raised the flag of revolt. It was a dangerous situation for Elizabeth, because the north was still more loyal to the old feudal nobles than to the crown. Northumberland and Westmorland were able to raise support quickly, whereas Elizabeth had no standing army to oppose them. The rebels occupied Durham and said mass in the cathedral. This made the rising appear like a crusade, though many of the rebels had joined the movement for other reasons. Then they marched southwards. Their immediate aim was to free Mary but Elizabeth acted quickly. She moved the captive queen from Tutbury castle in Staffordshire whilst her loyal nobles raised an army. The rebels quickly lost hope and scattered to their homes. The two earls fled into Scotland. The north was occupied by Elizabeth's troops, who stamped out the dying embers of revolt. Then followed the punishments: lands were confiscated and over eight hundred men executed. However, the queen was not content just to punish. Once and for all the north had to be brought under royal control. The earl of Huntingdon, a puritan, was appointed president of the council of the north. Under his energetic rule (1572–95), the feudal independence of the north was at last destroyed.

THE BULL OF EXCOMMUNICATION: 1570

The crisis was not yet over. In February 1570 Pope Pius V issued a bull which deposed and excommunicated Elizabeth—in other words her subjects were no longer bound to obey her. The pope's action was understandable. He could not continue to tolerate the government of England by a heretic—a heretic who moreover was becoming the acknowledged defender and protector of the protestants in Europe. That the pope had delayed so long before taking action was partly due to the hope that Elizabeth would become a catholic. That hope had long since gone. It was also due to Philip II, who preferred to see a protestant on the throne rather than the pro-French Mary. When Pius V finally went ahead and excommunicated Elizabeth, all hope of success had gone. The English catholics were few in number; most of them preferred loyalty to Elizabeth and a quiet life, especially after the dreadful punishments of the previous year.

Unfortunately a few did not. In 1570 the duke of Norfolk became party to another plot organised by De Spes and Ridolfi. Their plans and aims were much the same as those of 1569: Norfolk was to marry Mary and remove Elizabeth. Mary, the pope, and Philip II approved of it. But once again Cecil's spies uncovered the details of the plot (1571). Ridolfi and De Spes were expelled from England. Norfolk was arrested, tried for treason, and condemned to death. For a while he languished in the Tower, whilst Elizabeth made up her mind what to do with him. She was loath to execute such a great noble, but when parliament met in 1572 it forced her hand. The commons, shaken by the Ridolfi Plot, saw that Elizabeth (and with her their protestant Church) would be in constant danger so long as the queen of Scots lived. They demanded Mary's execution. Elizabeth would not consent to this, but she had Norfolk put to death (June 1572), in order to appease them. She could not ignore the fact that the crisis of these years (1568–72) marked the end of the period of toleration.

XIII

THE DRIFT TO WAR : 1572–85

ALTHOUGH relations between England and Spain were rapidly worsening, Elizabeth wished to avoid war. She had not the money to pay for one, and she doubted the country's strength to resist Spain. There was an even greater danger. France and Spain might combine in response to the Bull of 1570 which had called upon the catholic rulers to depose Elizabeth. So she sent Walsingham across the Channel to secure an alliance with Catherine de Medici. She chose the right man for the job. Francis Walsingham, who became one of her greatest ministers, was a devoted puritan. He was filled with a hatred of Spain and the pope, and was anxious to save England from what he regarded as their wicked schemes.

Walsingham was successful and the Treaty of Blois was signed in April 1572. It required that if either country was attacked the other should come to its aid. Walsingham had reason to be satisfied: if England was attacked by Spain, France was bound to help her. But in August his hopes appeared to be dashed by the Massacre of St. Bartholomew. The massacre resulted from Catherine de Medici's resentment at the influence which the Huguenot leader, Coligny, had come to exercise over the young king, Charles IX. She joined the Guises and planned with them the assassination of Coligny and the other Huguenot leaders who were then in Paris. On 24 August, St. Bartholomew's Day, the murders were duly carried out, but the Paris mob regarded them as the signal for a general slaughter of Huguenots. The other cities of France copied Paris' example.

The massacre was greeted with joy by the catholic princes of Europe. Elizabeth was horrified. The Treaty of Blois seemed worthless, for how could any protestant trust Catherine de Medici? In fact all was not lost. Many Huguenots had escaped the slaughter and lived to fight another day. The religious wars went on and Catherine, who soon reverted to her former hostile attitude to the Guises, would not risk a war with England as well. So the Treaty of Blois survived.

ELIZABETH AND SPAIN: 1570–80

Although Philip and Elizabeth continued to work secretly against each other, they were anxious to avoid war. But already their subjects had come to blows 'beyond the line' (this was the line drawn by Pope Alexander VI and which, by the Treaty of Tordesillas in 1494, divided the New World between Portugal and Spain). The restless adventurers who sailed from the west country ports of England were not deterred by the disaster of San Juan de Ulua which only strengthened their resolve to break the Spanish monopoly. Francis Drake led the way. He successfully ambushed a Spanish treasure train on the Panama isthmus (1572). In 1578–9 he plundered Spanish ships and settlements in the Pacific. On his return Elizabeth knighted him on board his famous ship, the *Golden Hind*. In this way she showed to all the world that she would not accept Spain's monopoly in the New World.

Many other adventurers, at one and the same time pirates, patriots, and protestants, took part in this unofficial war against Spain. They sailed from the sheltered harbours of Devon and Cornwall to plunder Spanish ships in the Atlantic, the Bay of Biscay, and the Channel. When Spain protested, Elizabeth insisted that it was not her fault – that her seamen would not obey her. She fooled no-one, least of all Philip II. He showed remarkable patience in putting up with this state of affairs for so long. There was little else he could do. His prime concern was with the revolt of the Netherlands. Until it was ended, he had neither time nor money to spare on a war against England.

ELIZABETH AND THE NETHERLANDS: 1572–78

Elizabeth did not like the Dutch or the Huguenots – they were not only rebels but also intolerant Calvinists. Yet she knew that once Philip had conquered the Netherlands he would turn his attention to England, and that if the Guise family crushed the Huguenots they would join forces with him. Elizabeth was gradually driven, by sheer necessity, into a distasteful alliance with subjects who were in rebellion against their anointed kings. But she gave her assistance secretly, for fear of arousing her enemies to war. When, after Coligny's death, Henry of Navarre became the new leader of the Huguenots, he also became the ally of Elizabeth who sent him money and arms. She adopted the same policy in the Netherlands, where Philip was finding that William of Orange's Dutch rebels were tough opponents. The Spanish generals made little progress. In 1573 Philip recalled Alva and in his place put Requesens, who fared no better. When Requesens died, in 1576, his unpaid soldiers mutinied and sacked Antwerp. The 'Spanish fury' was a disaster for Philip, because the southern provinces, hitherto neutral, now joined the rebels.

Requesens' successor, Don John of Austria (1576–8), failed to retrieve Spanish fortunes, and when he died in 1578 the end of the Dutch revolt seemed as far away as ever. This is just what Elizabeth wanted and she continued to aid the rebels with money and arms. Although she wanted to keep this a secret from Spain, Philip knew well enough what she was up to. Despite this he was still anxious to avoid war. His only chance of defeating England lay in a successful invasion. The English had no troops capable of standing up to a Spanish army. But his veterans had to get to England first, and to do so they would have to overcome Elizabeth's great sea-captains. Philip simply had not enough ships, and he could not afford to buy more. So war was out of the question.

Nevertheless Philip did not remain idle. He stirred up discontent in England and contributed troops to a papal expedition to Ireland (1579–80). When Elizabeth continued to interfere in the Netherlands and New World, Philip encouraged plots to assassinate her—even Mary Stuart on the throne was better than Elizabeth, who now stood out as the defender of Europe's protestants and the chief obstacle to Philip's ambitions.

THE COUNTER-REFORMATION AND ENGLAND: 1570–80

In 1570 the forces of the Counter-Reformation launched an offensive against Elizabeth, the signal for it being Pope Pius V's Bull of Excommunication. The purpose of the bull was to depose the queen and in this it failed miserably. However, in 1575 she was faced with a new danger. Seminary priests began to arrive secretly in England; in 1580 they were reinforced by Jesuits from an English college at Rome. The Jesuits in particular presented a formidable challenge to the government. They were zealous, able, and dedicated. Although most of them, like Edmund Campion, simply came to minister to the English catholics, one or two, such as Robert Persons, interfered in politics too. Persons spent his life scheming the downfall of

Elizabeth: he encouraged Spain to invade England, supported Philip II's daughter as heir to the English throne, and even plotted to murder the queen. Elizabeth and her privy council believed that these priests had come to spread treason and discontent. So the missionaries were relentlessly hunted down. When they were caught, torture, imprisonment or death was their lot. But others took their places.

THE PROBLEM OF IRELAND

The problem of Ireland was added to Elizabeth's other worries. When she became queen Ireland's condition was almost as bad as it had been on her grandfather's accession (1485). But nothing could be done until she had broken the resistance of the tribal chiefs and Anglo-Irish families. In short, Ireland had to be conquered. It took her the whole of her reign to do just this. It was not for want of trying, but she was short of money and tried to win her Irish wars as cheaply as she could. Campaigns against rebels dragged on and on because the Irish were experts in guerilla warfare. Even if they were stupid enough to fight a pitched battle (which they usually lost) they would withdraw to the bogs or mountains, where the English dared not follow. English deputies stuck doggedly to the task, but they did so with such harshness, such savagery, that Ireland became one of the sorriest aspects of Elizabeth's reign.

The first challenge to Elizabeth's authority occurred when a violent and primitive chieftain, Shane O'Neill, made himself master of Ulster (1562–6). He had ideas of ridding Ireland of its English rulers, and to this end he sought help from Elizabeth's enemies, Mary Stuart and the pope. His ambitious schemes were only scotched when he was defeated by the queen's new deputy, Sir Henry Sidney, and murdered by some Scottish settlers. Thereafter Ulster ceased to be a threat.

There was trouble in the south too:

First revolt of the Geraldines, 1569–72. The earl of Desmond, lawless and greedy, ruled Munster with an iron hand. He was involved in many affrays and feuds, especially (as he was a Geraldine) with the earl of Ormond, a Butler. Sir Henry Sidney did not hesitate. He arrested Desmond and sent him to the Tower. During his absence Sidney introduced English officials into Munster to watch over the local chieftains. He also began to 'plant' (colonise) it. Large tracts of land were granted to courtiers and gentlemen such as Richard Grenville.

Sidney's actions did not pass without protest. Another Geraldine, James Fitzmaurice Fitzgerald, headed a revolt against the deputy (1569), but Sidney wore him down and forced him to surrender in 1572. Although beaten Fitzmaurice did not give up. He realised that without foreign help he could not hope to win. So in 1575 he went abroad to seek support from the catholic kings of Europe. His action marks a significant change in Irish politics. To the government's normal problem of inter-tribal warfare and rebellion was now added the threat of the Counter-Reformation.

However, for the time being English rule in Ireland was marked with success. Sidney had pacified Ulster and Munster, and extended Elizabeth's authority. Although he is usually overshadowed by his more famous son, Philip, Sir Henry Sidney was a man of remarkable ability. When his deputyship ended in 1578, Ireland was more peaceful than it had been for many years.

Second revolt of the Geraldines, 1579–83. However, peace only lasted so long as Sidney was there. Soon after his restraining hand was removed, trouble flared up again. James Fitzmaurice's mission to the catholic courts of Europe had at last been rewarded with success. In 1578 the pope equipped and dispatched an expedition to Ireland. However, its commander, Sir Thomas Stukeley, an eccentric adventurer, decided to join King Sebastian of Portugal, who had gone on a crusade in Morocco. Sebastian, Stukeley, and the papal forces perished in a crushing defeat at Alcazarquivir. Another expedition set out in 1579. It was led by James Fitzmaurice, and this time the pope sent a legate, Nicholas Sanders, to make sure things did not go wrong. This expedition did at least reach Ireland. Some of the Irish joined the invaders and in 1580 they were reinforced by a Spanish force. But their success was short-lived: Fitzmaurice was killed; the Spanish troops who held Smerwick surrendered only to be massacred in cold blood by Lord Grey, the English deputy; finally the embers of revolt were stamped out (1579–83). Unsuccessful though the pope's intervention had been, it had caused Elizabeth a good deal of worry and expense.

This time the Fitzgeralds were finished for good. The vast

territory over which they had ruled in Munster was granted to protestants who undertook to 'plant' it with English settlers—over half a million acres were distributed in this way. Sir Walter Ralegh was amongst those who received lands; so was the poet Edmund Spenser who wrote much of his greatest work, *The Faerie Queene*, on his three thousand acre estate at Kilcolman. As the English colonists moved into Munster they found a wasteland. Spenser painted a vivid description of the miserable condition of those who had survived the recent rebellion: 'Out of every corner of woods and glens they came creeping forth, for their legs would not bear them; they looked like anatomies of death, they spake like ghosts crying out of their graves, and a most populous and plentiful country was suddenly left void of man and beast.'

THE THROCKMORTON PLOT: 1583

In 1580 Philip successfully claimed the Portuguese throne on the death of King Henry (1578–80). He was now master of the two greatest colonial empires in the world. He had acquired Portugal's fine harbours, its sailors and its many fine ships. At last he had the strength to attempt an invasion of England if all else failed. Nevertheless he still preferred to toy with plans for the assassination of Elizabeth—it was cheaper and less risky. No excuses can be made for political murder, but it was widely practised at the time: Lord Darnley (1567), the duke of Guise and his brother (1588), and Henry III (1589), all died at the hands of assassins. Even a pope, Gregory XIII, called upon the English catholics to kill their queen.

Elizabeth's life was now in constant danger as the Throckmorton Plot serves to show. Francis Throckmorton, an English catholic, was the central figure in a conspiracy to remove Elizabeth from the throne. It involved many: the duke of Guise who was to invade England, the pope and Philip II who were providing the money, and Mary Stuart who would become queen in Elizabeth's stead. Francis Throckmorton acted as the link between Mary and Mendoza, Philip's ambassador in London. His task was to raise a revolt amongst the English catholics when the duke of Guise landed.

At last the leaders of the Counter-Reformation were sinking their differences and combining to destroy the woman who stood in their way. But all their scheming came to nothing. Walsingham's agents uncovered the plot. Throckmorton was arrested and tortured on the rack. He made a full confession which implicated Mendoza and Mary. Throckmorton was executed and the Spanish ambassador was ordered to leave England. Yet once again Mary Stuart escaped scot-free. Elizabeth still could not bring herself to execute another queen.

THE BOND OF ASSOCIATION: 1584

When William of Orange was assassinated,[1] Elizabeth's councillors took steps to prevent her meeting a similar fate. They drew up the Bond of Association, which was circulated throughout England for all who wished to sign. Those who did so bound themselves by an oath to obey the queen, to protect her from would-be assassins, and to prevent the succession of anyone 'by whom or for whom any such detestable act shall be attempted or committed'; and they were not to rest content until those plotting to kill the queen were themselves put to death. It was crude, and if Elizabeth had been assassinated it would have resulted in mob-rule and lynchings. But at the time it expressed the nation's devotion to her. It also warned Mary Stuart what would happen if she continued to plot against Elizabeth.

ELIZABETH AND FRANCE: 1572–85

The Treaty of Blois guaranteed the neutrality of France. Elizabeth could depend upon the goodwill of Catherine de Medici and the alliance of Henry of Navarre. But she also had a powerful enemy in the duke of Guise. When Mary Stuart had sat on the Scottish throne the Guises had been enemies of Philip II. Their common religious interest, however, was drawing them closer together. Elizabeth saw the danger and set to work to strengthen her already friendly relations with Catherine.

For the last time Elizabeth used marriage as a diplomatic weapon – and on this occasion the 'victim' was Catherine's youngest son, the duke of Alençon. In 1579 he visited England to woo the queen in person. Although he was deformed and his face was pitted with the scars of smallpox he did not lack intelligence or cunning. At court a series of gay, extravagant entertainments followed. Elizabeth showed great affection for the duke. She nick-named him her 'frog' and spent every day with him. Her councillors feared that she really meant to

[1] See page 123.

5

marry him. So did her subjects. Most of them were horrified at the idea of a French catholic consort. Some of them said so, but they were dealt with harshly. Elizabeth was not going to let them upset her plans. When a puritan, John Stubbs, published an attack on the intended marriage, both he and the printer were condemned to lose their right hands. Stubbs became a popular hero, and an angry crowd watched the punishment. When his hand was cut off Stubbs shouted, 'God save the Queen, and confound all evil councillors'.

Elizabeth did not intend to marry Alençon. But the courtship served its purpose: Catherine de Medici did not join in a general catholic attack on England and Elizabeth persuaded Alençon to help the Dutch. So the position stood until 1584. Then disaster struck: Alençon died. His death made the protestant Henry of Navarre heir to the French throne. Out of loyalty to his religion, Henry III joined with the Guises to prevent this, and the Guises in their turn signed an alliance with Philip II. Their common aims were: to destroy heresy in France and the Low Countries, and to prevent Henry of Navarre succeeding Henry III. At last the catholic forces had sunk their differences. If the Huguenots' resistance was stamped out, there was nothing to prevent the French king, influenced as he was by Philip II and the Guises, from mounting an attack on England.

ELIZABETH AND THE NETHERLANDS: 1578–85

In the Netherlands too the situation had become desperate. In 1578 Philip II sent Alexander Farnese, duke of Parma, to the Netherlands. He was the greatest general of the age. He was also a man of great common-sense. By offering generous terms, he persuaded the catholic states in the south to return under Spanish rule. Then Parma began, slowly but surely, to reconquer the seven rebellious Calvinist provinces in the north.

The Dutch looked around frantically for a protector. They asked Elizabeth to become their sovereign, but she refused for it would obviously lead to war with Spain. When they found a protector in the duke of Alençon (1580–4) he turned out to be a dismal failure. He suffered defeats at the hands of Parma and quarrelled with the rebels. Yet his death in 1584 was a blow to Elizabeth, for, as we have seen, it caused Henry III to ally with the Guises. Worse was to follow. In 1580 Philip had outlawed

William the Silent[1] and offered a reward for his murder. Since then William had survived several attempts on his life, but in July 1584 he was at last struck down by an assassin—and the rebels were left leaderless to face the threat of Parma.

The situation was critical. Elizabeth's enemies had united in a common effort to destroy heresy. At the same time the plight of her allies was desperate. Even at home Elizabeth was not secure. Conspirators threatened her life, whilst Philip II interfered in Ireland and Jesuit missionaries stiffened catholic resistance to her Church. She knew that if her allies were crushed the whole weight of the catholic offensive would fall upon England. So Elizabeth was forced into the open at last. She sent money and later troops to assist the Huguenots. Finally, in August 1585 she signed a treaty of alliance with the Dutch. She became their protector (not their queen). She promised to keep an army in the Netherlands and to pay for it until the war ended. In return her soldiers were allowed to hold Flushing and Brill. This alliance was tantamount to a declaration of war on Spain. The conflict which Elizabeth dreaded had finally come to pass.

XIV

ENGLAND AT WAR : 1585–1603

ELIZABETH now embarked upon a war the end of which she would not live to see. Her country was stronger than at any time since her father's reign; most of her people were whole-heartedly behind her; Burghley had built up a war-chest of some £300,000. Yet she stood in a position of extreme peril. Spain appeared to be far stronger. Philip II was using all the forces of the Counter-Reformation to destroy his political rival. Poor though she was, Elizabeth had to bolster up her allies in France

---

[1] The popular name for William of Orange.

and the Netherlands, quell rebellion in Ireland, and wage continual war at sea. And all the time she had to be ready to meet the threat of invasion. The likelihood of her success must have seemed very slight indeed.

THE NETHERLANDS: 1585–7

Elizabeth had to act quickly if she was to save the Dutch rebels, for town after town was falling to Parma's victorious Spanish troops. So she straightway sent an army under the earl of Leicester to assist them. However, Leicester achieved little of value. He quarrelled with the rebel leaders, and he showed himself to be an incompetent general. The army had moments of glory. It captured Axel. And it even repulsed Parma at Zutphen, where the young and chivalrous Sir Philip Sidney was killed. But the English army failed to stop Parma's victorious advance for long. Leicester continued to squabble with the Dutch. In 1587 he gave up his command and returned to England.

THE WAR AT SEA: 1585–6

The war at sea was more successful. In May 1585 Philip II had seized all English ships lying in Spanish ports. Elizabeth looked around for some way of getting her own back. She approved Drake's plan to seize Philip's treasure fleet as it sailed from America to Spain, and then to plunder Spanish ports in the Caribbean Sea. Setting sail from Plymouth he missed the treasure ships, but he ransacked the Cape Verde Islands, an important stopping place for Spanish ships coming from America, and carried out a brilliant raid on the West Indies (1585–6). Santo Domingo and Cartagena were captured and sacked, and many galleons sunk. Drake had once again demonstrated English superiority at sea, whilst Philip II had to spend precious time and money in making good the damage.

THE END OF MARY, QUEEN OF SCOTS

Elizabeth had consistently rejected all demands for the execution of the queen of Scots. But Sir Francis Walsingham knew that, if he could prove that Mary herself was plotting to kill the queen, then Elizabeth would have to get rid of her. He set about trying to trap Mary and it was not long before he succeeded.

Early in 1586 a government agent wormed his way into Mary's confidence. He carried letters for her to and from the French ambassador—but Walsingham read each one before it was delivered. In this way he came across Babington's Plot. Anthony Babington was a Roman catholic and a devoted follower of Mary's. With five other catholics he plotted to kill Elizabeth, and asked for the Scottish queen's consent. When Walsingham received Mary's reply, giving her approval, he had all the evidence he wanted. Babington and his friends were seized and made to confess by torture. They were tried and executed. In October a special body of judges, appointed by Elizabeth, found Mary guilty and condemned her to death.

Although Elizabeth was still reluctant to execute Mary, she gradually gave way before the united demand of her privy council, parliament, and people. Her behaviour at this time showed her at her worst. First she signed the death-warrant, but refused to part with it.[1] Then she tried to persuade Mary's gaoler to murder her—but to his credit he refused. She gave the warrant to her secretary, William Davison, and told him to keep it. However, Davison and the other councillors secretly sent it to Fotheringay Castle where Mary was imprisoned. On 7 February 1587 the queen of Scots was beheaded.

When Elizabeth heard the news she flew into a furious rage. Davison was fined and sent to the Tower for parting with the warrant. Yet she must have realised when she gave it to him that he would use it. In fact, Elizabeth used him as a scapegoat.[2] She knew that Europe would be horrified by the death of one queen at the hands of another. Now she could tell the world that the execution had been carried out without her consent. Certainly Europe was shocked. But not even France took up arms to avenge Mary's death.

THE SPANISH ARMADA

Elizabeth had become Philip's arch enemy. She had harried his ships in the Channel; she had interfered in Spain's affairs in the New World and the Netherlands; she had become the leader

[1] An execution could only be carried out if the death-warrant was produced at the scene of execution.
[2] He was later released from the Tower. She did not reappoint him as secretary, for that would be to tell the world that she approved of what he had done. But he did not pay the fine and he drew his salary for the rest of his life.

and protector of Europe's protestants. To cap it all she had now put to death another queen. All attempts to assassinate her having failed, Philip decided to depose her by the conquest of her kingdom. It would put an end to English piracy, give him control of the Channel, and enable him to crush the Dutch rebels. England under his rule would be restored to the Roman catholic faith. So 'the enterprise of England' took shape.

Philip no longer lacked the resources and a suitable pretext for conquest. Portugal gave him the extra ships he needed. Pope Sixtus V blessed the Armada and so turned it (in appearance) into a crusade against the heretic Elizabeth. And Mary Stuart was no more. Furthermore Mary had acknowledged the Spanish king, not her own son James, as her heir, whilst Philip himself claimed descent from the Plantagenets. He declared that, as rightful king of England, he was coming to depose the 'usurping heretic' Elizabeth and restore the true faith.

All that remained was to organise the Armada. The marquis of Santa Cruz, Spain's greatest sailor, was appointed to prepare and lead it. As usual, Philip was short of money.[1] Nevertheless he scraped together as much as he could, and Santa Cruz pushed on with his preparations.

Elizabeth now took a hand. She approved Sir Francis Drake's proposal to attack and destroy Santa Cruz' ships at Cadiz (1587). It was a simple and daring plan which relied on the element of surprise. When Drake's fleet sailed boldly into Cadiz harbour it was crowded with ships: some belonged to the Armada, others were merchant vessels. As the Spanish ships were practically undefended, the English did as they pleased. Thirty ships were sunk including Santa Cruz' flagship, and great quantities of ores were destroyed. For six weeks his ships patrolled the coast, paralysing Spanish shipping. The English fleet then sailed for the Azores where it captured a Portuguese merchant ship, the *San Felipe*, rich in spices, silks, and jewels. And in June Drake returned to Plymouth. As he later boasted, he had singed the king of Spain's beard. Even Philip II was forced to admire the dreaded 'El Draque'. Certainly his work at Cadiz delayed the Armada for another year.

The Armada preparations received another setback when

---

[1] He received large sums of silver from the New World. However, his income was swallowed up by the revolt in the Netherlands and the normal costs of running his vast empire.

Santa Cruz died in February 1588. At once Philip II chose the duke of Medina Sidonia as his successor. The duke was a devout catholic, and a member of one of the greatest noble families in Spain. But he was not a seaman. He begged to be relieved of the post: he knew nothing about warfare or the sea; he was always sea-sick and caught colds; besides there were other more experienced men able to do the job better than he. But Philip would have no one else. So the duke loyally took up his command without further protest.

Medina Sidonia found the Armada in a pitiful state. There were not enough ships, stores, or men; above all he lacked powder and shot. Many of his ships were old, slow, and clumsy, whilst much of the food was rotten. However, in three months he worked wonders. He obtained more guns and fresh supplies. Soldiers and sailors were recruited and more ships added to the fleet as it gathered at Lisbon. By May the Armada was as ready as it would ever be. It now consisted of a hundred and thirty ships large and small, carrying eight thousand sailors and nineteen thousand soldiers. On 20 May Medina Sidonia put his trust in God and led forth the Armada.

Medina Sidonia had received clear instructions from his king. He was to sail up the English Channel, as far as the 'Cape of Margate'. There he would be joined by the duke of Parma with an army from the Netherlands. Parma's veterans would be ferried across the Channel in flat-bottomed barges, protected by the Armada, which itself carried reinforcements. In other words his task was to assist in an invasion, to strike at England where she was weakest—on land.

Elizabeth was ready and waiting. By May she had two fleets at sea: a small force under Seymour and Winter patrolled the Channel off the Thames estuary; the main body was concentrated at Plymouth under the admiral, Lord Howard of Effingham. Howard and his captains (Drake, Hawkins, and Frobisher) wanted to attack the Armada whilst it lay in Spanish ports. The queen, however, was loath to leave the Channel undefended. When in July she reluctantly allowed them to sail for Spain they were driven back by unfavourable winds. It was just as well: although the Armada had been scattered by a violent storm off the Spanish coast, it had re-formed at Corunna and set sail again on 12 July – and a week later it sighted the Lizard.

The English were taken by surprise. Their ships were trapped in Plymouth by unfavourable winds and tide, and the Armada had the weather-gauge. By the time Howard's ships warped out of Plymouth Sound, the enemy had sailed past into the

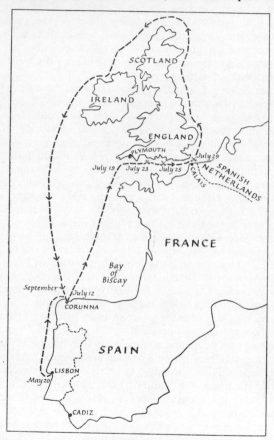

THE SPANISH ARMADA

Channel. However Medina Sidonia was slowed down by his heavily-laden hulks. The English ships, swifter and more manoeuvrable, soon regained the weather-gauge, which they kept for the rest of the campaign. So the Armada moved slowly up the Channel. Close on its heels came Howard's fleet, watching and waiting for the chance to strike a fatal blow.

The two fleets did not seem to be unevenly matched. Medina Sidonia had nearly seventy warships, some of which were old and unseaworthy. Pinnaces (small vessels used for scouting) and hulks full of supplies made up the rest of his fleet. The English force was even larger. Its strength lay in its fifty fighting ships: some were the fine new royal galleons built by Sir John Hawkins, the others private men-of-war and merchantmen from London. A hundred or more small craft accompanied them. There was no great difference in the size of the warships in the two fleets. The Spanish vessels were taller because of the castles built fore and aft to house soldiers. Yet many English ships were as large and heavy and the biggest vessel in either fleet was Frobisher's *Triumph*.

The real difference lay in their tactics. Most of the Spanish captains were used to an older kind of warfare, practised in the Mediterranean. There the ships were packed with troops whose task was to board the enemy vessels and capture them. But the ocean-going galleon and the cannon had revolutionised warfare. Speed, skill in sailing, and accurate gunnery were now essential, and the English were expert in these matters. Here was the Armada's real weakness. Its warships were more cumbersome than those of its opponent, and its slow-moving supply-ships slowed down the whole fleet. The faster English vessels were able to attack and withdraw at will. Furthermore the English had more guns, especially for long-range shooting. Both sides were anxious about their supplies of powder and shot, the Spaniards more so. These factors determined their tactics: the Spaniards vainly trying to board, and the English standing off and hammering them with long-range guns.

Despite these disadvantages the Armada was a tough opponent. Howard wrote, 'their fleet consists of mighty ships and great strength'. Medina Sidonia showed his mettle. He formed his ships into a crescent. The tips consisted of the strongest fighting ships, whilst the defenceless transport ships were shielded in the centre by galleons. It was a clever defensive formation, and for a week all the efforts of Howard's sea-dogs failed to break it. During that week three battles were fought: on 21 July, on the 23rd (off Portland Bill) and on the 25th (off the Isle of Wight). But the Armada was not diverted from its purpose.

5*

It pushed on until on 27 July it anchored off Calais. At once Medina Sidonia sent word to Parma that the Armada was ready and waiting.

Meanwhile both sides took stock of their position. The Armada had been outgunned and some of the best galleons had taken a severe beating; worst of all its supplies of shot and powder were almost spent. Howard too was worried. His ships had suffered little punishment, but the Armada was still strong and undefeated. They had used up nearly all their shot without sinking a single Spanish galleon. As the Armada waited for Parma, time was running out.

Parma did not come. His army was ready to embark in a fleet of barges, but Dutch warships were blockading the coast. Until they were driven away he could not move. This was the fatal flaw in Philip's plan. He knew of Parma's plight, yet he had done nothing to remedy it. Medina Sidonia could do nothing: the small Dutch vessels patrolled in water too shallow for his galleons. He refused to give up, but did not know what to do next. The English forced the next move upon him. During the night of the 28th they drove some fireships into the closely-packed Armada. The Spaniards were panic-stricken. They cut their cables and ran eastwards before the wind. By dawn they were scattered over a wide area. The fireships had done what the English cannons had failed to do: they had broken the Spanish formation.

Next day, off Gravelines, Howard's galleons went into the attack. They had received fresh supplies of ammunition, and they were able to fire at close range with deadly effect. The Spanish galleons fought valiantly: as they ran out of shot, the soldiers on board fought on with muskets and arquebuses. Nevertheless the odds were against them, and finally Medina Sidonia broke off the fight. His ships had had enough.

The Armada's plight was desperate. Some of its ships had been sunk or stranded on the coastal sandbanks. Most of the survivors were battered and leaking, and their ammunition was spent. There was nothing left but to run for it northwards up the east coast of England. The English pursued them. As Howard wrote, 'Their force is wonderful great and strong, and yet we pluck their feathers little and little'. Medina Sidonia decided to try to save as many of the king's ships as possible. As the Armada was too weak to battle its way through the English fleet to the Channel the only way home was around the British Isles. Little did the duke know that the English were very short of ammunition. But they 'put on a brag countenance' and continued to chase the Spaniards as far as the Firth of Forth. Then the English turned away, satisfied that the enemy would not try to land.

Meanwhile Elizabeth and her councillors had not been idle. When the Armada appeared in the Channel a chain of beacons was lit to warn the whole country that the enemy was near. Each county mustered troops, London assembled its train-bands, and at Tilbury the earl of Leicester commanded an army twenty thousand strong. Elizabeth reviewed Leicester's soldiers and encouraged them with defiant words:

> I am come amongst you as you see, at this time, not for my recreation and disport, but being resolved, in the midst and heat of battle, to live or die amongst you all, and to lay down for my God and for my kingdom and for my people, my honour and my blood, even in the dust. I know I have the body of a weak and feeble woman, but I have the heart and stomach of a king, and of a king of England too, and think foul scorn that Parma or Spain, or any prince of Europe should dare to invade the borders of my realm.

Even as she spoke the Armada was fleeing around the northernmost tip of Scotland. The danger had passed.

Medina Sidonia led the remnants of his fleet on the long, nightmarish journey home. One battered galleon after another foundered, then sank. Water and food ran short and sickness spread. Even when the Armada had rounded Scotland the worst was not over. Stormy seas and the treacherous rocky coast of Ireland claimed many victims. Thousands of men drowned. The Irish tried to protect and help those who struggled ashore, but most of them were caught and killed by English soldiers. In spite of these enormous losses, sixty-seven ships straggled into Spanish harbours in mid-September.

Medina Sidonia had failed – but he had done his best. He had been sent on a mission which was bound to fail, because Philip had ignored Parma's needs, and he had been given a force too weak to defeat the English. Yet he displayed great ability and courage, especially on the long trek home.

The jubilant Elizabeth issued a victory medal, inscribed 'God breathed and they were scattered'.   No mention was made of the part played by the sea-dogs.   Their performance disappointed the nation.   Everyone had expected them to sink more ships. In fact they had done their work well: the Armada was finished, even before the Atlantic storms completed the job.

THE WAR AT SEA: 1589–1603

(*1*) *The Counter-Armada of 1589.*   In 1588 Philip II failed to conquer England.   In 1589 Elizabeth went over to the attack. A large number of ships and soldiers were collected and Drake and John Norris were put in command.   The counter-armada had three aims: to destroy the survivors of the Armada, which were refitting in Spanish ports, to support the claim of a pretender, Don Antonio, to the throne of Portugal, and to pick up as much booty as possible.   The Elizabethans were confident of success   Yet the expedition was a complete failure: valuable time was wasted in an attack on Corunna; an attempt to capture Lisbon was badly handled by Drake and Norris; the Portuguese made no attempt to rebel in support of Don Antonio.   With nothing achieved the expedition returned to England.   The queen was furious, the more so because the young earl of Essex, her latest favourite, had disobeyed her and joined the expedition. One thing was clearly proved: Philip II was unable to conquer England, Elizabeth was equally incapable of breaking Spain.

(*2*) *The Spanish revival.*   The Armada marked the revival of Spanish sea-power, rather than its end.   Philip II strengthened the defences of his colonies and built more ships.   He also organised the convoy-system: the treasure-fleet was to collect at one American port and be escorted to Spain by a large escort of warships.   Gone were the days when English raiders could seize undefended treasure-ships.   In the years that followed few rich prizes were taken, except for the *Madre de Dios*—which was sailing from the Far East, not America.   Indeed on one occasion, in 1591, the tables were turned.   A Spanish fleet set sail to meet and escort the treasure fleet home.   At the Azores it met instead a small English force under Lord Thomas Howard.   All the English ships made good their escape except for one, Sir Richard Grenville's 'Revenge', which stayed to fight it out.   Throughout the day the battle raged.   And the 'Revenge' only surrendered when her captain lay dying.   She had been hit eight hundred times, and half her crew was dead.   But the Spaniards paid dearly for their victory: two of their galleons had been sunk and a thousand men killed.

The fight of the 'Revenge' became immortal; it was nonetheless a sign of the Spanish revival. Another sign was the fate of the English expedition to the Caribbean in 1595. A powerful fleet set sail under the joint command of Drake and Hawkins, the two greatest sailors of the age. Everyone expected complete success. But they were old, and they continually squabbled. Furthermore, Philip II's efforts had made his colonies a tougher nut to crack. Their attacks on Spanish ports were repulsed and the raids produced little plunder. Both Drake and Hawkins died at sea and the fleet returned to England, unsuccessful and empty-handed.

Philip II hit back. His soldiers burned villages on the Cornish coast. Fresh armadas set sail for Ireland in 1596 and 1597, only to be scattered by gales. The Spanish revival had gone a long way and Philip seemed to have completely recovered from the disaster of 1588. But before England's first great maritime age passed away, it had one last flourish.

(3) *The Cadiz Expedition: 1596*. In June 1596 Essex and Howard of Effingham led an expedition to attack Cadiz. They found the harbour crowded with merchant ships; but they also found it well fortified with gun-batteries and over thirty warships. Nevertheless they attacked and won a complete victory. Cadiz was taken, ransacked and burned. The Spanish ships, part of a new armada being prepared by Philip, were captured, sunk, or scuttled by their captains. It was a great blow to the Spanish king's reputation and his losses made him bankrupt. Even so Elizabeth was not pleased. She always expected her naval expeditions to produce a profit as well as a victory. And this had not brought back as much booty as she had hoped.

(4) *The Islands Voyage: 1597*. Profit and defence remained Elizabeth's main objects in the sea war. So, in 1597, she despatched a further expedition to destroy yet another of Philip's armadas and to capture the Spanish treasure fleet at the Azores. However, the commanders, again Effingham and Essex, simply carried out an inefficient search for the treasure ships—which they just missed—and sailed back home again. They had not bothered to deal with the new armada (it actually set sail for England, unknown to Essex, but it was scattered by a storm), and they had lost their chance to break Philip, who

could not manage without his annual supply of silver from America.

After this experience Elizabeth refused to organise any more large-scale expeditions. Instead the fighting was left to hundreds of privately owned ships which turned pirate in the hope of plunder. So the war at sea fizzled out in the last years of the queen's reign.

THE WAR IN THE NETHERLANDS: 1587–1603

After Leicester's futile campaigns Elizabeth was content to appoint professional soldiers to command her army in the Netherlands. Lord Willoughby and Francis Vere lacked Leicester's airs and graces, but they were tougher and abler. Nevertheless they were no match for the duke of Parma, who continued his advance into the rebellious provinces. However, he was not allowed to give his whole attention to the job: in 1588 he had to divert troops for the Armada, and later he had to fight in France in support of the Guises' Catholic League. During his absences from the Netherlands the Anglo-Dutch army was able to recover much of the lost ground. Parma died in 1592, and thereafter Philip II had little hope of recovering his lost provinces. However, fighting was to continue for many years, because Spain was too proud to admit defeat. Elizabeth remained true to her promise and for the rest of her reign an English army under Francis Vere fought side by side with the Dutch. By 1603 it had helped the new rebel leader, Maurice of Nassau, to expel Spanish forces from the whole of the north Netherlands.

THE WAR IN FRANCE: 1589–1603

In 1589 Henry III was assassinated. Thus the Huguenot Henry of Navarre became King Henry IV of France. Naturally the Catholic League, the Guise faction, and Philip II refused to recognise him. Henry appealed to Elizabeth for aid. In spite of her other heavy war expenses, she sent him troops and a loan of £20,000 (1589). On their side the Guises called in Parma to help them. Elizabeth had to give Henry as much help as she could. If Henry IV was overcome, the Catholic League could aid Philip against the Dutch rebels and their English protector.

In 1590 Spanish troops invaded Brittany. Elizabeth dispatched a force under 'Black' John Norris to resist them and it stayed there for six years (1590–5). In the following year the queen gave way to the earl of Essex who was anxious to display his ability as a soldier. She sent him with an army to hold Normandy, where he wasted time, money, and men in a futile siege of Rouen. Both campaigns were meant to keep the French coast in friendly hands. Necessary though this was, it was yet another drain on Elizabeth's limited resources. Fortunately Henry IV made sure of success by turning catholic. Many catholic Frenchmen rallied to him, in order to drive the hated Spaniards out of France. In 1595 the queen was able to withdraw her forces from French soil. Three years later Henry IV brought peace to France by signing the Treaty of Vervins with Spain.

THE WAR IN IRELAND: 1595–1603

Ireland remained subdued for over a decade after the last Geraldine revolt. It was fortunate for Elizabeth that at this time, when the catholic offensive against England reached its peak with the Armada, Philip II paid no attention to Ireland. Nevertheless it remained the chink in Elizabeth's armour, as Tyrone's rebellion served to show. In 1595 Shane O'Neill's successor in Ulster died. Hugh O'Neill, earl of Tyrone, who had been raised at Elizabeth's court until 1585, now succeeded to his inheritance. He was very ambitious, for he meant to make himself master of Ulster and even beyond. Tyrone was also very able and so very dangerous. He was a born leader of men, and organised an efficient army which was much larger than the English forces in Ireland. Whereas other Irish leaders were headstrong and impulsive, he preferred to play a waiting game. His army rested in the hills during the winter, and emerged in the spring to ambush his enemies or attack them in the rear. He also had a powerful ally in Hugh Roe O'Donnell of Tyrconnel. The plight of the English was desperate. Elizabeth sent reinforcements under the veteran Sir John Norris. But the situation went from bad to worse. Norris died (1597). In 1598 Sir Henry Bagenal was surprised by Tyrone at Yellow Ford, on the Blackwater River. Bagenal was killed and his army routed. This was the only serious defeat suffered by the English in Ireland during Elizabeth's reign.

Its effects were immediate and serious: the rebellion spread and took on the appearance of a national rising. In the south a Geraldine, 'the Sugane'[1] earl of Desmond, had been nursing a burning resentment at the loss of his family's fortunes. Now he rose in revolt and slaughtered the English planters in Munster. In the north Tyrone stood supreme after his victory. If he had wished, he could have swept the Pale with fire and sword. Instead he chose to await the arrival of Spanish troops, promised by Philip II.

Tyrone's delay saved Elizabeth. Her privy council acted quickly. It persuaded a war-weary parliament to provide the money for a large army. But who was to lead it? Elizabeth's favourite, the earl of Essex, clamoured for the post. He hoped to crush Tyrone and return, covered in glory, to a grateful queen who would shower him with rewards. Elizabeth was reluctant to let him go. She liked to have her favourite at hand and perhaps she thought that he was not the best man for the job. She was right. Nonetheless she finally gave in and made him her deputy and commander of her army. It was a doubtful honour. Tyrone was a tough opponent and all Ireland was embittered by the policy of 'planting'. However, Elizabeth had spent lavishly on troops and arms, whilst Essex himself was a dashing leader. So hopes were high when he departed for Ireland.

On his arrival in April 1599, Essex was more concerned to make himself popular and admired than to fight Tyrone. He knighted large numbers of his followers, and spent the summer in stately procession through Munster. But Tyrone was in the north. The queen sent angry messages, ordering him to attack the rebels. Instead he negotiated a truce with Tyrone: there was to be no fighting for six months during which time Tyrone was to have a free hand to act as he pleased. Essex had practically handed over Ireland to Tyrone; he may have been guilty of even worse things, for he discussed English politics with the Irish rebel—although whether he was plotting treason will never be known. Certainly Elizabeth was furious at the way in which he wasted away her expensive army. The headstrong earl felt that he must defend his behaviour. In September 1599 he left his army and hurried back to the queen's court.

Essex never returned. He was succeeded by Charles Blount, Lord Mountjoy, a man of very different calibre. He was a tough and able soldier and at once set to work to restore order.

[1] Sugane means straw rope, that is a rope which is weak and snaps easily. It was a reflection on the character of this weak and cowardly earl.

He sent an army to put down revolt in Munster, whilst he invaded Ulster (1600). He placed himself between Tyrone and Tyrconnel, whose combined forces were much larger than his own. Tyrone was penned in his earldom by new forts. Before Mountjoy could attack him, however, a Spanish[1] force arrived at long last. Unfortunately for Tyrone, the Spanish veterans landed at Kinsale, at the other end of the country. There they were besieged by Mountjoy. Tyrone and Tyrconnel marched to relieve the Spaniards, but the lord deputy routed them. In one battle he had broken the rebellion. Tyrconnel took refuge abroad. In 1602 the Spanish garrison surrendered, and Tyrone fled to the mountains. During the last months of the old queen's life Mountjoy wore down the remaining rebels. Tyrone's lands were ravaged and he was starved into submission. In 1603 just after Elizabeth's death, the proud earl gave himself up.

The story of Tudor Ireland is not a pleasant one. Too often it involves the baser instincts of greed, deceit, and dishonesty; it involves, also, fire, destruction, and much useless killing. But by 1603 Elizabeth's deputies and soldiers had closed for the time being the weak spot in her defences. Ireland had been pacified by fire and sword and the Counter-Reformation defeated. For the first time the English ruled all Ireland. On the other hand Elizabeth spent enormous sums of money in order to maintain her authority in Ireland; consequently she had little to spare for the other theatres of war during the last years of her reign. Furthermore Elizabeth had not crushed Ireland's loyalty to the pope. Its people detested protestantism as the religion of their hated rulers, and the old faith had become the symbol of their national resistance. Roman catholic they were and would remain despite the many attempts of England to crush it underfoot. Furthermore the savagery used by the English, the religious persecution, and the repeated confiscations of Irish lands: all these produced a bitterness towards the new protestant settlers which was to divide that unhappy country for over three hundred years.

THE WAR: CONCLUSION

Elizabeth has often been criticised for the way she ran the war—in particular that she was mean with her money, even

[1] Philip II died in 1598, but his son, Philip III, carried on the war against England.

keeping her ships short of cannonballs and powder during the fight with the Armada. The truth is that she was poor. Yet she sent armies to Ireland, France, and the Netherlands. Furthermore they were better equipped and clothed than any other in Europe; and the soldiers got their pay more regularly than the Spaniards did. However, she preferred naval expeditions. They were organised on a joint-stock basis[1] and so gave the queen the chance to earn some cash. The queen has also been blamed for being too cautious. The sea-dogs wanted to attack treasure ships and sink Spanish galleons. But Elizabeth's first concern was for the defence of England, and quite rightly she always insisted on this.

Europe regarded England's achievement as little short of remarkable. Spain appeared to be much the stronger power. Yet England—with God's help—had scattered Philip's ships, devastated Spanish shores, and helped Henry IV and Maurice of Nassau to victory.

The war had profound effects. Elizabeth had kept her country independent and her Church secure. At the same time her soldiers and sailors had not been able to strike a really decisive blow against Philip. As England was an island, the war could only be decided at sea. Thus the conflict between England and Spain was the first great naval war, and as yet neither side had learned how to make full use of sea-power. So the tedious war dragged on until James I ended it in 1604.

[1] The ships were given and the expenses paid by investors who also shared any profits.

XV

THE TWILIGHT YEARS

THE first thirty years of Elizabeth's reign were full of achievement: most of her subjects were united; under her leadership her Church was established and took root; the threat from Scotland was ended. She avoided war and gave England time to build up her strength and confidence. The exploits of her seamen resounded through Europe. Trade boomed, farming flourished, and industries grew. And when war came England was strong enough to throw back the might of Spain. True, the reign had its darker side: hungry peasants, armies of beggars, persecuted catholics. But at least the darker side was less apparent before 1590.

Disillusionment came in the 1590's. Bad harvests pushed up the price of bread for three years (1594–6). Many died of famine and others rose in revolt. There were several severe outbreaks of plague[1] in London and other towns. Meanwhile, against this background of natural disaster, the war dragged on. At first men had been willing to help pay for it, especially when the threat of invasion loomed large. But English expeditions, except for the Cadiz voyage in 1596, were as unsuccessful as the Armada. The Spanish revival meant fewer profits too. Finally, Ireland continued to swallow up men's reputations, money, and lives. And Tyrone's rebellion cast a shadow over the last years of the reign. Men began to grumble about heavy taxes. In fact, many of the queen's subjects were becoming sick and tired of war.

MONOPOLIES

Even the government was coming under fire. The cost of the war was more than Elizabeth could bear alone. Parliamentary grants and the efforts of her ministers increased her revenue to nearly £400,000 a year. But her expenses grew even faster and by 1600 she was spending £300,000 a year in Ireland alone. In order to raise more money she sold monopolies, or the sole right

---

[1] This was the bubonic plague, or Black Death, which first swept through England in 1349–50. Annual outbreaks continued in the unsanitary towns until the late seventeenth century.

to make or sell articles, to her courtiers. Some men held monopolies in unusual things: aniseed, ox shin-bones and calamine stone. But others had the sole right to sell salt, tin, fish, and other necessities of life. The monopolists could charge very high prices, which the people had to pay as they could not buy elsewhere. There were complaints in the house of commons in 1597. The queen promised to look into the matter, but did nothing. By 1601 the complaints had grown to a storm of protest, and when parliament met it was united against monopolies. It could not deny that the queen had the right to grant them—it was indeed a very old right of the crown. At the same time it was right when it complained that monopolies harmed trade and put up prices. It also objected to this new way of raising money without its consent. Sir Robert Cecil, Elizabeth's chief adviser since Lord Burghley's death in 1598, scolded the commons for their unruly behaviour, 'more fit for a grammar-school than a Court of Parliament'. But the members of parliament were bent upon putting an end to monopolies. And they did. Elizabeth was alarmed and gave way as graciously as she could. She cancelled the most harmful ones. Those who had suffered at the hands of monopolists were allowed to sue them in court. The commons were delighted. Indeed Elizabeth had been very clever. She had not lost the right to grant monopolies in the future. And she had made herself popular once again with her subjects:

> Though God hath raised me high, yet this I count the glory of my crown, that I have reigned with your loves.

The queen's words pleased the commons, but this did not alter the fact that her prerogative had been openly attacked. Furthermore she had lost this battle. It was a sign of things to come.

A NEW GENERATION

In the years after the Armada Elizabeth lost most of her old and trusty servants. Leicester died in 1588, followed by Walsingham (1590), Drake and Hawkins (1595), and finally Burghley himself (1598). For forty years Burghley had served the queen faithfully. She had always trusted him and listened to his advice—and the great achievements of the reign were probably due as much to him as to Elizabeth herself. She still had great need of him. But he died and she was left alone to face new and serious problems.

THE ESSEX REBELLION

Robert Devereux, earl of Essex, was Leicester's nephew. He came to court in 1577 and soon gained the queen's favour by his good looks and dash. He was made master of the horse, earl marshall, and privy councillor, and he was showered with money and lands. When Leicester died (1588) and Ralegh[1] was disgraced (1592), there was no one else to rival him for Elizabeth's friendship. His warlike exploits made him a popular hero. He fought bravely at Zutphen (1586), and his success as leader of the Cadiz expedition in 1596 made him the idol of the Londoners. Indeed Essex appeared to have a great future before him.

The earl had many good qualities: he was charming, generous to his friends, and quick to gain men's trust. But he also had faults which were to be his downfall. He was spoilt and ambitious for glory. Worst of all he had to take first place in everything; he was of 'a nature not to be ruled'. Therefore he hated Sir Robert Cecil (Burghley's son), the queen's chief adviser after 1598. But Essex failed to understand the queen. Fond though she was of him, she would not give him any real power. He was rash and overbearing.[2] Instead she preferred Cecil, who was obedient and cautious (but also cunning and Essex's enemy). When she had to appoint new ministers, she chose Cecil's friends. Essex was furious. He hoped that success in war might make Elizabeth change her mind. But his naval expedition of 1597 failed to capture the Spanish treasure-fleet. It was Elizabeth's turn to be angry. When, at a council meeting, he rudely turned his back on her, she treated him like a little boy and boxed his ears. Essex rounded on her and half-drew his sword. This made her more convinced than ever that Essex was not fit to have power.

Tyrone's rebellion offered Essex the chance to redeem himself, but his campaign in Ireland in 1599 was a failure, whilst his secret talks with Tyrone smelt of treason. When he hurried back to the court to explain his behaviour, Elizabeth received him politely. But soon afterwards the blow fell. He was imprisoned for nearly a year and lost all his offices.

Desperate, Essex plotted rebellion. His object was to remove Cecil and his friends, and to force the queen to do his bidding.

---

[1] Ralegh married one of the queen's ladies-in-waiting without her consent.
[2] Once, when Elizabeth made him angry, he told her that 'her conditions were as crooked as her carcase'.

At Essex House in the Strand the earl and his chief supporter, the earl of Southampton, laid their plans. The queen could no longer ignore what was happening. She sent some of her councillors to see what Essex was up to. But he locked them up. Then, sword in hand, he dashed with his followers into the City to raise revolt. The Londoners made no move to help him. They adored their earl, but were not going to get mixed up in a futile and treasonable uprising. So the revolt collapsed, and he surrendered to the queen's soldiers (February 1601).

Essex was tried and found guilty of treason. He believed to the very end that Elizabeth could not bring herself to execute him. But he had tried to seize all power for himself. Elizabeth, as queen, would not tolerate such behaviour. So Essex went to the block.

THE END

Elizabeth ruled for two more years. They were marked by one more important achievement, the Poor Law of 1601. A lonely and tired queen, she had completed her life's work. She was no longer in touch with the new temper of the times and did not like the changes she saw going on around her. She had not changed, but the times and conditions had. As Sir Walter Ralegh said, she was 'a lady whom time had surprised'. England needed a younger monarch with fresh ideas.

In February 1603 she was taken ill. She had never named her successor and still refused to do so. It was taken for granted, however, that James VI of Scotland, Mary Stuart's son, would succeed her. Cecil was already secretly in touch with the Scottish king, preparing the way for him.[1] Elizabeth died on 24 March 1603. At once a messenger galloped away on the long journey to Scotland to give the glad tidings to James. The Elizabethan age had ended—although its greatness had faded away ten years before.

QUEEN ELIZABETH: A SUMMARY

No one can deny the greatness of Elizabeth. It was revealed in so many ways:

(*1*) She knew how to choose loyal and able servants.

---

[1] Elizabeth would have been furious if she had known. So the letters were written in code: James was always referred to as [30] and Cecil as [10].

(*2*) Her favourites were given authority and riches. But they had to work hard for them—and none of them, not even Essex, controlled the government. The real work of governing was left to reliable servants like Burghley, and afterwards to Robert Cecil.

(*3*) She established friendly relations with Scotland, and paved the way for its union with England under James VI.

(*4*) Elizabeth rescued England from its decrepit state in 1558; and she gave it time to grow strong before it was plunged into war. Furthermore she gave a boundless confidence to her people. Many, including the puritans, worshipped her as the symbol of England's new greatness.

(*5*) Elizabeth did much to lay the foundations of England's navy and empire. She gave money, advice, and friendship to explorers, sailors, and merchants. She had John Hawkins build her a small fleet of the finest ocean-going ships Europe had ever seen. And although she was too poor to bear the costs of colonising, she encouraged Ralegh and others who were interested.

(*6*) Throughout her reign Elizabeth had sought to unite her people, protect her Church, and keep England independent of any foreign prince (or pope). The great measure of success which she achieved is the best proof of her greatness.

On the other hand Elizabeth's rule was by no means perfect. Indeed some of her policies stored up great trouble for the future: in particular her harsh treatment of the puritans made them hate the Church of England and its bishops, whilst by selling lands to pay for the war she made the crown even poorer than before. She left behind her a restless parliament, anxious for a greater share in the task of governing, and recusants grown desperate by the heavy fines imposed on them. All these problems needed to be solved. It remained to see whether the new king could do so.

THE HOUSE OF TUDOR

HENRY VII = Elizabeth of York

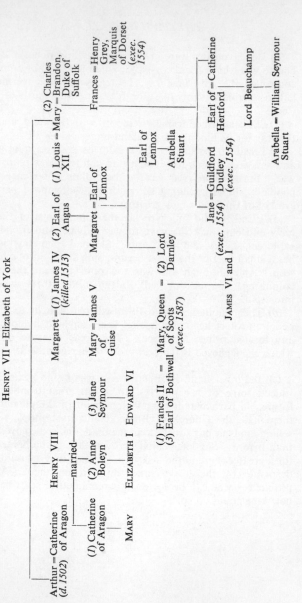

THE HOUSE OF VALOIS

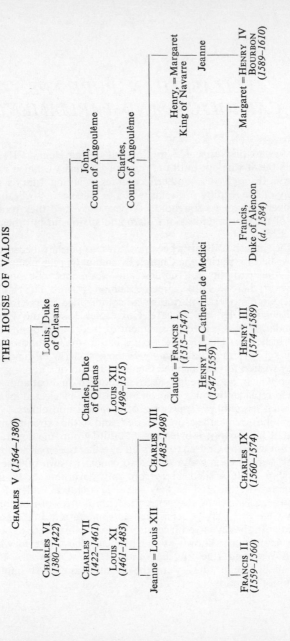

CHARLES V *(1364–1380)*

CHARLES VI *(1380–1422)*

CHARLES VII *(1422–1461)*

LOUIS XI *(1461–1483)*

Jeanne = Louis XII

CHARLES VIII *(1483–1498)*

Louis, Duke of Orleans

Charles, Duke of Orleans

LOUIS XII *(1498–1515)*

Claude = FRANCIS I *(1515–1547)*

HENRY II = Catherine de Medici *(1547–1559)*

John, Count of Angoulême

Charles, Count of Angoulême

Henry, = Margaret King of Navarre

Jeanne

Margaret = HENRY IV BOURBON *(1589–1610)*

FRANCIS II *(1559–1560)*

CHARLES IX *(1560–1574)*

HENRY III *(1574–1589)*

Francis, Duke of Alencon *(d. 1584)*

XVI

ELIZABETHAN PURITANS, CATHOLICS, AND PARLIAMENT

PURITANS

CALVINISM first appeared in England during Henry VIII's last years but it was not until the reign of Edward VI that it rapidly spread through the southern counties. During Mary's reign, many of the leading protestants fled to Geneva or to Frankfort, another Calvinist stronghold. When Mary died they returned, full of the extreme ideas of Calvin and anxious to put them into practice.

The English Calvinists became known as puritans because they all wished to 'purify' the Church by eliminating the many abuses and the catholic ceremonies and vestments. Beyond this, however, there was little agreement among them. The Frankfort exiles were moderate puritans who commanded a large following in England; led by Richard Cox, John Jewel, and Edmund Grindal, they accepted government of the Church by the queen and bishops. The Genevan exiles had a smaller following, but their supporters included many of the best clergy in the country. They wished to establish the Genevan system of Church government which had already been introduced in Scotland. This would replace the rule of queen and bishops by elected local and national assemblies, consisting of ministers and elders. These assemblies were called 'presbyteries', and so the extreme puritans became known as presbyterians. A third group, the 'separatists', did not wish the Church to be ruled by either queen or presbytery. They wanted each congregation to choose its own minister and worship as it wished, free from any governing body in the Church. In the 1580's they grew in number under Robert Browne, a Norwich preacher, and Henry Barrow of London, but they were successfully persecuted and suppressed by the government. In the seventeenth century the separatists were to become very important; known as independents they were to win the Civil War and rule England under Oliver Cromwell. But in Elizabeth's reign they were the smallest and least important group of puritans.

Elizabeth naturally disliked the beliefs of the puritans. She could not permit the separatists to ignore her rule of the Church, while her personal liking for vestments and ceremonial made her hostile to the puritans in general. Above all she could not accept presbyterianism, which would deprive her of power in the Church. But in 1559 all but one of Mary's catholic bishops resigned, rather than serve in a protestant Church. The only clergy suitable to replace them were the exiles. So Elizabeth had to choose many of her twenty-five new bishops from the moderate puritans: Cox was given Ely, Grindal London, and Jewel Salisbury. As her archbishop she chose a very moderate protestant, Matthew Parker.

Most of Elizabeth's new bishops felt bound to uphold the new Church, established by the Elizabethan Settlement of 1559. But the rest of the exiles were dissatisfied with it: the presbyterians still wanted to establish a Genevan church; the moderates disliked the remaining ceremonies and Prayer Book of 1559, which ordered the clergy to wear vestments. Elizabeth and the puritans were bound to clash, and it was not long before the first open quarrel occurred between them. Puritan ministers disliked the surplice, cope, and other vestments which they had been ordered to wear. Many of them ignored the command and conducted services in plain black gowns. Elizabeth forbade this, and in 1566 Archbishop Parker issued his 'Advertisements', a set of rules on the vestments to be worn by ministers. The puritans protested, but in 1566-7 Elizabeth enforced her will through the bishops. She had won, but the 'vestment controversy' left the puritans with a permanent bitterness towards the bishops.

It is surprising that the years following the puritans' defeat marked the great age of active puritanism. Its influence spread, bills were introduced in parliament for the reform of the Church, and puritan pamphlets circulated in large numbers. It even spread to the queen's court and government. Courtiers, including the earl of Leicester, favoured it. Sir Francis Walsingham, Sir Francis Knollys, and other members of the privy council were puritans; even Lord Burghley sympathised with them. Presbyterianism, the sect of extremists, grew in strength. It included some of the best ministers in Elizabeth's Church and attracted many more. Led by Thomas Cartwright, a Cambridge professor, the presbyterians demanded the establishment of the Genevan system of church government. Yet, so long as

Elizabeth and Archbishop Parker continued to oppose them, they had little chance of success.

Their opportunity came in 1575, when Matthew Parker died. Elizabeth chose Edmund Grindal, archbishop of York, as his successor. It was one of the rare occasions on which Elizabeth made a wrong choice. Grindal favoured some of the reforming ideas of the puritans, and saw no harm in the new development known as 'prophesyings'. These were meetings which were intended to train the clergy in the Scriptures. The puritans controlled the meetings and used them to spread their own ideas. Elizabeth saw the danger in these prophesyings and ordered Grindal to put a stop to them. The archbishop refused, because he regarded them as harmless and saw their value in training the clergy. Thereupon she suspended him from office in 1576, and the Church remained without a leader for seven years. Elizabeth herself did not forcibly suppress the meetings, but just allowed things to drift. So the puritans were able to develop their organisation without hindrance, and by 1582 they were well on the way to creating an unofficial presbyterian organisation within the Anglican Church. The basic units of this organisation were the 'classes' or local groups, which had grown out of the 'prophesyings'. It was planned to create provincial and even national synods above them.

In 1583 Grindal died. This time Elizabeth made no mistake when she appointed John Whitgift as his successor. Whitgift was a believer in firm discipline and upheld government of the Church by the queen and bishops. He was bitterly opposed to the puritans and had quarrelled with Thomas Cartwright their leader at Cambridge. By 1586 he had begun an active persecution of them. In particular he aimed to destroy the presbyterian organisation of classes. For this purpose he used the court of high commission which had been set up in 1580 to compel the puritans to conform. Whitgift introduced three articles: royal supremacy of the Church, the 1559 Prayer Book, and the Thirty-nine Articles. The clergy had to accept them if they wished to remain within the Church. Ministers were examined before the high commission, and those who refused to accept the articles were expelled.

The puritans naturally resisted Whitgift's measures, and in 1588–9 a series of letters attacking the bishops were published. Their author was unknown but he signed himself 'Martin

Marprelate'. As a strict censorship existed, the author had the letters printed on a secret press. They were widely read, because of the witty and abusive way in which they ridiculed the bishops. The government regarded them as both dangerous and seditious and made great efforts to locate the secret press. Eventually it was discovered at Manchester. Yet the government failed to detect the writer's true identity, which has remained a mystery ever since.

The letters of Martin Marprelate probably did more harm than good to puritanism. They were naturally deplored by Elizabeth and her councillors, courtiers, and bishops. Even the moderate puritans disliked the abuse they contained. In any case Whitgift won. In 1588 John Field, the organiser of the presbyterian classes, died and the movement collapsed. Moderate puritans accepted the three articles, but many presbyterians refused and so were expelled from the Church.

Elizabeth's victory was to have grave consequences in the seventeenth century. Driven from the Church, puritan ministers became chaplains to merchant companies and families of the gentry. Unable to oppose the crown's religious policy within the Church, puritan laymen still found their way into parliament and continued the attack there. So James I and Charles I were faced with a growing puritan opposition among the gentry, merchants, and parliament. Elizabeth's victory spelt disaster for the early Stuarts.

ROMAN CATHOLICS

In 1558 the puritans were members of the Elizabethan Church. They remained within the Church trying to reform it, although some of the puritan clergy were later expelled by Whitgift. The position of the Roman Catholics was fundamentally different. They remained outside the Church and obedient to the pope's supremacy. Yet Elizabeth hoped to win them over to her new Church by a policy of leniency. She was helped by the fact that the catholics received no guidance from Rome during the early years of her reign. She refused to enforce the existing penal laws against catholics and avoided collecting fines for recusancy (failure to attend Anglican Church services). Her moderation bore fruit: many became Anglicans whilst the rest became devoted to their queen.

Mary Stuart's arrival in England in 1568 brought to an end

Elizabeth's hope of winning over the rest of the Roman catholics by her policy of toleration. Mary's claim to the English throne was supported by some English catholics, who were implicated in the Northern Rebellion of 1569. Although the rebellion was led by discontented feudal nobles, many of their followers were catholics. The revolt was crushed, but in the following year danger came from another quarter. Pope Pius V issued his Bull of Excommunication which commanded catholics to depose Elizabeth and freed Englishmen from their allegiance to her. The English catholics were faced with the terrible choice of supporting their queen or the pope. In fact some of them practised their religion quietly and remained loyal to Elizabeth, but her privy council naturally feared that they would obey the papal bull. The Ridolfi Plot, a conspiracy to assassinate Elizabeth and make Mary queen, confirmed the government's fears, especially as such a great figure as the duke of Norfolk was again involved. Parliament and privy council demanded the execution of Mary, but Elizabeth would only agree to the death of Norfolk (1572). Parliament also clamoured for harsher recusancy laws but Elizabeth refused as she did not wish to drive the whole catholic body into opposition against her. Nevertheless the persecution of catholics intensified during the 1570's, and the existing recusancy law was more harshly enforced by protestant J.P.s.

The lot of the catholics became an unpleasant one: they had to pay recusancy fines; government spies and informers kept a constant watch on them; their houses were searched and they were questioned, threatened, even imprisoned. Those who wanted to lead a quiet life became Anglicans. Only the strong remained loyal to their faith and even they weakened: they had no one to advise them, no priests to say mass and hear confessions. Lord Burghley was hopeful that, without priests to guide them, all the catholics would drift into the Church of England.

Elizabeth still tried to distinguish between loyal catholics and those who were prepared to obey the papal bull. She wished to tolerate the former and punish only those who were guilty of treason. However her desire for toleration was frustrated by new developments. In 1568 William Allen, an English catholic exile, founded a college which began its life at Douai, in the Spanish Netherlands, and later moved to Rheims. Its purpose was to train priests who were to stiffen the faith of English catholics. The first of these seminary priests landed in England in 1575 and soon showed success in preventing a further decline in the number of catholics.

In 1579 a college similar to that of Douai was founded at Rome. It was controlled by the Jesuits whose first mission, led by Edmund Campion and Robert Persons, arrived secretly in England in 1580. Campion was a saintly and courageous man, interested only in the saving of souls. When he landed in England, he issued a declaration known as 'Campion's Brag', in which he set forth the aims of the Jesuit missionaries: their task was to give spiritual guidance to the catholics and to convert protestants from 'vice and ignorance', but not to engage in politics. Unfortunately his companion, Robert Persons, took part in intrigues against Elizabeth and encouraged Spain to invade England. The privy council naturally feared not only Persons but all the missionary priests as traitors, sent to carry out the Bull of Excommunication. In any case the distinction between heresy and treason was not a clear one. Burghley and Walsingham did everything in their power to track down and seize the popish priests. The government had few paid spies, but many people were willing to turn informer in order to receive the rewards which the government paid. Many were arrested; but for eighteen months Campion evaded capture as he moved secretly amongst catholic families, saying mass, hearing confession, and encouraging them to remain true to their faith. Eventually he was betrayed and arrested. During his imprisonment Campion displayed great courage: he was offered his freedom on the condition that he adhered to the protestant faith—but he rejected the offer; tortured on the rack he refused to reveal the whereabouts of his associates. Together with some other priests he was put on trial for treason, found guilty, and executed at Tyburn on 1 December 1581. In the government's eyes they were traitors. To the Roman catholic Church they were martyrs who died for their faith.

The government's fear that the Jesuits had come to England to overthrow Elizabeth was heightened by the action of Pope Gregory XIII. He attempted to enforce the Bull of 1570 by sending an expedition of papal and Spanish troops to Ireland. It was intended to be the first step towards Elizabeth's downfall, but the invasion was crushed in 1580. Nevertheless to the privy council it seemed that the papal expedition and the Jesuit mission had the same object in view: the destruction of Elizabeth's protestant Church and State.

Parliament also responded to this new catholic threat. In 1581 it passed an act which increased the fine for recusancy from one shilling to twenty pounds a month. The act also declared that it was treason for a person to become a catholic or to obey the papal bull.

The position of the catholics worsened during the 1580's. The Throckmorton Plot (1583) and the Babington Plot (1586) led not only to the execution of Mary Stuart, but also to the arrest and imprisonment of many catholics. After 1585 England was at war with Spain. All catholics were regarded as potential traitors, especially the missionaries. In 1585 all Jesuits and seminary priests were ordered to leave the country within forty days. If they were caught after this period, the penalty would be death. They refused to go and the government continued to hunt them down until the end of the reign. The lay catholics suffered from the heavy recusancy fines, yet most of them remained loyal to the government, even during the great crisis of the Armada. Elizabeth continued to boast that no catholics were punished for their religion, and it is true that the sternest measures were reserved for the priests and lay catholics who committed treason (over two hundred being executed during the reign). Nevertheless persecution did increase and lukewarm catholics adopted Anglicanism to avoid ruin. The defeat of the Armada ended any hope of a catholic restoration. By the end of Elizabeth's reign the Roman catholics had dwindled to a very small minority. Most of them were anxious to be recognised as loyal subjects who had remained faithful to their queen, even during the crisis of 1588. They wanted only to be left alone in the quiet practice of their religion.

ELIZABETH AND HER PARLIAMENTS

(1) Religion. Elizabeth's parliaments were less submissive and more willing to question royal policy than they had been in the time of Henry VIII. Throughout her reign she was faced with a puritan opposition, which hoped to achieve its ends by careful organisation. It was the puritans who forced Elizabeth to accept a more extreme protestant Church settlement than she desired. Even then they were not satisfied. In the commons

they kept up a constant demand for the abolition of vestments and ceremonies, for a new Prayer Book, and even for the Genevan system of Church government. When parliament was dissolved they continued to agitate for reform through sermons and pamphlets. Elizabeth found it difficult to quell this opposition, because parliament was now in a strong position. It had carried through all the religious changes since 1529 and so could claim that, as it had made the Elizabethan Settlement, it also had the right to alter it. Indeed, it was only with great difficulty that Elizabeth was able to keep her Church intact.

(*2*) *Elizabeth: the Succession Problem.* Religion was not the only source of friction. Parliament wanted Elizabeth to marry and produce an heir, or at least to name someone other than Mary Stuart as her successor.[1] At times these urgent questions were raised in the commons. This usually incurred Elizabeth's anger. She had little patience with these 'restless heads, such unbridled persons whose mouth was never snaffled by the rider'. Yet occasionally she would raise the hopes of anxious members with tactful charm, declaring that she would take a husband. 'I will marry as soon as I can conveniently, if God take not him away with whom I have a mind to marry.' Elizabeth would not openly declare her intention to remain single. She realised the diplomatic value of marriage and was maintaining peace with the catholic princes of Europe by holding out the prospect of marriage to one of them. As she grew older the marriage problem became unimportant. The succession question remained to vex relations between the queen and her parliaments. The commons still wanted Elizabeth to name her successor, but she preferred to remain silent. Indeed if she named James VI of Scotland as her successor, she only did so on her death-bed.

(*3*) *How Elizabeth 'managed' Parliament.* During Elizabeth's reign the self-confidence of parliament steadily grew. More and more gentlemen were entering the commons. Despite laws to the contrary, they were elected for many boroughs as well as for the shires. These men were the natural leaders of society. Many were deeply interested in politics, some had been trained in law, a number were ardent puritans, and all were of an independent temper. Small wonder is it that Elizabeth's parliaments were often critical and aggressive. The commons,

1 See pages 101-103.

6

led by puritans like Thomas Norton and the Wentworths[1], were willing to criticise royal policy, resist abuses, and protect parliamentary privileges.

Elizabeth, faced with such fractious parliaments, was forced to pay great attention to parliamentary management. She did not try to pack the commons with members who would support her. However, she always made sure that some of her privy councillors were elected to the lower house. Sir Francis Knollys and Sir Christopher Hatton, Sir Francis Walsingham and Sir Walter Mildmay were popular and experienced councillors who were usually able to lead the commons, guiding debates and the discussion of bills.

They were assisted in their task by the speaker who was chosen by the queen and officially elected by the commons. The speaker had great influence: it was he who determined the topics to be debated, the bills to be discussed, and the members who were to speak. The privy councillors' task of managing the commons was made easier by the new procedures which developed in Elizabeth's reign. It became the accepted practice to give a new bill three readings. After the second of these readings, it was placed in the hands of a committee which would discuss it in detail and amend it if necessary. Because of their experience and prestige most of the privy councillors were chosen to sit on the committees. There they could influence the other committee members to accept government bills and to modify or reject measures of the ardent puritans.

Despite all these safeguards the puritans sometimes swept aside the advice of privy councillors and forced through their own measures. The queen was then forced to fall back on the lords. Some of the older aristocracy might oppose her. But most of the peers were created by the Tudors and the bishops were chosen by the queen. They remained loyal to Elizabeth who could rely on them to throw out puritan bills which had passed the commons.

As a last resort, if the lords failed her, Elizabeth could use the royal veto to reject bills. Of greater value than this, however, was her own skill in parliamentary management: she crushed the opposition with an angry outburst or won them over with

[1] Paul and Peter Wentworth were brothers and outspoken puritans. Peter criticised the queen on several occasions for limiting freedom o speech in the commons; for this he was imprisoned in 1576, 1586, 1591 and 1597.

honeyed words; when she was forced to surrender she did so gracefully and without loss of face.

(4) *Elizabeth: Conclusion.* In any case, on most important issues apart from religion queen and parliament were in close harmony. Even the puritan opponents of Elizabeth's religious policy were fanatically devoted to her. When the pope excommunicated her in 1570 they helped to enact a statute which made it high treason for any man to call her a heretic or a usurper. In 1584 they took an important part in the formation of the Bond of Association to protect her, and they kept up a constant clamour for Mary Stuart's death, because she was a continuous threat to Elizabeth's life.

The queen and her subjects were allied in defence of their national Church and independent nation-state. In face of the Roman catholic danger, first from France and then from the pope and Spain, Elizabeth and parliament drew ever closer together. However, during the closing years of her reign the commons grew bolder; they condemned royal monopolies and complained about the heavy taxation necessitated by the war against Spain. Elizabeth found the task of controlling parliament more difficult. She was old and bad-tempered, and the younger generation in the commons was impatient of her cautious ways. Yet she retained much of her skill and tact in parliamentary management whilst the bond of affection between queen and subjects prevented any serious clash. This affection had grown and matured during more than 40 years of rule. Nowhere is it more clearly displayed than in the 'golden speech' which she made at the closing ceremony of parliament in 1601:

> I do assure you there is no prince that loves his subjects better. There is no jewel, be it of never so rich a price, which I set before this jewel; I mean your love.

TUDOR ENGLAND

XVII

THE PRICE RISE

CAUSES OF THE PRICE RISE

THE sixteenth century was a time of great economic and social change. The prime cause of these changes was the price rise (or inflation). The prices of all products rose, especially foodstuffs. By 1600 the cost of wheat, cheese, herrings, and beef was over 4 times that of 1500, whilst the price of bricks, slates, and other building materials had increased threefold.

Prices did not increase steadily, but in fits and starts. This can be understood if we accept a basic economic law: that inflation occurs when the amount of coinage in circulation increases whilst the amount of goods for sale remains the same; likewise prices go up if the supply of goods decreases. Thus sudden additions to the circulating coinage caused rapid spurts in the price rise. Henry VIII's action, in spending his father's treasure hoard on wars against France and Scotland (1512–14), had this effect. Later his income became much larger when he received the old papal taxes and monastic lands. Before the Reformation this money had gone to Rome, but now it was spent by the king in England. Even this increased income was not enough to meet the expense of his renewed wars with France and Scotland (1542–6). Henry was forced to sell many of the monastic lands and the nobles and gentry brought out their private hoards of treasure to buy them. With all this additional money in circulation prices naturally rose rapidly.

The price rise was most serious during the 1540's and 1550's when the cost of wheat doubled. This rapid increase was helped by the government's policy of debasing the coinage. Debasement was a practice whereby the old silver coinage was called in by the government and reminted into new coins, which contained less silver. This gave the government a profit, because it was left with a surplus of silver which it minted into new coins. But it also increased prices and the expenses of government. Wolsey's debasement in 1526 and a whole series of debasements between 1544 and 1551 had this effect. By calling in the coinage and issuing in return fewer coins, which contained more silver, Northumberland (in 1551) and Elizabeth (in 1560) stopped the price rise. This halt was only temporary, however, for prices rose by a further 60 per cent during Elizabeth's reign. They reached a peak during the 1590's when several bad harvests reduced the amount of wheat for sale.

The most important cause of inflation was not war or debasement. It was the discovery of vast new sources of silver by the Spaniards in Central and South America. Spain was flooded with the precious metal. Spanish trade with the rest of Europe caused this silver to circulate quickly and this was bound to affect England whose most important export, cloth, was sold at Antwerp, the financial centre of the Spanish empire. Elizabeth could steady prices for a few years, but she could not stop the flow of silver from the New World. So prices went up and up.

THE EFFECT OF THE PRICE RISE

The inflation affected people in different ways. It benefited the farmers, merchants, and owners of industry who produced foodstuffs or manufactured goods for sale; the price of their goods increased and they grew wealthy. As the price of food rose more rapidly than anything else, it was the farmers in particular who made great profits.

Others did not fare so well. Wage earners suffered because their wages always rose more slowly than their expenses. But the greatest losers were the landlords. During the Middle Ages, when prices had been stable, it had suited many landowners to rent out their lands. By this means they had been certain of a steady income without the trouble of farming the land. However the price rise forced them to make more money out of their property. Although they could try to raise rents, it was more profitable to regain their estates and farm them themselves. They also tried to add to their possessions, and the sale of lands belonging to the monasteries, bishops, and crown gave them many opportunities to do so. Those landlords who succeeded

in regaining their lands exploited them for profit.   There were
two main ways of doing this: by improving farming methods
and by rearing sheep.

THE IMPROVEMENT IN FARMING METHODS

Much attention was paid to new methods of farming in Tudor
England.   Hops were introduced and turnips were advocated.
The horse began to replace the ox as the most important working
animal on the farm.   *Five Hundred Points of Good Husbandry*,
a book on agricultural improvements by an East Suffolk farmer,
Thomas Tusser, showed the great interest in new farming
methods.   Five editions were sold during Elizabeth's reign alone.

SHEEP REARING

The effect of the new farming methods was very gradual.
The landlords, short of cash, found a quicker way of making
more money: this was to change over from arable farming to
sheep rearing.   It was cheaper, because one shepherd could tend
a whole flock and the sheep were easy to feed.   The profits were
very high, for English wool was the best in Europe, and it was in
great demand in both Flanders and the growing English cloth
industry.   Naturally many of the nobles and gentry, whether
they were landlords, tenants, or men who farmed their own lands,
decided to change to sheep rearing.

THE OPEN-FIELD SYSTEM

Those who tried to make improvements in their farming
practice were hampered by the open-field system.   Although
this system did not cover the whole of England, it prevailed in
the Midlands, south Yorkshire, the south of England (except
Kent and the west country) and East Anglia, which were the
most fertile parts of the country.   In these areas each village had
several large, unenclosed, arable fields.   Most villages had two
or three fields, although some had more.   They were divided
into strips, shared out amongst the peasants.   Originally each
man's strips were scattered singly in the fields.   By exchanging
them with each other, however, many peasants had managed to
group them together.   The lord also had a number of strips,
known as his demesne; it had at one time been tilled by the
peasants, but this labour service had long since been commuted
for cash payments.

The fields were farmed in rotation. If there were three fields, two would be sown with spring and autumn crops of wheat, oats, and barley, whilst the other lay fallow. In the spring field peas and beans were also grown. Each year, a different field

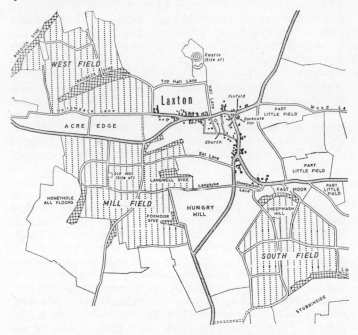

OPEN FIELDS AT LAXTON, NOTTINGHAMSHIRE
From 'Guide to Laxton' by permission of the Controller of Her Majestys' Stationery Office

was left fallow, enabling it to recover after its exhaustion by yielding a corn crop. In addition to the fields, there was usually a stretch of common land, a meadow, and some woodland. These belonged to the lord, but the peasants had certain customary rights: to graze a fixed number of their cattle and sheep on the common land, to receive a share of the hay from the meadow, and to collect brushwood for fuel in the woods.

The disadvantages of the open field system were many. Much

time and effort was wasted in moving from one strip to another. The traditional methods of farming could not be changed without the lord's consent. In any case communal farming prevented change, for when a field had been harvested it was thrown open for use as pasture by the livestock of the village; this meant that no individual could experiment with different crops which might take longer to ripen. Despite these disadvantages the system had been adequate in the early Middle Ages, when peasants and lords were concerned only with producing enough food for themselves. In the fourteenth and fifteenth centuries many began to practise commercial farming, that is they tried to grow enough food to produce a surplus, which they could sell in the local market. The open-field system was wasteful and not suited to this. It was even less suited to the conditions of the sixteenth century, when the price rise forced all men to farm their land for profit.

ENCLOSURES

The adoption of better farming methods and sheep rearing required a drastic change in the existing open-field system. Improvements could only be made by consolidating land, that is by grouping a farmer's strips together in one compact block. Thus the enclosure movement became a serious problem. It had in fact begun during the fourteenth and fifteenth centuries due to the overseas demand for English wool. 'Enclosure' itself was not harmful for it simply meant the erection of a fence or hedge around a plot of land. Normally, however, the term covered the practice of consolidating land and turning it into pasture. Such consolidation was often achieved only at the expense of the peasants' rights.

Enclosure was first practised by prosperous peasants. They consolidated their arable land by buying and exchanging strips and then put hedges round it. Some lords adopted the practice and enclosed common land which they used for raising sheep. This deprived the peasants of their grazing rights. Many could not make a living from their arable land alone, so, when they lost the right to graze livestock, they sold their strips and went to seek work in the towns or became beggars. The enclosure of common land caused widespread discontent especially during the 1540's when prices soared and the lords were desperately seeking ways to make more money. There were frequent enclosure riots and, in 1549, Ket's Rebellion in Norfolk, where the nobles and gentry had not been enclosing but overstocking the common land with their own livestock. The peasantry had been compelled to reduce the number of animals which they could graze there. When they rebelled under Ket's leadership, this headed their list of complaints.

Some lords even enclosed parts of the open fields. They bought strips and evicted peasants in order to obtain compact blocks of land which were then enclosed for pasture. The peasants drifted to the towns or wandered the country as robbers or beggars. In the Midlands, where the practice was most widespread, some villages became completely deserted. Time and time again the Tudors tried to prevent this kind of enclosure, since it would have harmful effects on the country. It was forbidden by Henry VII in 1488, whilst Wolsey sent out commissioners with instructions to put an end to the practice. A few offenders were fined and some hedges were uprooted, but enclosing continued unabated.

During the 1540's the high price of wool encouraged more and more lords to enclose. However, the practice was condemned by the duke of Somerset who was supported by a group of men calling themselves the 'commonwealth party'. They included preachers, such as Hugh Latimer, but their leader was John Hales, a minor government official who founded a free school in Coventry. Hales blamed all the difficulties of the time on to the greed of enclosing landlords: they had caused poverty and depopulation of the countryside by evicting peasants, whilst their conversion of so much arable land to pasture had led to a shortage of corn. However the commonwealth men were mistaken in their diagnosis: (*1*) They exaggerated the amount of enclosing which was going on. (*2*) They confused cause and effect since they did not realise that the price rise was forcing the landlords to do these things in order to save themselves from disaster. Nevertheless Somerset agreed with Hales' arguments and chose him to lead one of the commissions which he appointed in 1548. These commissions were sent to the midland counties, where they enforced the laws against enclosures, broke down hedges and ploughed up new pasture. But the fall of Somerset and triumph of Warwick, who was himself an encloser, brought about a complete change of policy. Hales and his followers fled abroad and enclosing was allowed to continue.

6*

Mary (1553–8) and Elizabeth (1558–1603) continued the traditional hostility of the Tudors towards enclosure. Some of their subjects still supported them. In 1581 a pamphlet called *A Discourse of the Common Weal* (well-being) *of this Realm of England* was published. It was an outspoken complaint against enclosures:

> I have knowen of late a docen plowes with in lesse compasse than six myles aboute me laide downe with in theise seven yeares; and wheare forty persons had theire lyvinges, nowe one man and his shepard hathe all. By theise inclosures men doe lacke livinges and be idle.

The author regarded as particular villains those men who converted good arable land to pasture:

> Yea, those shepe is the cause of all these mischieves, for they have driven husbandrie oute of the countrie, by the which was encreased before all kynde of victuall, and now altogether shepe, shepe.

In spite of the efforts of the Tudors and their supporters enclosing continued. To enforce the laws against it, they had to rely on the justices of the peace who were often themselves enclosers. Though they could not prevent others from doing it, at least the Tudor rulers refused to harm the peasantry by enclosing their own lands.

The enclosure problem has often been exaggerated. It did not occur outside the area of the open-fields and only nine counties were seriously affected. It was most widespread in Northamptonshire and Huntingdonshire and even here only 13 per cent of the land was enclosed. Indeed the face of England did not greatly change, for no more than 3 per cent of the country was enclosed during the sixteenth century. Most of this was carried out before 1550. In the second half of the century sheep rearing became less profitable, because too much wool was produced and prices fell. Enclosure became less frequent and some stock-farmers even changed back to arable farming.

LAND TENURE   HoMe FARM

During the Middle Ages many lords had leased out their demesnes. The price rise now forced them to try and regain their lands in order to exploit them themselves. This was easily done, because, when leases expired, the lords could simply refuse to renew them. A lord's demesne usually consisted of scattered strips in open fields. If he wished to raise sheep, he had to find some means of obtaining a compact block of land. He could try to buy land from the peasants, but they were making large profits from their strips and were unwilling to part with them. The only alternative was to turn the peasants off their lands. Some were freeholders who could not be evicted so long as they paid a small, fixed, annual rent. Others were copyholders, whose right to their land was written in the records of the manor court. So long as they possessed a copy of their recorded right, their lord could not harm them. But some copyholders held land for the duration of three lives only. When the term expired a landlord could drive out his tenant by a heavy increase in the entry-fine.[1] Furthermore, many of the peasants were tenants-at-will, who held their land for as long as it pleased the lord. He could raise their rents and even evict them.

Since the freeholders and most copyholders were protected by the law-courts, they could continue to farm their lands without interference. Many became prosperous and some even entered the ranks of the gentry. The fate of the tenants-at-will was more unpleasant, for many of them were evicted. Some of them were hired as farm-labourers or shepherds, but others drifted to the towns or became beggars. These evictions marked the beginning of the break-up of the peasantry, although it did not finally disappear until the eighteenth century.

THE CROWN

The crown was the greatest loser in the price rise. Henry VII had built up a large income and even saved a sizable fortune. His son gained an enormous income when he became Supreme Head of the Church. Yet inflation and the misgovernment of the 1540's and 1550's weakened the crown's financial position. When Elizabeth became queen, most of the monastic lands had been sold. She was still the greatest landowner in England but most of her estates were leased out for fixed rents. Meanwhile the cost of her court, army, navy, and government steadily increased. In brief, she was faced with the problem of a largely fixed income and rising prices.

[1] The entry-fine was a lump sum paid by the tenant when his contract was renewed.

Elizabeth was in desperate need of money, but found few fresh ways of raising more. She could summon parliament but taxation was unpopular. In any case those parliamentary grants which she did obtain were inadequate, especially during the long war with Spain (1585–1603). To pay for the war Elizabeth sold many of the crown estates, but this naturally made her regular income smaller. The only effective way of making ends meet was to cut down expenses as far as it was possible. Although she loved pomp and ceremony, Elizabeth was forced to scrape and save. Sometimes her thrift caused difficulties, as on the occasion when she kept her ships short of ammunition during the Channel fight with the Armada. But Elizabeth was not miserly. She was simply a poor queen who tried to make a little go a long way.

Despite her thrift the crown's financial position grew worse. She passed on to James I a debt of over one hundred thousand pounds and a reduced income. As the nation grew richer, the crown grew poorer. This was to have very important consequences in the next century when the policies of the Stuart kings were opposed by parliament. The increasing dependence of the crown on parliament for money made it possible for the commons to try to control royal policy.

THE NOBILITY AND GENTRY

During the sixteenth century the fortunes of the nobility and gentry varied greatly: many prospered and some declined. Energetic nobles and gentlemen made fortunes from land. Others increased their wealth by trading, marrying their children into wealthy merchant families, and obtaining offices, privileges, and rewards from the crown. At the same time those who were extravagant, inefficient, wasteful, or just unfortunate, underwent a decline. The spendthrift earl of Oxford lost all that he possessed. Lord Berkeley sold his estates to pay his debts and went to live with his mother-in-law as a paying guest at ten shillings a week. Such men as these paid the penalty for their extravagance and were ruined.

THE PROBLEM OF THE 'STURDY VAGABONDS'

For the first time in English history the government was faced with a serious unemployment problem. As there was no form of relief for the unemployed they were forced to become vagabonds. There had always been people who preferred to beg rather than do an honest day's work. During the sixteenth century they were joined by the victims of political and economic change: retainers who were dismissed after the Wars of the Roses; skilled craftsmen who were prevented from getting work by the guilds; peasants evicted by enclosing landlords, and weavers who had been thrown out of work by slumps in the cloth industry. The dissolution of the monasteries did not increase the ranks of the beggars because most of the monks and friars were given pensions or offices in the new Church. But it worsened the position of the existing beggars by ending the distribution of charity.

Beggars, travelling singly or in groups, became a common feature of the Tudor rural scene and children cried:

> Hark! Hark! The dogs do bark.
> The beggars are coming to town

As pedlars, fortune-tellers, tinkers, and actors, they attempted to make a living. Bands of vagabonds became the terror of the countryside as they roamed looting and stealing livestock. However, the number of beggars has often been exaggerated both by contemporaries and by modern historians. The Tudor government with its new standards of public order and peace may have seen the problem as more serious than it actually was.

That the early Tudors regarded vagabondage as a serious problem is certain, but the harsh treatment of beggars shows that they misunderstood the cause. Vagabonds were regarded as idlers who simply did not wish to work. When caught, they were whipped, placed in the stocks, and then sent back to their own parishes. Gradually it was recognised that some were not unemployed through any fault of their own. Norwich, York, and other towns introduced schemes of poor relief. London classified its poor in three groups: the industrious poor, who were given employment; the sick and insane, who were cared for at Bridewell and Bedlam; the sturdy idle vagabonds, who were still harshly punished.

The government slowly followed the example of the towns. An act of 1531 retained the harsh treatment of idle vagabonds, but gave the justices of the peace the power to grant begging licences to the impotent poor. In 1536 came the first real recognition of the State's responsibility to the unemployed. An act of parliament recognised that help should be given to those who were industrious but could not find work, and to the impotent poor who needed hospitals and charity. The former were to be given materials with which to work, whilst the old, sick, and insane were to be kept by the parish. Naturally the able-bodied but idle beggars were to be punished. This system was to be financed from money collected by churchwardens on Sundays. The act of 1536 was an important step forward. It established the first official organisation of poor relief by the State—but charity remained voluntary.

Voluntary alms-giving did not produce adequate money to pay for this scheme. There was a gradual move towards compulsory charity, which was finally established in 1572. Four years later counties and cities were forced to establish houses of correction in which idle beggars were to be set to work. They also had to provide stocks of hemp and other materials to enable the industrious poor to work. Many of these earlier acts were temporarily combined to deal with the crisis caused by the bad harvests of the 1590's.

Finally, the most important features were embodied in a permanent Poor Law passed in 1601. Poor relief in each parish was to be administered by four overseers (chosen by the justices of the peace) and the churchwardens. They were to apprentice pauper children, provide stocks of materials for those willing to work, and place the impotent poor in almshouses. Money was to be raised by a compulsory poor law rate, imposed by the local justices; but charity was still to be encouraged. As the act provided for all who were paupers through no fault of their own, begging was no longer considered necessary. So it was strictly forbidden. And the sturdy vagabond was still to be treated harshly. When caught, he was to be whipped 'until his back be bloody', then forced to return to his birthplace. If this was not known, he was to be sent to a house of correction until work was found for him. This famous law remained the basis of poor relief until the nineteenth century.

XVIII

INDUSTRY AND TRADE
IN THE SIXTEENTH CENTURY

In the sixteenth century most people still lived and worked in the countryside. Land was still the most precious possession of Englishmen. But changes were apparent. Towns were growing: London by far the largest, then Norwich, York, and Bristol. Old industries were having a new lease of life whilst new ones were making their appearance. It is to those that we must now turn.

Conditions were suited to the growth of industry in sixteenth century England. The country had plenty of raw materials: coal, iron, timber (though this was rapidly being used up to make charcoal and build ships and houses), and water power. And there were many hundreds of skilled craftsmen in the towns, able to make goods of the highest quality. These advantages had existed in the Middle Ages. Yet it was not until the sixteenth century that there was much industrial activity. There were several reasons for this:

(*1*) The price rise, which encouraged manufacturers to make more goods.

(*2*) As new continents were discovered, so they were colonised. The new colonies would take many years to build up their own industries—in the meantime they provided new markets in which English goods could be sold.

(*3*) Even at home the demand for manufactured goods was increasing, for many Englishmen had more money to spend than they had ever had before; furthermore the population was growing.

(*4*) The Tudors blessed England with over a century of freedom from civil wars—and they did something to quell even normal lawlessness. Business men became confident that it was safe to invest money, and did so.

(*5*) There was more money available for investment. There were no banks to make loans, but moneylenders and merchants were willing to do so. They made large sums of money by trade, piracy, or farming, and lent them out in return for interest; others started industries on their own account.

(6) Englishmen began to take advantage of the many inventions of Renaissance Europe: the printing press; a Dutch loom which mass-produced ribbons; the stocking frame; pumps (worked by horses) which drained the coal-mines, and many others.

(7) Raw materials and finished goods could be carried about freely and cheaply in England—unlike France where there were tolls between most provinces.

(8) The wise economic policy of the Tudors.

THE ECONOMIC POLICY OF THE TUDORS

The Tudors accepted the fashionable economic theory of the time, known as 'Mercantilism'. This theory was concerned above all with the nation's well-being, and it can be summarised as follows. There was a fixed amount of wealth in the world. Thus if a country became richer, it did so at the expense of others. However, to become richer it had to export more than it imported. And this could only be achieved by developing its own industries: manufacturing those goods which in the past had come from other countries, and making more articles for sale abroad. Most men regarded gold and silver as wealth. This is not so, for precious metals are only what we term a means of exchange: a piece of gold is in itself useless; its only value lies in what it will buy in the way of foodstuffs, clothes, or other goods. However, that they did not understand this matters little: what is important is that, in order to increase their store of bullion, Englishmen made and sold more and bought less from abroad.

More than anyone else it was William Cecil, later Lord Burghley, who put Mercantilism into practice. He encouraged new industries and developed old ones. In particular he wanted England to make its own arms and ammunition, and this became urgent as Spain grew more powerful and menacing. As yet the queen still bought her cannon and gunpowder from abroad. But Burghley changed all that. He sold the monopoly for making gunpowder to George Evelyn, a Surrey gentleman, and from Evelyn's mills came the gunpowder which Howard's fleet used to defeat the Armada. Burghley encouraged the making of cannon. But the best cannon were made of brass (an alloy of copper and zinc). The Germans were experts in these matters, so Burghley encouraged them to come to England. They discovered copper in the Lake District and zinc in Somerset. A company was set up to make brass and in 1568 the queen gave it a monopoly. By the end of Elizabeth's reign English cannon had the reputation of being the finest in Europe.

THE REVIVAL OF OLD INDUSTRIES

There were other new industries: glass and needle making, silk weaving, and extracting salt from sea-water. However, some of the older industries[1] took on a new lease of life too. Tilers, bricklayers, and plasterers were busy building more comfortable homes for the nobles and gentry. In the Wealden forest of Sussex and Kent over one hundred forges and iron mills produced iron. (They used charcoal for smelting aud when most of the timber was used up in the following century the industry declined, never to recover.) In the Mendips lead was mined in greater amounts, as new methods of draining the mines were introduced.

For the first time coal became very important. It had been used in the Middle Ages, but only in small amounts to warm the houses of the rich. However, as England's forests rapidly dwindled more and more people burnt coal in their hearths. Most of the coal came from mines on the north coast, near Newcastle. From there it was transported by sea, especially to London—thus Londoners called it 'sea-coal'. There were other mines in the Midlands, but they were less important than Newcastle whose output rose to over thirty thousand tons a year.

The dockyards of England had never been so active: they built warships for the queen and her sea-dogs, merchant vessels, colliers (to carry sea-coal), and also fishing boats. Under the early Tudors most English seamen fished off the coast or around Iceland. However, two events changed their habits: the herring shoals shifted westwards to new feeding grounds off the east coast of England, and in Elizabeth's reign the English successfully fought Spain for control of the Newfoundland fishery. With new fishing grounds English fishermen were able to catch and sell herring and cod in large quantities. The government was anxious to encourage fishing; after all, the fishing fleets were

[1] Some of the older industries declined, especially tin-mining which had been important in Cornwall since pre-Roman times. The biggest deposits were on the surface; as these were exhausted, deep mines had to be sunk to find more. This cost a lot of money—and often investors lost heavily.

training schools for sailors, so in 1548 an act required people to eat fish on Fridays and Saturdays, and in 1563 Cecil added Wednesday to the list.

THE CLOTH INDUSTRY

Since the twelfth century wool had been by far the most important industry in England. Thousands were engaged in it, shepherds, spinners, weavers, and merchants. Originally most of the wool had been exported to Bruges, Ghent, and the other towns of Flanders, where it was made up into cloth. A native cloth industry had grown up, however, centred on York, Norwich, and the villages of the Cotswolds. This resulted in less wool being exported. However, the English weavers only made 'white' cloth, which was still sent to Flanders to be dyed and finished. So the nature of the trade had changed, but the volume had not diminished, and this was so until the sixteenth century.

In the time of the Tudors there were important new developments. Flanders suffered during the Dutch revolt against Spanish rule. It caused the decay of the great banking city of Antwerp, where the English merchants sold their wool and white cloth. Trade was often interrupted as Anglo-Spanish relations grew worse. Finally, Antwerp never recovered from the 'Spanish Fury' of 1576. The English cloth towns benefited, for, as sales to Flanders declined, they began to dye the cloth themselves. New cloth towns which produced coarse cheap cloth flourished in Lancashire, the west country, and the West Riding of Yorkshire. However, prosperity was not universal: in the old centres, which specialised in fine cloth, the selfish behaviour of the gilds[1] strangled the industry.

The cloth industry was organised in a variety of ways. The domestic or 'putting-out' system was organised by local merchants who did not assist in the actual processes of making cloth. They were the entrepreneurs (middle-men), who bought the wool, passed it to the spinners in their cottages, collected the spun yarn, distributed it among the cottage weavers, and so on through the dyeing and finishing stages; finally they marketed the cloth. The greatest clothier of this type was John of Winchcombe, known as Jack of Newbury. However, one or two clothiers were bringing their employees and machines together under one roof—in other words, they set up factories. William Stumpe's

[1] See page 171.

factory in Malmesbury Abbey (which he bought when it was dissolved) employed over a hundred men. However, this was exceptional—factories were to remain few and far between until the Industrial Revolution.

THE MIDDLE–CLASSES IN INDUSTRY

Not only the merchants were setting up new industries and lending money to improve others; nobles and gentlemen were doing the same. The earl of Shrewsbury owned lead mines and Sir Philip Sidney's family made glass, iron, and steel, whilst Sir Francis Willoughby had coal mines in the Midlands. And over them all stood the Tudors, who encouraged them and sometimes lent a helping hand.

THE GILDS

The gild was common to most medieval towns. It was an association of cloth workers, goldsmiths, or other craftsmen, and it was formed to protect the craft in which they were engaged. Each gild had a local monopoly in its own craft. Thus only the members of a clothworkers' gild could make and sell cloth. In this way it protected its members from too much competition. (In the Middle Ages this was quite reasonable because the population was small and there was only a limited number of customers.) It also punished its members for making shoddy goods, so both customers and employers were protected against bad workmanship.

However, the gilds had become too restrictive. The rich merchants, who controlled them, were unwilling to admit new members; instead they preferred to share the profits of their craft amongst as few as possible. Such attitudes were out of date in the sixteenth century when the discovery of the New World meant new markets, Europeans were buying more English goods, and England itself had a more prosperous, growing population. The craft-gilds could not produce enough to meet this growing demand. As we have seen, enterprising craftsmen moved to places where there were no gilds. They flourished, but the old gilds decayed, and their selfishness and greed hampered the growth of industry in their towns, which also went into decline. When the Tudors realised that the gilds were no longer capable of controlling industry and trade, they took on this task themselves.

THE STATUTE OF APPRENTICES

The Tudors were just as anxious to regulate economic life as the gilds had been, and in 1563 Elizabeth, William Cecil, and parliament tried to do it by means of the Statute of Apprentices (or Artificers). This act did not contain much that was new: it simply brought together a lot of old statutes in an attempt to draw up a complete labour code.

(*1*) It tried to put an end to idleness and at the same time ensure that farmers had enough workers: all able-bodied persons between 12 and 60 years of age and especially beggars were liable to work on the land. Certain crafts were made exempt, but even these could be called upon to help with the harvest.

(*2*) Elizabeth feared and mistrusted change. She believed that each man was born to a certain rank in life. He had rights, but he also had obligations. Above all he ought not to rise above his station: a craftsman should not become a merchant, and a peasant should not try to achieve the status of a gentleman. So the Act of Apprentices was designed to keep each man in his place. Only landowners' sons could be apprenticed to goldsmiths, drapers, mercers[1] or ironmongers; whereas those whose fathers were landless could only become farm labourers or rural craftsmen[2], or enter the building trades. Each man was to stay in his birth-place and remain in the same job, and to ensure this employers had to hire their workers for at least a year.

(*3*) Craftsmen who had moved away from the gilds were free from interference. Often they made goods of inferior quality, partly because they did not bother to give their workmen a thorough training. The act attempted to raise the standard of workmanship: in every trade and craft boys were to be apprenticed for seven years before they could be accepted as craftsmen.

(*4*) Justices of the peace were empowered to fix rates of wages annually. Hours of work were also laid down: from dawn to dusk in winter, and twelve hours a day in summer.

The act had some success. It tended to protect the poor man. Thus it gave him reasonable wages, and it lessened the danger of unemployment. But in the long run it was really ineffective.

[1] Mercers bought and sold many articles, but chiefly textiles.
[2] Rural craftsmen included blacksmiths, carpenters, hedgers, and thatchers.

Evicted peasants still drifted to towns in search of jobs; slumps in the cloth industry caused clothiers to dismiss workers; the number of beggars increased. Finally, new crafts arose to which the act did not apply. So its effect was limited, but it remains the best example of the Tudors' passion for order and control.

CONCLUSION

The Tudors wanted England to be prosperous and contented. Like parents, they guided and encouraged their subjects. New industries appeared, old ones revived, mines were opened, and fortunes were made. The Tudors disliked some of the changes, but they were not strong enough to stop them. However, we must not exaggerate the amount of change. Industries were still few and scattered. London apart, English towns were small, and most men still lived and worked in the countryside. Nonetheless the developments in Tudor England were helping to pave the way for the Industrial Revolution which changed the face of England in the eighteenth and nineteenth centuries.

TRADE

In 1485 England was a rather poor backward country on the edge of Europe. She traded chiefly with Flanders, and her only important exports were wool and cloth. By 1600 she had become a commercial power to be reckoned with. Her merchants were trading in the New World, Russia, and the Far East, while London was overtaking Antwerp to become Europe's greatest port. Such a remarkable change needs to be explained:

(1) The most important factor was the development of new trade routes around Africa and across the Atlantic, which England was well placed to exploit.

(2) The price rise meant greater profits for merchants. So they invested more money in the search for new markets and sea routes.

(3) The interruptions in trade with the Netherlands caused English merchants to look elsewhere for reliable markets.

(4) A strong national feeling drove on English merchants and sailors. They sailed the oceans, ignoring the rights of others as they looked for ways of making money.

(5) The Elizabethan government did all in its power to assist the merchants. William Cecil and the queen were mercantilists; they saw that England had to export more than she imported.

So Elizabeth granted charters to companies to trade in the Levant and East Indies; she appointed a London merchant to make a trade agreement with the Turkish Sultan; she made another merchant, Thomas Gresham, her agent in the Netherlands,[1] and she even engaged in trade herself. She took care to protect her merchants. In the past the Hanseatic League had lent money to English kings in return for privileges, and under Mary Tudor its merchants paid lower custom duties than the English. But in 1558 Elizabeth cancelled its privileges. Later the Venetians tried to hinder English ships in the Mediterranean. Elizabeth forbade them to import currants into England; instead the right was given to the Levant Company. Small wonder that the English merchants were loyal to their queen.

WOOL AND CLOTH

During the Middle Ages the Merchant Staplers monopolised the export of wool. However, since 1400 wool had gradually given way to cloth as England's chief export. Consequently the Staplers had declined. In their place a newer company, the Merchant Adventurers, had risen to importance. The Adventurers dealt in cloth. By Henry VIII's reign they dominated English trade; eventually they obtained a monopoly. Most of the Adventurers were Londoners. So the highly profitable cloth trade passed under London's control. However, the company's troubles were not over. Trade with the Netherlands was frequently interrupted, especially when they revolted against Spanish misrule. Antwerp never recovered from the 'Spanish fury' of 1576. When this old and well-tried market failed them, the Adventurers were forced to go to Germany, the Americas, and even further afield to find new ones.

THE ORGANISATION OF TRADE

In the sixteenth century fewer merchants traded alone. They had always travelled in convoys for safety. Now they organised themselves into groups. In some cases they did so at the behest of the crown. The Tudors liked to control the sale of the most important products; thus it was much easier to keep an eye on

[1] In the past Gresham had obtained loans for Edward VI and Mary, when they were short of money; now he did the same for Elizabeth. He also helped to improve the coinage; and later he built an exchange (a place where merchants could meet to discuss business). Elizabeth performed the opening ceremony and titled it the Royal Exchange.

the sale of wool or cloth if it was restricted to one company rather than left in the hands of hundreds of independent merchants. So the Staplers and Adventurers were given monopolies, which were protected by the government. In return the monarch took a share of their profits in taxes, and sometimes borrowed money from them.

A second kind of organisation was the joint stock company. A number of men (merchants, but also courtiers, landowners, and even the monarch) would pool their money to finance a voyage. If it produced a profit, each man would receive a share, and his profit would vary according to the amount he had invested. At first it was a temporary practice: merchants would get together for one voyage at a time. However, they came to see the advantages of a more permanent organisation. So the regular joint stock company came into existence: of these the Muscovy Company (1555), the Guinea Company (also 1555), and the Levant Company (1581) were the most important.

LONDON

To a large extent London governed itself. It was ruled by a mayor, aldermen, and a common council, all of whom were chosen by the wealthier citizens, and who were responsible for the protection of the City's economic interests.

London's trade and industry were organised in the livery companies. Many were old (e.g. the goldsmiths and the mercers), others were new (e.g. the stationers). But they were all flourishing, some richer than they had ever been before. A livery company differed from a craft-gild in several ways: it had a royal charter which gave it a monopoly and left it free to organise its trade; it included craftsmen who made the wares and great merchants who sold them (and who also ruled the company).

Thus London was a great power in the land. Its population rose rapidly, from seventy thousand in 1485 to over two hundred thousand in 1600. It was also a very rich city, taking trade away from other towns. It was a place where the needy Tudors might go to borrow money. Above all it had an independent spirit and jealously guarded its rights; whilst in its city militia, the 'train bands', it had an army larger than any that the king could quickly muster. Indeed one of the secrets of the Tudors' successful rule was their friendship and co-operation with the merchants of London.

XIX

THE ENGLISH AT SEA

In the Middle Ages the Mediterranean Sea was the centre of the world's trade. The merchants of Venice, Genoa, Florence, and the Levant[1] bought and sold goods in Europe, North Africa, and the Middle East. In particular they controlled the richest of all trades, the spice trade. Spices were necessary to medieval men to make their food palatable. Few had any idea how to cook a decent meal, whilst much of the meat which they ate was salted to preserve it. Therefore merchants could always be sure of a ready market for their pepper, cinnamon, nutmeg, and cloves, which were brought, together with ivory and silk, overland from Asia to the ports of the Levant.

During the fifteenth century the Turks overran the lands at the eastern end of the Mediterranean. They were Moslems and hated the Christians, so they closed the overland route to the east. European merchants were forced to seek an alternative route to the fabulous wealth of Cathay and the East Indies. And it was this which gave rise to the remarkable voyages of discovery.

As new, cheaper, and safer sea-routes to the Spice Islands were discovered, the days of the Mediterranean's greatness came to an end. Venice, Genoa, and the Levantine ports declined. Their place was taken by those countries which were on the Atlantic seaboard and so had easy access to the new trade routes. Portugal, Spain, France, England, and the Netherlands were the great colonial and maritime powers of the future.

PORTUGAL

Portugal took the lead in exploration and discovery. This was due to the vision and effort of a Portuguese prince, Henry the Navigator (1391–1460). He was interested in mapmaking, encouraged trade, planned voyages, and discussed the many problems of sailing with merchants and sailors. Prince Henry was not interested in founding an empire; he simply wanted to

[1] The eastern Mediterranean region.

find a south-east passage to the Spice Islands. He did not live to see this achieved. But before he died Portuguese seamen were feeling their way southwards along the African coast. By 1485 they were building forts and depots along the coast of West Africa in order to exploit the gold and ivory of this region.

The route to the Indies remained the chief quest of the Portuguese. Their unceasing effort was soon rewarded. Bartholomew Diaz rounded the Cape of Good Hope (1486) and Vasco da Gama reached India (1497–8). The Portuguese were determined not to share the benefits of this new route with anyone else. When Albuquerque captured Goa (1510)[1] and Malacca (1511)[2], he turned them into fortified bases, which the Portuguese used to protect their monopoly. By 1520 they were masters of the Indian Ocean, rulers of an empire, and controllers of the route around the Cape. As a result, they were selling spices in Europe at lower prices than the Venetians could offer.

SPAIN

Spanish seamen were jealous of Portugal's success, so they explored westwards to find a new trade route to Asia. Christopher Columbus, a Genoese sailor, led the way. He offered his services to the king of Portugal, but failed to persuade him to finance a voyage across the Atlantic. He turned to Ferdinand and Isabella and this time he was successful; so it was as a sailor in Spanish pay that he discovered Cuba (1492). As a result of his voyages not only Cuba but also the Bahamas, Hispaniola, and Dominica were claimed for Spain. It was confidently believed that they lay off the Asiatic coast and were therefore part of the 'Indies'.

Portugal and Spain were becoming rivals in trade, and friction grew between them. King John II claimed that Columbus' discoveries were part of the Azores and so belonged by right to Portugal. Pope Alexander VI ruled that all new lands more than a hundred leagues west of the Azores belonged to Spain, and that those to the east belonged to Portugal. John II protested at what he regarded as an unfair decision—after all the pope was of Spanish birth. By the Treaty of Tordesillas (1494), Ferdinand agreed to move the dividing line farther west,

---

[1] On the west coast of India.   [2] On the Malayan coast.

EXPLORATION AND DISCOVERY

WILLOUGHBY AND CHANCELLOR 1553

JOHN DAVIS 1585
FROBISHER 1576
JOHN CABOT 1490

SEBASTIAN CABOT 1508-9
OF THE CABOTS

JACQUES CARTIER

CHRISTOPHER COLUMBUS 1492

VIRGINIA

MEXICO
NOMBRE DE DIOS PANAMA

PERU

DRAKE

MAGELLAN'S EXPEDITION

GUINEA

BARTHOLOMEW DIAZ 1486
VASCO DA GAMA 1497-8

LINE MARKING THE
POPE'S DIVISION OF
THE WORLD

LINE ESTABLISHED
BY TREATY OF
TORDESILLAS

DRAKE

CAPE OF GOOD HOPE

SURAT
BOMBAY
GOA

MALACCA

DRAKE 1577-80

MAGELLAN 1519-22

Portuguese colonies

Spanish colonies

thus giving Brazil to Portugal. Though friction continued between the merchants of the two countries, this treaty prevented any likelihood of war.

The Spaniards rapidly explored and colonised the Caribbean. They established settlements in the West Indies, in South America, and on the Panama Isthmus. But Spanish sailors still searched for a passage to the Spice Islands: Amerigo Vespucci (who gave his name to America); Balboa who crossed the Isthmus, so becoming the first white man to see the Pacific (1513); Juan Diaz de Solis who explored the Brazil coast down to the River Plate. Finally Magellan rounded South America, passed through the treacherous straits (named after him), and entered at last the Pacific. He sailed on until he reached the Spice Islands. Although Magellan was killed in a fight with natives in the Ladrone Islands, his lieutenant del Cano brought the ships safely back to Spain via the Cape of Good Hope. As the expedition had also started from Spain, del Cano became the first captain to sail around the world. He had proved—what many already believed—that the world was a globe. Further-more, he had opened up a new south-west route to the East Indies. However, it was little used as it was so long. Spanish merchants preferred to bring their tropical riches from the Spice Islands to Panama and carry them across the isthmus to Nombre de Dios. There they were loaded on to other ships bound for Spain. This is why English sailors became so keen to raid central America.

During the reign of Emperor Charles V the Spaniards established their vast American empire. It was mainly the work of a few adventurers. Hernando Cortes, with a handful of men, conquered the ancient kingdom of the Aztecs in Mexico (1519–22). Francisco Pizarro conquered the Incas of Peru (1532). The mines in Mexico and Peru were to provide the enormous amounts of silver which enabled Spanish kings to pay their armies and build their fleets. Meanwhile other Spaniards occupied what are now Chile and Argentina. The Spanish kings would tolerate no interlopers in their new empire. They claimed that the Treaty of Tordesillas gave them sole rights over the Americas (except Brazil), and they held that it was the right of the finder to occupy vacant land. As we shall see, the latter was an argument used against them by the English.

FRANCE

France's role in the New World was less important. Some small colonies were established in Florida and Brazil. Jacques Cartier explored the St Lawrence and claimed Canada for France. In the later sixteenth century, however, French activities were limited to fishing off Newfoundland and privateering on the Spanish Main.

ENGLAND: EXPLORATION UNTIL 1547

England was a latecomer in the field of discovery and colonisation. In the fifteenth century her energies were drained away in the Hundred Years' War and the conflict between Lancaster and York; the only voyages of note were those from Bristol in search of the legendary Atlantic island of Brazil. Henry VII's reign brought with it more settled conditions. Merchants were able to turn their attention to the task of finding new markets. In particular this was true of Bristol, which took the lead in such matters until Edward VI's reign. In 1496 Henry VII granted a charter to some Bristol merchants to discover new lands and if possible a new passage to the East Indies. The Portuguese monopolised the south-east route around the Cape of Good Hope, and, as Spain was an ally, Henry VII forbade the merchants to use the south-west route. So they searched for a north-west passage instead.

In 1497 the Bristol expedition sailed under the command of John Cabot, a Genoese sailor, and his son Sebastian. The Cabots found the mainland of the New World, explored the coast of Nova Scotia, and discovered Newfoundland. But they did not find a way round North America. Two years later John Cabot sought a north-west passage around Greenland and Labrador, but again without success. Sebastian Cabot carried on the search. In 1508–9 he thought that he had found the much sought-after way through. In fact it was only Hudson's Strait. Enthusiasm declined. Cabot left England and entered the service of Spain. Nothing else was achieved until Edward VI's reign.

WHY ENGLAND BECAME A MARITIME POWER

(*1*) England had a long sea-coast and many sheltered harbours, especially in the west country. Furthermore, there were rich fishing grounds nearby in the North Sea and English Channel, and in her fishermen England already had a large number of skilled and experienced sailors. Most important of all, when the New World was discovered England found herself astride the trade route between Europe and the Americas. She was assured of a great future as an oceanic power, if only her kings and people seized the opportunity.

(2) The Tudor kings were willing. All of them, except for Mary, gave active encouragement to the search for new lands and markets.

(3) The merchants needed little encouragement. They attempted to find a route to the Indies, because they wanted to share in the profitable spice trade. Many were anxious to find new markets for their goods, and during the sixteenth century they searched as far afield as the Americas, Russia, India, and Burma. Others were as active in their search for gold, silver, and other riches. Indeed the hope of finding a silver-mine was one of the greatest inducements to English explorers.

(4) The exploits of Spanish and Portuguese sailors fired the imagination of Englishmen. Sir Thomas More's *Utopia* was an imaginary land in the New World. Richard Hakluyt a clergyman, John Dee an astrologer, and Thomas Hariot, the greatest English scientist of his time, wrote enthusiastically about the new discoveries. Shakespeare's *The Tempest* was inspired by an eye-witness account of a storm in Bermuda. This fascination with the New World led many adventurous English spirits to follow in the footsteps of the first explorers.

(5) At first, religion was a factor of no importance. But when England became protestant, her rivalry with Spain in the New World acquired something of the character of a holy war. Men like Drake believed that when they sank Spain's ships, or plundered her colonies, they were striking a blow against the Roman catholic Church.

(6) During the Middle Ages, England was noted for its military power. The national heroes were warrior-kings such as Edward III and Henry V. This military tradition lingered on after the loss of all continental lands except Calais, the symbol of a great military past. But Mary Tudor's loss of Calais (1558) and Elizabeth's failure to regain it marked the end of English ambitions on the continent. The country threw itself whole-heartedly into the pursuit of trade and new conquests overseas.

THE SEARCH FOR A NORTH-EAST PASSAGE TO THE INDIES

Henry VIII's reign saw little maritime activity. William Hawkins, a west-country man, began a profitable trade with the Guinea coast, where he bought ivory to exchange in Brazil for Brazil wood and popinjays. But there was little else. Activity revived under Edward VI. English merchants, like Hawkins, were trading in Morocco, the Guinea coast and other parts of Africa. Guinea was Portuguese, but English merchants denied their claim to own the entire coast and began to trade with the natives for gold and ivory. It was a dangerous business. Hakluyt wrote, 'if they took us in those ports they would use us as their mortal enemies'. Far better for the English if they could find another route to the east.

Sebastian Cabot had failed to find a north-west route. Now he pinned his faith on a passage to the north-east. When the Muscovy Company was formed Cabot, now very old, became its governor. The company's object was to open up trade with Muscovy (Russia) and, if possible, reach the Indies. In 1553 an expedition set sail, under the command of Sir Hugh Willoughby and Richard Chancellor. It was paid for by a large number of merchants and nobles, including the duke of Northumberland. As the ships sailed down the Thames, past Greenwich Palace, they fired a salute to Edward VI. The boy king died soon after. So did Willoughby, trapped in the Arctic ice. However, Chancellor was more fortunate. He reached Muscovy and was entertained at the court of Czar Ivan the Terrible in Moscow. By his voyage he had found a new market for English cloth merchants; a profitable trade with Russia soon developed, and between 1557 and 1563 Anthony Jenkinson opened up further trading contacts as far as the Caspian Sea. Yet Chancellor had failed to discover that elusive passage to the Indies. And he himself was killed on a further voyage to Muscovy in 1557.

ELIZABETH I: 1558–1603

Mary Tudor, wife of Philip of Spain, restrained the activities of English sailors for fear they might harm her husband's interests in the New World. But with the accession of her sister Elizabeth there dawned the first great age of English sea power.

The Elizabethans' interest in the sea was focused upon three things in particular:

(*1*) the search for a north-west passage.

(2) the use of the south-west passage. English merchants became interested in it when they failed to discover a northern route to the Indies. However it had two great disadvantages: it was very long, and it was in the Spanish sphere of influence.

(3) trade with the Spanish empire.

THE SEARCH FOR A NORTH-WEST PASSAGE

Some men still believed that it was possible to sail round Canada and so penetrate to Cathay and the Indies. The failure of Chancellor to reach the east by way of Russia had caused others to consider this idea anew. In 1566 Sir Humphrey Gilbert wrote a *Discourse for a Discovery for a New Passage to Cathay*. In it he expressed his firm belief in the existence of a north-west route. Gilbert's theories were put to the test by Martin Frobisher. In 1576 he sailed up the coast of North America and reached Baffin Island. He found what he insisted was a westward channel to Asia. However, he did not explore it, and in fact it was only a deep bay. Nevertheless he aroused great interest, by bringing back what he—and everyone else—thought was gold ore. Frobisher led two more expeditions and each time his ships returned loaded with ore. But no gold was extracted and his search for precious metals ended in ridicule. Frobisher had also reached Hudson's Strait. At last he thought that he had found the north-west passage. But interest was declining. When John Davis' expedition failed to find such a passage in 1585, interest died. It was left to the explorers of the seventeenth century to take up the challenge again.

THE SPANISH EMPIRE IN THE NEW WORLD: 1567–85

For most of Elizabeth's reign it was the Spanish empire which attracted men most. English merchants explored to find new markets—but it was more profitable to poach on existing ones. This explains John Hawkins' voyages in the 1560's.[1] We have already seen how he was treacherously attacked by the Spanish viceroy at San Juan de Ulua. It ended peaceful trading with the Spanish empire—so far as Philip II was concerned it had never begun, because he insisted on a monopoly in trade in his empire. The silver of Peru and Mexico, the wealth of tropical products: these were too precious to allow other countries a share in them. At San Juan de Ulua he made his point, so the English turned

See page 112.

to piracy. They were not very reluctant to do so. There was something of the pirate in most English mariners.

For twenty years attention was focused on the Spanish colonies in the Caribbean. Whilst England and Spain remained officially at peace, English pirates and Spanish galleons fought a savage sea-war 'beyond the line'. It did much to bring about eventual war with Spain.

SIR FRANCIS DRAKE

Foremost amongst the Englishmen engaged in this unofficial war was Sir Francis Drake. He became a legend. And much of the legend is true, for he was a great sailor and a born leader of men. He was with John Hawkins at San Juan de Ulua and narrowly escaped with his life. From then on he made his aims quite clear:

(*1*) to break Philip II's monopoly. He claimed that the Spaniards had no right to claim a monopoly over vast territories, much of which they had not even occupied.

(*2*) to avenge his cousin John Hawkins and to reimburse him for his losses at San Juan de Ulua.

(*3*) he was a protestant crusader, who kept John Foxe's[1] *Book of Martyrs* in his cabin. This was not unusual in the conditions of war in the Spanish Main. When English sailors were captured they were tried by the Inquisition and burnt at the stake as heretics. Spain turned the struggle at sea into a religious war. It suited Drake.

(*4*) he denied that he was a pirate. He fought for the queen who often gave him (secret) permission to rob Spanish ships. As his expeditions were financed by others he had to show a profit for the investors—and gold and silver was always welcomed by the needy queen. Yet it cannot be denied that Drake had an eye for a quick profit—and he waxed rich on his exploits in the Spanish Main.

DRAKE'S RAID ON PANAMA: 1572

After the disaster at San Juan de Ulua, Hawkins retired to build ships and organise a navy for the queen. So Drake took the lead. In 1572 he planned to seize Nombre de Dios and plunder its treasure house, which was full of silver from the Spanish mines. The attempt failed. Undaunted, Drake ambushed a treasure train which was crossing the Panama

[1] See page 195.

Isthmus. This time he was successful, and he returned to England with a fortune in silver. Those who copied him were less successful. When John Oxenham attempted a similar exploit in 1576 the Spaniards were ready for him, and he was captured and hanged.

DRAKE'S VOYAGE AROUND THE WORLD: 1577–80

Drake now turned his attention to the Pacific. There Spain was unchallenged and had no need for defences. Her ships and colonies were unarmed and ripe for plunder. The queen consented to his plan for a descent upon the Pacific, because 'I would gladly be revenged on the King of Spain for divers injuries that I have received'. She helped to pay the costs of the expedition (though she hid the fact from Spain), but she made him share the command with an adventurer, Thomas Doughty. In November 1577 he set sail with three ships. At first things went badly. Doughty stirred up discontent amongst the crews. Near the Straits of Magellan Drake held a court-martial. Doughty was found guilty of mutiny and executed. Having restored order, Drake successfully passed through the treacherous straits. But on entering the Pacific his small fleet was scattered by a storm. Only one ship survived, Drake's 'Pelican', which he now renamed the 'Golden Hind'.

Alone, Drake sailed up the Pacific coast of South America. Here lay the Spanish empire, rich beyond belief and unprotected. He plundered towns, destroyed shipping, and captured the 'Cacafuego', a large merchant vessel laden with gold, silver, and jewels. Drake continued to sail northwards, until he reached California. He named it New Albion and claimed it for the queen. Having tried, and failed, to find the western end of the north-west passage, he sailed across the Pacific to the Spice Islands, and thence home across the Indian Ocean, round the Cape of Good Hope and up the African coast. When the 'Golden Hind' entered Plymouth Sound, Drake hailed a passing vessel to ask, 'Is the Queen alive or dead?' Elizabeth was very much alive. She welcomed the £500,000 which she received as her share of the profits. The other investors were rewarded many times over. And Drake himself got £10,000.

The results of Drake's voyage:

(*1*) It was in itself a remarkable achievement, for he was the first Englishman to sail round the world.

7

(2) It demonstrated the lack of Spanish defences in the Pacific. Other men were tempted to follow Drake. Thus Thomas Cavendish captured a richly laden galleon, the 'Santa Anna', and returned to England with a vast profit. However, the Spaniards soon tightened up their defences, and most of the other fortune hunters met with failure and even death.

(3) Drake opened up the prospects of trade with the Spice Islands.

(4) He showed that, although England had entered late in the race for sea-power, she was fast catching up.

THE CARIBBEAN AFTER 1580

The best days of English piracy were already passing away. Philip II was strengthening the defences of his colonies. As war with Spain loomed near, the queen employed the sea-dogs to harass Spain in the Caribbean and especially to stop the flow of silver to Philip II who needed it to finance his war preparations. This was the object behind Drake's brilliant raid on the Spanish West Indies in 1585. Thereafter, however, Elizabeth concentrated on defence. Her sea-captains were kept chafing in English ports and hovering off-shore, to meet the Armada when it came. The naval engagements and campaigns of the following years belong to the history of the war against Spain.[1] They involved no new discoveries, no exploration, no search for new markets. The later Elizabethans had turned either to war or to colonisation.

A last touch of the Elizabethan zeal for discovery is to be seen in Sir Walter Ralegh's expedition to Guiana in South America (1595). Ralegh was seeking the fabulous wealth of Eldorado, an ancient city. He explored Trinidad and travelled three hundred miles up the Orinoco river. He brought back a few samples of gold and tales about the warlike Amazon women.[2] But he had not found Eldorado.

ELIZABETHAN COLONISATION

The objects in founding colonies were often the same as those in going on voyages of discovery: to set up bases from which to

[1] Chapter XIV.
[2] He also told of a race of men, the Ewaipanoma, with 'eyes in their shoulders, mouths in the middle of the breasts and hair growing backward through their shoulders'. Shakespeare must have heard the tales: in *Othello* he wrote about a race of men 'Whose heads do grow beneath their shoulders'.

attack the Spanish treasure fleets; to combat the growing colonial power of Spain; and to find gold. Too often no attention was given to raising crops and trading. Colonies were also useful as dumping-grounds for the surplus population, especially soldiers, paupers, and even criminals. It is not hard to see why every Elizabethan attempt to found a colony failed. Yet they were important, for from their mistakes men learned what was needed to establish successful settlements.

Colonisation was favoured by popular writers especially Richard Hakluyt who feared Philip II's power and wished to see his countrymen 'settle' North America. His most famous book was the *Principal Navigations and Discourse of Western Planting*, in which he wanted the State, not private people, to organise and pay for colonisation. The queen did not heed him. She was too poor. But the men of the west country followed his lead.

(1) Sir Humphrey Gilbert and North America: 1578–82. In 1578 Elizabeth permitted Sir Humphrey Gilbert to occupy any lands not already held by a Christian king.[1] His first expedition suffered severely at the hands of Spanish galleons and fled back to England. However, he persisted. In 1582 he set sail again for the New World with 4 ships. Gilbert arrived at St. John's, Newfoundland, which he claimed for the queen. Then he sailed south, seeking a suitable site for a colony. But when his store ship sank, the only thing he could do was to return home. During their return passage a violent storm endangered the ships. With great courage, Gilbert tried to prevent panic amongst his crews. He sat in the stern of his ship, calmly reading a book; and he called out to his sailors, 'We are as near to heaven by sea as by land'. Nothing more was seen of him, for his ship went down in the storm.

(2) Sir Walter Ralegh and Virginia: the expedition of 1585. Ralegh was a young man of great pride and talent, who had risen by his wits. His pride had made him many enemies. But his intelligence and good looks had made him the queen's latest favourite. She gave him lands in Ireland and made him captain of her guard. The many gifts which he received from her enabled him to play an active part in colonisation, in which he was deeply interested. He took up where Sir Humphrey Gilbert had left off. The queen gave him a charter which empowered

[1] Elizabeth would not recognise Philip II's claim to North America as his subjects had not colonised it.

him to set up a colony in North America. In return for Elizabeth's aid, he proposed to name his colony 'Virginia'.

In 1585 his first expedition sailed from Plymouth. Ralegh did not lead it, because the queen wanted to keep her favourite at court. Instead Sir Richard Grenville commanded the fleet of 10 ships. He successfully landed the hundred and seven settlers on Roanoke Island.[1]   But the colonists had a hard time. They were too late to sow seed; they had a bad winter; and they soon got on bad terms with the Indians.   In June 1586 Drake stopped at Roanoke Island on his way home from his raid on the Spanish West Indies. The colonists chose to return to England with him and hastily left the island. The colony had failed. Yet Ralegh had learned an important lesson. Most of his settlers were soldiers, who were more interested in privateering, fighting Spain, and finding gold. To succeed, a colony needed families who were willing to settle, build homes, and farm the land.

(3) *Ralegh and Virginia: the expedition of 1587.*   Ralegh's second expedition carried a hundred and fifty settlers to Roanoke Island.   This time the colony was to consist of families farming the land, not wage-paid soldiers who lived by piracy and war. Despite this precaution the colonists soon ran short of food. Their governor, John White, returned to England to obtain supplies. Although Ralegh agreed to send relief ships, it was 1588, the year of the Armada, and no vessels could be spared. Furthermore, Ralegh was short of money.   A group of London merchants came to the rescue. They agreed to finance the colony, and in return Ralegh gave them the right to trade there. However, it was not until 1591 that the merchants were able to send three relief ships.   On their arrival they found that the colonists had gone and their settlement had been destroyed. Their fate has remained an unsolved mystery.

Once again Ralegh had failed. Yet he lived to see a successful colony of Virginia established in James I's reign.   And the men who founded it drew upon his experience.

THE ROLE OF THE ELIZABETHAN MERCHANTS

The English seamen owed much to the merchants in Elizabeth's reign.   It was they who paid for expeditions to find new routes to the Indies, and who helped to finance the voyages of Drake and others who were seeking plunder on the Spanish Main.

[1] Off the coast of modern Virginia.

The merchants' efforts were not confined to lending money. Some of them went out to look for new markets. Thus in 1583 John Newbury and Ralph Fitch travelled overland to India. Fitch even reached Malaya. He returned with wondrous tales of the east which caught the imagination. His journey led to the foundation of the greatest of all companies, the East India Company. Lesser companies were formed too, such as the Muscovy Company and the Turkey (later the Levant) Company (1581). Indeed the English merchant-class must take much of the credit for making Elizabeth's reign the first great maritime age in English history.

CONCLUSION

Spain and Portugal had a long start in discovery, exploration, and colonisation, but by the end of the sixteenth century the English were overtaking them. Drake and Cavendish had circumnavigated the world; English ships traded in Africa, the Far East, and the Americas, despite national monopolies and rivalries; the first tentative attempts at colonisation had been made. But the seamen were not alone—the queen encouraged them, granted charters, bestowed knighthoods, contributed money to ventures (but mainly to those which might bring a profit). She was a friend to John Dee and Richard Hakluyt. That she did not do more was due to lack of money and her many other commitments, especially during the long war with Spain. Many others followed her example: councillors like Walsingham, Hatton, and even cautious Burghley; the earls of Leicester and Oxford and other nobles; gentlemen and of course many merchants. From the skill and courage of the sea-dogs and the money and trust of the investors there came the birth of the British Empire and England's naval supremacy.

XX

THE ENGLISH RENAISSANCE

THE OLD AND THE NEW

THE Renaissance did not break with the past. It contained much that was new, mixed with much that was old. Some men put more trust in reason than in faith—that was new. But most people had a strong belief in witches and astrology—and that was so very old. The Renaissance, like most great changes, kept much that was good—and bad—from the past.

THE EARLY RENAISSANCE

The Renaissance in England passed through two phases: in the late fifteenth and early sixteenth centuries, there was a revival of interest in the classics.[1] The humanists were, as we have seen, the sponsors of this movement: Grocyn and Linacre popularised Greek; Dean Colet refounded St Paul's School and put Greek in the timetable. But they did not look forward. When Sir Thomas More wrote *Utopia* and Erasmus criticised the Church, each was seeking to break with the ugly changes in sixteenth century life and return to the standards of a happier, purer past.

THE LATER RENAISSANCE

The second phase had its climax in Elizabeth's reign. Englishmen were no longer content merely to study the classics. They began to write poetry and plays, to compose, and to paint for themselves. Naturally they were deeply influenced by the classics; they were also influenced by the artists and thinkers of sixteenth century Italy. But they did not forget their own past. Old English traditions were joined with the 'new learning'. The result was an age rich in the arts, science, thought, and education.

EDUCATION

When men studied the classics they were stirred by ideas new to them. They learned to doubt some of the fixed beliefs of the

[1] 'Classics' refers to the works of the poets, thinkers, and playwrights of ancient Rome and Greece.

Middle Ages, and so they began to seek out the truth. Some turned to science and astronomy, others to geography and history. One natural product of this curiosity was a greater interest in education. Schools flourished and teachers took on a new importance. New, more interesting teaching methods, made famous by Roger Ascham's book *Scholemaster*, replaced the old humdrum 'learning by heart'. Great attention was naturally given to the teaching of princes. Edward VI and Elizabeth both received the best Renaissance education that the time could offer. It was based, of course, on the classics—and they were guided by John Cheke and Roger Ascham, the best teachers of the day.

The Reformation was a great blow to education in England. Many schools in monasteries and chantries were dissolved. But the fact that many people were interested in education saved the day. Some of the chantries' property went to found Edward VI Grammar Schools. Some older establishments survived, Eton and Winchester among them; new schools were founded too, the most famous of which were Shrewsbury, Rugby, Harrow, whilst many of the large towns established free grammar schools. Nor did the universities remain unchanged; new colleges[1] were established, to which laymen went in increasing numbers.

In education the Church no longer had a monopoly. Laymen were now in charge of the schools. Scholars and artists found patrons in the king, his nobles, and gentlemen. Fewer people went to university to train for the Church; instead the sons of gentry went—and then on to the Inns of Court[2] to acquire a smattering of law, so useful in administering their estates. So the number of educated laymen grew. This was made possible above all by the introduction of printing. William Caxton set up the first printing press in England in 1476, and by the 1550's a flood of pamphlets, histories, poetry, plays, and English Bibles were being printed. The Church before and after the Reformation was not intolerant of these matters (except where religion was concerned): Polydore Vergil (1470–1555), a papal agent, wrote a history of England; Hakluyt, an Anglican chaplain, produced books on English voyages; and, in Elizabeth's reign, Archbishop Parker was a great patron of scholars.

1 Elizabeth founded Trinity College, Dublin.
2 The Inns of Court were the training-schools for lawyers.

THE ROLE OF THE COURT

The court was the fountain-head of culture. Tudor rulers were hard and ruthless—but they were also educated and cultured. Henry VIII was an amateur theologian, friend of the humanists, and a musician of sorts, though he also liked the more robust pursuits, such as hawking and wrestling. Elizabeth was the most cultured of them all. To Ascham she was 'among them all the brightest star'. She could speak French, Italian, Latin, and Greek as well as English. When in 1597 the Polish ambassador offended her, she rebuked him angrily in a flood of Latin. Her courtiers—and most of all the ambassador—were amazed.[1] She was a great patron of the arts: she sat for portraits; she employed composers to write music for services in the Chapel Royal; she imported Italian musicians to provide lighter music. She loved drama too, so companies of actors were hired to perform plays, specially written to entertain her.

The queen's court followed suit: nobles and gentlemen wrote verse, some of it very fine—amongst them were the earl of Oxford, Sir Philip Sidney, and Sir Walter Ralegh. The earl of Southampton was Shakespeare's patron, the Dudley brothers (Leicester and Warwick) formed companies of actors to please the queen. Indeed her court (and her father's too) was a brilliant affair. It was thronged with ministers and soldiers, poets and swordsmen, courtiers and sea-dogs, in fact most of the great men and women of the day. Many were gorgeously attired,

> With silken coats and caps and golden rings,
> With ruffs and cuffs and farthingales and things;
> With scarfs and fans and double change of bravery,
> With amber bracelets, beads and all this knavery.

Jewellery was worn by men and women alike.[2] Some men, usually puritans, disliked such extravagance. But it was all to some purpose, for the pomp and spectacle of the court added to the queen's dignity and made her appear more important.

ARCHITECTURE

In architecture too the Tudors took the lead. Wolsey built Hampton Court in red brick with its courtyards, great hall, and

---

[1] When she had ended she cried, 'God's death, my Lords! I have been enforced this day to scour up my old Latin.'
[2] Sir Walter Ralegh always wore pearls.

twisted Tudor chimney stacks. When he fell, it was acquired by Henry VIII, who also built the palaces of St James, Bridewell, Nonsuch, and Whitehall.[1] This royal activity was a sign of the age. The Reformation ended the great era of church-building. Men were more concerned to build for themselves. So courtiers erected stately homes in stone or brick: the Cecils' Hatfield House, Sir Thomas Lucy's Charlecote Hall,[2] and the earl of Shrewsbury's Hardwick Hall. (Most of them had pillars, archways, and decoration reminiscent of ancient Greece and Rome—a sign that the Renaissance influenced the builders.) Gentlemen put up comfortable manor houses. In the towns, too, old gloomy buildings were replaced by new, stout, half-timbered ones, with plenty of windows. Whether great or small, houses were being built for comfort.

PAINTING

There were few good painters and the only one whom we might call great was Hans Holbein, court artist to Henry VIII—and he was a German. In Elizabeth's reign Nicholas Hilliard painted miniatures which were very popular, and the queen herself sat for him.

MUSIC

Church music remained popular: partly because the queen liked it (she hated the puritans' plain services); also because William Byrd (1543–1623) was busy composing music for services in the Chapel Royal. Very sensibly it did not worry her that he was a Roman catholic; she was only interested in his music. Other composers were active, some in writing madrigals;[3] and playwrights were inserting songs in their plays— so Shakespeare gave us 'Where the bee sucks there suck I' and many others.

PROSE AND POETRY

The great glory of the English Renaissance was its literature. The early sixteenth century, however, showed little promise of

[1] The banqueting hall, built in James I's reign, is all that remains.
[2] Lucy's home was near Stratford-on-Avon. When a young man, Shakespeare is reputed to have been fined for poaching on Lucy's estate.
[3] Another sign of the Renaissance influence, for madrigals began in Italy. A madrigal is an elaborate part-song of five or six parts.

what was to come.　There were few prose writers of note, apart from Sir Thomas More.　And there were no good poets.　Even the court poet, John Skelton (1460–1529), could only write simple childlike verse—and he had a poor opinion of his own work:

> My rhyme be ragged
> Tattered and jagged
> Rudely rain-beaten,
> Rusty and moth-eaten

However, in the last years of Henry VIII's reign the effect of the Renaissance was felt.　Sir Thomas Wyatt, the father of the rebel in Mary's reign, and Henry Howard, earl of Surrey, who was executed in 1547, introduced the sonnet[1] from Italy.　In doing so they gave England its first sample of fine native poetry for many years.

The harvest came in Queen Elizabeth's reign.　Elizabethans were interested in so many things and wrote about them.　Serious history books were written:　Richard Holinshed chronicled England's varied past; so did Richard Grafton and a London tailor, John Stowe, who spent much of their time in futile quarrels.　Grafton accused Stowe of 'counterfeiting my volume'.　Stowe replied that his enemy 'hath but picked feathers from other birds next in his reach'.

Others concentrated on local histories:　Richard Carew wrote on Cornwall, William Lambarde on Kent and John Stowe proudly described London.　They worked hard to collect their information.　Stowe wrote, 'It hath cost me many a weary mile's travel, many a hard earned penny and pound, and many a cold winter night's study'.　Towering above them all was William Camden, whose *Britannia* was a fascinating survey of the whole of Britain.

There were geographers too:　John Speed with surprisingly accurate maps, John Dee writing on Terra Australis (a continent which, he believed, existed in the South Seas), and Hakluyt, arousing men's interest in the New World.　Naturally there were a great many works on religion—it was something in which nearly all Elizabethans were intensely interested.　However, some of the books were abusive:　Roman catholics attacked Anglicans, and puritans attacked everyone.　Things were

---

[1] A poem of fourteen lines.

printed which today would put the author into court on a libel charge. Amongst the better works were the *Book of Martyrs*[1] (by John Foxe, an ardent puritan), describing the sufferings of protestants under Mary Tudor, and Richard Hooker's book which defended Elizabeth's new Church.

Few subjects remained untouched: there were biographies and memoirs; books on education (some of which condemned beating, and others proposed education for women), archery, vagabonds, and health (especially hints on how to avoid catching the plague); even London's underworld was described—by Robert Greene (1560–92), the first professional journalist. Much of it was dull, even unreadable. But it all showed that, for the first time, there was a reading public.

The reign did not lack poets either. Edmund Spenser was one of the men who planted Ireland. It was there that he wrote *The Faerie Queene*, most famous of Elizabethan poems; there too that he met a fellow-poet, Sir Walter Ralegh. Together they came to England, to publish Spenser's work.[2] Sir Philip Sidney was a very different kind of man: young, handsome, and dashing, the toast of the court. He was as much the chivalrous knight in his poetry as in his heroic death on Zutphen field. There were many lesser poets. Some wrote long histories, and others love poems in flowery and affected language. But greater than any of them was Shakespeare: in the intensity of feeling and the beauty of his verse he had no equal.

DRAMA

Medieval Englishmen liked stage performances. They watched their fellows enact scenes from the Bible, and simple stories which pointed a moral; citizens of York and other cities performed miracle plays; peasants took part in dumb-shows. However, nearly all plays were concerned with religion, and there were no professional actors, no permanent theatres. As in so many other things there was no change until Elizabeth's reign. And then it was the schools and universities which led the way. At the Inns of Court the lawyers amused themselves in play-acting, whilst the headmasters and university dons wrote plays (modelled on the classics), which were acted by their pupils.

[1] After the Bible it was the most popular book in England.
[2] The queen gave Spenser a pension.

It was not long before the companies of children were performing before Elizabeth at court. However, they were not without rivals. As we have seen, some of the courtiers gathered together players to perform for the queen. So the adult companies came into being, which when they were not at court toured the country or performed in the courtyard of the Boar's Head, the Mermaid, and other London taverns. However, they found it hard to make a living. The mayor and aldermen of London were puritans who regarded play-acting as wicked: one said that 'the cause of sin are plays'; another that plays contained 'nothing but profane fables and scurrilous behaviours'; yet again that they caused riots and helped to spread the plague. They did everything to hinder or prevent performances from taking place—and often succeeded. However, the problem was solved when James Burbage built the Theatre in Shoreditch (1577). Others followed: the Curtain, also in Shoreditch, the Swan and Globe in Southwark, and finally the Fortune. All of them were built in places over which the mayor and aldermen had no control. In any case Elizabeth would not allow anyone to ban plays in the new theatres—except at 'time of divine service' or when the plague was about.

London now had its first permanent theatres, open to the sky but with covered galleries for spectators. The Londoners loved it. They flocked to see stories of kings and wars, angels and devils, fairies and lovers, murder and revenge. And there appeared on the scene a band of young men, ready to write plays for these eager theatregoers. They took their plots from the classics and copied the methods of the Roman playwrights. But they wrote often in verse[1] and always in English. They made our language a thing of beauty—and in the process they gave us some of our finest poetry.

Thomas Kyd (1558–95) showed the way. He was no poet, but his exciting bloodthirsty plays were very popular. On his heels came the 'university wits', a group of young men from Cambridge, with new and very witty plays. Also from Cambridge came Christopher Marlowe, a rather more sinister figure. He had been a secret agent for Walsingham; he mixed with thieves and cutpurses, and it was whispered about that he did not believe in God.[2] However, he was also a great writer of

---

[1] They wrote in blank verse – i.e. poetry with rhythm but no rhyme.
[2] To many men this was even worse than being a heretic.

plays. *Tamberlaine the Great* was the story of a savage conqueror from Asia who created a vast empire; and *Doctor Faustus* tells of the man who sold his soul to the devil. His plays had everything: action, colour, excitement—and the finest poetry before Shakespeare.

Marlowe was killed in a tavern brawl in 1593. Six years before, William Shakespeare had left his home town of Stratford-on-Avon to make his fortune in London. He had already written a lot of poetry and several plays when, in 1596, he joined the company of the lord chamberlain. He stayed with it until 1612, and during that time he wrote nearly thirty plays, most of which were also acted at court. The company performed at the Theatre until 1599; then they pulled it down, carried the timbers to Southwark—and there built a new and better theatre, the famous Globe.

In his wit, his plots, his poetry, Shakespeare excelled all others. Fat drunken Falstaff, 'that huge bombard of sack, that father ruffian'; Prince Hal, going to war 'in thunder and in earthquake like a Jove'; Lady Macbeth, her hands bloodstained with the murder of her king: heroes or villains, they enthralled audiences of Shakespeare's day. They have done so ever since.

THE EARLY STUARTS

✦✦✦✦✦

XXI

THE FIRST OF THE STUARTS

JAMES VI OF SCOTLAND

ENGLAND's new king had been raised in an atmosphere of suspicion, intrigue and violence; several of the regents, who ruled for James during his minority, were killed. Scotland was ruled by the nobles, who ignored James, and the presbyterian ministers who bullied him—one, Andrew Melville, contemptuously called him 'God's sillie vassal'. When his minority ended, he worked patiently and skilfully to restore the power of the crown—and by 1603 he had succeeded in large measure.

When James of Scotland became king of England (1603), he united the two crowns in his person. But it was no more than a union of the crowns. England and Scotland were in no sense united: each kept its own law-courts and laws; Scotland retained its own parliament and privy council; English taxes did not apply north of the border; there was no agreement which allowed the Scots to trade on equal terms with English merchants. However, the union did bring certain advantages. Scotland and England would no longer wage war on each other. Even the lawless days of the Marches were numbered. Border raids petered out as James created an efficient force to police this turbulent region. The king aimed to achieve more than this: he tried to turn the personal union into a real union of the two countries. Unfortunately he failed, because the English parliament would not grant equal trading rights to the Scots. Nevertheless something was achieved: in 1607 Scotland's parliament gave Englishmen the rights of Scottish citizens, while a test case[1] in the English courts did the same for Scots in England.

[1] Calvin's case (1608).

In 1603 James came south to live in London, but he did not forget his native land and he laboured to improve its government. He kept a firm control over its parliament and council; parish schools were encouraged; Ulster was planted with Scots; and he introduced the office of justice of the peace into Scotland, though without much success. He intervened in religious affairs too. The Church of Scotland was presbyterian. It was governed by a number of synods, headed by the general assembly. James' policy was moderate but firm. At first he did not tamper with presbyterian doctrines. But he meant to control the Church, so in 1612 he introduced the office of bishop which had been abolished during the Reformation. His success encouraged him to go further. In 1618 he imposed the Articles of Perth on the Church. These Articles constituted an attempt to change the form of worship. They laid down rules on such matters as baptism and confirmation. One article in particular stirred up opposition: it required that men should kneel at communion. The presbyterians thought that this smacked of popery. James heeded the protests and wisely did not press the matter.

It is clear that whatever may be said of James' rule in England, a country of which he knew little, he showed a remarkable understanding of Scottish problems and a rare ability in dealing with them. As we shall see, his policy was a more sensible one than that which his son later tried to impose on the Scots.

JAMES I OF ENGLAND

England's new king was physically unattractive, even grotesque. His personal habits were unpleasant. He was dirty and untidily dressed. Such personal defects did not necessarily reflect on his abilities as a king. However, several of his failings were distinct disadvantages in a monarch. He was lazy. He had plenty of ideas, some of them inspired, but they were seldom put into practice; he simply could not be bothered to work them out in detail. He also lacked tact. James was a Scot who thought that he knew England better than the members of the house of commons. He presumed to lecture them on the laws and government of their own country. Above all he lacked dignity. He was aware of this and insisted that he should be shown the respect due to a king. In his clashes with the commons he often sacrificed the substance of power in order to keep the appearance of power—in other words, in order to preserve his dignity.

James' court at Whitehall revealed a similar lack of dignity. The king and his consort, Queen Anne (daughter of the king of Denmark), led the way with their merrymaking and lavish spending. The courtiers followed suit. Sir John Harington, the late queen's godson, regretted the change. He wrote a caustic account of the king of Denmark's stay at Whitehall Palace in 1606:

> In good sooth, the parliament did kindly to provide his Majestie so seasonably with money, for there have been no lack of good livinge, shows, sights, and banquetings from morn to eve.

The visit was marked by excessive drinking and 'childish buffoonery'. At one feast the Danish king collapsed, because 'wine did so occupy his upper chamber'. It was not surprising that parliament was unwilling to vote the king money, if he misused it in this way.

Despite his gaiety at court, James was serious-minded. He saw himself as father of his people, and he sternly lectured them on matters which aroused his disapproval. For example he detested smoking, which he condemned as 'a custom loathsome to the eye, hateful to the nose, harmful to the brain, dangerous to the lungs, and in the black stinking fume thereof nearest resembling the horrible Stygian smoke of the pit that is bottomless'. In the same way James, a capable theologian, preached to his subjects that kings were like gods. Little did he realise that his preaching did nothing but arouse resentment. Likewise his lecturing on matters of government raised and defined serious problems. But James could not resist the temptation to lecture. He did so frequently—and familiarity breeds contempt.

James also had much to recommend him. He had wisdom and in some matters he was far ahead of his time: he wanted to tolerate the Roman catholics, to bind England and Scotland more closely together, and to establish peace in Europe. He was also more cautious and less obstinate than his son, Charles. Yet James was a very inconsistent man: although he had some enlightened ideas, he was superstitious and believed in witches; he was wise and often shrewd, but he was easily duped by flatterers. It was as the English Solomon that he saw himself, yet his dealings with parliament often lacked common sense. Perhaps that astute French king, Henry IV, understood James best when he called him 'the wisest fool in Christendom'.

THE PROBLEMS WHICH FACED JAMES IN 1603

James' inheritance was not trouble-free: England was still at war with Spain; discontented Roman catholics and puritans all hoped to be favoured by the new king; the royal treasury was empty and burdened with Elizabeth's debts. The king's lack of money was to be a perennial problem. The slow increase in his income was not enough to offset his growing expenses, and the position was aggravated by rising prices, his own extravagance and the needs of his family. James was in a quandary. It was generally accepted that the king should live within his means and only ask parliament for more money in an emergency. The simple fact was that the medieval method of providing the king with money was quite out of date. His hereditary revenues were just not enough, and although parliament was ready to criticise the king's policies and to advocate wars, it was not disposed to vote him the necessary money.

Parliament had matured and become more self-confident. If James was to rule successfully, he had to treat it with caution and restraint. It was James' unfortunate mistake that he did not.

XXII

JAMES I
RELIGION AND FOREIGN AFFAIRS

THE BYE AND MAIN PLOTS: 1603

AT first the new king made few changes. He retained most of Elizabeth's advisers, and he placed particular trust in Burghley's son, Robert Cecil. However, one or two Scots were brought in and Sir Walter Ralegh, captain of the king's guard, was dismissed.

For years men had dreaded Elizabeth's death which might bring the bloodshed and disturbance of a disputed succession. But James had succeeded peacefully, and his new subjects rejoiced. Nonetheless, opposition there certainly was, and almost at once the king had to deal with plots against him. The Bye Plot was planned by a Roman catholic, William Watson. It had as its object the kidnapping of the king, who would be forced to promise leniency towards the catholics as the price of his freedom. It had little hope of success. In any case the Jesuits, who were Watson's enemies, revealed the plot to the privy council. The conspirators were duly executed.

The Main Plot was more dangerous: James was to be deposed in favour of Arabella Stuart, a descendant of Henry VII's daughter Margaret Tudor. Lord Cobham, the author of the plot, lost his nerve. He gave the privy council details of the conspiracy and claimed that Sir Walter Ralegh was involved. Cobham and his fellow plotters were imprisoned or executed. As for Ralegh, he was sentenced to death after an unfair trial. It seems that he had known of the plot, but had not taken an active part in it. Perhaps James himself doubted Ralegh's guilt, because he suspended the sentence. Instead Ralegh was confined to the Tower, where he passed the time making medicines and writing a history of the world.

In 1616 Ralegh was released to search for Eldorado. This was the city of gold which he was certain existed up the Orinoco river in Guiana. The Spanish ambassador, Gondomar, who had great influence over the king, made a violent protest claiming that Guiana was Spanish. James was impressed. He warned Ralegh that if he harmed the Spaniards in any way his suspended sentence would be carried out on his return. Undaunted the old Elizabethan set sail. However, when he reached Guiana he was taken ill. He had to remain behind, whilst a search party which included his son went up the Orinoco to find Eldorado. They followed a route which should have by-passed the local Spanish settlement. Unfortunately the Spaniards had moved their town, which now barred the way of the search party. There was a clash in which some Spaniards were killed, as well as Ralegh's son and some of his officers. Ralegh had to return home without the gold which might have softened the king's displeasure. When Gondomar demanded that Ralegh be punished, James agreed. He was at that time negotiating for the marriage of the Spanish infanta to his son Charles—and he was not going to let Ralegh upset his plans. In 1618 the suspended sentence of death was carried out. It was the end of the last of the great Elizabethans, a man who was unorthodox, daring, anti-Spanish and warlike—all qualities which James I detested.

THE GUNPOWDER PLOT: 1605

The catholics, who had suffered heavily at the hands of Elizabeth's government, hoped that the new king would treat them more leniently. Indeed James was tolerant, although parliament was not. He relaxed the stringent laws against them, but the effects of this generous act were unforeseen. Catholic priests flocked into England. This James could not allow, because they upheld the view that heretical kings should be deposed or assassinated. Furthermore the Bye Plot encouraged James to enforce the penal laws more strictly.

Some of the catholics became desperate at the prospect of renewed persecution. A group of them, gentlemen from the Midlands, resolved to take drastic action. They were led by Robert Catesby, a man of great charm and ability, and included recusants who had paid heavily for their religion. They were joined by Guido Fawkes, a soldier of fortune, who came from an old Yorkshire family. The plotters planned to blow up the house of lords when the king, lords, and commons were present at the ceremonial opening of parliament. The country's protestant leaders would perish at one blow, and the catholics would take advantage of the ensuing confusion to seize power. They imagined—as so many conspirators had believed in the past—that the rest of the catholics would rise in arms to support them. The conspirators rented a house adjoining the house of lords and began the slow arduous task of tunnelling beneath it. Soon an easier method presented itself: a ground floor room beneath the parliament house became vacant. Catesby hired it. His followers placed in it over one and a half tons of gunpowder in barrels which were carefully covered with firewood and coal.

The day fixed for the opening of parliament, 5 November 1605, drew near. The plotters were confident of success. Then one of them, Francis Tresham, committed a fatal mistake. He wrote to his brother-in-law, Lord Mounteagle, warning him not to attend the opening ceremony: 'I say they shall receive a terrible blow, the parliament, and they shall not see who hurts them.' Mounteagle showed the letter to the privy council. On 4 November a search was made and Guido Fawkes was discovered, watching over the store of gunpowder. He was tortured to make him reveal the names and whereabouts of his fellow-conspirators. But they had already given themselves away: when they learned of Fawkes' arrest, they tried to raise a revolt. It was a feeble attempt. Some of them were killed and the rest rounded up; with 'Guy Fawkes' they suffered the penalty for traitors (1606).

James was now willing to listen to parliament, which all along had been anxious to persecute the catholics. In 1606 new penal laws were passed. Recusants were not allowed to hold government offices, they could not become lawyers or doctors, and they were forbidden to come within ten miles of London. For some years these laws were enforced. When James began negotiations for a Spanish marriage match, however, they were relaxed, to the great chagrin of parliament.

THE CHURCH OF ENGLAND

The Anglican Church, established by the Elizabethan Settlement of 1559, had been forced to fight on two fronts. The Roman catholics condemned its protestant doctrines and the royal supremacy. On the other hand, the puritans believed that the reformation had not gone far enough. In matters of doctrine, however, there had been little to choose between the loyal and satisfied Anglicans and the puritans: both were Calvinists.

In James I's reign the Anglican Church began to change. Stern Calvinist ideas had been all very well in Elizabeth's day, when her Church was threatened by the Counter-Reformation. But the threat had passed and with it the need for such strict and rigid beliefs. In these circumstances the Arminians[1] came to the fore. They included some of the finest men of the day, among them Lancelot Andrewes, bishop of Winchester (1555–1626). In doctrines and ceremonies they moved nearer to the Roman catholic Church: they rejected predestination and adopted the doctrine of free will instead (i.e. that man can attain

[1] Derived from James Arminius, a Dutch professor of theology who led a reaction against the strict and gloomy Calvinists of the United Provinces.

salvation if he so desires); they accepted that the Bible was the source of truth, but that the teachings of the Church were an invaluable guide. They also saw that 'beauty of ceremony' helped to draw men closer to their God. So they favoured music, images, and vestments. The puritans, however, saw in these changes an attempt to revive the hated and feared popery.

The Arminians upheld the doctrine of the divine right of kings. They accepted the royal supremacy and exalted the bishops. In return the king defended them against the attacks of the puritans. There emerged an alliance of king, bishops, and Arminians, and the commons were faced with what they suspected was the twin threat of absolutism and popery.

THE PURITANS

By 1603 the puritans had been subdued for the time being. The great majority of them were still moderates, men who accepted the rule of the bishops and worshipped in Anglican churches. A few 'slight reforms' in the form of worship would make them content. There were two groups, however, who would not be so easily satisfied, the separatists (or independents) and the presbyterians. The former were as yet unimportant, whilst the presbyterian clergy had been hounded by Whitgift. Some had left the Church—in many cases to become chaplains to families of merchants and gentlemen. Others had remained and they, like the moderates, now hoped that they would get from James the reforms that Elizabeth had refused them. After all, had he not been reared by presbyterians?

In 1603 the puritan clergy, moderates and presbyterians, presented the millenary[1] petition to James. It requested 'the redress of divers abuses of the Church' and desired some moderate reforms: (*1*) that the sign of the cross in baptism, the use of the ring in the marriage ceremony, and bowing at the name of Jesus should not be obligatory. (*2*) as for vestments, that 'the cap and surplice be not urged'. (*3*) that 'the Lord's Day be not profaned'. (*4*) 'that none hereafter be admitted into the ministry but able and sufficient men, and those able to preach diligently'. (*5*) that certain abuses be reformed, pluralism abolished, and 'that men be not excommunicated for trifles and

[1] So-called, because it was supposed to contain the signatures of a thousand puritan clergymen.

twelvepenny matters'. No mention was made of presbyteries, the bishops were not condemned, and no changes in doctrine were proposed.

It was indeed a moderate programme. The puritan clergy claimed that they were not seeking 'a disorderly innovation, but a due and Godly reformation'. Undoubtedly many Englishmen thought so too. Elizabeth had refused to give way on these matters, and the result had been a good deal of puritan discontent, which expressed itself in parliament and in the Church. James stood at the parting of the ways: he could come to terms with the puritans and so absorb them into the Church as loyal Anglicans, or he could persecute them and so drive them into active opposition. He appeared to favour the former when in 1604 he summoned 4 puritan divines, the archbishop of Canterbury and 7 bishops to meet at Hampton Court—at least he was willing to hear their point of view.

In the presence of the king, who presided over the conference, they debated the points put forward in the millenary petition. James was not unsympathetic to some of their requests: he consented to authorise an English version of the Bible, and he conceded that 'a preaching ministry is best'. But he was sensitive about criticism of the bishops who enforced the royal supremacy over the Church. When one puritan referred to presbyteries, James was reminded of the Scottish presbyterians whose Church had been free from royal control and who had often presumed to lecture to him. He feared that the puritans wanted the same system in England. It would mean the abolition of bishops and the end of the royal supremacy—or as James pithily expressed it, 'No bishop, no king'. He was stirred to anger:

A Scottish presbytery as well agreeth with a monarchy as God and the Devil. Then Jack and Tom and Will and Dick shall meet, and at their pleasures censure me and my Council and all our proceedings. Stay, I pray you, for one seven years before you demand that of me, and if then you find me pursy and fat and my wind-pipes stuffed, I will perhaps hearken to you.

He closed the conference, warning the puritans: 'I shall make them conform themselves or I will harry them out of the land.' James was as good as his word. 'What intractable men do not perform upon admonition, they must be compelled unto by authority.' The new archbishop of Canterbury, Bancroft, expelled over three hundred nonconforming puritan clergymen from their livings.

The Hampton Court conference achieved little. Only one of the puritans' proposals was acted upon: in 1611 the new authorised version of the Bible was published. The conference was more important for what it failed to achieve. James had lost a golden opportunity to unite the Church by absorbing the moderates into it. Instead some had been expelled, others left of their own accord, whilst many became more uncompromising and extreme in their religious beliefs. Some even left the country and emigrated to the New World, where they could worship in their own way. The puritan clergy had suffered their final defeat in the Anglican Church. Instead of giving up the struggle, however, they transferred the fight to parliament and encouraged the growing number of puritan laymen there with advice, sermons, and pamphlets. Thus the religious discontent united with the growing political opposition to James in the commons.

FOREIGN POLICY

James I had Spanish sympathies. He liked to pose as the peacemaker in Europe. These two considerations dictated his foreign policy. Thus, in 1604 he ended the expensive and indecisive war with Spain. With an empty treasury it was the only sensible thing for James to do. Nonetheless it outraged the war-hungry men like Ralegh, and it offended the national feeling against Spain. Parliament, and the puritans in particular, continued to press for an aggressive anti-catholic policy.

During the early years of his reign, James' foreign policy was protestant enough to satisfy even parliament. In 1612 he joined the Protestant Union, a league of German princes against the Hapsburg emperor, and in the following year he married his popular daughter Elizabeth to Elector Frederick of the Palatinate, leader of the German princes. Yet times had changed since Elizabeth's reign, when England had been the ally of the protestant United Provinces against catholic Spain. Now the Dutch were becoming a powerful trade rival. They were competing with the English in the fisheries of the North Sea and in the rich markets of the East Indies. When, in 1623, the

Dutch killed some English settlers at Amboyna in the Spice Islands, it aroused much bitterness in England.

In the same way England's relations with Spain changed. The reason for this lay in Germany, where catholics and protestants were drifting towards civil war. Philip III of Spain would be obliged to assist the emperor, who was his cousin and leader of the catholic cause, if such a conflict occurred. He was worried by the encouragement which James gave to the German protestants. There was a danger that England might throw her weight on the protestant side, in the event of a religious war in Germany. To prevent this he dispatched the wily and astute count of Gondomar to James I's court. Gondomar quickly discovered James' weaknesses: his love of flattery, his fear of war, and his desire for toleration. He exploited these weaknesses to establish a commanding influence. As a result James changed his policy. He ceased to help the German protestants. Instead he began to contemplate an alliance between England and the Hapsburgs which might avert the impending war. And when in 1615 he decided that it was time for his son Prince Charles to marry, it was to Spain that he turned for a suitable bride. A marriage between Charles and the Spanish infanta[1] would cement the new Anglo-Spanish friendship, whilst James greedily hoped for a large dowry.

The proposed Spanish match bedevilled English politics from 1615 to 1623. The English people disliked and feared it. Catholic Spain was still the national enemy. Parliament disliked the idea too and said so in no uncertain manner. But James pushed on with his scheme. He had obstacles to overcome, however, for Philip III made exorbitant demands: any children of the marriage were to be brought up in the catholic faith, and the English catholics were to be given freedom of worship. James was afraid to promise such things publicly. He went as far as he dared to meet Philip's demands, and had Ralegh executed as a sop to injured Spanish pride.

In 1618 James' difficulties were increased by events in the Holy Roman Empire. The Empire lacked any sort of unity. There was constant friction between the princes and their overlord, the emperor: the former sought greater freedom from imperial control and the latter tried to strengthen his authority over them. Nor had there been unity in religion since the

[1] The infanta was the eldest daughter of the reigning Spanish king.

Reformation. The princes were grouped into two camps, catholic and protestant. The catholics were led by the Hapsburg emperor; the protestant leader was James I's son-in-law, Frederick. Tension between the two groups mounted. In 1618 the old emperor died. His successor was Ferdinand, another Hapsburg, who had been trained by the Jesuits and was noted as a fierce persecutor of protestants. In the early sixteenth century a Hapsburg emperor, Charles V, had become king of Bohemia. Although the Bohemian crown was elective, each Hapsburg emperor since that time had also become king of Bohemia too. However, many of the Bohemians were protestants, who feared Ferdinand's reputation. When he became emperor, they refused to accept him as their king. Instead they offered the crown to Frederick of the Palatinate, who accepted. So began the Thirty Years' War.

In 1619 Ferdinand gathered an army to deal with this rebellion against his authority. Frederick appealed to James for help. The English were wildly enthusiastic in the elector's favour, but their king was not. He was unwilling to set a bad example to his own people by assisting a rebel against his overlord, whereas his subjects were more concerned to strike a blow for the protestant cause.

Ferdinand overwhelmed Frederick's army at the battle of the White Hill (1619). James still refused to help him. He hoped to persuade Spain to join with him in bringing the war to an end. His hopes were soon dashed, however, when Spanish troops invaded the Palatinate in support of the emperor. Englishmen could not understand their king. Why did he not help his son-in-law? In fact, he dreaded the prospect of war and he could not afford the cost of one. Above all, Gondomar was still dangling the bait of the Spanish match before his eyes. James firmly believed that, if the marriage was arranged, he could then persuade the Spaniards to surrender the Palatinate.

Parliament met in 1621. James obtained from it some much-needed money and some unwelcome advice on foreign affairs. The commons was wholeheartedly on Frederick's side. Undoubtedly they expressed the opinion of most Englishmen. Yet James chose to disregard them and pressed for the conclusion of the Spanish match. In order to hurry things up, he allowed Charles to go to Spain and conduct his wooing in person (1623). The whole episode was both romantic and absurd.

Charles and the duke of Buckingham, who was the king's
favourite, travelled incognito as 'Tom and John Smith'. They
crossed France and late one night arrived in Madrid. All their
efforts were in vain. The Spaniards insisted on further concessions for the English catholics. Charles tried to meet their
demands and made promises which he knew he could not keep.
But when the Spaniards refused to restore the Palatinate to his
brother-in-law he broke off the negotiations. When the two
men returned to England empty-handed, bonfires were lit and
the country rejoiced that the shadow cast by the Spanish match
had been lifted.

James always regarded political rebuffs as personal insults.
Therefore he was willing to go along with Charles and Buckingham who were bent on war with Spain. Preparations were set
on foot: in 1624 parliament willingly voted subsidies; alliances
were signed with the Dutch and the Danes; arrangements were
made for Charles to marry a French princess, Henrietta Maria.
An army, under a German mercenary soldier, Mansfeld, was
assembled and sent to win back the Palatinate. But the soldiers
were unpaid, ill-trained, and badly equipped. As some deserted
and many more died of disease, the army dwindled and achieved
nothing of value. When James died, he left Charles with a
costly war on his hands. Parliament had at last got the war that
it wanted. Yet were the Stuarts capable of conducting it
successfully?

XXIII

JAMES I AND THE CONSTITUTION

FAVOURITES AND MINISTERS

WHEN James became king he placed his trust in Robert Cecil,
later the earl of Salisbury, who had helped to smooth his path to
the throne. Cecil was cautious and capable, and an able

financier who tried hard to place his royal master's finances on a sounder footing.

Salisbury died in 1612. Thereafter James' government passed into the hands of favourites. The distinction between a minister and a favourite should be made clear: a minister was a trusty counsellor to whom the king gave great authority because of his ability; a favourite was a close friend to whom the king gave power and wealth as a token of friendship. By chance, a favourite might also be a capable minister. Unfortunately James' favourites were not. The first of them was a penniless Scot, Robert Carr. He was charming and handsome, but unscrupulous and greedy. James lavished money and lands upon him. He made him Viscount Rochester and later earl of Somerset. When Carr became infatuated with Frances, wife of the earl of Essex, James enabled her to procure a divorce. Then she and Carr were married. The country was scandalised, but James treated his subjects' opinions with scant respect.

Carr's supremacy at court was challenged when George Villiers was introduced to the king in 1614. He was the son of a Leicestershire gentleman. At once James took a liking to his good looks and flattering ways. Carr saw him as a rival and he became sullen and ill-mannered towards the king. James warned him, 'I had rather have a conformable man with but ordinary parts, than the rarest men in the world that will not be obedient.'

Carr fell from favour when he and his wife were accused of the murder of Sir Thomas Overbury who had tried (unsuccessfully) to persuade Carr, his close friend, not to marry Lady Essex. Carr and his wife were found guilty (1616). James saved them from the gallows, but they were imprisoned in the Tower, whilst Carr was stripped of his offices. It was scandals of this kind that robbed the crown of the dignity and respect which the Tudors had given it.

Carr's dismissal made way for Villiers. Once again James made the fatal mistake of allowing his favourite to run the government. Villiers became duke of Buckingham and lord high admiral. Those who wanted offices had to come to him, and he distributed his favours in truly royal manner. In fact Buckingham was not incapable, but power and money went to his head. Like all favourites he was liable to work for his own advancement rather than for the country's interest. As James grew old, Buckingham won the confidence of Prince Charles, thus ensuring he would stay in power when the old king died.

After Salisbury, only two other ministers are worthy of mention: Francis Bacon, whom we shall meet later, and Lionel Cranfield. Cranfield was a rich London merchant, whom James called upon in 1618 to rescue him from his great indebtedness. He successfully put the king's finances in order. The revenue was increased by selling monopolies and levying higher customs duties; the king's debts, £900,000 in all, were paid; by economies at court he made the royal income equal expenses. The grateful James made him earl of Middlesex and lord treasurer. But Charles, Buckingham, and Queen Anne resented the fact that Cranfield had cut down the cost of entertainments at Whitehall. In 1624 they co-operated with parliament to impeach and imprison him. With Cranfield's downfall went the king's last chance to balance his budget.

THE DIVINE RIGHT OF KINGS

Tudor kings claimed that they had been ordained by God to rule—that they ruled by divine right. At the same time they recognised that they had to rule in accordance with the laws of the land. The king's rights, his prerogatives, were considerable, but they could not be used to put aside the common law except in an emergency. This then was the view prevailing in the sixteenth century, and it was harmless enough.

James too believed that kings were appointed by God. He told parliament: 'The state of Monarchy is the supremest thing upon earth; for kings are not only God's lieutenants upon earth and sit upon God's throne, but even by God himself they are called gods.'

Unlike the Tudors, however, he went on to claim that this put him above the law, i.e. that the laws were his and whilst they applied to his subjects they did not apply to him. James had written and published a book on the subject. In it he wrote: 'And as ye see it is manifest that the King is overlord of the whole land, so he is master over every person that inhabiteth the same, having power over the life and death of every one of them. For although a just prince will not take the life of any of his subjects without a clear law, yet the same laws are made by himself.' He spoke as if parliament did not exist.

[*Continued on p.* 217

SUPPLEMENT OF ILLUSTRATIONS

PLATE I

HENRY VII, artist unknown (*National Portrait Gallery*).
HENRY VIII, after Hans Holbein (*National Portrait Gallery*).
CARDINAL WOLSEY (*National Portrait Gallery*).
THOMAS CROMWELL, after Hans Holbein (*National Portrait Gallery*).

PLATE II

FOUNTAINS ABBEY (*Aerofilms and Aero Pictorial Ltd.*).
OPEN FIELDS AT LAXTON (*Aerofilms and Aero Pictorial Ltd.*).

PLATE III

EDWARD VI, school of Holbein the younger, in Windsor Castle.
MARY TUDOR, by Antonio Mor (*Prado Museum, Madrid*).
ELIZABETH I, artist unknown (*National Portrait Gallery*).
MARY, QUEEN OF SCOTS, French school (*National Portrait Gallery*).

PLATE IV

CARTOON DEPICTING DR. WILLIAM PARRY'S UNSUCCESSFUL PLOT TO
KILL QUEEN ELIZABETH, 1585 (*British Museum*).
THE EARLIEST STAGE OF THE ARMADA CAMPAIGN, 1588 from *Expeditionis
Hispanorum in Angliam vera descriptio.* (*British Museum*).

PLATE V

THE SWAN THEATRE, c. 1600, by Johannes de Witt, in Arend van
Buchell's 'commonplace book' (*University Library, Utrecht*).
LORD BURGHLEY AND HIS SON, SIR ROBERT CECIL, from Lord Salisbury's
collection, by permission.

PLATE VI

ELIZABETH AT THE CLOSING OF PARLIAMENT, from Sir Simonds D'Ewes'
Journals of the Parliaments of Queen Elizabeth, 1682 (*British Museum*).
AN ENGLISH ARMY ON THE MARCH IN IRELAND, from John Derrick's
The Image of Ireland (*Library University of Edinburgh*).

PLATE VII

PART OF VISSCHER'S ENGRAVING OF LONDON, 1616. (*Guildhall Library*).
ROYAL SIGNATURES, from originals in the House of Lords Record Office.

PLATE VIII

SIR WALTER RALEGH AND HIS SON, WALTER. (*National Portrait
Gallery*).
SIR FRANCIS DRAKE. (*National Portrait Gallery*).
SIR FRANCIS DRAKE'S 'GOLDEN HIND'. (*Mansell Collection*).

EXPLANATORY NOTES

PLATE II (*Top*). This was one of the larger monasteries which surrendered to the king in the years following the Pilgrimage of Grace. The abbot was deposed in 1536 and executed in the following year for inciting revolt in the North. Its impressive ruins still stand after 400 years and bear witness to the strength and permanence of monastic buildings. Notice the large monastic church and tower on the left. In the foreground are the long, low living-quarters of the lay brothers.

(*Bottom*). Apart from Braunton Great Field in North Devon, this is the only surviving example of open-field farming in England. Notice the contrast between the hedgeless open fields divided into strips in the foreground, and the enclosed fields, hedged and much smaller, in the distance.

PLATE IV (*Top*). Obviously drawn by a protestant: Dr. Parry carries the Pope's absolution for the evil deed which he plans to commit; in the background the traitor receives his just deserts.

(*Bottom*). The Armada is sailing up the Channel in crescent formation, with the Cornish coast to the North. Ahead are the English ships working their way out of Plymouth harbour; they are depicted again rallying in the rear of the Spanish fleet. Seeking to attack, they straggle in a long line; but the Spanish crescent is a tight defensive formation, with the transport ships in the centre and the strong galleons at the tips, ready to ward off attacks.

PLATE V (*Left*). The only surviving contemporary drawing of the interior of an Elizabethan theatre. Notice the open-air stage with sheltered recess and balcony. The audience sat in the three-tiered covered galleries, running from either side of the stage around the circumference of the theatre; the groundlings paid less and stood in the open court around the stage. Above flies a standard bearing the sign of the swan. (See Chapter XX.)

PLATE VI (*Top*). The queen is seated on the throne beneath a canopy. Behind her, on either side from where they can whisper advice to her, stand her councillors. The white-bearded lord chancellor, whose duty it is to deliver the queen's speech to the assembled parliament, stands at her right hand; around the throne stand heralds and court officials carrying her cap and sword. At the foot of the steps to the throne are four woolsacks covered in red cloth. The sack nearest the throne is for the lord chancellor; opposite this is a bigger sack on which sit four royal clerks keeping a record of proceedings. On the other two sacks sit councillors and judges; behind them are the members of the house of lords. On the queen's right are her bishops and on her left her nobles, whilst other noblemen stand behind the clerks. At the lower end of the house is a rail, 'the bar', at which the commons stand with the speaker in the front row on a small dais— he will make the closing address to the queen.

(*Bottom*).   Notice the different types of weapon in use: the pike, spear, lance, sword and dagger—and especially the musket.

PLATE VII (*Top*).   The Thames was London's highway, carrying vessels of assorted shapes and sizes, spanned by London Bridge, London's only bridge until the eighteenth century.   This is crowded with houses and at the southern end is the Bridge Gate, bristling with the heads of criminals and traitors on pikes.   On the South bank is Southwark with its great church of St. Mary; and further West, Shakespeare's Globe and the Bear House.   On the North bank stands the western half of the City of London dominated by the old Gothic St. Paul's. As the picture indicates, it was a crowded city of jostling buildings, prickly with spires.

PLATE X (*Top*).   The palace of Nonsuch, designed and built for Henry VIII, was erected on the site of the village of Coddington which was depopulated and demolished for this purpose.   Begun in 1538, it was not completed until after 1556.   The palace—None Such—owed its name to its ornate and extravagant decoration which was unequalled in Tudor England at that time.

PLATE XIII.   The arrangement of both armies was quite conventional: cavalry on the wings, and in the centre a mixture of musketeers and pikemen (whose long pikes can be seen).   The New Model Army is drawn up in battle array in the lower half of the picture; it holds Naseby and its baggage camp can be seen in the lower left-hand corner. Oliver Cromwell and Prince Rupert command the cavalry on the right wings of their respective armies.

PLATE XIV (*Top*).   These show the first victims (1); the mass exodus from London (2 & 3); the Plague at its height with its enormous toll of human life (4–8); and the return of the refugees as the epidemic subsided (9).

PLATE XV (*Bottom*).   The view is from the South Bank (and is of the same area as that shown in Plate VII).   It was from Southwark that Samuel Pepys viewed the Fire, describing it as 'one entire arch of fire from this to the other side the bridge, and in a bow up the hill for an arch of above a mile long'.   The Fire began in Pudding Lane, just to the right of London Bridge.

Above.   King Henry VII

Below.   Cardinal Wolsey

Above.   King Henry VIII at the age of 49

Below.   Thomas Cromwell

Fountains Abbey, Yorkshire

Open fields at Laxton, Nottinghamshire

Above. King Edward VI. *Above.* Queen Mary I
Reproduced by gracious permission
of Her Majesty the Queen
Below. Queen Elizabeth I *Below.* Mary Queen of Scots

A cartoon portraying Dr. Parry's unsuccessful plot to kill Elizabeth, 1585

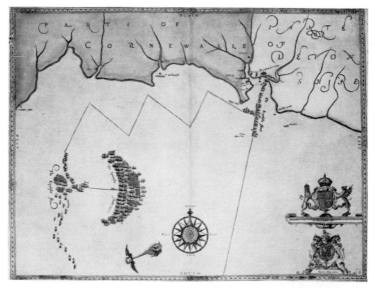

A map depicting the earliest stage of the Armada campaign, 1588

Lord Burghley and his son, Sir Robert Cecil

The Swan Theatre c. 1600

Elizabeth at the closing of a session of Parliament

An English army on the march in Ireland

Part of London, as seen from the South Bank, 1616

Royal signatures: from left to right they are those of Henry VII, Henry VIII, Edward VI, Mary Tudor and Elizabeth I

Above.   Sir Francis Drake

Left.   Sir Walter Ralegh and his son, Walter

Below.   Sir Francis Drake's ship, the Golden Hind

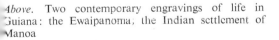

Above. Two contemporary engravings of life in Guiana: the Ewaipanoma, the Indian settlement of Manoa

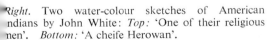

Right. Two water-colour sketches of American Indians by John White: *Top:* 'One of their religious men'. *Bottom:* 'A cheife Herowan'.

X

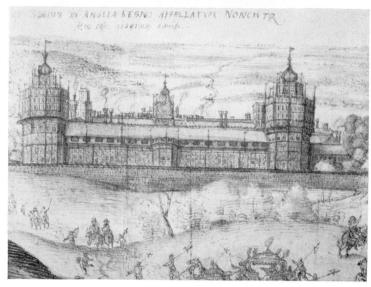

Nonsuch Palace, Surrey

Queen Elizabeth dancing with the Earl of Leicester

Reproduced by permission of the Rt. Hon. Viscount de L'Isle, V.C., from his collection at Penshurst Place, Kent

The first three Stuarts: James I, Charles I and Charles II

The Declaration of Breda, 1660

Charles I's letter assenting to the execution of the
Earl of Strafford, 1641

Above.   Archbishop Laud in 1635

Below.   Oliver Cromwell

Above.   Thomas Wentworth, Earl of Strafford

Below.   John Pym

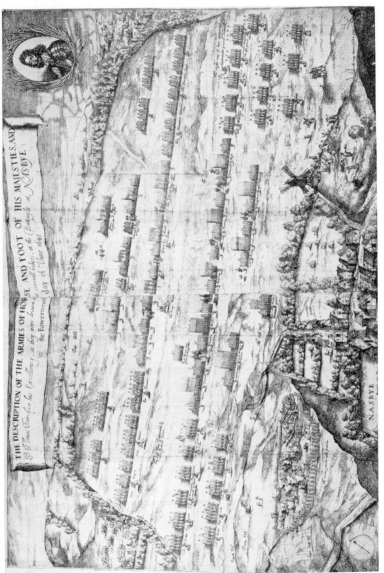

The opposing armies drawn up before the battle of Naseby, June 1645

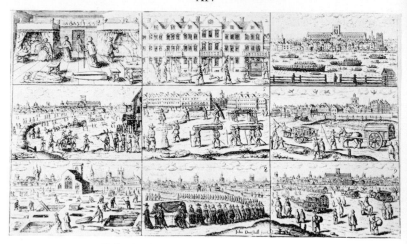

Episodes from the Plague in London, 1665

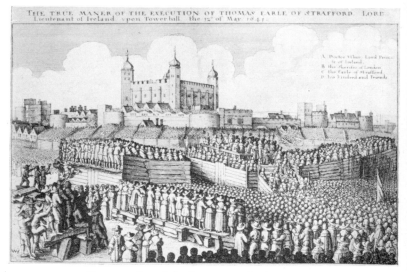

The execution of the Earl of Strafford, May 1641

The four days battle, June 1–4, 1666

The Great Fire of London, 1666

William Harvey demonstrating the circulation of the blood
to Charles I

James, Duke of York with his first wife, Anne Hyde, and his daughters,
the Princesses Mary and Anne. *Reproduced by gracious permission of
Her Majesty the Queen*

James held that it was sinful to oppose the king, his argument ran: 'It is atheism and blasphemy to dispute what God can do; so it is presumption and high contempt in a subject to dispute what a King can do, or say that a King cannot do this or that.'

Dutiful subjects ought to receive good government gratefully; and the king's actions must be accepted without murmur, for kings are 'accountable to none but God only'.

He did acknowledge that a wise king would not rule in arbitrary fashion: 'A king leaves (ceases) to be a king and degenerates into a tyrant as soon as he leaves off to rule according to his laws.' Yet supposing that a king had no wish to rule by the laws, the subject had no means of redress, because it was sinful to oppose him. This was indeed dangerous stuff to put about.

The English constitution was vague and ill-defined. Nowhere were the king's rights or parliament's privileges laid down. The Tudors had taken advantage of this to extend their authority quietly, and they had wisely refrained from discussing their rights. Not so James, who was incurably talkative. He insisted on defining matters of government and philosophising about his rights. In this way he drew attention to them at a time when many felt that the crown's authority should be reduced. And although he had every intention of ruling by the laws of the land, his uncompromising claim that he was above the law simply aroused men to oppose him: lawyers rushed to uphold the supremacy of the law, and the commons flew to the defence of their privileges.

James' theory of divine right was not out of tune with the political beliefs of his time. Absolutism was on the march in Europe. But James was unwisely ignoring the changes which were going on around him: a richer gentry seeking a voice in government; a widespread feeling that the king had more than enough power; a self-confident parliament; his own poverty which frequently forced him, despite 'the divinity that doth hedge a king', to go cap-in-hand to the commons for money.

JAMES I AND HIS PARLIAMENTS

James' relations with parliament, especially with the commons, were beset with thorny problems. Most of the members of the lower house were country gentlemen. During the sixteenth century they had become experienced in local government and they had served in the army and navy. They were educated and some had a knowledge of the law. A number of them were puritans. They were men of independent temper, ready to criticise the king's government—and there were several issues on which they were more than willing to do so. Some of them we have already considered:

(*1*) James' theory of divine right: Although James did not intend to put his theories into practice, the commons did not know this. They feared an attack on their privileges, even the end of parliament itself—and his tactless comment, that as he gave them their privileges he could also take them away, hardly helped to improve relations. The result was growing friction between a king claiming novel power and a parliament desirous of reducing his existing power.

(*2*) The religious problem: James was an Arminian, inclined to tolerate catholics but unsympathetic to the puritans. Parliament was bigoted in its hatred and fear of popery, but it favoured the puritans whose strength in the commons was growing. Under puritan leadership the lower house demanded fresh penal laws against the catholics, set its teeth against the Spanish marriage match, and clamoured for a war in aid of Elector Frederick.

(*3*) Money: The commons believed that the king ought to live of his own, and when he did not they put it down to his extravagant court and his favourites. His poverty provided them with a powerful weapon. They would offer him subsidies on condition that he first redressed their grievances. 'Redress before supply' was the commons' most effective weapon in their struggle with the early Stuarts.

(*4*) The power and incompetence of the king's favourites.

The parliament of 1604: the commons' privileges. Before the elections, James had issued a proclamation warning 'that there be not chosen any persons bankrupt or outlawed, but men of known good behaviour'. Despite this the electors of Buckinghamshire chose Sir Francis Goodwin, an outlaw. James annulled the election and ordered a new one to be held. The commons challenged this decision and claimed that they were the true judges of elections to their own house. James told them in effect to mind their own business, and that in any case they derived their privileges from him. The commons could not accept this opinion as to the origin of their privileges: if the king granted them, he could also take them away again. James had got his facts right, but his tactlessness had changed an election dispute into a major debate on the rights of king and commons. The matter was only settled when he recognized the right of the lower house to judge disputed elections. In return the commons agreed to a new election in this case. James had lost the first clash with parliament.

As a result of their differences with James, the commons drew up 'the form of apology and satisfaction'. Although it was never presented to the king, it is important as a statement of their views on their privileges, which 'are our right and due inheritance'. They explained that it was necessary to keep a constant watch over their rights: 'the prerogatives of princes may easily and do daily grow; the privileges of the subjects are for the most part at an everlasting stand'. The apology was written in respectful terms. Nonetheless the commons were behaving like an experienced schoolmaster, who instructs his new pupil on the rules and customs of the school.

Another privilege was challenged in this parliament, though not by the king. The Tudors generally accepted that members of parliament had freedom from arrest for debt whilst parliament was sitting. When Sir Thomas Shirley, a member of the commons, was seized by creditors, the house ordered his release and imprisoned those who had had him arrested. The king upheld the commons' action. Nevertheless this first session of parliament was not an harmonious start to the reign.

The parliament of 1610: impositions and the Great Contract. In 1606 parliament met under the shadow of the recent Gunpowder Plot. It co-operated with the king to pass new laws against the catholics. The parliament of 1610, however, was a much stormier affair due to James' money problems. By 1606 his worsening financial position had caused him to turn his attention to trade. He already received customs dues (an hereditary right of English kings) and tunnage and poundage (a duty granted to each king for life by parliament).[1] James now imposed extra duties on imports. A merchant, John Bate,

[1] Originally a duty on every 'tun' of wine and pound of wool, leather, and other articles.

refused to pay the new charge on currants. The dispute was taken to court where the judges decided that, in order to regulate trade, the king had the right to levy customs duties as he saw fit (1606). Certainly there was no law which forbade these 'impositions'. The judgement was important for two reasons: it confirmed James' right to impose extra duties without parliament's consent; and the chief judge ruled that he had the right to do so because he was an absolute king—the judges were upholding divine right. Such a judgement threatened to give James a supply of money over which parliament had no control.

James proceeded to abuse the decision of the judges. They had recognized his right to levy impositions in order to regulate trade, but he did so with the object of raising money. In 1608 he issued a book of rates in which duties were increased on many articles. Despite this his debts, which totalled £300,000, forced him to recall parliament in 1610. The commons were less concerned to grant him money than to debate impositions. James angrily ordered them to stop on the grounds that they were discussing his prerogative. When the commons hotly resisted him, however, he gave way. In the debate which followed, they made their views quite clear: king in parliament, not the king alone, was the sovereign power and it alone could impose new taxes. If the king was in need of money, he should go to parliament for it.[1]

The commons also considered Salisbury's scheme to place the crown's finances on a firmer basis. With James' approval he offered to surrender feudal dues in return for payment of the king's debts and an annual sum of £200,000. However, James greedily demanded more than £200,000. The commons, angry over impositions and suspicious of the king, were unwilling to grant even that amount. When further disputes arose over religion, James dissolved parliament with his financial difficulties unsolved. The Great Contract had much to recommend it: it might have modernised the crown's finances and enabled the king to do his job properly, and it would have brought to an end feudal dues which irritated so many landowners.

[1] This was all very well, but requests for money were unpopular in peace-time. Even if he obtained a parliamentary subsidy it would not be enough. It should have been, but most of the landowners were under-assessed or paid nothing. The gentry, a majority in parliament, made sure of this.

The 'addled'[1] parliament: 1614. James sold monopolies and titles[2] and continued to levy impositions. But in 1612 his financial expert, Salisbury, died, and two years later he was forced to summon parliament again. His unsuccessful attempt to tamper with the elections resulted in a turbulent session. The complaints of the commons about monopolies, impositions, and favourites were only silenced when James dissolved parliament without obtaining supplies.

The parliament of 1621: monopolies and impeachments. Once again James had to use benevolences, monopolies, and other dubious and unpopular expedients to make ends meet. Yet he was only saved from financial disaster by Lionel Cranfield, who by 1624 had made him solvent for the first time. Long before then, however, James had called parliament again (1621). He had been prompted to do so by the European situation. The Palatinate was being overrun by the Hapsburgs. As the commons wanted James to help his son-in-law, he hoped to get a subsidy from them on the strength of this. Instead they launched forth into a furious attack on monopolies and courtiers.

Under pressure from the commons Elizabeth had removed the most harmful monopolies and allowed the rest to be challenged in the law courts. Since 1611, however, James had revived the sale of monopolies. They were not always harmful: some protected the owners of new inventions; others were used to control the making of arms and gunpowder. But monopolists always raised prices. The commons wanted to punish them. However, they had no right to try anyone, except for a breach of privilege. So they revived their old right of impeachment which had not been used since 1459. The process was simple but effective: they presented the accused person to the lords and charged him with certain offences, and he was then tried by the upper house. In this way the most notorious monopolist, Sir Giles Mompesson, was sentenced to imprisonment for life, a fine of £10,000, and the loss of his property.

Parliament now found a more important victim. Francis Bacon, Viscount St Albans and lord chancellor, was accused of

[1] So-called, because it produced nothing.
[2] In 1611 James created the title of baronet which he sold for £10,000 apiece.

receiving bribes. He had been in the habit of accepting presents from suitors who appeared before him in court. Sometimes they were gifts from grateful men after Bacon had judged in their favour. Occasionally, however, he had accepted gifts from suitors before he delivered judgement. In Bacon's defence this must be said: that his judgements were against these suitors despite their gifts, and that it was a common enough practice amongst judges to take presents. Nevertheless he was impeached. He begged the lords, that their sentence 'may not be heavy to my ruin but gracious and mixed with mercy'. Little mercy was shown. He was fined £40,000, imprisoned in the Tower, and disqualified from holding any public office. James pardoned him, but deprived him of the chancellorship. His public career was over.

Bacon's impeachment was very important. The commons had found a way to exercise control over the king's ministers and to bring his 'evil counsellors' to justice. Instead of being responsible to the king alone, as they had been in the past, they were now held to be responsible to the laws of the land as well.

Parliament now turned its attention to foreign affairs and in a petition presumed to give James advice. In doing so it was trespassing on the king's prerogative. He was furious: 'None therein shall presume henceforth to meddle with anything concerning our government or deep matters of State, and namely not to deal with our dearest son's match with the daughter of Spain.'

Elizabeth would have said much the same sort of thing. But parliament had come far since then. The commons presented another petition to the king, in which they complained that the king 'doth seem to abridge us of the ancient liberty of parliament for freedom of speech'. Naturally it did not serve to put James in a better temper. With his usual tactlessness, he reminded the commons: 'We are an old and experienced King' who was not in need of their advice. He told them that, 'You meddle with things far above your reach' and that, 'Your privileges were derived from the grace and permission of our ancestors'. The last was a threat to the commons' liberties, which could not go unchallenged. The result was the famous Commons' Protestation of 18 December 1621:

> That the liberties, franchises, privileges and jurisdictions of
> Parliament are the ancient and undoubted birthright and

inheritance of the subjects of England; and that the arduous and urgent affairs concerning the King, State, and defence of the realm and of the Church of England, and the maintenance and making of laws, and redress of mischiefs and grievances are proper subjects of debate in Parliament; and that every member of Parliament hath freedom of speech to propound, treat, reason, and bring to conclusion the same.

This was too much for James who dissolved parliament and tore the Protestation from the commons' journal. Yet no action of his could alter the facts: the commons had at last claimed the right to discuss all matters of State, and not merely those subjects placed before them by the king.

The parliament of 1624: harmony restored. In James' last parliament relations were more harmonious. Charles and Buckingham, who had virtually taken over the government from the old king, wanted war with Spain. Parliament was only too willing to vote supplies for a policy which it had demanded for years. Charles and his favourite also encouraged the impeachment of the able treasurer, the earl of Middlesex. Finally, James gave his approval to a law annulling all monopolies, except patents for new inventions. It was a signal victory for parliament over the prerogative.

JAMES I AND THE JUDGES

The courts were the king's. So were the judges, who were appointed by him and held office 'during his pleasure' (that is to say, he could dismiss them whenever he pleased). In the early years of James' reign they regarded themselves as royal servants and, as Bate's case showed, they upheld James' ideas of kingship. In this they were opposed by the lawyers who sat in the commons. The lawyers argued that James was not an absolute king, but that he was below the law. The most famous of these lawyers was Sir Edward Coke. He had served in Elizabeth's government, and James made him a judge. Coke was a man of unpleasant character: greedy and cruel, servile to the king's favourites and harsh in his judgements. But he proved to be the great defender of the common law against James' encroachments. He wanted the judges to be not just the spokesmen of the king, but impartial referees in disputes between the king and his subjects. When James tried to influence the judges in cases concerning him, Coke challenged his right to do so. By 1616 James had had enough. He dismissed Coke and appointed Francis Bacon in his place. Bacon was a man of very different calibre, a philosopher and essayist, scientist and lawyer. Where Coke was learned, Bacon had genius; where Coke was narrow-minded and selfish, Bacon was open-handed and generous. They were indeed bitter opponents: they had been rivals for office, and had wooed the same woman. On both occasions Coke was the winner; but in 1616 Bacon had his revenge—and two years later he became lord chancellor. However, James did not make good use of Bacon's brilliant mind; he listened only to Buckingham. Furthermore, Coke had the last laugh, when he had the satisfaction of seeing his rival impeached and humbled.

Bacon and Coke represented two schools of thought, those of king and parliament. The former accepted that normally the king must abide by the law, but in times of emergency he could override it to protect his subjects. Bacon saw the judges as 'lions under the throne', upholding a king who like Solomon ruled wisely in the interests of the people. Parliament's function was simply to vote money and laws and to give advice when asked. Coke, on the other hand, denied that James could ignore or ride roughshod over the laws. Even the king had to obey the law. Bacon looked back to the government of the Tudors; Coke looked forward to the rule of parliament.

CONCLUSION

James I's relations with his parliaments set the scene for the great battles of his son's reign. The clashes had been numerous, but two issues were basic: religion and the form of government. At Hampton Court James lost the last chance to put an end to religious strife. Thereafter, whilst the Arminians grew in strength, the puritans gave up their attempt to reform the Church from within; instead they left it and prepared to overthrow it from without. In matters of government the old Tudor compromise had gone. King in parliament had been the sovereign then. Now James claimed sovereignty for himself alone. So parliament, wanting a greater share in government, was moving towards the same claim for itself. As yet there had been little change in practice. But parliament had asserted its right to debate matters of state; it had used 'redress before supply' and revived impeachment. Above all it had advanced in self-confidence to a point where it was willing to challenge the king openly.

The Stuarts' greatest danger was that the religious and political opposition to their rule had combined. The puritans had wrested control of the commons from the king. This was, in large measure, James' own fault. He did not ensure that he was represented in the commons by capable privy councillors. As a result leadership of the house passed to the puritans under Edwin Sandys. James could not even rely on the lords to assist him. The favour he had shown to upstarts like Villiers irritated the old noble families, who in their turn opposed the courtiers and favourites and upheld the pretensions of the commons.

By 1625 the Stuarts and parliament were drifting apart, and as they defined their positions there was less and less room for compromise. The views of Bacon and Coke reveal the opposing positions they had taken up. When James I died, the situation called for a man with great vision, common-sense, and a willingness to compromise. Charles I was not that man.

XXIV

CHARLES I : 1625–29

THE CHARACTER OF THE NEW KING

CHARLES I was James I's second son. Prince Henry was raised as heir to the throne, whereas the younger brother was intended for the Church. Henry was extremely popular: he was a keen protestant and a friend of Sir Walter Ralegh. If he had lived to become king he might well have averted or postponed the disastrous conflict with parliament. But he died in 1612.

Charles had been a backward child; he did not learn to talk until he was five, and only walked when he was seven. Such backwardness left its mark on Charles the man: he walked with a limp, while more serious in a public figure was an impediment of speech, which made him reserved and unwilling to talk—and which some people took to be haughtiness.

The new king differed greatly from his father. Dignified, sensitive, and cultured, he turned Whitehall into a centre of the arts, where writers of masques, actors, and painters were always welcome. However, it did little to please parliament and the puritans: the former noted with disapproval that Charles spent lavishly on the arts, and the latter detested the play-acting of which the king, queen, and courtiers were so fond.

Those who knew Charles well adored him. Indeed he had much to commend him as a man: he was a faithful husband and devoted father, whilst to his friends and servants he was gentle and kind. And, as the tragic events of his reign were to show, his courage and his devotion to the crown were never in doubt.

However, he had grave defects as a king. He lacked the easy bluff manner of the Tudors. In any case he felt that as a king he should be aloof and distant; to mix freely with his subjects would be to destroy the dignity of the crown. He was vacillating, and easily swayed by the second-rate men in whom he put such great faith, whereas the advice of his ablest and most loyal supporters was usually ignored—until it was too late. Above all he was obstinate: he believed that he had a divine mission to perform and he was determined to do so, come what may. James I had been flexible, able to play for time or give way when the odds were against him. Charles rigidly adhered to his high principles regardless of criticism and opposition.

Charles' divine mission was simple. He had inherited the crown's prerogative and the royal supremacy over the Church. His duty was to preserve them intact and hand them on to his heir. He believed that a king had the right and duty to govern and his subjects had the duty to obey. James had enjoyed philosophising about such things; Charles with his natural reserve did not. But James did confine himself to the realm of theory; Charles tried to put his ideas about divine right into practice—and at a time when his subjects favoured a reduction in the king's power. Unfortunately he believed that the rightness of his mission allowed him to regard public opinion as of no account. He declared, 'I owe the account of my actions to God alone.' His subjects were required by God to obey the king—or else suffer dire punishment at His hands. When Englishmen opposed his policies and enquired into matters of government he treated them with dishonesty and duplicity—and felt that he was justified in doing so. He failed to see how unpopular his government was becoming—and like his father he believed that opposition was caused only by a few 'fiery and popular spirits'.

Charles typifies the difference between the Stuarts and the Tudors: the former had more attractive personal qualities but lacked political understanding, whereas the Tudors were less likeable, but more statesmanlike.

The new king was saddled with an expensive war against Spain. He decided to ask the commons to finance it—after all it was really their war. There was some justice in this. But Charles' actions, prior to the meeting of parliament, created an atmosphere of mistrust. Buckingham was as strong in royal favour as ever—and as lord high admiral the conduct of the war against Spain was in his hands. Furthermore, Charles, as a result of his father's negotiations, married Henrietta Maria, daughter of Henry IV of France. In secret clauses in the marriage treaty he agreed that the princess and her household could attend mass; that he should relax the penal laws against the English catholics; that England should, if required, help Louis XIII against his enemies, including the Huguenots. This marriage was a remarkable piece of folly. The Stuarts thought that English opposition to the Spanish match had been due to the traditional hatred of Spain. Charles was oblivious of the fact that, as Henrietta Maria was a Roman catholic, she would be equally objectionable to his subjects. And, although the clauses of the marriage treaty were secret, the commons suspected their existence. In the long run this marriage was to dog the king's chances of success: the queen, Charles' 'evil genius', led him into unwise actions, made his government unpopular, and aroused the popular belief that his court was riddled with popery.

In James I's reign the king's control of parliament had collapsed. Leadership of the commons had passed to the opposition: some were puritans, others were simply desirous of good government. New leaders were now coming to the fore, among them John Pym, Sir John Eliot, Sir Dudley Digges, and Denzil Holles. They were young, determined, uncompromising puritans. Another prominent critic of the government was Sir Thomas Wentworth. He was no puritan but he was anxious to promote good government.

CHARLES' FIRST PARLIAMENT: 1625

Parliament met in June, 1625. At once there was trouble. The commons voted a mere £140,000 to the king. Worse still, it granted tunnage and poundage for one year only. This was an additional grant of customs duties, which was made to the king in the first parliament of his reign. Formerly it had always been granted for life. The commons had broken with tradition in a way that was bound to cause friction between king and parliament. It was foolish. It was also dangerous. Just as the commons had claimed, in James' reign, that the king's grant of privileges was a mere formality, so Charles might take the same attitude over their granting of tunnage and poundage—and in fact he did, for in the years to come he levied it without parliament's consent.

The commons were more concerned to criticise the government. They distrusted Buckingham and they were suspicious of the terms of Charles' marriage. The war was being mismanaged; in any case, if the king was fighting for protestantism why did he tolerate the English catholics and send ships to help Louis XIII against the Huguenots? Charles in his turn was angered by the commons' unwillingness to pay for a war which they had for so long demanded. In August 1625 he dissolved parliament.

THE CADIZ EXPEDITION: 1625

Charles decided that a dazzling feat of arms would make parliament more amenable. So the government planned an expedition to Cadiz. He had deliberately revived the policy of the Elizabethan sea-dogs in an attempt to appeal to parliament. The fact that so many Elizabethan expeditions had failed was ignored or forgotten. Buckingham organised the expedition. He had already done much to improve the navy. He had reduced its cost yet increased the number of ships. But Lord Howard of Effingham, victor over the Armada in 1588, who had been admiral before Buckingham, had in his later years let the fleet go to ruin. Buckingham did his best, but he lacked the money to equip and supply the fleet properly. Criminals and beggars, hungry and half-naked, were pressed to man the ships. Many of the vessels were merchantmen, which were of little use in a fight. Viscount Wimbledon, a soldier, led the expedition which was a miserable failure. The food was foul; disease broke out amongst the crews. A landing was effected, but the soldiers were more interested in the abundant Spanish wines which they found. The army dissolved in general drunkenness and indiscipline—and its only achievement was a successful withdrawal to the ships. It returned to England in disgrace.

CHARLES' SECOND PARLIAMENT: 1626

Charles' treasury was empty. A parliament had therefore to be summoned, and he had not gained the glorious victory which might have persuaded the commons to dip deep into their purses. He did his clumsy best to make parliament compliant. The opposition leaders were appointed sheriffs.[1] He also tried to stop the earl of Bristol, Buckingham's enemy, from taking his seat. But his efforts were to no avail. The lords insisted on Bristol's inclusion. Though the commons' normal leaders were absent, Sir John Eliot came forward to lead them. He was extreme in his views and bitterly condemned the Cadiz fiasco. He had witnessed the expedition's return to Plymouth where men had fallen down and died of exhaustion in the streets. Eliot genuinely though unjustly believed Buckingham to be responsible for the mismanagement of the war. He told the commons, 'Our honour is ruined, our ships are sunk, our men perished; not by the sword, not by the enemy, but by those we trust.' He proposed that they should impeach the king's favourite. The commons needed little persuasion. They charged Buckingham with 'exorbitant ambition' and neglect of 'his office and duty' as admiral. 'The dominion of the said seas is thereby in most eminent danger to be utterly lost.' Charles saw that no money would be forthcoming unless he sacrificed his favourite to the commons' wrath. He preferred to dissolve parliament.

King and parliament were rapidly drifting apart. The attacks on Buckingham were really attacks on Charles, who was well aware of this. One of his councillors told the commons, 'His Majesty cannot believe that the aim is at the Duke of Buckingham, but findeth that these proceedings do directly wound the

[1] As the sheriff's duty was to supervise elections to the commons he could not offer himself as a candidate.

honour and judgement of himself and his father.' Charles warned them, 'Now you begin to set the dice, and make your own game; but I pray you be not deceived, it is not a parliamentary way, nor is it a way to deal with a King. Remember that Parliaments are altogether in my power for their calling, sitting, and dissolution.'

GOVERNMENT WITHOUT PARLIAMENT: 1626–8

To make financial matters worse Charles now found himself at war with France. In 1625 he had hoped for an Anglo-French expedition to free the Palatinate from the Spaniards—France and Spain were then at war. However, trouble arose soon after he had married Henrietta Maria. Although Charles had promised to lend Louis XIII some ships he was unwilling to implement the promise. He knew that Louis intended to use them against the Huguenots of La Rochelle[1] who were in rebellion, so he found excuses to delay the dispatch of the ships. When they finally sailed, the crews refused to fight fellow-protestants. Louis XIII in his turn was unwilling to help Charles recover the Palatinate. In 1626 he made peace with Spain. Thereafter relations rapidly deteriorated. Each country accused the other of piracy in the Channel. Charles enforced the penal laws against the catholics in order to please parliament (1626). He expelled his wife's French attendants and ordered the seizure of all French ships in English ports. English vessels in French ports suffered a similar fate. By 1627 the two countries were at war.

Buckingham's plan of war was to co-operate with the Huguenots against their king. He organised, and this time led, an expedition to assist La Rochelle. His first target was the island of Rhé, situated outside the port. But it was ably defended by the French and Buckingham was repulsed with heavy losses. Later in the year he sent a second expedition. In the meantime, however, Louis XIII's great minister, Cardinal Richelieu, had begun a siege of La Rochelle. He had erected large earthworks. These partly blocked the narrow channel linking the city to the sea. The English commander, Denbigh, was baffled and made no attempt to attack.

Buckingham's expeditions had achieved nothing, but they still had to be paid for. The government tried to cut its expenses:

[1] An important port and fortress on the west coast of France.

soldiers were raised by the counties and billeted in private houses around the south coast ports. Indiscipline amongst them forced the government to impose martial law on the southern counties. (When martial or military law was imposed, the ordinary laws were suspended and both civilians and soldiers were subject to it.) Fresh ways of raising money were sought. Tunnage and poundage was levied without parliament's consent. Ship-money[1] was collected from the sea-ports. Charles also demanded a forced loan from the richer classes. It was widely resisted, but some who refused to pay were imprisoned. Five gentlemen or 'knights', led by Sir Thomas Darnel, complained that they had not been told the cause of their imprisonment, so they demanded to be released on bail. The 'Five Knights Case' in 1627 became a test-case which involved the liberties of the subject, for, as a lawyer complained, if a man could be arrested without cause shown and then refused bail, he might languish in prison forever. The judges, however, gave their verdict in the king's favour: he was entitled to commit people to prison and keep them there without trial, for the security of the State. He did it by 'that absolute power that a sovereign hath, by which a king commands'.

The judges were as usual legally correct. The king's prerogative could be used at his discretion in an emergency. To protect the state in such emergencies he could declare martial law, imprison people without trial, and so on. However, because he was at loggerheads with parliament, the king was forced to turn the emergency prerogative into the weapon of day-to-day government. It was a clear threat to the liberties of the subject. As the knights' lawyers argued, Charles' action was contrary to the Magna Carta, which declared 'that no freeman shall be imprisoned without just cause'.

CHARLES' THIRD PARLIAMENT: FIRST SESSION (1628)

Despite the various expedients for raising money Charles' expensive wars and growing debts forced him to summon parliament yet again. When it met, it had many grievances to consider: not only the recent misuse of the prerogative, but also the growth of Arminianism (which many saw as a return to popery). The commons decided to insist on 'redress before supply'. They drew up the famous Petition of Right which

1 See pages 237-238.

embodied their complaints. If the king signed it, they would grant him the money he so sorely needed. Charles hedged and tried every ruse to avoid signing. But the commons persisted and in the end he gave way.

The Petition requested four things of the king:

(*1*) 'that no man hereafter be compelled to make or yield any gift, loan, benevolence, tax or such like charge,' without the consent of parliament.

(*2*) 'that no man shall suffer arbitrary imprisonment without cause shown'.

(*3*) that in future soldiers and sailors should not be billeted on private persons.

(*4*) that martial law should never again be imposed in time of peace.

Although parliament had won its first victory since the act against monopolies (1624), it was a hollow victory. A few abuses had been prohibited, but the Petition had not touched on the fundamental problem: what the form of government was to be in the future. It had obstructed Charles' policies. The government could no longer pursue an active foreign policy without its consent. At the same time parliament had not yet attempted to wrest from the king the right to rule. In other words, whilst parliament had no right to govern, it prevented the king from doing so.

With the Petition signed, the commons kept their promise and granted supplies to the king. Charles saw a chance to establish better relations with them. However, they had not finished with his government yet. They attacked Buckingham, they criticised the Arminians, and they called into question Charles' recent levy of tunnage and poundage, which was deemed a breach of the Petition. Charles was disillusioned. In June 1628 he prorogued parliament until the following year.

Shortly afterwards, as Buckingham prepared a third expedition to La Rochelle, he was murdered. The assassin was a naval officer, John Felton. He was a frustrated, ambitious, and melancholy puritan, but to the country he was a hero who had rid England of its tyrant. Buckingham's death brought to an end his war policy. The fleet sailed to La Rochelle in time to watch the city surrender to Cardinal Richelieu. Once again it returned having achieved nothing. It was the last military venture against the French.

CHARLES' THIRD PARLIAMENT: SECOND SESSION (1629)

With Buckingham dead there was a chance that the commons might be more amenable. Instead they met in a mood of grim determination. They criticised the religious and foreign policies of the king: in effect they were demanding the right to influence, even control, royal policy. Sir John Eliot and Sir John Pym might have argued that this was self-defence against the divine right theories of the Stuarts. Nonetheless they were demanding a power which no Tudor parliament had ever possessed. The king was entitled to govern as he saw fit, subject to the laws of the land and the criticisms of parliament, but the commons were trying to make him govern as they saw fit.

The commons were angry with Wentworth who had changed sides and entered the king's government, and they were afraid of the strength of the Arminians, some of whom, such as Laud and Montague, were being given high offices in the Church. They were also incensed against tunnage and poundage; the government had continued to levy it and when John Rolle, a merchant, refused to pay, his goods were seized. Rolle was a member of the commons who demanded that his goods be restored to him. Charles had had enough, and he decided to adjourn parliament. However, Eliot forestalled him. His supporters locked the doors of the house of commons, and while the speaker was held down in his chair[1] he put to the members three resolutions which were passed amidst shouts and cheers: that whoever brought in any 'innovation of religion' or sought 'to extend popery or Arminianism' was 'a capital enemy of the king and kingdom'; similarly, whoever advised the levying of tunnage and poundage without parliament's consent, or who paid it, was both a capital enemy and a betrayer of England's liberties.

Charles now took his revenge. He dissolved parliament, and imprisoned the chief culprits. Sir John Eliot died in prison in 1632, whilst the others were not released until 1640. Meanwhile Charles had made a grave decision: henceforth he would rule alone and without parliament.

THE SIGNIFICANCE OF CHARLES' FIRST THREE PARLIAMENTS

(*1*) Charles believed that his difficulties with the commons were due to a few 'turbulent and ill-affected spirits' who 'mask and disguise their wicked intentions, dangerous to the State'. 'Some

[1] The speaker could end a meeting of the commons by standing up.

few vipers' were upsetting the good intentions of the 'wise and moderate men of that house'. It was a common failing of the Stuarts not to see the widespread support which their critics had.

(2) The Tudor system of government had been effective in its day: the king ruled; parliament voted money and criticised the government; together they made laws. This arrangement no longer worked. The king could not rule with parliament any longer: either the king alone must be sovereign, or parliament would snatch that sovereignty from him. The partners had become competitors for supremacy.

(3) Tudor England had seen the rise of a large number of gentlemen, pushing, able, and greedy. The crown had co-operated with them in the conduct of local affairs and war. James I and Charles I tried to carry on in co-operation with them, but they failed in their attempt to do so. This was due to many things: differences in religion, in foreign policy, and in their ideas of what prerogative was; the Stuarts' defects of character, and the short-sightedness of parliament which never looked like taking financial reform in hand. The gentry, seeking to influence a government with which they were dissatisfied, were unwilling to give the king enough money to govern properly. By 1629 the Stuart attempt to co-operate with the gentry had broken down.

(4) The king was losing support in the country especially amongst those who mattered most, the gentlemen and merchants. He could expect to command the support of Anglicans and nobles, but even amongst them his position had been weakened. Some devout Anglicans disapproved of the queen's catholicism, others were disturbed by the growth of Arminianism. There was discontent amongst the nobles too. They disliked the sale of peerages to upstarts and the reckless grants of lands and money to favourites. A 'country party' had grown up. It consisted of dissatisfied peers such as the earls of Bedford, Warwick, and Essex, puritans all, and co-operated with the puritan leaders in the commons. Charles was blind to the growing opposition as he prepared to rule by himself.

XXV

THE PERSONAL RULE OF
CHARLES I: 1629–40

THE KING'S DEFENCE OF HIS ACTIONS

CHARLES issued a proclamation justifying his decision not to summon any more parliaments. He had done everything possible 'to take away all ill understanding between us and our people', but the commons were more interested in 'a multitude of questions raised amongst them touching their liberties and privileges'; and they had spent their time in 'blasting our government'. He ended by accusing the commons of aiming 'to erect an universal over-swaying power to themselves, which belongs only to us, and not to them'. Having justified himself, Charles turned his back on parliament forever—or so he hoped.

CHARLES' PERSONAL RULE: WAS IT A TYRANNY?

The eleven years of personal government have been called a 'despotism' and even a 'tyranny'. Neither is true. The law did not require regular parliaments. Parliament was summoned and dismissed at the king's discretion. Furthermore, Charles was not arbitrary. He promised to observe the law and usually he did so. Certainly he did not intend to rob his subjects of their rights and property. However, many saw the dangers of personal government. It was only in parliament that subjects could raise their grievances and complain of injustices. Without it criticism was silenced. The law-courts did not provide an alternative. Whenever the king's rights were questioned, the judges decided in his favour, and those who did not were liable to be dismissed. With the judges on his side and parliament falling into disuse, the king could move towards absolutism without anyone to stop him.

One further point may be made in Charles' favour. Parliament did not directly represent the whole people: the upper house consisted of landed nobles and bishops; the commons, elected by the propertied classes, contained a large majority of landowners with a smaller number of moneyed men. Since 1603 parliament had demanded warlike policies for which it would not pay, and it had adopted a selfish attitude towards the poorer and weaker of the king's subjects. In short, it had worked in the interests of the landowners. Charles believed that he could do better. He would ally himself with the merchants and govern in the interest of all.

THE AIMS OF CHARLES' GOVERNMENT: 1629–40

The objects of Charles' government may be listed as follows:

(*1*) to uphold the king's supremacy over the Church and to enforce uniformity in matters of doctrine—the latter meant the persecution of nonconformists.

(*2*) to uphold the rights of the crown.

(*3*) to protect the liberties of all the king's subjects, especially of the poor. The government wished to enforce the poor law and acts relating to apprentices and enclosures. It believed that property owners had duties as well as rights, taking the view that it was not the fault of the poor that they were poor, and that, therefore, it was the duty of their more fortunate brethren to provide for them. Such a policy was generous and high principled. In the circumstances, however, it was unwise, for it alienated the rich and the strong. When the king found himself in need of help, there was little that the poor could do to aid him against his powerful enemies.

(*4*) to maintain peace and so promote trade. This would require a stronger navy than Charles as yet possessed.

(*5*) to remain solvent—an essential if Charles intended to rule without parliament.

The king's subjects were to play a passive role. They were not to share in government, but simply to accept the benefits of Charles' rule with gratitude and to obey his commands.

CHARLES' FINANCIAL POLICY

Charles' treasurer, Richard Weston, later the earl of Portland, had three tasks: to reduce expenses which then stood at £600,000 a year, to remove the king's debts, and to balance the annual budget. In 1630 the expensive and humiliating wars were brought to an end. Fraud was checked and the expenses of the royal household were reduced. The crown's debts were eliminated: some creditors were paid with grants of land, monopolies, or royal offices; others were simply ignored.

Various devices were used to bring in more money. The sale of offices, pensions, and land continued as before, and the king still levied tunnage and poundage. Some of the measures were unpopular. An act of Edward I's reign required that every landowner whose land was worth more than £40 a year should become a knight and pay the fees which this involved, or else suffer a fine for refusal. Charles enforced it, to the great annoyance of the gentry. Statutes against enclosure were put into effect and offenders were fined. Other measures were also legally questionable. Thus the old forest rights of the king were revived. In the Middle Ages much of England had consisted of royal forests. Landowners had encroached on them, however, and by the seventeenth century they were only a fraction of their former size. Charles now restored them to their ancient limits: Rockingham Forest was increased from 6 square miles to 60 whilst most of Essex was found to be royal forest land. Nobles and gentlemen whose ancestors had made encroachments were forced to pay large fines—the earl of Salisbury was fined £20,000. As a result Charles lost the goodwill of both the gentry and nobility.

The king's financial policy also endangered his friendly relations with the merchants, for whom he did so much in other ways. His advisers had found a way to evade the Monopolies Act (1624) which they now put to profitable use: courtiers snapped up monopolies which entitled them to make or sell silk, starch, linen, soap, tobacco, wines, beer, coal and a host of other articles; then they forced up prices and sold inferior products.

These devices caused widespread discontent, but it was ship-money which first caused men to resist the government openly. Ship-money was an old and well-established tax, paid by coastal towns in ships or cash. It enabled the king to strengthen his fleet in time of emergency. The right to levy it was not questioned. As recently as 1624 it had been imposed without opposition. Charles wanted to reinforce his fleet to deal with the Barbary pirates, who were plundering and sinking English vessels. So in 1634 ship-money was levied as usual on the ports. It was again imposed in 1635 and 1636, but on these occasions the inland counties too were required to contribute. It was on the way to becoming a new regular tax, levied without parliament's consent. It was all spent on the navy, which became strong enough to end the pirate menace. Yet this did not prevent it from being unpopular. John Hampden, a Buckinghamshire gentleman, refused to pay the twenty shillings which was demanded of him. His trial was a very important test case, which determined whether ship-money, as levied by Charles, was legal. The judges decided in the king's favour, but it was a hollow victory because 5[1] of the 12 judges declared for Hampden (1637).

Nevertheless the verdict caused alarm. The majority of judges declared that the king had the right, in time of emergency, to tax his subjects without consulting parliament, and that the king was sole judge of whether or not an emergency existed. It seemed to give him the right to tax as he pleased. It was a dangerous claim to make, and one which his enemies did not forget.

FOREIGN POLICY

The government's foreign policy was dictated by domestic politics. As it was necessary to avoid costly wars, peace treaties were signed with Spain and France (1630). Secondly, Charles wished to promote trade. It would make his regime popular and increase his revenue from the customs. Both objects could best be achieved by a policy of friendship towards the Spanish king. It would help the English clothiers who were selling textiles in Spain, whilst the ships of the Levant and East India companies could sail without fear of attack. In any case the conditions of Elizabeth's reign had gone. Spain was no longer a real threat, whereas the Dutch were becoming serious competitors in trade. Charles' policy suited both his purse and England's needs.

Many men thought that religion was more important than trade. Good protestants disapproved of Charles' friendship with Spain. They wanted him to lead the protestant states in a war to expel the Spaniards from the Palatinate. Charles could not afford such a policy, however, without financial aid from parliament. He preferred to remain neutral whilst the Thirty Years' War exhausted Europe. His policy made England insignificant on the continent; nevertheless it gave her peace, helped trade, and enabled the king to rule without parliament.

[1] In fact only two declared that ship-money was illegal. The other three judges objected to the method of collection.

Over one issue only was Charles prepared to risk war: his claim to sovereignty in the Channel. He insisted that only England had the right to maintain a fleet there. All foreign vessels should strike their flags as a sign of respect to his ships. To enforce his claims Charles used his 'ship-money fleet'. It was only successful because the Dutch and French were absorbed in the Thirty Years' War. Later, when Charles was distracted by the rebellion in Scotland, the Dutch seized their opportunity and destroyed a Spanish fleet in English coastal waters. It revealed how worthless was the king's claim to be master in the Narrow Seas.

THE KING'S MINISTERS AND THE POLICY OF THOROUGH

Charles was surrounded by intriguing courtiers, most of whom were mediocre and all of whom were greedy for riches and power. However, a few of his advisers were men of ability: Richard Weston, Bishop Juxon (who succeeded Weston as Treasurer in 1635), and above all Sir Thomas Wentworth and William Laud.

Wentworth had a love of order which could only be achieved if the government was strong. He recognised that supreme power was normally vested in king and parliament together. But he upheld the king's right to set aside the laws in an emergency, for the good of all. He preferred government by king, lords, and commons, but only if parliament held the same position as it had in the Tudor system. Recently it had been advancing claims for more power, so he was content to see it put aside until its members were in a more dutiful frame of mind.

Laud and Wentworth were advocates of the policy of 'thorough'. This meant that they favoured 'paternal government'.[1] It must be efficient, strong, and strict. It was to enquire into corruption, root out dishonesty, and crush all opposition. They did not merely preach thorough; they practised it as well, Laud in the Church, Wentworth in northern England and Ireland.

It was in the 'Addled Parliament' of 1614 that Wentworth entered public life. He was no puritan but in the following years he became a severe critic of the government, especially in

[1] Government in which the king can be likened to a father and his subjects to his children. The father rules for the good of all his children and protects them from danger; the children are obedient and grateful

the early years of Charles I's reign. He was imprisoned for refusing to pay a forced loan; he helped to force the Petition of Right upon the king; he condemned the folly and incompetence of Buckingham. However, he came to realise that co-operation between king and parliament had ended in deadlock which could only be broken by strengthening one or the other. He chose the former and changed sides, partly to satisfy his ambition but also in order to improve Charles' government. Charles made him a viscount as a reward. His former allies never forgave him for deserting them.

Wentworth was the strong man of the government. He was forceful and domineering, an able administrator who enriched and strengthened his royal master. At the same time he had a quick eye for personal profit, made a fortune, and became the king's greatest subject. But serious defects of character undermined his achievements. He was boastful and vain, and he had no understanding of other human beings. As he built up the king's authority, his harsh tactless manner alienated powerful royalists.

WENTWORTH IN THE NORTH: 1628–33

In 1628 Wentworth was made president of the council of the north. Under the Tudors, the council had done much to bring order to the turbulent north. Between 1603 and 1628, however, it had fallen a prey to factions. It had become a weapon of injustice, and the councillors had lined their own pockets at the expense of the people over whom they had been set to govern. Wentworth meant to change all that.

His aims were: to uphold and strengthen the crown, to protect the weak and the poor against the great men of the land, and to enforce the poor-law and other social measures. His rule was marked by strictness and a sense of justice. He had the right to hold a court, just as the privy councillors did in star chamber. There he meted out justice sternly and the poor knew that they would get a fair hearing. Indeed he appeared to delight in punishing the great men, who, however, hit back whenever they could. Lord Fauconburg charged him with injustice, but was forced to shelter in London to avoid his wrath. Sir David Foulis, who had embezzled £5,000 of the king's money, accused the president of the same misconduct. Wentworth sued him successfully in star chamber, and he was fined £8,000. Disloyal or disobedient men were also brought to heel: when Lord Eure defied the king's sheriff, Wentworth besieged his house with cannon and soldiers until he submitted.

Wentworth's rule benefited the poorer people. He regulated wages, demolished enclosures, enforced the laws of apprenticeship, and even attempted to control outbreaks of the plague. The small farmer, the wage-earner, and the pauper were protected by him. For example, when the fens were drained, he championed the rights of the fen dwellers. He insisted that they should receive a fairer share of the drained land than the gentry had been willing to allow.

It might appear that Wentworth's rule in the north was a success. He had strengthened the king's authority and had given justice to the meanest of his subjects. But in doing so he had gained the reputation of a harsh, vindictive, and ambitious man. When landowners questioned or opposed his power, he had to punish them—it was his duty as the king's servant. Nonetheless he pursued them with a spitefulness which made him many enemies.

THE KING'S DEPUTY IN IRELAND: 1633–40

In 1633 Wentworth became lord deputy (the king's representative) in Ireland. Ireland had always been an expensive source of weakness to English rulers. He intended to make it rich and strong, so that it might 'supply the king's wants' and add to his power.

The new deputy was faced with a complex problem. Ireland was turbulent and lawless, the scene of constant struggle between three groups: the native Irish, the 'old English' led by the earls of Ormonde and Clanricarde, and the 'new English'.[1] The last-named were protestants who had settled on land which had been confiscated from Irish Roman catholics, especially rebels. In Elizabeth's reign Munster and Leinster were colonised in this way. Under James I it was the turn of Ulster, where the two Irish earls of Tyrone and Tyrconnel ruled. As a result of a disagreement with the English government they fled to Spain, never to return. James regarded their land as forfeit. Ulster was planted by English and Scottish protestants. A large stretch of land, renamed Londonderry, was given to the corporation of London. The Irish catholics, persecuted for their

[1] For a full description of the three groups see pages 16-17.

religion and dispossessed of their land, had a deep and abiding hatred for the new English settlers.

Despite these difficulties, Wentworth made many improvements. He removed dishonest judges, put an end to corruption in the government at Dublin, and once again defended the poor. The Irish parliament enacted social measures: houses of correction were set up for 'sturdy beggars'; acts were passed against fraud, blasphemy, and kidnapping; men who bribed or bullied juries were to be severely punished.

The lax protestant Church of Ireland also felt the deputy's heavy reforming hand. Clergy of the better sort were encouraged to come over from England. The landowners were made to disgorge lands and tithes which they had acquired, and this property was then used to supplement the income of the clergy.

Wentworth tried to modernise Ireland and make her more prosperous. Roads were built and bridges repaired. He encouraged the manufacture of woollen blankets and rugs, and he invested his own money in the linen industry. The Irish Sea was cleared of the Spanish, English, and French pirates who preyed upon shipping, and smuggling was checked. As a result, trade flourished and the king's customs revenue increased from £23,000 to over £50,000 a year.

Ireland became one of the pillars of Charles' government. In the past it had been a drain on his treasury; under Wentworth's tireless management it turned into an important source of revenue. Wentworth also provided Charles with a first-class body of soldiers. In 1633 the Irish army was ragged, undisciplined and unpaid. He left it well-equipped, trained, and efficient. Recruited from the Roman catholics it was a constant source of fear to English protestants, who thought that Charles might bring it over to crush opposition to his rule.

Nonetheless Wentworth failed to build up the king's power on a firm foundation. Men obeyed him because he was strong and fearless, but few liked him and to his many enemies he was known as 'Black Tom Tyrant'. He gave Ireland the most efficient government it had known for many a long year. Yet he managed to alienate every group in the process:

(*1*) The Irish feared him. He wanted to make Ireland prosperous and protestant, but this could not be done so long as most of the land remained in the hands of the native Irish, who tilled it in primitive fashion. So he planned to plant Connaught, a vast area in the west of Ireland (i.e. to evict the Irish occupiers and grant the land to protestant settlers). When Elizabeth and James I confiscated Irish lands and colonised them they had an excuse for their actions: they were punishing rebels. But Wentworth intended to do it in time of peace, when there was no sign of rebellion. The Irish quickly learned to hate him, although he was recalled to England in 1640 before he had time to colonise Connaught.

(2) The old English, most of whom were catholics, were similarly threatened by Wentworth's scheme. Only one of them, the earl of Ormonde, remained faithful to the deputy and the king.

(3) As a devout protestant Wentworth favoured the new English settlers. Yet he even made enemies of their leaders. Lord Loftus was imprisoned for unjust behaviour whilst a judge. The earl of Cork was forced to surrender Church property. Lord Mountnorris was sentenced to death for insulting him.

As in northern England, he showed a singular lack of understanding for other people in Ireland. He had nothing but contempt for the Irish; he detested the Scottish presbyterians who had settled in Ulster; he deplored the selfishness and greed of the new English settlers. During his 6 years in Ireland he overcame them all. But they were to win in the end.

LAUD AND THE CHURCH OF ENGLAND

William Laud, the son of a draper, was educated at Reading grammar school and then at Oxford, where he soon became well known for his love of learning. The duke of Buckingham became interested in him and persuaded James I to make him bishop of St David's. The king mistrusted him, however, and would advance him no further, 'because I find he hath a restless spirit, and cannot see when matters are well but loves to toss and change, and to bring things to a pitch of reformation floating in his own brain'. Charles I had no such misgivings. He was in complete agreement with Laud's views and made him bishop of Bath and Wells, then bishop of London (1628), and finally archbishop of Canterbury in 1633.

Laud had much to commend him. He was energetic, and unselfishly devoted to the Anglican Church. He was broad-minded in matters of doctrine—like Elizabeth, he only wanted men to conform outwardly. Before him he always had the vision of the Church as he wanted it to be: a Church embracing everyone, organised and efficient, administered by a dedicated priesthood and with the same ceremonial everywhere.

He was a stern disciplinarian. The widespread laxity which he found shocked him. Services in many churches were thinly attended, and members of the congregation slept or spat, gossiped or gazed at the latest fashions. Churches decayed through lack of money, some were even deserted. Even St. Paul's cathedral was abused by merchants and tradesmen who met to discuss business there. In many cases the clergy were no better: many were ignorant, uneducated, and lazy; some were guilty of moral misconduct. Laud was not the man to ignore such goings on. Offenders, lay and clerical alike, were punished by the Church's courts. His strictness enabled him to raise the standards of the clergy. He cared little that he made himself unpopular in doing so.

The Church was poor. Some of the bishops were so poverty-stricken that they were driven to take drastic steps—the bishop of St. David's stripped the lead from the roof of his palace and sold it. The lower clergy presented a sorry picture too. A vicar's livelihood depended on his glebe (the plot of land which he farmed) and tithes (payments in foodstuffs made by the parishioners to the vicar). In many parishes, however, the gentry had acquired the right to receive the tithes, paying the vicar only a fraction of their real value. The gentry paid the Church only £7,000 a year for tithes which were worth £150,000. In order to eke out their money clergymen held several livings and, as a result, parishes had to put up with an absentee vicar who only put in an occasional appearance. Yet when Laud tried to increase the Church's share to a moderate £10,000 he aroused widespread anger and opposition.

Laud came into violent conflict with the puritans. It was unavoidable. As an Arminian he upheld the doctrine of divine right. He also worked for 'the beauty of holiness' in his Church. God's house should be beautiful. So he insisted on vestments, images, pictures, and altar hangings in the churches. The communion table was placed at the east end of the church and railed[1] off. Anglican rights were conducted in a solemn and

[1] The puritans thought that this encouraged idolatry. They preferred the table placed in the centre of the church.

reverent fashion. To the puritans these changes signified a move towards popery. They believed that the king's court was a nest of catholics with Laud in the centre. When the pope offered to make Laud a cardinal their suspicions appeared to be confirmed. The bishops were a particular object of hatred to the puritans. It was the bishops—or at least most of them—who carried out Laud's instructions and persecuted them. Furthermore, they surrounded themselves with pomp and splendour. Laud always travelled with 40 or 50 mounted attendants. At the Hampton Court conference the puritans had only demanded a few changes in the rites of the Church. Since then their persecution by the bishops, especially Laud, had driven many of them into extreme opposition; now some of them were presbyterians who wanted to abolish the office of bishop 'root and branch'.

The archbishop worked for uniformity. Everyone had to conform to the rites and vestments of his Church. But it was precisely this that the puritans would not do. Consequently puritan clergy were turned out of their livings and their preachers were suppressed. By control of the pulpit and the Press Laud hoped to silence his critics.

Those who dared to criticise Laud's regime were punished in the court of high commission (the prerogative court of the Church) or star chamber. The most notable were: Alexander Leighton, who wrote bitter attacks on the bishops, John Bastwick and John Lilburne, William Prynne, who criticised the queen's love of theatricals,[1] and Dr. Henry Burton, who called the bishops 'upstart mushrumps'. The punishments inflicted by star chamber were barbarous. Lilburne got off lightly, being whipped, pilloried, and imprisoned; but the rest suffered mutilation, heavy fines, and life-imprisonment. In the past star chamber had protected subjects from injustice, but as Charles I used it to persecute his opponents it became an object of fear and hatred. Charles and Laud failed to realise that their puritan critics had widespread support. Fear of popery, dislike of the archbishop's severity, hatred of all the bishops: all went to swell the opposition to Laud's rule.

[1] Many puritans were very narrow-minded. Some even wanted to prevent people from working or playing on Sundays. James I had not agreed. In 1617 he issued the Book of Sports which permitted those who had attended church on a Sunday to engage in certain lawful pastimes and pleasures. Puritan opposition continued but in 1633 Laud reissued the book.

THE FAILURE OF THROUGH

Wentworth and Laud were efficient but unpopular. Opposition was not destroyed but only driven underground. When the king was finally forced to summon parliament in 1640, the smouldering discontent burst into flame and destroyed the results of 11 years' patient work.

The policy of thorough was adopted in the north, in Ireland, and in the Church, but it had no influence on the government at Westminster. Charles listened to Laud's advice in religion but preferred to give his trust in matters of government to Francis Cottington, the duke of Hamilton, and other second-rate men. Furthermore, the king treated Wentworth with reserve. He trusted him and yet was overawed by him. Wentworth's great abilities 'might make a monarch rather afraid than ashamed to employ him in the greatest affairs of State'. At Whitehall all was mismanagement and corruption, frivolity and extravagance. The king remained oblivious and unseeing to the growing discontent with his rule. Only when his power was crumbling did he make Wentworth his chief adviser. But by then it was too late.

CHARLES I AND SCOTLAND

Charles' religious policy in Scotland proved to be his undoing. The Scottish Church was Calvinist in doctrine and presbyterian in government. With great skill James VI had introduced bishops to give him a measure of control over the Church. But he had been careful not to antagonise the presbyterians by insisting on changes in matters of doctrine.

Charles was not as wise as his father. He tried to recover some of the Church lands, which had been seized by the nobles after the Scottish Reformation. His motive, worthy of praise, was to increase the stipends (salaries) of the clergy. But it had the effect of destroying the alliance between king and nobles on which James had depended. Worse was to follow. When Charles visited Scotland in 1633, he disliked the plain services. Influenced by Laud, he decided that rites and doctrines there ought to be brought into line with those of the Church of England. A new book of canons (Church decrees) imposed uniformity of worship (1635). And in 1637 a revised prayer-book was introduced. It was bound to receive a hostile reception from the Scots, who found Laud's Arminianism too much akin to popery for their liking. When the Prayer-Book was used for the first time in St. Giles' Cathedral in Edinburgh it caused a riot. Tradition has it that one, Jenny Geddes, started the disturbance when she threw a stool at the minister and shouted, 'Wilt thou say mass in my lug'? The Prayer-Book was everywhere resisted, and ministers who persisted in its use were roughly handled.

Charles was determined to have his wishes obeyed. But the Scots were not idle. They formed a number of 'tables' or committees to govern Scotland. In 1638 the Scottish National Covenant was drawn up, and signed by a large part of the nation. Those who signed it promised to resist, to the death if need be, any attempt to change the presbyterian Church. They rejected the new canons and Prayer-Book as contrary to the Word of God, to acts of the Scottish parliament, and 'to the intention and meaning of the blessed reformers of religion in this land'. The recent innovations 'do tend to the re-establishing of the popish religion and tyranny'. However, they swore their loyalty to the king, vowing that they would give their lives to defend him and his authority. The National Covenant indicated that resistance to the Prayer-Book had become a national revolt. It also demonstrated the folly of Charles' policy, which had caused the Scottish nobles, clergy, and people to unite against him.

Even Charles realised that, as he lacked an army to coerce the Scots, he must conciliate them. He agreed to summon the general assembly and the Scottish parliament. It soon became clear, however, that the time for compromise was past. When the assembly met, it tried to restore strict presbyterianism. And when the duke of Hamilton, who was the king's commissioner, dissolved it, the assembly refused to break up. It went on to annul not only the Prayer-Book and canons but also the Articles of Perth, and it even abolished episcopacy. All the fruits of James VI's patient scheming were destroyed. As Charles refused his assent to these acts, the issue could only be resolved by war.

THE FIRST BISHOPS' WAR: 1639

Both sides made military preparations. The Scots had every advantage. They were convinced of the rightness of their cause and united in defence of their Church. When the covenanters' army was formed, the nobles came with their retainers and volunteers flocked to join. Among them were many experienced soldiers, veterans of the Thirty Years' War. One of them, Alexander Leslie, was appointed to command the army. The Scots prepared for war, 'preaching, praying and drilling'.

'I mean to be obeyed,' said Charles. But these were empty words without an army to enforce his will. The treasury lacked the money to meet such an emergency. Somehow the government scratched together a force, but it was lacking in discipline and equipment. Unlike the covenanters, Charles' soldiers did not feel that they were fighting for a noble cause. Although they advanced as far north as Berwick, they grumbled and looked mutinous. Many of them were unpaid. Each day more deserted. With his army in this condition Charles dared not risk a battle. Instead he came to terms with the covenanters. By the Treaty of Berwick (June 1639), both sides agreed to disband their armies, whilst Charles promised that Scotland's religion should be determined by the general assembly. So ended the bloodless First Bishops' War.

Charles had no intention of observing the treaty, but he pretended to co-operate with the Scots whilst he searched for ways to muster an army capable of defeating them. He had no qualms about such dishonest behaviour. The doctrine of divine right taught him that subjects who took up arms against their prince not only committed treason, but also sinned against God. Therefore he was entitled to use fair means or foul to bring them to order. In the following years Charles practised deceit so often that his opponents could place no trust in any of his promises.

The general assembly proceeded to settle religion: it confirmed all that it had passed earlier that year. Although Charles gave his assent to its acts, he meant to annul them as soon as he gained the upper hand. Meanwhile Wentworth was recalled from Ireland to become his chief adviser, and the king honoured him with the earldom of Strafford. He insisted that the Scots had to be crushed. He advised the king to call parliament in order to obtain the necessary money.

THE SHORT PARLIAMENT: 1640

In April 1640 parliament met. The king believed that he could obtain money by appealing to the national pride of the commons. He was sure that their desire to defend the kingdom would overcome their dissatisfaction with his government. But he misread the temper of the nation. The puritans regarded the Scots as their allies. Furthermore, redress of grievances was uppermost in the thoughts of the commons. Opposition to the king was led by John Pym, a Somerset squire, who had first entered parliament as long ago as 1614. He had been involved in all the constitutional conflicts in the 1620's. During the years of personal rule he had kept in close contact with other opponents of the government. Furthermore, in 1630 he had joined with the earls of Essex and of Warwick, Lord Saye and Sele, and Oliver St. John to form the Providence Company. Its object was to establish a refuge for puritans on Providence Island in the Caribbean, but it suffered from Spanish depradations, a factor which made Pym hostile to Charles' policy of friendship with Spain. Now he had an opportunity to put forward his own grievances and those of his countrymen. The king's request for money was ignored. Instead Pym made a lengthy speech in which he listed all the objectionable and illegal acts of the government. He showed himself to be a master of tactics. His speech appealed to the disgruntled commons who spent their time discussing their many complaints. The king tried to bargain with them. He offered to levy ship-money no more, if they would vote supplies. Instead they prepared to petition him against the war. Charles' reply was to dissolve parliament when it had sat for only three weeks.

THE SECOND BISHOPS' WAR: 1640

The king did not waver. His personal rule would continue and by some means or other he would raise a fresh army against the Scots. Laud issued some new canons which declared his support for Charles' policy. He declared that rebels 'shall receive damnation'. Some of the canons were aimed at the puritans, especially the restrictions on preaching. Others imposed practices already in use in the Roman catholic Church. Nothing could have been more unwise at this time.

Strafford advised the king to take the offensive against the covenanters. 'You have an army in Ireland, you may employ here to reduce this kingdom.' But Charles did not bring over the Irish. Threats, loans, ship-money, and other devices enabled him to muster an English force. Yet he could not afford to equip and feed his soldiers properly, nor even pay them regularly. Time was running out. The Second Bishops'

9

War began when the Scots crossed the border in force. Charles hurried north with his sullen army but without the good wishes of his people. The nation's hopes were with the Scots.

In August the covenanters advanced to Newburn on the Tyne, where they routed the English soldiers who opposed them. They occupied Newcastle, swept on through the northern counties, then sat down to wait upon events. Charles' position was desperate. His only possible course of action was to call parliament, but he wanted to avoid this at all costs. He summoned a great council of peers, a device commonly used by medieval kings before parliament developed. The council advised him to summon parliament. It also negotiated the Treaty of Ripon: the covenanters were to occupy Northumberland and Durham until their grievances were redressed, and in the meantime they were to receive £850 a day for expenses. If the Scots were not co-operating with Charles' opponents in England, they were certainly in sympathy with them. They knew that Charles would have to call parliament to obtain the money. If parliament chose to put 'redress before supply', he would not dare to resist them. There was no way out of the dilemma. Therefore the king summoned parliament. It meant the end of his personal rule, of the policy of thorough, and eventually of the divine right of kings.

CIVIL WAR AND REVOLUTION

❖❖❖

XXVI

THE LONG PARLIAMENT : 1640–42

THE parliamentary elections were held in an atmosphere of great excitement. The king and his opponents realised how much was at stake, and both sides did everything possible to get their friends elected. John Pym did some modern electioneering. He rode round the country, recommending suitable candidates to the electors. The king fared badly. The country was filled with complaints against his government, and almost everywhere his supporters were defeated.

Parliament met on 3 November 1640—and it was destined to last until 1660. From the beginning it was hostile to the king. Many and diverse were the grievances which united the commons: Charles' devices for raising money, Laud's inquisitorial courts and his apparent love of popish practices, catholicism at court, and Strafford's harsh justice. The lords too had their grievances: the forest laws had offended some, whilst Essex, Bedford, and others were puritan opponents of Laud. The king and his advisers stood alone. In 1640 there was no possibility of civil war because no one was prepared to support the king.

At once the commons insisted on redress before supply. The king was trapped and this time he could not escape. Pym condemned the recent misrule and proposed that parliament should punish the 'evil counsellors' who had threatened their liberties. His tactics were clever, because he ignored the religious issues which were bound to divide parliament. He concentrated instead on grievances, a subject on which all were agreed.

THE TRIAL OF STRAFFORD: 1641

Pym led the attack on the king's advisers. Windebank and Finch were threatened with impeachment but escaped abroad. Laud was imprisoned in the Tower, whilst Prynne, Bastwick, Burton, and his other victims were released to add to the popular feeling against him. But Strafford was the main object of the attack. He was the only one of the king's ministers who was really dangerous and ruthless; he had made many enemies in the north and in Ireland, and the commons' hostility to him was no doubt sharpened by the memory of his desertion in 1628.

Pym and his friends put about a rumour that Strafford was plotting to use force against the king's opponents.[1] Parliament was whipped into a state of fear. So Strafford was arrested and impeached, and in March 1641 he was brought to trial in Westminster Hall on a charge of high treason. In the past treason could only be committed against the king. In this case Strafford was accused of attempting to overthrow the fundamental laws of the kingdom and to destroy the liberties of subjects. His offence was against the people, not against the king. Pym had invented a new theory of treason to suit his needs—and by his definition even a king could be adjudged a traitor.

The trial lasted three weeks. During that time not only Strafford but also 'thorough' and Charles' ideal of paternal government were on trial. Strafford was accused of many offences: misusing the king's money and encouraging papists, tyranny in Ireland and giving evil counsel, fomenting war with Scotland and advising against the calling of parliament. The most serious accusation was that he meant to use the Irish army to impose the king's will in England. In 1640, when Strafford had advised Charles to use the Irish 'to reduce this kingdom', he was referring to Scotland. Pym claimed, however, that he meant England. There is no reason to doubt that Pym, Hampden, and others sincerely believed in the rightness of their action. They saw in 'Black Tom Tyrant' a threat to the nation's liberties. At the same time many false and malicious charges were made by the earl of Cork and others whose greed and selfishness had been offended by Strafford.

[1] In fact Strafford was planning to impeach the opposition leaders for treasonable correspondence with the covenanters during the Short Parliament.

The impeachment failed, because the commons could not substantiate their charges. But the parliamentary leaders could not let him escape; whether he was guilty of treason or not, he would be a threat to them so long as he lived—as the earl of Essex said, 'Stone dead hath no fellow'. They introduced a bill of attainder, which declared Strafford to be guilty of high treason for trying 'to introduce an arbitrary and tyrannical government against law'. Pym manoeuvred the bill through the commons, though not without incident. There were rumours of a plot by Charles' courtiers to use soldiers against parliament. Once, when a floor-board cracked, a member shouted that he smelt gunpowder and everyone rushed, panic-stricken, to the doors.

The lords seemed less likely to approve the bill. But Pym astutely chose this moment to reveal the news of the courtiers' plot, and as a result the upper house passed it. There only remained the king. He had promised Strafford that his life would be spared. Now the London mob howled round White-hall Palace, mouthing threats against the queen. It was Strafford himself who provided Charles with the answer to his dilemma. In a letter he wrote:

> To set your Majesty's conscience at liberty, I do most humbly beseech your Majesty for prevention of evils which may happen by your refusal to pass this bill; and by this means to remove this unfortunate thing, forth of the way towards that blessed agreement which God I trust shall ever establish between you and your subjects.

The king, released from his promise, signed the bill in order to save his wife. In May 1641 Strafford went to his death on Tower Hill before a crowd of over two hundred thousand. At the end he vowed that he had been loyal to both king and people.

Strafford's enemies had been unscrupulous, dishonest, and immoral in the methods which they employed to get rid of him. They were convinced, however, that Strafford had to die for the good of England, and that so long as he lived he would continue to advise the king 'that he was loose and absolved from rules of government'. Charles never forgave himself for sacrificing his minister. 'My lord of Strafford's condition is happier than mine,' he said. Certainly he had added to his reputation for being untrustworthy.

THE ATTACK ON THE KING'S PREROGATIVE: 1641

Cried Pym, 'He hath given us Strafford then he can deny us nothing.' The commons could now safely proceed to the redress of grievances. It had already passed the Triennial Act, which required that parliament should be summoned at least once every three years, regardless of the king's wishes. And in May the king assented to an act which declared that the 'Long Parliament' should not be prorogued or dissolved without its own consent. He was completely at the mercy of his opponents.

The financial devices of his government were next attacked: the commons voted tunnage and poundage, but an act prohibited any future levy without parliament's consent. Ship-money was declared illegal and the judgement against Hampden was reversed. Landowners could no longer be forced to purchase knighthoods. The royal forests were reduced to the limits which existed in 1623. These acts deprived the king of the means of ruling without parliament.

In July 1641 the prerogative courts were abolished: star chamber, the council of the Marches in Wales, and the council of the north. It was the end of conciliar government. Parliament also destroyed the court of high commission, the weapon with which Laud had disciplined the Church and enforced Arminian practices. Finally it ruled that no new prerogative courts should ever be erected.

These laws, which were passed by virtually unanimous consent in 1641, marked the permanent contribution of the Long Parliament to English government. The many political and religious enactments, which came afterwards, were destroyed in 1660, but the acts passed before August 1641 remained. In theory parliament restored government as it had been before the Tudors. In fact they ended the possibility of personal rule, because of the king's lack of money; they guaranteed a regular place for parliament in the government of the kingdom, and they protected the liberties and property of the richer subjects of the king.

THE SPLIT IN PARLIAMENT

August 1641 saw the parting of the ways. Until then parliament had been united in its determination to limit the king's power. Thereafter a rift appeared and two parties formed: one stood for Church and king, the other for puritanism and the political ideas of Pym. Disunity first resulted from the religious issue. With Laud imprisoned and the high commission abolished, the people were free to express their dislike of Arminian practices. They tore up communion rails and destroyed images. Puritan preachers insisted that the Sabbath be observed. They threw away their vestments and put an end to ceremonial. Beyond this violent hostility to Laud's rule, however, there was no agreement. Pym and his puritan followers wanted a State Church, regulated by parliament, without bishops, and intolerant of other sects. A variety of new sects sprang up, whilst the presbyterians and independents rapidly grew in strength. Devout Anglicans defended episcopacy and the royal supremacy.

This division in the nation's religious opinions was reflected in parliament. In December 1640 London petitioned it to abolish the bishops. When the 'root and branch' petition was debated, the commons temporarily divided into the friends and enemies of episcopacy. It was only after August 1641, when the king's power had been curtailed, that the split became deep and permanent. In both houses there was growing opposition to the more advanced reforming ideas, and it was led by the king. Charles had sacrificed Strafford and surrendered much of his power, but in religion he stood firm. Royal supremacy, the Anglican rites, and the bishops were causes for which he was prepared to die.

CHARLES' VISIT TO SCOTLAND: 1641

Between August and November Charles was in Scotland. The object of his visit was to raise support for his cause among the nobles. He was at great pains to show his friendship and he worshipped in presbyterian churches. But all his efforts failed, because of the 'Incident'—this was a plot to kidnap the marquis of Argyle, leader of the parliamentary cause in Scotland. Nevertheless sympathy for the king was growing in England. Men were tired of paying taxes for the covenanters' army, whilst the arbitrary behaviour of parliament and the puritans' attacks on the Anglican Church were doing great harm to Pym's cause. Though some Anglicans might approve of attacks on the bishops, they rushed to defend their rites and form of worship.

THE IRISH REBELLION: 1641

In October 1641 the Irish catholics rose in rebellion. For nearly a century their protestant rulers had persecuted them and taken away their land, and Strafford's scheme to plant Connaught was the latest in a long series of such confiscations. Now the covenanters were supreme in Scotland, the English puritans had triumphed over their king, and the Scottish protestants in Ulster were assuming a threatening manner. The threat of renewed persecution drove the Irish catholics to revolt. There was no Strafford to stop them. As they rebelled, the system of thorough collapsed.

The rebels were joined by the soldiers of Strafford's army, which had been disbanded. Thousands of protestant settlers were slaughtered and many more died of cold and hunger. The rebels claimed that they had risen in defence of their religion, property, and liberties, but to the English it was a catholic conspiracy against English rule. Public opinion was inflamed by exaggerated reports of the horrors of the massacre. Both king and parliament were agreed that the rebellion must be suppressed. But here was the real difficulty: the commons, distrusting Charles, were afraid to give him money for an army which he might use against them. They were forced to demand that parliament should control the army. In trying to grasp the power of the sword they were in effect seeking to govern the country. Charles was able to pose as the defender of the laws against the revolutionary behaviour of parliament. It brought to his side the many men who still recognised him as rightful governor of the kingdom, although they approved of the earlier acts of the Long Parliament. To the defenders of the bishops were added the supporters of the king's prerogative (or what was left of it). So the royalist party was born.

THE GRAND REMONSTRANCE: 1641

Pym decided to go over the heads of the commons and appeal to his followers in the country. He drew up the Grand Remonstrance, which was addressed to the king but was intended for the people: the errors and evils of the government were recited, together with the ways in which parliament had redressed the nation's grievances. However, it went on to make more demands, and when it petitioned Charles to employ only 'such councillors as the parliament may have cause to confide in', it was claiming for parliament a complete control of the king's government. It also recommended a thorough reform of the Church by 'a general synod of the most grave, pious, learned, and judicious divines of this island'. The Remonstrance was not an appeal to the nation at large. It was biased and unfair to the king. It ignored the fact that he had conceded much, yet he had remained moderate and acted with due regard for the law. In fact it was Pym's attempt to rally his party in face of the growing support for the king.

The debate on the Remonstrance which took place in November revealed how deep was the rift. Anglicans argued for the king, so did moderate men like Lord Falkland and Edward Hyde. Ranged against them were the puritans and those men who, like Pym, wanted sovereignty (supreme power) for parliament in order to safeguard the recent gains. The discussion was heated. Men lost their tempers and on one occasion swords were drawn. 'I thought we had all sat in the valley of the shadow of death,' said a member afterwards. The Grand Remonstrance was approved by a narrow majority—but the fact that a hundred and forty-eight voted against it showed how far reaction had gone in the king's favour.

THE ATTEMPT TO SEIZE THE FIVE MEMBERS: 1642

At this time Charles nearly destroyed the image, which he had created of himself, as defender of the laws. When Pym planned to impeach the queen for intriguing with foreign powers, Charles lost patience and decided to impeach him. Pym, Hampden, Holles, Hesilrige and Strode, as well as Lord Mandeville, were charged with attempting 'to deprive the king of his regal power' and to set up 'an arbitrary and tyrannical power' over his people; furthermore, they had corresponded with the covenanters during the Short Parliament. Charles had blundered. It was legally doubtful whether the king could ask the lords to impeach them, for this was the traditional right of the commons. The angry peers refused to take action against the five members.

Charles was not sure what to do next, but the queen made up his mind for him: 'Go, you coward, and pull these rogues out by the ears, or never see my face more.' On 4 January 1642 Charles led several hundred armed men down to Westminster, where he entered the house of commons. But the five members, warned of his coming, had already taken refuge in London, which was a parliamentary stronghold. Charles found that 'all the birds are flown'. He had failed. Furthermore, he had committed a flagrant breach of the commons' privileges which served to unite the two houses against him once more.

9*

THE COMING OF CIVIL WAR: 1642

Six days later Charles left London and set up his headquarters at York, where he was joined by Edward Hyde. At first he received little support. His attempt to arrest the 5 members had shocked the nation. During the next 6 months, however, more and more men hurried to join him. He issued several proclamations, in which he claimed that he was the rightful ruler and that parliament was breaking the law. His claim was borne out by parliament's actions at this time: it attempted to govern the realm and issued militia bills for the raising of soldiers, whilst the commons behaved in an arbitrary fashion when it expelled royalist members.

In June 1642, parliament presented the king with an ultimatum, known as the Nineteen Propositions. Charles called it 'a mockery and a scorn', which would make him 'a mere phantom of a king'. Parliament was indeed trying to seize power. The prospect was so shocking that men flocked to his cause. War was now inevitable, for neither side would budge an inch. In July parliament voted that an army be raised under the earl of Essex. A month later Charles raised his standard at Nottingham. The Civil War had begun.

XXVII

THE CIVIL WAR : 1642–46

THE PARTIES IN 1642

As we have seen, the causes of war were many and varied. Religion and politics were not the only issues, though they were by far the most important. Local feuds, class rivalries, traditional loyalties all played their part. Indeed it is easier to determine those issues which did not start the war. The contending parties did not shed blood over ideals like Liberty or Democracy. And none but a mere handful of fanatics wanted to destroy the monarchy. Nevertheless it is possible to see certain broad differences between the two parties.

THE KING'S PARTY

The king's strength depended chiefly on the support of a faith and a tradition, of Anglicans who wanted to defend their Church and of those men with a deep-seated loyalty to the throne. Socially this meant most of the landowning class, especially the nobles, for the natural interests of an hereditary aristocracy lie with an hereditary king. Many of the gentry too joined Charles, some because they were Anglicans and others because they saw him as the only rightful head of the government. Sir Edmund Verney spoke for many gentlemen when he said, 'I have eaten the king's bread and served him near thirty years, and will not do so base a thing as to forsake him.' Some of the gentry had taken alarm at the growing arrogance and strength of the trades-men, small farmers, and apprentices—whom they called 'the lower sort of common people'. They rallied to the king to defend their traditional position as the governing class. In the towns there were few royalists apart from the ruling minorities of great merchants, to whom Charles had shown his favour during his personal rule, and in most cases these were now over-thrown by the lesser merchants and traders. Only the non-industrial towns, such as Oxford, York, and Worcester remained loyal.

THE PARLIAMENTARY PARTY

Whereas the king's support came from the countryside, the strength of the parliamentarians lay in the towns, amongst the tradesmen and shopkeepers, manufacturers and merchants of 'the middling sort', craftsmen and apprentices. This was due to the fact that the towns were strongholds of puritanism, for the puritans whether presbyterian or independent were against the king. This is not to say that there were no parliamentarians in the landowning class: thirty nobles and most of the yeomen fought against the king, and where puritanism was very strong, as in East Anglia, so did the gentry.

THE FUNDAMENTAL ISSUES

These social divisions were chiefly due to the great issues of politics and religion. The Civil War has often been called a struggle between the king and his parliament.   Yet eighty of the one hundred and thirty peers, and over one hundred and seventy-five members of the lower house fought for the king, whilst some sixty more M.P.s assisted him in other ways.   It was really a conflict between two parties in the ruling class to decide whether king or parliament should be supreme.   In religion it was a straight fight between the Church of England and its opponents. The Anglicans, especially the bishops, were royalists; the puritans were for parliament.   This drew to the king's party many men who were disgusted or frightened by the new and varied radical opinions which were being aired by some puritans.   On the other hand the puritans benefited from the popular hatred of popery, because the queen was an active papist and the English catholics were royalists.

THE IMPORTANCE OF SOCIAL CLASSES

Class-feeling often decided a man's loyalty.   Many yeomen disliked and envied the gentry.   Where the latter supported the king, the former might join the other side.   More important, as we have seen, many of the country squires were driven to support the king by the threatening manner of the lower classes. Nevertheless the Civil War was not a class war.   The traditional opponents are the cavalier and the roundhead: the former a swaggering young courtier of noble or gentle birth, the latter a crop-haired apprentice born of humble parents.   There is some truth in this.   The cavalier is the symbol of the landowners, the courtiers and nobles, nearly all of them royalists; the apprentice represents the townspeople, most of whom opposed the king. It is also misleading because both parties contained men of all classes.   It is worth remembering too that only a fraction of the population took an active part in the fighting.   Most men went about their own business and were often unaffected by the struggle.

PARLIAMENT'S GEOGRAPHICAL ADVANTAGE

A line drawn on the map from Hull to Bristol would indicate the territory controlled by the two parties.   Charles held the north and west, including Wales, an area which was poor, conservative, and backward.   Parliament was supreme in the south and east, which were richer, more populous and progressive.   The ports and towns were its strongest adherents— even Plymouth, Gloucester, Bristol, and the cloth towns of the

West Riding, all of which were in the king's territory. The division of the country in this way gives only a rough general picture of the regional strength of the two sides. Royalists and 'roundheads' had to contend with pockets of resistance and disloyal men in their own territories.

ENGLAND IN 1642

PARLIAMENT'S INITIAL SUPERIORITY

Parliament had every advantage in 1642:

(*1*) It controlled most of England's wealth and population; above all it had London with its riches, its ships, and its train bands.

(2) Charles' ship-money fleet threw in its lot with parliament, which was able to blockade him and prevent him receiving help from abroad.

(3) The king was short of money. He controlled only the poorer regions and heavy taxes might lose him the support of even these. The universities gave him their gold plate and nobles like the duke of Newcastle spent their own money in his service. But soon it was all gone. If Charles hoped to win the war, he had to do it quickly. In a war of attrition parliament, which commanded much greater resources, was bound to be the victor.

THE TWO ARMIES

The king had the better cavalry. His nobles and gentlemen were horsemen born and bred, and their commander was the dashing Prince Rupert, who was the son of Elizabeth of the Palatinate and therefore Charles' nephew. He was a born leader of men, a strategist, and a fiery spirited cavalry commander. Unfortunately he quarrelled with the other royalist leaders and created a good deal of bad feeling in the king's camp. On the field of battle he lacked discipline and restraint. He would drive the opposing cavalry from the field and then proceed to plunder the enemy's baggage train, with never a thought of returning to help the infantry. His impetuosity was to rob the king of victories and eventually lead to disaster.

Although parliament could afford a larger army, and its infantry was superior in numbers to the king's, it was weak in cavalry. Furthermore, its commanders were half-hearted nobles. The earl of Manchester lamented, 'If we beat the king ninety and nine times, yet he is king still; but if the king beat us once we shall all be hanged.' The earl of Essex was of the same opinion. They did not want to inflict a complete defeat on the king, but hoped to reach a satisfactory compromise with him.

THE CAMPAIGN OF 1642

The king's lack of money determined the course of the war. He had to end the struggle quickly, so he decided to make a dash for London. He found his way barred by Essex's larger army at Edgehill. Rupert's cavalry routed the enemy horse and pursued them across country, leaving the infantry of both sides to fight it out. He returned at nightfall just in time to save the king's soldiers from a complete defeat—but too late to win the battle. It was really a drawn fight, but Essex left the royalists in possession of the field and retreated towards London. The king followed. At Turnham Green his way was once again blocked by Essex, who was supported this time by the train

The moſt Illuſtrious and High borne PRINCE RUPERT, PRINCE ELECTOR, Second Son to FREDERICK KING of BOHEMIA, GENERALL of the HORSE of Hs MAJESTIES ARMY, KNIGHT of the Noble Order of the GARTER.

A cartoon depicting Prince Rupert, Charles I's cavalry commander (*British Museum*).

bands of London. He gave way before an army twice as large as his own and retreated to Oxford which became the royalists' capital for the duration of the war. Although Charles appeared to have got the better of the first encounter, his chances of success had suffered a serious blow. He had failed to take London—and as time went by and his money dwindled, he would find it ever more difficult to keep his army in the field.

THE CAMPAIGN OF 1643

Charles, well-aware that London was the key to victory, planned a three-pronged attack on it. He was to move eastwards from Oxford along the Thames valley, Sir Ralph Hopton would advance from Devon, and Newcastle was to march south from Yorkshire. The plan failed. Hopton's westcountrymen refused to advance any farther than Bristol, because they were afraid that the parliamentary garrison at Plymouth might sally forth and destroy their homes whilst they were absent. Newcastle captured Gainsborough and Lincoln, despite a minor defeat at the hands of a cavalry commander, Oliver Cromwell; but he too had to retrace his steps to stop enemy raids from Hull. As there was not no hope of capturing London, Charles decided to besiege Gloucester instead. But Essex led the train bands across country to relieve it, and the king was forced to withdraw. As the earl retraced his steps, he found the royalist army waiting for him at Newbury. In a desperate battle he forced his way through and returned to London. Lord Falkland, one of the noblest figures on either side, was killed at Newbury. He died loyal to his king but anxious for peace.

Elsewhere the king's forces were victorious. Newcastle routed the Fairfaxes, father and son, at Adwalton Moor and captured the puritan cloth towns of Yorkshire—only Hull remained in parliamentary hands. In the west Hopton overran Devon, another royalist defeated Waller at Roundway Down, and Prince Rupert forced Bristol to surrender.

PARLIAMENT'S ALLIANCE WITH THE SCOTS: 1643

Although the king's power was at its height neither side seemed able to win a decisive victory. They both searched for allies. Charles gained the support of the Irish catholic rebels, who gave him £30,000 and some soldiers who changed sides at the first opportunity. This alliance did more harm than good. It seemed as if Charles had thrown in his lot with popery, whilst his opponents were able to pose as the defenders of protestantism.

Pym had negotiated a more successful agreement with the Scots. Having obtained what they wanted—recognition of their liberties and their religion—they had withdrawn from the north of England in August 1641. They were still willing to cooperate with Pym's party, but the price of their assistance was high: it was the establishment of presbyterianism in England.

Pym was willing to pay the price. Parliament established the Westminster Assembly, a body of presbyterian ministers and Scottish representatives, to consider changes in the service and government of the Church. It also approved the Solemn League and Covenant, by which it bound itself to 'the reformation of religion in doctrine, worship, discipline and government, according to the Word of God and the example of the best reformed Churches'. The wording of the Covenant was vague and in time this was to lead to trouble between the allies. Nevertheless it sufficed for now. In January 1644 a Scottish army swept south across the border.

JOHN PYM

In 1643 the parliamentary party lost its ablest politicians. Hampden was killed in a skirmish at Chalgrove Field, and Pym, the master-organiser and schemer, died. More than any other man John Pym was responsible for the great changes in government in the seventeenth century. He had put an end to the possibility of personal rule in the future, and he had taken the first steps in that process which transferred sovereignty to parliament. At the same time he must take much of the responsibility for the Civil War. Under his guidance the commons had attacked the bishops, published the Grand Remonstrance, and tried to wrest from the king his right to govern. In the long run Pym's policies led to parliamentary government; in the short term they caused Englishmen to kill each other.

THE ASSOCIATIONS

Despite Pym's death 1643 marked the turn of the tide. For the second time Charles had failed to take London and now time was running against him. His treasury was empty, his unpaid armies were shrinking, and all the time parliament was becoming stronger. At first it had relied for soldiers on the county levies, each county being required to raise a body of troops. Although they were brave enough in battle, they were only amateurs, and they were unwilling to serve outside their counties for they were chiefly concerned to protect their homes. Parliament tried to overcome this problem by grouping the county levies into three associations (1642-3). The armies thus formed were free to move about within the area of their own associations. The most famous of them was that of the Eastern

Association, which was commanded by the earl of Manchester.[1] At Marston Moor its cavalry was to prove itself superior to the flower of Rupert's horse. In addition parliament now commanded the services of the Scots, and it benefited from the military genius of Oliver Cromwell.

OLIVER CROMWELL

Oliver Cromwell was a Huntingdonshire squire of comfortable means. He once told the commons, 'I was by birth a gentleman living neither in any considerable height nor yet in obscurity.' His family was certainly famous for he was a descendant of Thomas Cromwell, hammer of the monks and architect of the Tudor Revolution in Henry VIII's reign. He was a puritan of the independent type, favouring religious toleration for all except the papists.

In 1628 Cromwell represented Huntingdon in the commons and in the Long Parliament he sat for Cambridge. Pym found in him a loyal follower. He supported the 'root and branch' bill and the proposal that parliament should control the militia in Ireland and England, and he voted for the Grand Remonstrance. But it was in the Civil War that he showed his true worth. A great cavalry leader, he created out of the Eastern Association the finest body of horsemen in England. His soldiers were chosen not for their social position but for their godliness and zeal. 'I had rather have a plain russet-coated captain that knows what he fights for and loves what he knows, than that which you call "a gentlemen", and is nothing else.' They were better armed, trained, and disciplined than any other soldiers in the war, and they were full of fervour for the puritan cause. Cromwell required them to observe high moral standards. Drinking and swearing were severely punished. But his soldiers were free to hold and express a variety of religious opinions.

Cromwell, like many puritans, was convinced of the rightness of his cause. Absolutism, bishops, and religious intolerance were evils to be destroyed. This could only be done by inflicting a complete defeat on Charles. He would have none of the half-hearted methods of Essex and Manchester, vowing that if he saw the king in battle he would shoot at him. When Marston Moor gave him the chance to inflict a crushing blow, he took it.

[1] An army formed from the levies of seven counties: Norfolk, Suffolk, Essex, Cambridgeshire, Hertfordshire, Huntingdonshire, and Lincolnshire.

Then as always he was certain that God was on his side. After the battle he wrote, 'God made them as stubble to our swords.'

THE CAMPAIGN OF 1644

In 1644 the fate of the king's cause was decided in Yorkshire. The Scots marching south, and the Eastern Association, joined forces with another army under Sir Thomas Fairfax. The duke of Newcastle was outnumbered and retired into York where he was besieged by the combined armies of parliament. Rupert boldly marched to his relief and rescued him. Together they faced the enemy at Marston Moor in July 1644. A surprise attack, followed by a bitter struggle, gave parliament a complete victory. Cromwell's 'men of God' defeated Rupert's 'men of honour'. Newcastle's white-coated infantry were annihilated. After the battle Newcastle fled overseas. Marston Moor decided the outcome of the war. Charles lost the north of England, together with many men and guns.

In the south the king made a last desperate bid to take London. Sir Ralph Hopton marched eastwards to join the royalists in Kent and Sussex, prior to an attack on the City; but Hopton's defeat ended the attempt. Nevertheless parliament failed to take advantage of its recent great victory. Charles defeated Waller at Cropredy Bridge in the west and pursued Essex into Cornwall, surrounding him at Lostwithiel. Essex escaped and his cavalry fled to Plymouth, but his infantry surrendered and were disarmed. Although Essex and Manchester attacked Charles at Newbury in October, their half-hearted conduct enabled him to escape.

DISAGREEMENT BETWEEN PARLIAMENT AND THE ARMY: 1645

Although the war was not yet over, the rebels were beginning to quarrel among themselves. Parliament, in which the presbyterians were strong, was bound by the Solemn League and Covenant to establish the presbyterian Church in England. It prepared to introduce the Directory of Worship to replace the Book of Common Prayer, and to compel everyone to use it. Its generals, Essex and Manchester, were anxious to come to terms with Charles. They would restore him to his throne on certain conditions. In February 1645 parliament negotiated with him at Uxbridge. It demanded the control of the army, the right to appoint his councillors, and the establishment of a presbyterian Church. Charles refused to surrender his supremacy over the Church or his prerogative. He told his opponents that 'they were arrant rebels and their end must be damnation, ruin, and infamy'. So the war continued.

Parliament's views were not shared by the army. It was the stronghold of the independents, who hated the intolerance of the presbyterians. Their leaders, especially Cromwell, wanted the complete destruction of Charles' forces. By 1645 Cromwell had tired of his leaders' lack of enthusiasm. He advised the commons that, unless effective steps were taken to end the war quickly, the nation would come to hate parliament. He wanted an efficient army under an able and devoted commander. Parliament responded by creating the New Model Army, which consisted of twenty-two thousand men under Sir Thomas Fairfax. It was not confined to one area but was free to move about the country. It was staffed with competent and zealous officers and at first it was well and regularly paid. To get rid of the parliamentary generals, the commons passed the Self-Denying Ordinance (in April 1645). All members of the two houses were to surrender their military commands, but Fairfax was free to reappoint those whom he wanted. Essex and Manchester retired, but Cromwell was reappointed. The war effort was now in the hands of determined men.

THE END OF THE CIVIL WAR: 1645-6

The New Model Army achieved immediate success, routing Charles' army at Naseby in June 1645. Most of the Midlands passed under parliamentary control. Apart from Devon, Cornwall, and North Wales, only some scattered castles, fortified country houses, and centres like Oxford remained loyal to the king. The New Model Army proceeded to force the remaining royalist strongholds into submission. In 1646 Charles gave himself up to the Scots at Newark; when Oxford surrendered shortly afterwards, the Civil War was over.

SCOTLAND AND THE CIVIL WAR

Prior to the Civil War the king had no support in Scotland. Almost everyone of importance had signed the National Covenant, to which they remained true despite the king's blandishments when he visited Scotland in 1641. The Covenant, however, was a declaration of loyalty to the king as well as to the presbyterian Church. Many men were repelled when the covenanters entered the Civil War on the side of parliament; amongst them was the marquis of Montrose, who was a loyal covenanter but also a loyal subject. In September 1644 he took up arms in support of his king, and at the head of a small army

ENGLAND IN 1645

he won a series of resounding victories over the marquis of Argyle's covenanters: at Tippermuir, Aberdeen, Inverlochy, and Kilsyth (August 1645). Despite these successes his army gradually dwindled, until the covenanters, reinforced by part of the earl of Leven's Scottish army, overwhelmed him at Philiphaugh (September). Montrose's flight to the continent ended the king's cause in Scotland for the time being.

XXVIII

KING, ARMY, AND PARLIAMENT
1646–49

AT the end of the war a captured royalist, Sir Jacob Astley, told his victorious opponents, 'You have now done your work and may go play, unless you will fall out amongst yourselves.' And indeed the victors did fall out; let us take a look at them and their opinions:

(*1*) *The Scottish army* had successfully defended presbyterianism north of the border. It also wanted to see the same religion established in England, as parliament had promised in the Solemn League and Covenant. In January 1647 the Scots handed over Charles to parliament in return for £400,000 and withdrew into Scotland. Nevertheless they watched anxiously to see if parliament would carry out its promise, and they still accepted monarchy as the only possible form of government.

(*2*) *The English presbyterians*, who were conservative in politics, hoped to restore Charles if he would consent to the establishment of presbyterianism as the sole religion in the kingdom. Socially they were strong amongst the merchants, traders, and manufacturers of London and other towns. Politically they were powerful in parliament, where they were by far the largest party. The departure of royalists and Anglicans in 1642 had served to increase their importance there. They had abolished episcopacy and executed Archbishop Laud (1645); they had appointed the Westminster Assembly, signed the Solemn League and Covenant, replaced the Book of Common Prayer by the Directory, and introduced assemblies to govern the Church.

(*3*) *The independents* had grown from small beginnings. In Elizabeth's reign everyone had despised and persecuted them. As late as 1640 they were a small minority; but during the Civil War they had multiplied rapidly, especially among the soldiers, and by 1646 they had gained control of the New Model Army. The independents included many sects with varied religious beliefs, but they had common ideals, especially the 'liberty of tender consciences', the right of each congregation to choose its own minister and to govern itself.

In politics many of the independents were radical. Amongst them were men with advanced and even wild ideas: the quakers who were pacifists; John Lilburne and his levellers; Gerrard Winstanley, whose 'diggers' were communists; the fifth monarchists, fanatics who believed that Christ's kingdom was soon to be established on earth. The rich and respectable presbyterians despised and feared the independents' dangerous political opinions. As events were to show, this contempt and fear were not altogether justified. True, the radicals of the army were 'mechanics' (craftsmen), small yeomen, shopkeepers, and apprentices. But the generals included gentlemen like Cromwell and Ireton, who were genuinely horrified at the dangerous opinions of their soldiers.

THE KING

Charles' party had been broken in war, and his generals had fled abroad. He stood alone, beaten but unbowed. He refused to surrender either his rights as a king or his supremacy over the Church, and he would not desert episcopacy. He was willing to make a pretence of giving them up, however, in order to deceive his enemies. He believed that he could snatch victory from defeat by playing off the victorious parties against each other. Parliament and the army had been allies in war, but were becoming rivals in peace. Charles hoped to bargain with each of them in turn, in order to procure the best possible terms. This policy of intrigue and deceit was dangerous. He believed himself to be indispensable—on one occasion he told his enemies, 'You cannot be without me.' Perhaps that was true in 1646. Few men, except for a handful of republicans, would have contemplated executing their king or abolishing the monarchy. But his behaviour between 1646 and 1648 caused everyone to distrust him and many to seek his death.

CHARLES AND THE SCOTS: 1646-7

First Charles tried to bargain with the Scots, but without success. Whilst he was their prisoner, he also negotiated with parliament, which offered to restore him if he agreed to the establishment of presbyterianism, control of the army by parliament for 20 years, and the punishment of his leading supporters. Charles rejected the terms as unacceptable. In January 1647 the Scots sold him and withdrew, and for the time being they ceased to be an important factor.

PARLIAMENT AND THE ARMY FALL OUT: 1647

Parliament and the army failed to work together to make a political settlement pleasing to the majority. Instead they became instruments in the hands of rivals, the presbyterians and independents. The formation of the New Model Army and the passing of the Self-Denying Ordinance had been defeats for the presbyterians. As the war was over they saw a chance to regain their supremacy. In May 1647, parliament declared its intention to disband the army without paying the arrears in wages. The soldiers were allowed to volunteer for an expedition to Ireland.

The army mutinied and the generals joined with the ordinary soldiers to oppose parliament's decision. A general council was formed, consisting of the generals, some junior officers, and 'agitators' who were elected by the soldiers to present their grievances. It drew up the Solemn Engagement, by which the army refused to disband until it had obtained such concessions as the council considered fit and just. To strengthen their hand, the generals sent Cornet Joyce with a body of cavalry to seize the king at Holmby House in Northamptonshire. The army declared that it was not 'a meer mercinary army' but a force created to defend the liberties of the people. And it demanded the withdrawal of 11 leading presbyterians from the commons. Parliament gave way when the army threatened to march on London.

THE HEADS OF PROPOSALS: 1647

Now it was the army's turn to negotiate with the king. In August it presented its harsh terms, known as the Heads of Proposals. Parliament was to control the army and navy and to choose the king's ministers for 10 years, whilst royalists were to be debarred from government offices for 5 years. The army was prepared to permit the return of a State religion with bishops and the Book of Common Prayer, although other religious sects were to be tolerated. Charles refused to consider the Proposals, because he was holding out for better terms from parliament. Thenceforth the generals did not trust him.

THE ARMY OCCUPIES LONDON: 1647

The army was being forced to intervene in politics. London, a presbyterian stronghold, made parliament receive back the 11 expelled members. Independents were forced to fly to the safety of the army. The generals lost patience and marched on London. They turned out the leading presbyterians and restored the independent members. With soldiers in London and Fairfax in command of the Tower, parliament had to do as it was told.

THE AGREEMENT OF THE PEOPLE: 1647

The troubles of the army generals were not yet over. The radical rank and file thought that the Heads of Proposals were too moderate. The levellers drew up the Agreement of the People, in which they demanded democratic rights and equality before the law for all men. During the summer of 1647 the generals and agitators met in Putney church and discussed their ideas. The debates revealed a deep rift between the conservative generals and the men whom they commanded. Cromwell was so alarmed that he ended the discussion and ordered the agitators to return to their regiments. It was the end of the general council. In future the army was to be governed by a clique of generals without reference to the opinions of their soldiers.

THE SECOND CIVIL WAR: 1648

In November 1647 Charles escaped from the army and fled to Carisbrooke Castle on the Isle of Wight, where he signed the Engagement with the Scots. He was to establish presbyterianism for three years and during that time he was to persecute the independents. In return the Scots agreed to invade England to crush the New Model Army. The presbyterian-royalist alliance made possible a second civil war.

Pre-arranged revolts occurred in Kent, Essex, and Wales. The navy mutinied and many of the ships went over to the king's side. In July the duke of Hamilton's force of Scots invaded England. The New Model Army faced the new threat alone. Despite this the king's supporters had little hope of success. The presbyterians and royalists distrusted each other. There was disunity in Scotland, where many men denounced the nobles who had signed the Engagement. Therefore Hamilton's Scots were not the fervent covenanters whom Leslie had led in the

First Civil War. They were inexperienced soldiers, ill-equipped, badly led, and with little stomach for the fight.

The New Model Army was still an efficient disciplined force with brave and able leaders. Fairfax was able to crush the royalists in Kent and Essex. Cromwell quelled resistance in Wales and then marched north to destroy the Scottish army at Preston, so bringing to an end the Second Civil War (August 1648). The army of the independents stood triumphant as the presbyterians in parliament made a last futile attempt to reach a constitutional settlement with the defeated king.

THE TRIAL AND EXECUTION OF THE KING: 1648–9

Charles was doomed. The fruitless Second Civil War had simply resulted in more killing and an aftermath of great bitterness. Among the soldiers there was universal agreement that no mercy should be shown to him. William Goffe, a radical soldier and preacher, insisted that it was their duty 'to call Charles Stuart, that man of blood, to an account for that blood he has shed'. Cromwell and his fellow-officers agreed and determined to put the king on trial. They were convinced that this course was the only just one. Their victory in the First Civil War had been a clear sign that God was on their side, but the king had chosen to ignore His judgement.

The army leaders realised that the trial had to be legal, as well as morally right. However, the presbyterians, who had been the king's allies in the recent war, might not co-operate. In December 1648 Colonel Pride and a force of musketeers were sent to the house of commons where they excluded the presbyterians, leaving a remnant of about one hundred independents. This remnant, known popularly as the Rump, was entirely in sympathy with the army. It set up a court to try the king for attempting 'to erect an unlimited and tyrannical power to rule according to his will and to overthrow the rights and liberties of the people'. To this end he 'hath traitorously and maliciously levied war against the present parliament and the people therein represented'. The new definition of treason which had first been used against the earl of Strafford was now applied to his master.

The trial of the king in Westminster Hall was a mockery of justice. A parliament, by now completely unrepresentative, had created a tribunal with one hundred and thirty-five partisan judges, who were concerned not to try but to get rid of him. Cromwell had already sworn, 'We will cut off his head with the crown upon it.' When the court met, Charles refused to acknowledge it until the judges could tell him by what authority it met. Naturally they could not do this for the only person who could legally convene such a court was the king. Likewise he refused to plead and during the trial he took his stand as the defender of the people's liberties, which were being challenged by military usurpers. After three days the president of the court, John Bradshaw (who was wearing a bullet-proof hat), sentenced the king to death for treason. On 30 January 1649 he was led out to his execution.[1]

THE EFFECTS OF THE KING'S EXECUTION

During his last days, Charles' belief in the divine right of kings did not waver. At his trial he claimed 'that no earthly power can justly call me (who am your king) in question as a delinquent'; whilst on the scaffold he declared that 'subject and sovereign are clean different'. So Charles I was executed, a martyr to his Church and to his prerogative. With him died the divine right of kings. But at the same time there was born fresh hope for the royalist party, which was now centred on the late king's son, Charles II. No matter what his faults were, Charles I won much sympathy during his last days. The army which brought him to his death was already an expensive and unpopular burden. Its treatment of him and especially his execution deprived it of much of its support. Charles saved the monarchy by his death, while his regal bearing during and after the trial made a deep and favourable impression on contemporaries.[2] Even his execution might be termed a personal triumph:

> He nothing common did or mean
> Upon that memorable scene

His death sent a thrill of horror around Europe. It angered the Scots and disturbed Englishmen. But the independents did not waver. They did not kill the king because it was convenient or

[1] He was executed in Whitehall, on a scaffold built against the Banqueting Hall.

[2] After his death there was published *Eikon Basilike*, a book purported to have been written by Charles, describing his thoughts during his last days alive. Fifty editions were printed and sold in a year. Milton wrote a reply, *Eikonoklastes*, but only three editions were sold.

necessary. The generals believed that it was a righteous punishment for his sins against God. Now that they had removed the author of England's troubles, they could build a new State more to their liking.

XXIX

THE COMMONWEALTH AND PROTECTORATE : 1649–60

THE COMMONWEALTH ESTABLISHED

THE execution of the king opened the way to a republic.[1]   The Rump condemned the office of king as 'unnecessary, burdensome, and dangerous'.   It regarded the house of lords as 'useless and dangerous'.   Therefore it abolished both.   Instead the power of the executive was to be wielded by a large council of state, consisting of members of the Rump and a number of army officers.   Legislative power was vested in a single assembly, the Rump.   One of its first enactments was to declare that England and its people were a Commonwealth 'without any king or house of lords'—in other words a republic.

The new government was in the hands of a few independents, backed by the army.   It was conscious that it was surrounded by enemies: royalists, catholics, Anglicans, and presbyterians all had good reasons for hating it.   Stern measures were taken to secure its position.   All men over the age of 18 were required to take an oath promising to be 'true and faithful' to the Commonwealth.   Even the members of the council had to make a promise of loyalty.   A new Treason Act was passed, and a savage censorship was imposed on the Press—an action which angered the poet Milton, who was a loyal independent but a champion of individual liberty.

[1] Strictly speaking, this meant government without a king.   But there were two kinds of republican: those who wanted government by an assembly (the commons); and those who wanted rule by a single person (but not a king) and an assembly.

The government's severity at this stage was understandable. Its continued existence was everywhere threatened and not only in England. Ireland was still in the grip of rebellion. Scotland was disillusioned by the success of the tolerant independents and alienated by the execution of their king. On the seas royalist privateers under Prince Rupert harried and plundered English merchant ships. The Commonwealth also had good reason to fear that the Stuarts might obtain help from the monarchs of France and Spain who had been shocked by the execution of a fellow king. Even in the United Provinces, another republic, there was a widespread feeling of disgust, and when the Commonwealth's ambassador, Isaac Dorislaus, was murdered by royalists at the Hague, the Dutch helped the assassins to escape. The new government had no time to think about the pressing religious and political problems until it had overcome the threats to its security.

IRELAND

Ireland had been in a state of rebellion since 1641. The rebels simply sought freedom from the oppressive rule of the protestants. They were not royalists and Charles' attempt to enlist their aid during the Civil War had been a pathetic failure. After the war, parliament appointed Michael Jones as its governor in Ireland. Although his force was small, he profited from the feuds and rivalries which split the rebels. The duke of Ormonde, who was leader of the royalists, was able to unite them for a short time, but his joint rebel-royalist force was defeated by Jones at Rathmines in 1649. In the same year the Rump gave Cromwell the task of conquering Ireland. By the time he arrived in Dublin with twelve thousand men, Jones' victory had already removed the one army which was capable of opposing him in the field—the remaining Irish forces were garrisoning the chief towns and ports. Cromwell spent the winter reducing the towns on the west coast. He stormed Drogheda and Wexford and put the garrisons to the sword. By the rules of war a defending force which refused to surrender when called upon to do so could be slaughtered when the town was captured, and in both cases Cromwell had given them a chance to capitulate. However, he did not justify his actions on these grounds. The massacres were 'a righteous judgement of God upon these barbarous wretches, who have imbrued their hands in so much innocent blood'. Like other puritans, he believed that he was an instrument of God, carrying out His judgements on His enemies. The massacres had one salutary effect: they caused the other towns to surrender without resistance and so shortened the war. Having occupied the west coast and struck fear into the rest of the country, Cromwell could safely leave Henry Ireton to complete the work of conquest. In 1650 he returned to England.

After the conquest, which was completed by 1652, came the settlement. The Rump's policy was not original, for it continued the practice of plantation which the Tudors had begun. Two and a half million acres of land belonging to the Irish rebels were confiscated. They were granted to those who had lent money to the government and to soldiers in lieu of their arrears of pay. Many of the rebels were pardoned, but in 1652 the Rump enacted that some of their leaders, especially Ormonde, were not included, whilst others were to forfeit some of their estates. It proceeded to rule Ireland in an enlightened fashion. Her merchants were allowed to trade freely with England and her colonies and in foreign markets, and she was given thirty seats in the British parliament at Westminster. The protestant Church in Ireland was reformed and staffed with devout ministers. Justice was administered impartially and law and order were restored. In 1652 Ireland was depopulated and impoverished. The good government of the following years enabled her to recover from this sorry state. But it did nothing to remove the deep-seated causes of discontent; if anything it aggravated them. The Roman catholics were not forced to attend protestant churches, but they could not hear mass and their priests were caught and exiled. Religion, coupled with the land settlement, perpetuated the bitterness between the Irish and their English governors.

SCOTLAND: 1649–58

Meanwhile matters had come to a head between the English independents and the Scottish covenanters. Since the Bishops' Wars Scotland had been virtually ruled by the intolerant presbyterians through the kirks. Although they claimed to be loyal to the king, they had gone to war against him in order to ensure the triumph of their religion in both countries. Since 1646, however, their hopes had faded. The Rump and the army, who together governed England, had no intention of falling in with their wishes. They believed in religious tolera-tion, an idea which was hateful to the covenanters.

The execution of the king caused a final rupture between the two countries. The Scots proclaimed his son, Charles II, as king not only of Scotland but of England too. Charles was in France, where his father had sent him along with the rest of the royal family. From there he negotiated with both the Scottish royalists under Montrose and the presbyterians who were led by the marquis of Argyle. The latter would only support him if he agreed to impose their religion on England and Ireland. Charles preferred to put his trust in Montrose, whom he publicly disowned in order not to alienate the covenanters, but to whom he gave secret encouragement. Montrose was eventually defeated at Carbisdale, betrayed to his enemies, and hanged (May 1650). Charles turned back to the presbyterians. Being less principled than his father, he signed the Covenant whilst aboard a ship bound for Scotland. The presbyterians were not satisfied that he was sincere. When he landed, they obliged him to declare that his catholic mother had been guilty of idolatry. That done, they were willing to take up arms in his cause.

Cromwell wanted to avoid a war with the Scots and he appealed to them for a peaceful settlement of their differences. When they refused, he reluctantly invaded Scotland. He found in Leslie, commander of the covenanters, a skilled and experienced opponent who trapped him at Dunbar. Cromwell was caught between the sea and the hills in which the Scottish army was encamped. But the Scots came down from their strong position to prevent his escape along the coastal road, and there he routed them. Three thousand fell and ten thousand more were captured, whereas the English losses amounted to no more than 30 men (September 1650). The battle of Dunbar was a severe shock to the covenanters. God had given His judgement against them, because, as many believed, He was displeased with their intolerance. It also ended their attempt to impose their religion on England.

Charles II did not despair. He raised a fresh army, composed this time of both royalists and presbyterians. Immediately he found himself threatened by Cromwell, who had conquered the central lowlands and advanced to Perth. As the road to the south was unguarded, however, Charles seized his opportunity and invaded England. But his presence aroused little enthusiasm amongst his subjects. Everyone was sick of war, whilst many men still feared the Scots as the traditional enemy. Meanwhile Cromwell had turned south in pursuit. He caught up with the Scots at Worcester where by 'God's crowning mercy' he routed them (September 1651). Charles became a hunted fugitive. No-one betrayed him, although the government offered a reward of one thousand pounds for his arrest. He was smuggled across England by loyal friends and eventually reached Brighton, where he found a ship to take him back to France. His followers were less fortunate, for many of them were transported to the sugar plantations of the West Indies.

After Worcester, Scotland lost its independence. Cromwell's lieutenant, George Monck, rapidly conquered the country, which was officially united with England and given 30 seats in the British parliament. The defeated Scots were treated leniently. A few leading royalists lost their estates, but there was no general seizure of property. Severe punishments were reserved for the rank and file. The presbyterian Church was not suppressed, although it was deprived of the power to persecute other sects. As in Ireland, the English government ruled Scotland with efficiency and fairness: Scottish merchants were free to trade anywhere; the law courts were administered impartially; the highlands were reduced to order. Nevertheless heavy taxes and English garrisons made the Scots only too aware that they had lost their independence. Though they gave no more trouble, they remained hostile to English rule.

THE END OF THE RUMP: 1653

By 1652 the Commonwealth had vanquished most of its opponents. Ireland and Scotland had been conquered and pacified. Robert Blake, in command of the fleet, had chased Prince Rupert's privateers from the Irish Sea and the English Channel. Now Cromwell could turn his attention to the pressing problem of a constitutional settlement.

The Rump was totally unrepresentative, and the whole government rested on the swords of the army. This had been good enough as a temporary arrangement, but it would not do as a permanent settlement. The majority of Englishmen were tired of the heavy taxes needed to maintain the army and were hostile to the regime. Cromwell was well aware that a permanent constitutional settlement could only be made by broadening the basis of the government's support. It could be done by making parliament more representative and by passing worthy reforms.

It was unlikely that either could be achieved so long as the Rump remained in being. A few of its members were corrupt, many of them were more concerned with making fortunes, all wanted to perpetuate the power which they had enjoyed for so long. Yet they did nothing to justify the continuance of their power. Reforms were pressing: the law courts were slow and expensive, and many of the laws were unnecessarily harsh. But all that the Rump did was to lay down savage penalties for sins. Although many admirable ideas were aired, they were not carried out. Furthermore, it did not attempt to heal the wounds caused by the Civil War; on the contrary, it drove many men into opposition. After the battle of Worcester, it spoilt any chance of reconciling the royalists when it confiscated the estates of many of Charles II's supporters. Landowners were frightened when it proposed to abolish tithes. And the levellers and diggers were angered by its failure to carry out the reforms which they demanded.

Even the independents were sickened by the inaction of the Rump. Yet there was little that they could do about it because, by the law of 1641, the Long Parliament could not be dissolved without its consent. The army officers grew impatient and pressed the members to draw up a bill for a new assembly. They did so but the chief object of their bill was to prolong their own power: present members were to keep their seats, and they were empowered to judge whether newly-elected members were fit to take their seats. Cromwell warned them not to pass it. When they ignored his advice, he went down to the commons with a body of musketeers and turned them out, saying, 'You are no parliament, I say you are no parliament. I will put an end to your sitting.' John Bradshaw, who was a member of the council of state, warned him, 'You are mistaken to think that the parliament is dissolved; for no power under heaven can dissolve them but themselves; therefore take you notice of that.' Cromwell's action was perhaps necessary, but it had shown that England was really being governed by the army. Bradshaw had put his finger on the great weakness of the regime: that England would only respect and support a legal and constitutional government not ruled by the sword.

10

BAREBONE'S PARLIAMENT: JULY —DECEMBER 1653

Cromwell's action aroused no outcry; as he said, 'There was not so much as the barking of a dog.' The independents welcomed it for it gave them their long-awaited chance to establish 'the rule of the saints'. Everything depended upon Cromwell, who as commander-in-chief of the army was the only legal authority left in the country; he alone could decide what form the new government would take. As a practical man he wanted to give England a permanent constitutional settlement; the army and civilian government had to be separated and the country governed by known laws and institutions. But Cromwell was also an idealist, believing that the army had a divine mission to purge the country of corruption and sin. England would be governed best by 'godly men'. For the time being his idealism won. The independents of the local churches were invited to nominate suitable men for a new parliament. The army leaders sifted the nominees and chose a hundred and forty of them, of whom only 5 were from Scotland and 6 from Ireland. These men formed Barebone's Parliament (named after one of the members Praise God Barbon, a London leather-seller). England was now to be subjected to the rule of the saints.

Barebone's Parliament, which was as unrepresentative as the Rump, proved to be a failure. Idealists do not usually make practical men of affairs, and these were what were needed. It passed some salutary reforms. The court of chancery was abolished; it had been costly and dilatory—and twenty-three thousand cases, some thirty years old, were still waiting to be heard. It introduced civil marriage, and ordered the registration of births, marriages, and deaths. Nevertheless it soon caused trouble. It was slow to pay the army's wages and arrears, and it voted to abolish tithes—a foolish move which would upset landowners at a time when Cromwell was seeking more support for the regime. Major-general Lambert and the other dissatisfied generals persuaded their friends and the more moderate members in parliament to meet early one morning and surrender their powers into Cromwell's hands.

The unsuccessful experiment of Barebone's Parliament showed that government by godly men did not work. The rule of the saints was over, and thenceforth the practical vein in Cromwell came to the fore.

THE PROTECTORATE ESTABLISHED: 1653

The army officers now drew up the Instrument of Government, which was England's first written constitution. Government was to be by a lord protector, a council of state, and parliament; thus it followed closely the traditional form of government. Cromwell was to be protector for life. He would exercise executive power with the help of the council, and he was to receive £200,000 a year for the expenses of government, as well as money for the army and navy. Special care was taken not to put the control of the army into the hands of one man; Cromwell was to share it with parliament.

A single-chamber parliament was to impose taxes and make laws, but could not alter the constitution. Cromwell was not given the king's absolute veto, but was only enabled to hold up new laws for twenty days. Parliament had to meet every three years, and then each session was to last at least 5 months; thus regular sessions were ensured. It was to consist of four hundred and sixty members, of whom Scotland and Ireland were to have 30 each, and the seats were redistributed in order to make it more representative. The franchise, too, was reformed. The senior army officers were not diggers or levellers but landowners. They gave the vote in the counties to all men who owned property (land or merchandise) worth more than £200; and in the towns they restricted it to the governing bodies (corporations). The result was a much smaller electorate than in the past: many of the forty shilling freeholders were disfranchised, whilst royalists were debarred from the first 4 parliaments of the Protectorate, and Roman catholics were excluded for ever. On the other hand the Instrument advanced the freedom of the individual in one respect, when it guaranteed liberty for tender consciences—except of course for Anglicans and catholics.

The Protectorate was a considerable improvement on the rule of the saints. It was more practical and realistic, and so had a greater chance of succeeding. It gave the protector only a limited power, which would satisfy those with unhappy memories of Charles I, while it might please the many men who yearned for the more traditional form of government. But it had weaknesses. First, none of the aspirations of levellers, diggers, and other radicals were satisfied. Secondly, it meant no reconciliation with the Anglicans. Thirdly, it made enemies of those republicans who wanted government by parliament alone.

Finally it made no allowance for any future changes which might be necessary; naturally the task of alteration would devolve on to the army again. Cromwell had got his constitutional settlement. It gave him less power than if he had ruled with the army alone; but he did not want to be a dictator, preferring to govern by consent rather than by force. Nevertheless the Protectorate was the creation of the soldiers, and Cromwell still appeared to be their nominee.

THE FIRST PROTECTORATE PARLIAMENT: 1654–5

Most of the members of this parliament held moderate views, because Barebone's Parliament had discredited the extremists; many were presbyterians. They accepted Cromwell as head of the executive, but proceeded to criticise the rest of the Instrument of Government. Cromwell persevered. He told them that they could not revise the fundamentals of the constitution. These were: government by parliament and a single person; their joint control of the army and navy; the limited life of each parliament; religious toleration. He warned parliament that he would resist any attempt to overthrow them. Rather than give them up, 'I can sooner be willing to be rolled into my grave and buried with infamy, than I can give my consent unto'. He required the members to sign an engagement to be faithful to the regime and the protector and not to alter the government. However, some of them remained critical. They decided to draw up a list of 'damnable heresies' which everyone was to reject, and 20 articles of faith which all were to observe. They demanded that the army should be reduced in size and made subject to parliament's sole control. Cromwell informed them, 'Discontent and dissatisfaction have been more multiplied within these five months of your sitting than in some years before.' So saying he dissolved parliament.

THE RULE OF THE MAJOR-GENERALS: 1655–6

There was widespread discontent with the Protectorate. A royalist rising in Scotland was suppressed in 1654. Levellers, republicans, and royalists were in alliance against 'the tyrant Oliver Cromwell', and hoped to profit from his disputes with parliament. Disloyalty spread. Unpaid soldiers joined plots against the regime. A rebellion was planned, but Cromwell and his reliable officers scotched it and imprisoned the leaders.

Only in Salisbury did the royalists under Colonel Penruddock actually revolt, and there they were easily put down (March 1655).

To prevent further uprisings a new experiment in government was devised. England and Wales were divided into 11 districts, each commanded by a major-general with a military force at his disposal. The chief task of the major-generals was to defend and maintain the government. Recent events had convinced Cromwell that the royalists would never be reconciled to the Protectorate. He gave up his former lenient policy towards them and imposed a 10 per cent tax on their incomes. It was to be assessed and collected by the major-generals, who were also instructed to enforce the 'reformation of manners'—a project dear to the hearts of the puritans. They were to punish blasphemers, put an end to gaming, bear-baiting, and cock-fighting, reduce the number of ale-houses, and close the theatres. They did so with great enthusiasm, but their inquisitorial methods alienated the nation. Whatever the government of the Protectorate did in the future, it stood revealed as a military despotism. However, Cromwell had no intention of prolonging the rule of the major-generals. It was simply a stop-gap, and in 1656, a year before he was required to by law, he summoned another parliament.

THE SECOND PROTECTORATE PARLIAMENT: 1656–8
    The rule of the major-generals had had its effect. Many of the government's opponents were elected, and although a hundred of them were excluded, the remaining members were embittered by the recent arbitrary rule. Fear of the army prompted the majority to draw up the Humble Petition and Advice. This was a proposal for a new constitition, which would include a second chamber and make Oliver Cromwell king. It was a deliberate attempt to return to the traditional government which everyone knew and understood. If the petition succeeded, it would establish a government limited by law instead of the arbitrary rule of soldiers. Cromwell was tempted to take the crown, though not because he was ambitious. The petition was the work, not of the army, but of the nation's representatives in parliament. Here was a chance to rule by consent of the people. 'It is time to come to a settlement, and to lay aside arbitrary proceedings so unacceptable to the nation.'

In the end Cromwell refused the crown (May 1657). His chief support came from the independents and the army, and they were bitterly opposed to a monarchy. With parliament's approval he became hereditary lord protector instead; he accepted the rest of its petition, in particular that there should be a second chamber whose members were to be chosen by him, and that parliament should be secure from further purges. He believed that he had at last succeeded in making a permanent constitutional settlement.

In January 1658 the second protectorate parliament met again. In the meantime Cromwell had raised 40 of his supporters from the commons to the new second chamber. The members who had been excluded from the first session now returned. They were all opponents of the regime, republicans to whom only the Rump was legitimate. At once they began to debate the powers of the new chamber. After only a month Cromwell dissolved parliament, saying, 'And let God be judge between you and me.' He was finding that his government, no matter whether it rested on consent or force, was unacceptable to the nation. He intended to persevere and call parliament again, but before he could do so he fell ill, and died on 3 September 1658.

OLIVER CROMWELL: AN ASSESSMENT

The various experiments, which followed the dissolution of the Rump all failed because:

(*1*) although Cromwell wanted to govern by consent, he always reverted to force when he met obstacles. Thus his experiments appeared to be mere attempts to conceal the fact that England was governed by the sword—and the English hated this above all else.

(*2*) Bradshaw was right when he pointed out that parliament was the only authority which people would recognise and obey. To many men, and not only the republicans, the Rump was the last legitimate government.

Cromwell failed to lead England on to a new path of constitutional development. Yet his greatness, both as a general and a statesman, is undeniable. He was moderate and tolerant, practical and pious. But it was in the field of war that he made his first great contribution. The 'ironsides', the regiment out of which the New Model Army grew, was his creation; and he forged the army into a terrible weapon of war, disciplined, orderly, and inspired both by his leadership and religious enthusiasm. His soldiers' trust in him was justified, for he was a military genius—Marston Moor, Dunbar, and Worcester bear witness to this. As ruler of England for 5 years he had a dual responsibility: to God and to the well-being of the people. To the best of his abilities he endeavoured to carry it out.

A NOTE: THE SECTS

(*1*) *The Levellers*. The levellers held advanced political ideas. They were tolerant and republican[1]; in particular they believed that as the people were sovereign parliament should represent them; so they demanded a wider franchise. However, it would not be correct to call them democrats. When they asked for the vote to be given to all 'freeborn Englishmen', they did not mean wage-earners and paupers. The levellers had many followers in the rank and file of the army, and it was to the generals that they presented their proposed reforms in the Agreement of the People. The generals, however, were propertied men. They believed that only those with 'a permanent fixed interest in this kingdom' (i.e. those with land or engaged in trade) should have 'a share in that power that shall dispose of all things here'.

The leader of the levellers was John Lilburne (1614–57). His ideas brought him little but trouble. Star chamber flogged and imprisoned him. Cromwell crushed the levellers' mutinies in the army and the Rump sent him into exile, threatening him with death if he came back. 'Freeborn John' did return. He was put on trial but acquitted. The London populace and even his guards greeted the verdict with joy. Lilburne's views had little chance of acceptance, but his love of freedom would be praiseworthy in any age.

(*2*) *The diggers*. The diggers were primitive communists. Although the levellers wanted more men to have political rights, they respected the existing social order. But the diggers went further and sought to abolish private property, so that the fruits of the earth might be shared equally by all. Under their leader Gerrard Winstanley they tried to put their beliefs into practice. At St. George's Hill, not far from London, they farmed the land communally, each man taking a share of the produce. The Rump would not tolerate such dangerous practices. The army

1 They wanted government by a single elected assembly.

drove them off the land, destroyed their dwellings, and so brought the experiment to an end. But Winstanley's belief in social justice survived in his book, *Law of Freedom*.

(3) *The fifth monarchy men*. They were dangerous fanatics who were to be found amongst the artisans and craftsmen in the towns, especially London. They believed that the world had seen the rule of 4 monarchies: of Assyria, Persia, Macedonia, and Rome. The fifth monarchy, which was the rule of Christ, was at hand. If government proved to be an obstacle to the establishment of Christ's rule, it must be overthrown. It seemed as if the fifth monarchists saw every government as an obstacle: they gloried in the downfall of the king, but found the Commonwealth and Protectorate no more godly than the old, and in 1657 Thomas Venner, a London wine-cooper, led an unsuccessful attempt to overthrow it. In 1661, after the restoration of Charles II, they tried again. Of all the sects, the fifth monarchists were the most fanatical and the least realistic. They offered nothing practical in the place of the government they would destroy, and their success would have led to anarchy.

XXX

FOREIGN POLICY DURING THE INTERREGNUM : 1649–58

ENGLAND played no part in European affairs between 1640 and 1649. Indeed there was a greater likelihood that Europe would interfere in English affairs on the king's side; Charles I's wife was French and his eldest daughter Mary married William of Orange. But aid was not forthcoming. France was involved in the Thirty Years' War, and although William gave a little help to Charles, the states-general, which ruled the United Provinces, favoured parliament. The execution of the king horrified Europe and revived the danger of armed intervention on behalf of his family. Once again, however, no European power was ready to go as far as to give active assistance to the new king, Charles II. By 1651 the republic had secured its position and was ready to play an active role in Europe.

THE DUTCH WAR: 1652–4

As the Dutch were republicans and Calvinists, they had much in common with the rulers of England. The Commonwealth even proposed a political union of the two States, but the offer was rejected because the regicide government was still unpopular. In any case the United Provinces with its empire and merchant marine was England's great commercial rival. It had taken much of the carrying trade during the Civil War, but now the Commonwealth meant to regain it. This was sound Mercantilism.[1] In October 1651 the Rump passed the Navigation Act. It forbade goods to be imported into Britain from Asia, America, and Africa, except in British ships; goods from a European country were to be carried either by ships of that country or in British ships. The act was an obvious blow at the Dutch carrying trade. Yet it was only one of the causes of the war which followed. Battle was also joined over the freedom of the seas. The English and French were engaged in piracy against each other. The English claimed the right to search neutral ships for French goods, but the Dutch seamen resisted attempts to enforce it. Several other causes are worthy of note: the long-standing commercial rivalry in the Far East; the murder of Isaac Dorislaus; the help given to the Stuarts; the refusal of Dutch vessels to strike their flags to the English in the Channel.

The war proved to be a great success. Although the Dutch had many more ships, most of them were merchant vessels, whereas the Commonwealth had doubled the number of its warships in the least three years. Many of the Dutch warships had to spend their time in convoy duty, but this was less of a problem to the English, whose merchant fleet was so much smaller. The war began in 1652. In November Blake was defeated by the Dutch admiral, Van Tromp, off Dungeness. Three months later, Blake gained his revenge when he beat Tromp off Portland. As a result, England gained control of the Channel and blockaded the United Provinces. Dutch trade was

[1] See Chapter XVIII.

slowly strangled.   When Tromp made a valiant attempt to break the blockade, he was defeated and killed (July 1653).   Although the Dutch sued for peace, the English merchants still wanted war and the protestant zealots insisted on a union of the two protestant States as one of the conditions of peace.   The Dutch were saved by Cromwell who took a leading part in the negotiations.   He offered more moderate terms, which the Dutch accepted (1654).   They agreed to salute English ships in the Channel, to give no more aid to the Stuarts, and to compensate merchants who had suffered losses at their hands.   The war was of great significance.   England was marked out as the great naval power of the future.   The Navigation Act protected her trade and, by the capture of nearly one thousand five hundred merchant ships, she had inflicted a blow on the Dutch from which they never recovered.

CROMWELL'S FOREIGN POLICY: 1653–8

During the Protectorate England adopted an aggressive foreign policy; for the first time since the reign of Queen Elizabeth she became a force to be reckoned with in European politics.   The country was favourably placed for such a policy; her army was probably the finest in Europe, and her navy was flushed with its success over the Dutch.   Cromwell aimed to do four things: to further the protestant religion in Europe; to harry the Stuarts wherever they were to be found and especially to prevent them getting a base for operations against England; to protect and encourage British commerce; to strike a blow at Spain which he saw as the catholic arch-enemy.

(1) *Religion.*   Cromwell carried his protestant zeal into foreign affairs.   He made peace with the Dutch, whom he saw as England's natural ally against the catholics.   But he failed to achieve a political union or even an alliance due to continued trading rivalry.   Despite this he hoped to erect a protestant alliance in Europe, and he signed agreements with Denmark and Sweden.   He also appealed to Mazarin, the first minister of France, to prevent the duke of Savoy slaughtering his protestant subjects.   Milton offered up a prayer to heaven:

> Avenge O Lord thy slaughtered saints,
> Whose bones lie scattered on the Alpine Mountains cold.

His prayer was answered when Mazarin did as Cromwell asked.

The protector's successful intervention enhanced his reputation amongst the protestants of Europe.

(2) *The Stuarts.* Blake's ships were already harrassing Prince Rupert's privateers. Portugal had allowed the royalists to use Lisbon as a base from which to prey on English ships. Blake forced the Portuguese to refrain from giving further assistance and to pay an indemnity (1652). Cromwell carried on the attack against the Stuarts: in 1654 the Dutch were compelled to close their frontier to them, and when England made a compact with France in 1656, Mazarin agreed to expel them. Charles II retaliated by signing a treaty with France's mortal foe, Spain (1656).

(3) *Commerce.* English merchants were protected by Blake's warships: in 1654 he destroyed the ships and forts of the dey of Tunis, and made him disgorge English prisoners. Much was done to encourage the growth of trade too. Favourable trade treaties were negotiated, especially with Sweden, which supplied England with hemp, timber, and other naval supplies. Later the Sound was opened to English shipping. In a treaty with Portugal, in 1654, favourable terms of trade were obtained. Cromwell also entered into negotiations with Spain. He wanted two concessions for English merchants: freedom to practise their religion in Spain, and the right to trade with Spanish colonies. 'This is to ask for my master's two eyes,' was the answer of a Spanish representative. Thereupon Cromwell dropped the project.

(4) *Spain.* The protector's outlook was essentially anti-Spanish. His demand for free trade and religious toleration was quite unreasonable; he was asking Spain to give up its two most prized possessions, its trading monopoly in its empire, and the absence of heresy in its dominions. When his demands were refused, Cromwell reverted to a popular Elizabethan project, an attack on the Spanish West Indies. An expedition set sail under William Penn and Robert Venables, its destination Hispaniola (1655). The attempt was a miserable failure; instead Jamaica was captured and colonised. When the Spanish king learned the news, he declared war.

In the conflict which followed the forces of the Protectorate were successful by land and sea. In 1656 Captain Stayner seized a Spanish treasure fleet off Cadiz, and in the following year Blake destroyed the ships of a second treasure fleet, this time off the Canaries. It was the last of Blake's many achievements, because he died as his ship sailed into Plymouth Sound (August 1657). In the same year Cromwell made an alliance with France. Their joint forces were to attack the Spanish strongholds in Flanders. England was to supply a fleet and six thousand men; in return she was to receive Dunkirk and Mardyke. The former would enable England to control the Channel and threaten the Dutch. Anglo-French co-operation was crowned with success. Mardyke was taken and Dunkirk besieged. A Spanish army was routed amidst the sand-dunes, as it advanced to its relief, and soon afterwards Dunkirk surrendered. In the same year Cromwell died, and England's warlike foreign policy came to an end.

CROMWELL'S FOREIGN POLICY: AN ASSESSMENT

In some ways Cromwell's policy was more suited to an earlier age. He still thought of foreign affairs in terms of religion, but after the Thirty Years' War, which ended in 1648, kings were less willing to go to war for their faith. Religious disputes were giving way to other considerations, such as territory and trade.

We may also accuse Cromwell of 'backing the wrong horse'. To preserve the balance of power in Europe, he should have supported Spain, which was the weaker power, against the growing strength of France; instead, it is often argued, he helped to make France so powerful that she became a threat to Europe's security. But few realised how great was the decay of Spanish power. In any case, if Cromwell had lived, England's military strength might well have been a curb on French power.

Cromwell's foreign policy achieved much that was good. He helped the growth of English trade, and pointed the way to his country's great future as a colonial power. And he had raised England's prestige from the depths to which it had sunk under the early Stuarts.

XXXI

THE END OF THE INTERREGNUM
1658–60

THE COLLAPSE OF THE PROTECTORATE: SEPTEMBER 1658—MAY 1659.
THE death of Cromwell in 1658 was the first in a series of events
which led to the restoration of the monarchy. Anglicans,
catholics, presbyterians, and royalists had opposed the regime
established in 1649, and the creation of the Protectorate had
made enemies of the diggers, levellers, and republicans too.
Cromwell's prestige and personality had held them in check but
he had failed to win them over by ending military rule and
establishing the principle that the army should not interfere
in politics (i.e. that the civil power should control the army and
not vice-versa).

Cromwell's successor was his son, Richard. He was honest
and well-intentioned, but he lacked the qualities needed for his
high office. As he did not inspire fear or respect as his father
had done, all the old opponents of the regime emerged again.
Republicans demanded a return to the Commonwealth, and
royalists wanted the return of the Stuarts. Furthermore,
Richard, as a civilian, did not have the respect and loyalty of the
soldiers. He had to battle with Fleetwood, Lambert, Desborough, and the other generals. They had become rich and
powerful. They were also ambitious and ready to use the army
to interfere in politics, setting up governments and pulling them
down. It was their arbitrary and selfish behaviour after
Cromwell's death that made the Restoration certain; people saw
that a return to government by king, lords, and commons was
the only way to avoid anarchy or the tyranny of the army.

The protector was in a difficult position. He was inexperienced
and weak, and he could only trust one general, George Monck,
who was commander-in-chief in Scotland. The other army
leaders meant to extort greater power from him. They
demanded that one of the generals, not the protector, should be
made commander-in-chief of the army, and that officers should
not be dismissed by either the protector or parliament but only

by a court-martial.[1] Such concessions would deprive the protector of control over the army. However, he did not lack support. In January 1659 a new parliament met. Most of the members were moderate men, many were presbyterians. They would prefer even the Stuarts to the rule of the sword. Both the protector and parliament showed themselves hostile to the army. No attempt was made to pay the soldiers' wages which were much in arrears. The commons even prepared to impeach the harshest of Cromwell's major-generals.

The army, too, had gained a new ally. The republicans hated the office of protector, which was too much like that of a king. They wanted a return to the Commonwealth with its Rump and council of state. So they threw in their lot with the army in the hope of overthrowing Richard Cromwell. Their hopes were realised when parliament went too far. It proposed to dismiss those officers who wanted to interfere with its meetings, and it resolved that the council of army officers should not meet whilst parliament was in session. Fleetwood acted as the generals' spokesman. He refused to accept parliament's proposals. Instead he summoned the regiments to him. Richard challenged this by ordering them to join him. Nearly all obeyed Fleetwood. So Richard gave way to the generals' demands and dissolved parliament (April). In May he restored the Rump. Then he resigned.[2]

THE RESTORED COMMONWEALTH: MAY 1659—MARCH 1660

The republicans had got their way. The army leaders too appeared to have obtained their ends. They petitioned the Rump to maintain religious toleration (except for Roman catholics and Anglicans), and to appoint Fleetwood as commander of the army. The Rump appointed Fleetwood, but insisted that parliament should continue to choose and promote officers. The army leaders had failed to realise that the men of the Rump—indeed of any parliament—were not going to make the army completely independent of the State, a free agent to interfere in politics whenever it chose. The Rump behaved as if the army should obey it in all things—and indeed this was essential if the country was to be governed by a stable civil

---

[1] A military court in which the judges were army officers.
[2] He became known popularly as 'Tumbledown Dick', because the whole system of government collapsed after his resignation.

government and not by the sword. The generals, however, would have none of it. Events moved towards another clash between the civil power and the army.

The royalists took advantage of these squabbles to raise a revolt in favour of Charles II. The presbyterians[1] joined them. However, the revolt was suppressed by Lambert, who regarded his victory as a sign that God was still with the army. He asked the Rump to dissolve itself and arrange for a new parliament to be elected; he also demanded virtual independence for the army. The Rump rejected the petition, whereupon Fleetwood and other generals met together and decided to support Lambert. The Rump still resisted. It was encouraged by the fact that General Monck upheld its supremacy over the army. Therefore it dismissed Lambert, Desborough, and other hostile officers. In October, Lambert descended on Westminster and turned the Rump out, just as Cromwell had done in 1653. Then the generals met to work out a constitution more to their liking. But their support crumbled. The governor and garrison of Portsmouth declared for a free parliament; so did the navy. Soldiers and civilians alike were tired of arbitrary rule. Fleetwood, with more commonsense than the rest, saw that their days of power were numbered. He recalled the Rump.

Now General Monck acted. 'Obedience is my great principle,' he said. He respected the authority of parliament and believed that the army should always obey it. He had already purged his own forces of unreliable officers. Now he told them that, until there was a free parliament, they would not get their arrears of pay. Having united his soldiers behind him, Monck began his march south. The other generals prepared to resist him. Lambert marched northward to obstruct his way. He received no help from the people, however, sickened as they were by heavy taxes, military rule, and the ambitions of selfish officers. The army, too, had long since lost the unity it once had. No longer was it fighting for great causes, but simply to satisfy the generals' thirst for power. It was not even being paid. Lambert's demoralised army dissolved in the face of Monck's determination—and on 3 February 1660 entered London, to end 'that intolerable slavery of a sword government'.

---

[1] There were no presbyterians in the Rump. They had been excluded by 'Pride's purge' in 1648 and so were hostile to this unrepresentative parliament.

Monck set an example by the respect which he showed for parliament. The Rump, however, was only an unrepresentative fragment, so he told the remaining handful of members that they should admit all the excluded representatives (i.e. royalists, expelled during the Civil War, and presbyterians). But the men of the Rump had not changed—they were still anxious to keep their places and power. When London supported Monck's proposal, they ordered him to punish the City by destroying its gates. Monck hated the task, but he did it in order to show the army that it must obey the civil government. Yet he saw that the members of the Rump were interested not in 'the liberties of the people', but only in their own power. He forced them to take back the excluded members. The City went mad with joy—and Londoners showed their contempt for the assembly by lighting bonfires and roasting rumps of meat. The excluded members formed a majority which dissolved the Rump in March 1660.

THE RETURN OF THE KING: 1660

Elections were held for a new parliament which would make a constitutional settlement. Previously Monck had not indicated what form he would like the settlement to take. But now he spoke for the restoration of the monarchy. Most men agreed with him, because it would put an end to arbitrary rule. Monck advised Charles II to make certain promises which would ensure parliament's support for his return. Charles agreed and embodied them in his Declaration of Breda. The Declaration made it clear that there would be no general revenge for past acts—so encouraging the king's many opponents to accept his return. And it stated that his promises were subject to parliament's approval—thus revealing that he intended to respect parliament's authority.

In April the so-called 'Convention Parliament' met. All were agreed that the king should be recalled. The presbyterians wanted to impose harsh terms on him, but they were in a minority. The majority preferred an unconditional restoration— so when Charles came back, it was as head of the executive and commander of the armed forces, not as a mere puppet. Parliament recognised Charles II as king (dating his reign from 30 January 1649) and implored him to return to England. In May he came, and on his thirtieth birthday he entered London. John

Evelyn, the diarist, wrote, 'This day his Majestie Charles II came to London after a sad and long exile and calamitous suffering both of the King and Church. I stood in the Strand and beheld it and bless'd God. And all this was don without one drop of bloud shed, and by that very army which rebell'd against him.'

THE SIGNIFICANCE OF THE INTERREGNUM

The interregnum was over. But it had wrought changes and left scars that could not be effaced:

(*1*) It had advanced parliament's authority and prestige. At the same time it had destroyed forever the possibility of absolute monarchy in England. No one forgot that Charles I had been executed—a fact which established that even kings could be called to account.

(*2*) The nation had learned to mistrust written constitutions and to detest military government. Thereafter it preferred the rule of law. In 1660 the nation returned to the old forms of government—and never again did it stray from the well-trodden path of traditional constitutional growth.

(*3*) Many political theories had been aired during the long period of revolution between 1640 and 1660. Some of them— like Lilburne's republicanism and Winstanley's communism— were popular amongst the lower classes. But they frightened the men of property who united to defeat them—and such ideas did not revive until the nineteenth century.

(*4*) The rule of the saints had been tried and found wanting. The country's revulsion at the puritans' reformation of manners led to a violent reaction in the looser morals and manners of the Restoration era. On the other hand the independents gave England its first lesson in toleration: presbyterians, quakers, baptists, and many other sects were free to worship in their own way, and in 1656 Cromwell permitted the Jews to return to England.[1] However, toleration was not extended to the Anglicans and Roman catholics. The Anglicans took their revenge after the Restoration. But many men were sick and tired of ideologies, theological hair-splitting, and persecution. Some lost interest in religion; others became sceptical. The one thing guaranteed to panic Englishmen into savage mood was popery.

(*5*) The Commonwealth and Protectorate were harsh regimes

[1] The Jews had been expelled by Edward I in 1290.

in many ways. Freedom of the Press and of speech were less, taxes heavier than ever they had been under the Stuarts. Charles I's 'extortion' during his personal rule (1629–40) produced £500,000 a year; taxation during the interregnum amounted to £4,000,000 a year—and still a large deficit was left, to be eliminated at the Restoration.

Yet there was much to commend in the experiments of the 1650's. Attempts were made to simplify the laws and reduce the costs of law-suits. Although no concessions were made to the egalitarian spirit of John Lilburne, the redistribution of parliamentary seats was the fairest devised before the nineteenth century. Government was more efficient, the civil service better organised—largely because the government received enough money to do its work properly. Law and order were maintained, even in Ireland and the highlands of Scotland. Finally Cromwell raised England's prestige in Europe and pointed the way to an imperial future.

RESTORATION
TO REVOLUTION

※

XXXII

THE RESTORATION : 1660

THE CHARACTER OF CHARLES II

In May 1660 Charles II returned to England to be greeted
with wild enthusiasm, but once the cheering was over serious
problems of government had to be solved. There was the
important task of making a constitutional settlement, and much
of its success would depend on the character of the new
king.

Charles II was handsome, healthy, and physically active.
Unlike his shy, proud, and withdrawn father, he was easily
accessible and friendly; he was witty, sociable, and loved to
converse on all manner of subjects with courtiers and politicians,
artists and scientists. Charles also differed from his father in
that he was cynical and immoral, no doubt as a result of his
experiences since the Civil War. He headed a dissolute court in
which the duchess of Portsmouth and other of his mistresses
exercised too much influence. Nonconformist preachers were
wont to thunder from the pulpit about the iniquities of the new
Babylon at Whitehall—and even some of the royalists agreed
with them. Yet it only distressed a minority; the rest regarded
the court's standards as those of the age.

The king was a shrewd politician. His experiences in exile
had taught him to study and understand other men. He was a
man of few principles, unscrupulous, and deceitful, and he was
prepared to use any means in order to stay on his throne and
avoid 'going on his travels' again. In the same way he would

sacrifice a capable and loyal minister if he happened to be unpopular. There were two principles to which he was unswervingly loyal: his right as a Stuart to be king, and 'legitimacy', the right of his younger brother James to succeed him if he had no heir. Little else mattered, as his attitude to religion shows. He was probably a catholic as his mother and brother undoubtedly were. His years of exile in France had strengthened his preference for the Roman catholic Church. Yet, if he was a papist, it remained a secret locked in his heart; he knew well enough how England hated popery, and he was not going to risk his throne for the sake of openly professing his beliefs.

Charles favoured absolute monarchy of the kind which Louis XIV had established in France, but he was lazy and unwilling to exert the sustained effort needed to do the same in England. Because he had no love for the hard work required by matters of State, some men thought him frivolous. They underestimated this unscrupulous king who, when occasion demanded, could fight with tenacity, patience, and great skill.

Charles has too often been maligned for his lack of principles and morals, but in these he was representative of an age which gloried in its freedom from restraint—no more major-generals, rule of the saints, or reformation of manners. Furthermore, he is too often remembered for these things alone. Several facts are worth noting: he did not seek revenge but insisted that the Restoration be grounded on moderation and law; by the exercise of skill and perseverance he left to his brother James a crown which he had greatly strengthened; in his patronage of science, architecture, and the arts, and in his interest in colonial matters, he represented the forward-looking materialist outlook of his people.

EDWARD HYDE, EARL OF CLARENDON

Edward Hyde had opposed the arbitrary acts of Charles I's government; in the Long Parliament he had joined in the condemnation of Strafford. But he was a man of moderate views. Alarmed by the uncompromising attitude of Pym and his followers, he joined the royalists to defend the Anglican Church and limited monarchy. He fought against parliament in the Civil War. After Charles I's execution he attached himself to the new king, accompanied him on the Worcester campaign, and then went into exile with him. He was convinced that one day the monarchy would be restored; and, when it happened, it was Hyde who with Charles' approval ensured that the Restoration was carried through without revenge. His great achievement was to restore not absolute monarchy but a balance of power between king and parliament, each with its assigned place in the constitution—and with their actions always based on the rule of law.

THE CONVENTION PARLIAMENT: 1660

The Convention[1] Parliament, consisting of the lords and commons, met in April 1660. It accepted Charles' Declaration of Breda, in which he promised four things: a general pardon, except for those whom parliament excluded; his consent to an act of parliament granting religious toleration; that all questions relating to land were to be decided by parliament; that the army was to receive payment of its arrears in wages by parliament. The Convention Parliament implemented some of these promises:

(*1*) *An Act of Indemnity* pardoned all who had taken part in the rebellion and the subsequent governments of the Commonwealth and Protectorate. There were only fifty exceptions, some of whom were regicides, of whom 11 were executed. As a token act of revenge the bodies of Cromwell, General Ireton, and Pym were removed from their tombs in Westminster Abbey, hanged at Tyburn, and buried beneath the gallows.

(*2*) *A land settlement* was made, though it pleased few. The republican governments had confiscated the property of the king and the Church, as well as the estates of many of the king's supporters. Others had suffered such heavy fines and taxes that they had been forced to sell their land in order to raise money. Naturally the returning royalists wanted their estates back. This was no easy problem to solve, because some of the confiscations and sales of land had taken place years before. Since then estates had changed hands one or more times, and the present owners, some of whom were in the Convention, had bought them in good faith. Although Charles wanted to give his faithful followers their due, he was in no position to antagonise such a large body of landowners by evicting them without compensation. The only solution was a compromise: the

---

[1] It was not a legal assembly, because the king had not summoned it; but after the many illegal acts of the past twenty years this mattered little.

property of the king and the Church was restored; so, too, were the estates which had been confiscated; but those royalists who had sold their lands did not receive them back.

It was a great blow to many of Charles' supporters, but it is clear that some people had to suffer in such a vast and complex land settlement. There was a great change in the landowning class. Many of the old landed families, mainly royalists, were replaced by the purchasers of the 1650's who were for the most part sympathetic to the parliamentary cause.

(3) *The financial settlement.* As we have seen, money was one of the main causes of strife between the early Stuarts and their parliaments. The crown's hereditary revenue was quite inadequate even for ordinary needs. Parliament was suspicious of the Stuarts' political ambitions and irritated by their extravagance and mismanagement, so it refused to give them as much as they required. Both James and Charles had been forced to adopt extortionate methods, which only made matters worse. The tax system needed a drastic overhaul, and the more up-to-date methods of the interregnum pointed the way (e.g. parliament had introduced excise duties). The king and parliament did their best to make a satisfactory settlement. Charles surrendered feudal dues and received instead an excise on wines and beer. Together with his other hereditary revenues, it was estimated to give him £1,200,000 a year.

Things did not work out that way. This sum was insufficient even for his ordinary expenses. In addition parliament had miscalculated, for the new arrangements failed to bring in the anticipated amount; so in 1662 a hearth-tax[1] was introduced to make up the deficit.

The crown was burdened with enormous immediate expenses, which included Charles I's debts, those which Charles II had incurred in exile, and the arrears of pay of Monck's army. Parliament voted nearly £1,000,000 for the soldiers, who were paid off and disbanded—except for some cavalry and the Coldstream Guards who went to form the nucleus of Charles' standing army.[2] But no money was forthcoming for the king's debts. Matters were made worse by his government which mismanaged its financial affairs; large sums were wasted by

---

[1] A tax of two shillings on every hearth.
[2] It began as a force of five thousand men, but was gradually increased during the reign.

him on his mistresses. The fiscal problem did much to destroy the new-found unity between king and parliament.

(*4*) The most important task of the Convention Parliament was to make *a constitutional settlement*. It declared that government ought to be by king, lords, and commons. It invited Charles to return to England and imposed no conditions on him. But this did not mean that Charles II would possess the same power as his ancestors. Gone was the paraphernalia of personal rule, because the statutes to which his father had assented down to August 1641 remained in force. The prerogative courts and councils, the non-parliamentary taxes had gone forever. When the Convention Parliament was dissolved in December 1660, it had already mapped out the main lines of the settlement which was intended to heal the rifts of the past 20 years.

(*5*) The Restoration made necessary *a constitutional religious, and land settlement in Ireland*. The union of England and Ireland was brought to an end. The form of government which had existed before 1641 was restored. Briefly it was this. A lord lieutenant, who was assisted by a council, governed in the king's name. The Irish parliament, in which only protestants could sit, made laws and voted taxes; it was strictly subordinate to the king, whose consent was necessary before its acts became law. Furthermore, the English parliament could make laws which applied to Ireland.

The religious settlement was a restoration of things as they had been before the Irish rebellion. The Church of Ireland (the Irish branch of the Anglican Church) regained its old supremacy. The presbyterians in Ulster were excluded from town corporations, and their ministers were ejected from their livings. The Roman catholics suffered the same disabilities, and the mass was once again prohibited. In practice, however, the catholics were free to worship quietly and even to hold public offices, because Charles' lord lieutenant, Ormonde, was sensible and tolerant.

The land problem was more complex. In the Cromwellian settlement, most of the catholics and many protestants were evicted; about one-quarter of them were compensated with lands in the west. 'The confiscated property was given to soldiers in lieu of pay, and to financiers who had made loans to the government; they were all protestants. The Restoration settlement could not satisfy everybody. The moneylenders and soldiers kept what they still held. Protestants who had been dispossessed by Cromwell received their lands back; so did the catholics who had not taken part in the rebellion of 1641—but first they had to prove their innocence. Although catholic rebels who had afterwards submitted to the king were promised compensation, they did not receive it. In 1641 the protestants had owned one-third of the good farmland in Ireland; after the Restoration settlement they held two-thirds.

Although the Convention's treatment of the Irish problem was selfish and shortsighted, it had accomplished much. But it left the thorniest problem of all, the religious settlement, to be tackled by a new parliament which would be summoned by the king.

THE CAVALIER PARLIAMENT: 1661–79

The Cavalier Parliament, which met in 1661, was to last for eighteen years. At first it was violently royalist. It passed an act which made treasonable any attempt to make war on the king or depose him. The idea was to make his person inviolable, and so to prevent a recurrence of the recent upheavals, and it ruled that it was unlawful even to resist him. In this way the doctrine of non-resistance came into being. The theory evolved that the king could do no wrong; his ministers were to be blamed for unpopular policies, for which parliament would impeach and punish them.

When parliament met, it consisted of two houses. The bishops and royalist peers were restored to the house of lords; elections to the commons were based on the old franchise and distribution of seats. Hyde wanted to revive the Tudor system of government, whereby parliament should meet only at the king's discretion to vote money, make laws, and give advice and constructive criticism, whilst the country was governed by the king and his council. But those days had gone forever. The Triennial Act of 1641 (and another confirming it in 1664) required regular sessions, and the great advance in parliament's authority since 1640 made it unlikely that members would be satisfied with such a limited role. At the same time the abolition of the prerogative courts and councils prevented the government from controlling the justices of the peace, who now became the real rulers of the countryside.

Charles was tolerant; he loved his bed-of-ease and felt that his subjects were entitled to enjoy theirs too. Unfortunately, the high churchmen were very prominent in the Anglican Church after the Restoration. Few of them were ready to come to terms with the puritans, preferring to drive them from the Church and persecute them. An attempt was made to bring the two sides together. Twelve bishops and the same number of presbyterians met in debate at the Savoy Palace, but the meeting broke up in rancour and disagreement.

Parliament met in the shadow of sectarian violence. In January 1661 Thomas Venner had led a band of fifth monarchists in an attempt to seize London and establish the rule of Christ. They were soon rounded up and Venner was executed; but any attempt to grant toleration after this was out of the question. Parliament feared that nonconformist[1] services would be a meeting-place for revolutionaries; its fears were increased by rumours of quaker sedition and presbyterian plots. The result was the Clarendon Code, a number of laws which were designed to render the nonconformists harmless:

(*1*) *The Corporation Act (1661)*, which required all members of municipal corporations to receive communion in accordance with Anglican rites; to renounce the Covenant; to swear the oath of non-resistance to the king. Parliamentary elections in the towns were usually controlled by the corporations. Thus the puritan sects were excluded from the commons; only royalist Anglicans could sit.

(*2*) *The Act of Uniformity (1662):* ministers and schoolmasters had to accept Queen Elizabeth's Prayer-Book with 'unfeigned assent and consent to everything' in it. Two thousand puritan clergymen gave up their livings and left the Church rather than submit.

(*3*) The nonconformists found serious difficulty in financing their ministers, who had no livings to support them. Many were restless and discontented; some took part in plots and even an abortive rising. Parliament retaliated by passing *the Conventicle Act (1664)*. Religious services, other than those using the Anglican rites, were prohibited on pain of imprisonment, or transportation for the third offence.

[1] The nonconformists were those people who refused to observe the Anglican rites and so left the Church with their ministers. Those sects which we term 'puritan' before 1660 (i.e. presbyterians and 'independent' sects, such as the quakers and baptists) are known after the Restoration as nonconformists.

(*4*) *The Five Mile Act* (*1665*) forbade the dispossessed ministers to preach, act as schoolmasters, or come within 5 miles of their former livings or any corporate town, unless they took an oath which was unacceptable to most nonconformists.

This code was incorrectly named after Edward Hyde, to whom Charles had given the earldom of Clarendon. He was not responsible, for it was swept into law by a parliament which feared a vigorous revival of the sects. It ended the attempt to comprehend everyone within the Church; the nonconformists remained outside, harassed by its penalties. Although their numbers declined, they remained an important factor in English life. Prevented from entering parliament, the law, and local government, they were forced to go into trade and industry to make their mark. Their puritan thrift and energy were admirably suited to this.

Political power and the professions remained in the hands of the royalist Anglicans, whilst the Church itself was strengthened by the restoration of its courts (except for the court of high commission). However, it had declined in importance. The Laudian system had gone in 1641; bishops no longer played a part in government; and the Church had deprived itself of the services of many able and devoted puritan ministers.

THE SIGNIFICANCE OF THE RESTORATION

(*1*) The Restoration marked England's rejection of thorough, rule by the army, and rule of the saints. Instead of paper constitutions and idealistic experiments Englishmen preferred the form of government which they knew and understood, that of king, lords, and commons. They chose law rather than the sword as arbiter.

(*2*) The king had lost all the instruments of personal rule. On the other hand he was not a figurehead. He retained the right to govern, choose his own advisers, summon and dissolve parliament, command the army and navy, wage war, and sign treaties. But he was bound now to observe parliament's wishes in many things. His ministers were responsible to it as well as to him. His foreign policy was influenced by the commons who controlled the purse strings. They also claimed the right to ensure that additional grants of money were spent for the purpose for which they were voted, and they set up a parliamentary audit to make sure. The control of the way in which supplies were spent in furtherance of the king's policy was the first step to parliament's complete mastery over the executive.

(3) Here then was the great problem posed by the Restoration. The monarchy had been re-established with the right to formulate and carry out policies. But it was hardly in a position to do so without parliamentary grants. Therefore parliament could obstruct, even prevent, policies with which it disagreed; yet it had no right to force its own policies on Charles, nor could it carry out projects of its own—government was the king's. In brief, parliament had the right and power to check the king's policies without being able to put any in their place. As Charles favoured Louis XIV and catholicism and as parliament was hostile to both there was every chance of a deadlock. The government could not function efficiently until either king or parliament had become sovereign, that is until one of them had gained complete control over both the executive and legislature—and that was to come in 1689.

(4) The Restoration brought back the old classes, nobles, bishops, and gentry. Society was once again led by the peers, whilst the countryside was ruled by the squires and the parsons. From the gentlemen were chosen the justices of the peace. They were now free from the constant supervision which had been exercised by the Tudors and the early Stuarts. They protected their own interests and the lower classes were compelled to obey their 'betters'. This rule of the justices was to last until the nineteenth century.

XXXIII

THE REIGN OF CHARLES II : 1660–85

THE EUROPEAN SITUATION IN 1660

In the seventeenth century Spain declined from its former position as the greatest power in Europe and France took its place. Between 1610 and 1661 two great French ministers, Richelieu and Mazarin, established absolute monarchy and made France the greatest power in Europe. They bequeathed to Louis XIV, who began his personal rule in 1661, the finest army in Europe, successful generals, plenty of money and absolute power. He chose to use his assets to make France the arbiter of Europe. Vain, ambitious, and eager for glory, he sought to advance the boundaries of France at the expense of his Spanish and German Hapsburg neighbours. Indeed he threatened to dominate Europe.

Yet this did not perturb Charles II who was anxious to be Louis' friend. His mother was a princess of France, and he had spent much of his exile there; he admired and envied the French king's power and secretly favoured his religion. Above all, his poverty led him to sell his friendship for French gold.

He displayed his friendship in several ways. In 1662 he married Catherine of Braganza, the daughter of the Portuguese king, who was an ally of France.[1] In the same year Dunkirk was sold to France for £400,000. Finally Charles married his sister, his adored Henrietta, to the duke of Orleans, Louis XIV's brother.

Charles' friendship with Louis XIV was unwise, because the French king was a threat to the peace and security of Europe. It was, however, only a continuance of Cromwell's policy, and it went hand-in-hand with Charles' dislike of the Dutch, a dislike which was shared by English merchants to whom the Dutch were old and hated trading rivals. On one thing king and parliament were agreed, that a war with the United Provinces was both necessary and desirable.

[1] Her dowry consisted of Tangier, which was abandoned in 1683, Bombay, and £800,000.

At first the king was intent upon the pursuit of pleasure, after his years in the wilderness. The task of government was left to the earl of Clarendon, who was honest, capable, and energetic. However he was unpopular. His almost-puritan morality was mocked by the easy-going courtiers. Parliament disliked him and the people mistrusted him. When he married his daughter Anne to James, duke of York, he was accused of ambition. When he sold Dunkirk to France many suspected that he had been bribed by the French to sell it, and that he had used the proceeds to build his fine mansion in Piccadilly. He became the scapegoat for all the shortcomings of the king's government.

The second Dutch war (1665-7) proved to be Clarendon's undoing. Although he was opposed to it, the merchants were anxious to strike another blow at their enemies. The war was not a success; and England was humiliated when the Dutch carried out a devastating raid on the fleet at Chatham. Parliament looked for a whipping-boy and found one in Clarendon. Charles was aware of his minister's unpopularity, and he was tired of the way Clarendon lectured him; so Clarendon was dismissed and parliament began to impeach him. Thereupon he went into exile in November 1667, and the last days of his life were spent in writing his *History of the Great Rebellion*.

THE SECOND DUTCH WAR: 1665-7

The second war with the Dutch was the result of commercial rivalry. Parliament had passed another Navigation Act in 1660, similar to that of 1651. English and Dutch merchants continued to clash in the East Indies, Africa, and North America, and in 1665 this friction led to war.

The early popularity of the war soon waned as merchants on both sides suffered heavy losses. The English war-fleet was not in good shape; although it had competent commanders in the duke of Albemarle (General Monck), Prince Rupert, and the duke of York, it had no one of the calibre of Blake or of the great Dutch sailor De Ruyter.

The English scored the first success when they crushed Opdam's fleet off Lowestoft (1665). In the same year they cornered De Ruyter, who was convoying a fleet home. He sheltered in the Norwegian harbour of Bergen. The king of Denmark, who also ruled Norway, allowed the English fleet to attack De Ruyter as

his ships lay at anchor.   However, a mistaken order caused the
Danish forts to fire on the English and drive them off.   The
following year saw the greatest battle of the war, when Albemarle
was defeated in a 4 day fight in the Channel.   He was quick to
recover and later in the year he gained a victory off North
Foreland.   Both sides were feeling the strain.   The Dutch were
short of money; London was demoralised by the plague (1665)
and the Great Fire (1666), and Charles' treasury was empty.   In
1667 he attempted to save money by laying up his warships at
Chatham.   The Dutch seized their opportunity; with great
daring they sailed up the Medway and created havoc among the
king's fleet.   Some ships they burned and others they towed
away including the great flagship, the Royal Charles.

The Medway disaster was the signal for the end of the war.
In July 1667 the Treaty of Breda was signed.   England gained
the New Netherlands, which she had captured during the war.
The Navigation Act was modified in favour of the Dutch, who in
return agreed to salute the English flag in the Channel.   The
treaty marked the end of the period of great economic rivalry
between the two countries.

THE POLICIES OF KING AND PARLIAMENT AFTER 1667

Despite the Treaty of Breda, Charles remained as hostile as
ever to the Dutch.   Whatever else may be said about his
behaviour, it cannot be denied that Charles cherished his
country's growing commerce and colonies.   He still feared the
economic strength of the United Provinces and hoped to secure
Louis' support in another war against them.

The attitude of parliament, the merchants, and the nation
was changing.   The second Dutch war had dampened their
desire for a further conflict with such doughty opponents.
Furthermore, the Treaty of Breda had settled the outstanding
differences between the two countries.   As Louis' power
increased, parliament became ever more concerned to check his
ambitions, and it saw the United Provinces as England's natural
ally.   Religion was an important consideration.   The Dutch
were protestants, whereas Louis XIV was an intolerant Roman
catholic who was busily persecuting the Huguenots.

Thus the year 1667 marked the parting of the ways: thereafter
parliament opposed France and favoured the United Provinces
while Charles remained a friend to Louis and an enemy of the

Dutch. It was parliament's policy that was most suited to the national interest for France was now the chief threat to England's security.

In 1668 Charles showed his skill as a politician, when he joined Sweden and the United Provinces in the Triple Alliance against Louis XIV who was at the time engaged in an invasion of the Spanish Netherlands. For Charles to oppose his friend, by allying with the Dutch whom he detested, may seem absurd. Yet his policy had not changed. By a show of strength he hoped to convince Louis that England's alliance was worth having. The ruse appeared to work. Louis seemingly bowed to the strength of the protestant alliance, ended his invasion of the Netherlands, and made peace with Spain. Shortly afterwards he opened negotiations for a treaty with Charles.

Now Louis turned his attention to the Dutch, whom he despised as protestants, merchants and republicans. In addition they had been his official allies against Spain in the past; yet they had joined a coalition against him. His vindictive nature would not rest until they had been punished; so Charles and Louis prepared to destroy the Dutch republic.

THE CABAL: 1667–73

When Clarendon fell, Charles made up his mind not to have another chief minister. Instead, he ruled with the aid of a committee, known as the Cabal from the initial letters of the ministers' surnames: Clifford, Arlington, Buckingham, Ashley Cooper and Lauderdale. It was a strange mixture of Roman catholics and men who once followed Oliver Cromwell. Sir Thomas Clifford was a papist of extreme opinions. He was willing to support any scheme, no matter how hare-brained, to restore his religion in England. The earl of Arlington was hostile to France. But he changed his opinions to please his king and finally became a papist. Buckingham, the son of Charles I's favourite, was bad-tempered and inconsistent:

> Stiff in opinions, always in the wrong,
> Was everything by starts and nothing long;
> But in the course of one revolving moon
> Was chymist, fiddler, statesman, and buffoon.
>
> *Dryden*

Ashley Cooper was able, and tolerant in religious matters. He was also unreliable and ambitious, dangerous and vindictive. He had served Charles I, deserted to parliament, and become a royalist again in 1660. Finally there was Earl Lauderdale, an ex-covenanter who was put in charge of Scottish affairs.

These unscrupulous and self-seeking men were Charles' chief advisers for the next 6 years. But he conducted foreign policy himself and did not always confide in them. Nor did the members of the Cabal act together. They were bound together only by their dislike of the Dutch and their loyalty to the king, who consulted them individually.

THE THIRD DUTCH WAR

Between 1667 and 1674 Charles pursued a policy which was designed to achieve those objects nearest to his heart: a war to annihilate the Dutch republic, toleration for the catholics, and a French pension which would free him from parliament. To this end he signed the Treaty of Dover with France, in June 1670, after long negotiations with his sister Henrietta Maria. The two kings agreed to conquer and partition the United Provinces. England was to provide a fleet and soldiers; in return she would receive Walcheren, Sluys and Kadzand. Charles was to declare himself a Roman catholic, when a suitable opportunity presented itself; Louis promised to give him £150,000 and six thousand French soldiers with which to quell any opposition which might arise. If this scheme had been revealed, it might have swept Charles from his throne. Parliament hated and feared popery, and it had executed his father for attempting to destroy the liberties of his subjects. Charles took every precaution. Only two members of the Cabal, Clifford and Arlington, were parties to the agreement. In order to deceive the nation, parliament, and his other ministers, this treaty remained a secret; Charles made public a bogus treaty which dealt solely with the plans for the proposed war.

Louis invaded the United Provinces in March 1672, and Charles' fleet also entered the war. Everything pointed to a quick victory. Nevertheless, the two kings failed to achieve their ends. The Dutch bravely resisted the invasion of their country; by opening the dykes they marooned the French army. William of Orange came forward as his country's saviour. He proved to be a great diplomat, for he organised a great coalition of States against Louis. Instead of gaining an easy success, the

French king found himself involved in a general war against half of Europe.

Meanwhile Charles II issued a Declaration of Indulgence in England (1672). He suspended all the penal laws against the catholics and nonconformists, who were granted freedom of worship. It seems unlikely that he intended to establish popery by force. He was sensible enough to realise that the use of French troops would only cause civil war and might lose him his throne. It is understandable, however, that his subjects should suspect the worst. His alliance with Louis XIV, the presence of papists on his council, the command of the fleet in the hands of his catholic brother: everything pointed to the apparent fact that the war was a cover for an attempt to restore Roman catholicism.

When parliament met in 1673 it displayed a profound suspicion of his intentions. Although it voted him £1,200,000 for the war, it compelled him to withdraw the Declaration of Indulgence. It also passed the Test Act (1673). This required the holder of any public office to take the oath of supremacy, to take communion in accordance with the rites of the Anglican Church, and to condemn the Roman catholic doctrine of transubstantiation. Few papists would do this; the duke of York resigned as lord high admiral and Clifford was obliged to leave the government. Shortly afterwards Ashley Cooper, who had been created earl of Shaftesbury in 1672, was dismissed. He had supported the war against the Dutch for economic reasons. But he was furious when he found out that he had been deceived over the secret Treaty of Dover. As an act of revenge he supported the passing of the Test Act, so Charles deprived him of his office. The Cabal collapsed, and Shaftesbury became the leader of the opposition to the king. There was nothing left for the government to do, but to make peace. By the Treaty of Westminster, in 1674, Charles could get nothing better than £180,000 from the Dutch, although the war had cost him £6,000,000.

The third Dutch war had an important effect on English politics:

(*1*) Although Charles' military alliance with France came to an end, he did not change his policy. Instead, he pursued it in secret, receiving a pension from Louis, in return for which he kept England neutral.

11

(*2*) England had given a clear indication that she would not allow her king to thrust popery on her; she would not even tolerate freedom of worship for the catholics. Charles, who was always ready to learn lessons from his experiences, gave up the attempt, although his private religious convictions remained the same.

(*3*) From 1674 can be dated the growth of a serious opposition to the king. It was centred upon Shaftesbury's 'country party', which hated and feared the twin threats of France and popery.

CHARLES II'S SECRET FRENCH POLICY: 1674-8

After the break-up of the Cabal in 1673, Charles appointed Thomas Osborne, the earl of Danby, to be his chief minister. Danby was a loyal cavalier who served his master well, putting the government's finances in good order and paying off its debts. He realised that the king could not govern properly unless he gained the co-operation of parliament. Therefore he used bribes to build up a following of 'king's friends' in the commons.

In foreign affairs Danby was hostile to France. He hoped to persuade Charles to adopt the protestant foreign policy which parliament favoured. To this end he arranged the marriage of Mary, the duke of York's eldest daughter, to William of Orange in 1677. However, the king was secretly conducting a policy quite different from Danby's. He was receiving money from Louis as the price of his neutrality, and whenever parliament pressed too hard for a war against France, he prorogued it. Thus England played no further part in Louis' war with the Dutch. The Treaty of Nymegen, which brought the war to an end in 1678, gave Louis further gains. England stirred uneasily at the sight of his continued success.

THE POPISH PLOT: 1678

It was now that the Popish Plot burst upon England. Most Englishmen had a lurking fear of Roman catholicism, some believed that the Fire of London had been the work of papists, and there were frequent rumours of French troops coming to restore the faith. Fear increased as Louis XIV grew stronger. The tense atmosphere engendered by this fear made even normally sane people believe the mixture of wild accusations and lies, which went to make up the Popish Plot.

The plot was invented by Titus Oates and Israel Tonge. Oates was an evil character who had changed his religion twice. He had been expelled from school and had failed to get a degree at Cambridge; later he had been turned out of a naval chaplaincy and then of a Jesuit college abroad. He had even been imprisoned for perjury. He returned to England masquerading as a doctor of divinity from the university of Salamanca in Spain, although he was now a 'good protestant'. His partner, Israel Tonge, was at least a genuine doctor of divinity from Oxford. Oates and Tonge placed before Sir Edmund Berry Godfrey, a justice of the peace at Westminster, details of a papist plot: the conspirators planned to assassinate the king, fire the City again, carry out a general massacre of protestants, and place the duke of York on the throne. Their story was clearly an invention, and some of their charges were fantastic. Charles II later questioned Oates and proved him to be a liar. But few men were as clear-headed as the king. People were ready to believe that there was a conspiracy, probably because they were willing to believe the worst of papists—Edmund Berry Godfrey, who was a devout protestant, certainly did. Shortly afterwards, however, he disappeared; later he was found, impaled on his own sword, in a ditch on Primrose Hill.

Godfrey's death was a lucky stroke indeed for Oates. Who else could have done this but the papists, in order to silence him? Panic spread. To Charles' amusement, cannons and soldiers were brought to Whitehall to guard him; less amusing was the witch-hunt for catholics which followed, one of the worst episodes of intolerance in English history.

The Popish Plot was a heaven sent opportunity for Shaftesbury. He knew that there was only one genuine plot: Charles II's plan to establish popery, the policy embodied in the secret Treaty of Dover. But it was the duke of York who presented the real threat to English protestants; he was heir to the throne and an avowed catholic. In order to discredit him Shaftesbury's country party stirred up popular hatred of the papists in London.

Titus Oates had a second stroke of good fortune, when he gained possession of letters belonging to Edward Coleman, the duchess of York's secretary. They showed that he had been in correspondence with the courts of Louis XIV and the pope; here seemed to be convincing evidence that the Popish Plot did exist. London gave way to a wave of anti-catholic madness.

Oates' accusations sent people to trial before the brutal lord chief justice, Scroggs. Three innocent labourers were condemned and executed for the murder of Godfrey; Edward Coleman, the aged Viscount Stafford, the saintly Roman catholic archbishop of Armagh and 7 Jesuits followed them to the scaffold. Altogether 35 men died between 1678 and 1681, victims to the wickedness of Titus Oates, the ambitions of Shaftesbury, and the blind hatred of popery.

Throughout the panic Charles II alone remained calm. But he was powerless to control events. The reign of terror had to run its course whilst he waited patiently for people to realise the folly of it all. His difficulties were increased in 1679, when the house of commons discovered that Danby had been corresponding with the French king. Although Danby had no love for France, he was also a loyal cavalier; against his wishes he had written to Louis about Charles' pension. The commons at once impeached him, but he was saved by the king who dissolved the Cavalier Parliament after a life of 18 years.

THE FIRST EXCLUSION PARLIAMENT: 1679

Charles foolishly imagined that an election might give him a more agreeable commons. Instead, the panic caused by the Popish Plot led the country to elect an overwhelming number of Shaftesbury's supporters. They imprisoned Danby in the Tower. But their chief intended victim, James, had wisely gone abroad. The king tried to conciliate Shaftesbury by bringing him into the government. But this did not prevent the country party from introducing a bill designed to exclude James from the succession. When it appeared likely that it would pass the commons, Charles dissolved parliament and dismissed Shaftesbury. The only useful piece of work done by this parliament was the passing of the Habeas Corpus Act, which required that anyone who was imprisoned should be brought to trial quickly. Thus the crown was prevented from detaining opponents in prison for a long time without a hearing.

THE SIGNIFICANCE OF THE EXCLUSION BILL

Until now Charles had not appeared as the open enemy of the country party. Indeed, as the Popish Plot was supposedly directed against him, Shaftesbury's men were, in effect, defending him. In fact they were entirely opposed to each other. Charles stood for popery, the French alliance, and legitimacy, but the country party proposed to deprive the catholic pro-French duke of York of his inheritance. Shaftesbury planned to do this by an exclusion bill, which would alter the succession in favour of a protestant.

However, he played into Charles' hands. He could have proposed that the duke of York be replaced by one of his two daughters, Mary and Anne. Mary, the wife of William of Orange, who was the great protestant champion and enemy of France, would have been a popular choice. Instead, Shaftesbury proposed the duke of Monmouth, an illegitimate son of the king by one Lucy Waters. Monmouth was a protestant, but he was vain, stupid, and self-seeking. Shaftesbury tried to strengthen the duke's claim by asserting that he was legitimate, and that the certificate of Charles' marriage to Lucy Waters was hidden in a mysterious black box. The nation was disinclined to believe the story. Furthermore, it was generally felt that, if James was to be excluded, it should be in favour of one of his daughters. Charles too would have none of it: though he adored his son, he sent him into exile.

As men grouped themselves around one or other of the two opponents, political parties came into being. Shaftesbury had for some time led a group known as the country party, because it represented the country against the party of the court. Its headquarters were in the Green Ribbon Club in the City, where it organised mob violence and distributed pamphlets against the king. It also petitioned him to summon parliament—and so its members became known as the 'petitioners'. Charles rallied round him a party of courtiers, men who upheld James' right to the throne and moderate people who were alienated by the violence of the country party. These men were known as 'abhorrers', because they abhorred (or detested) the petitions of their opponents. However, the two parties became popularly known as the whigs and the tories. These were originally terms of abuse: a whig was a humourless covenanter while a tory was an Irish Roman catholic robber. Yet it was these names which stuck. The whigs stood for exclusion, parliament, and protestantism (especially nonconformity); the tories represented legitimacy, the royal prerogative, and the Church of England.

THE SECOND EXCLUSION PARLIAMENT: 1680

Time was on Charles' side: as the panic of the previous months subsided, a feeling of shame and disgust spread. The false accusations of Titus Oates were seen for what they were, and the whigs' association with him discredited them too. By 1680 the extremists had had their day. The whigs did not give up and when parliament met in October 1680 they forced the exclusion bill through the commons. But the lords rejected it and Charles dissolved parliament.

THE THIRD EXCLUSION PARLIAMENT: 1681

Charles summoned a new parliament to meet in Oxford. This deprived Shaftesbury of the support of the City mob which had frightened members into following his lead. The whigs turned up armed to the teeth, with green ribbons in their hats, and guarded by armed followers. Charles was able to pose as the defender of law and order against the terrorism and violence of his opponents; as he told parliament, 'I have reason and law in my favour.' When the whigs prepared to bring in another exclusion bill, he once again dissolved parliament. It was his last, and it had only lasted a week.

CHARLES II'S PERSONAL RULE: 1681–5

When Charles dissolved the Oxford parliament, the tide was running strongly in his favour. The nation was now definitely hostile to Shaftesbury's party and its violent methods. Charles, who had waited patiently for this reaction, took advantage of it to strengthen his position. He ignored the Test Act and restored the duke of York to office. Faithful followers were promoted: one, Jeffreys, was made lord chief justice.

The king was determined to crush the whigs and nonconform-mists. Shaftesbury was tried for treason. Although he was acquitted, he deemed it wise to fly abroad, where he died in 1683. The government forced London and many other whig boroughs to surrender their charters, which were then remodelled to increase the king's control over them. The election of the governing corporations in these boroughs was now made subject to his approval. In this way he ensured that they would choose only his supporters to represent them in the commons. Charles had struck a shrewd blow at the whigs whose strength lay in the towns.

The extreme whigs, deprived of the constitutional means of opposing the king, turned to violence. In 1683 a number of them, including Monmouth and the earl of Essex, plotted to kill him as he returned to London from Newmarket. However, the 'Rye House plot', so called from the place where the king was to be surprised, was uncovered. Monmouth escaped, but many of the whig leaders were arrested. Essex committed suicide and Lord Russell and Algernon Sydney were executed—quite unjustly as it turned out, for they had not been involved in the plot—but they were prominent whigs and Charles seized the opportunity to be rid of them. The plot had strengthened the king's hand in several ways: he had removed the whig leaders, and 'whiggery' was now tainted with treason. He also took his revenge for the crimes of the Popish Plot: Titus Oates was imprisoned and many of his victims were freed.

Between 1681 and 1685 Charles went far along the road to personal rule. Louis XIV secretly paid him an annual pension. It enabled him to ignore the Triennial Act by which a parliament should have been summoned in 1684 and none met before his death in February 1685. On his death-bed he confessed to Father Huddleston, a priest who had sheltered him long ago after the battle of Worcester, and he was received back into the the Roman catholic Church.

The last 4 years of Charles' reign were a triumph for his skill, patience, and moderation. He had come to the throne in difficult circumstances; he had resisted attempts to reduce the royal prerogative even further; he had overcome formidable opposition from the whigs. Finally he had ensured that the crown would pass to his brother James, whom he left in a position of great strength:

(*1*) The opposition was broken and discredited.

(*2*) Any future parliament would contain a large number of the king's friends.

(*3*) With Jeffreys at the head of the law courts and with juries packed with royalists, the king could be sure of favourable verdicts in cases which concerned him.

(*4*) The king had a standing army at his disposal.

(*5*) Charles had shown that he could dispense with parliament for as long as he pleased, despite the Triennial Act.

Charles II's strength had rested on an alliance with those gentlemen who were tories (i.e. defenders of the king and the

Anglican Church). Whether James was successful or not would depend entirely on this alliance.

NOTES: THE GREAT PLAGUE AND THE FIRE OF LONDON

The Great Plague: 1665. The bubonic plague had scoured England periodically since 1349. No remedies were found. People fled before it if they could; otherwise they stayed—and many died. It took its toll in many towns and above all in London due to the prevalence of the black rat, which was the carrier of the disease. The great plague of 1665, although the last epidemic in London, caught the imagination of later generations because Samuel Pepys, John Evelyn, and others, witnessed it and recorded what they saw in diaries and journals.

As the plague spread rapidly during the spring a general exodus began: nobles, gentlemen and merchants fled with their servants and families; the king and his court moved to Oxford and then to Salisbury; many of the parish clergymen deserted their churches, their places being taken with great courage by the ejected nonconformist ministers. The rest of the people were left to face the plague. However, the archbishop of Canterbury stayed; so did the lord mayor and the duke of Albemarle, who was summoned by the king to keep order in the plague-stricken City.

London's streets were deserted. Business ground to a stand-still, industry and trade ceased, and ships were diverted to Amsterdam. Nothing could be done; the plague had to be left to work itself out. At its height during the summer, it claimed seven thousand victims in a week. It died down at the end of the year but revived in the following summer, by which time the victims probably numbered sixty thousand. It was then that the Great Fire purged London of the plague.

The Fire of London: 1666. The fire occurred in early September 1666, at the end of a long and dry summer. It began at the house of a baker, Farryner, in Pudding Lane. As a stiff easterly breeze drove the fire westwards, the Tudor city went up in flames and smoke. Pepys wrote, 'We stayed till, it being darkish, we saw the fire as only one entire arch of fire; it made me weep to see it. The churches, houses and all on fire and flaming at once.' It was only by blowing up enough houses to make a wide gap in its path, that the fire was stopped.

In 4 days the great conflagration swept through five-sixths of the City. It destroyed thirteen thousand five hundred houses, St. Paul's, 89 churches and the Royal Exchange, as well as schools, prisons, and hospitals. Nearly £10,000,000 worth of property was lost—£600,000 in rents alone. Few people were killed by the fire, but two hundred thousand were homeless. Many lost their entire wealth and were reduced to abject poverty.

At once plans were set on foot for rebuilding London. Some architects wanted to take this opportunity to erect a planned city. Sir Christopher Wren proposed Italian piazzas, fountains, and magnificent squares. Such schemes were rejected because of the cost and London was rebuilt on the old lines, with its warren of winding lanes and alleys. Parliament imposed a duty on coal to pay for new public buildings, but no help was given to house-owners who had to manage as best they could. Rapidly a new and finer city arose. The old dark wooden dwellings were replaced by taller houses, often of brick or stone. The fire rendered one great service: it cleansed London of the plague for the newer houses did not have the thatch and tapestry hangings that had harboured rats in the past. Wren had to content himself with erecting individual buildings; he built over 50 parish churches, 36 company halls, and St. Paul's. Indeed, it was Wren who was chiefly responsible for the beauty of the new City.

XXXIV

JAMES II : 1685–88

THERE was no resistance to the duke of York when he succeeded his brother as James II: most men recognised his hereditary right to the throne, no matter what their political opinions were, and there was widespread sympathy for him after the treatment he had suffered at the hands of the whigs. Yet in less than 4 years he lost his crown. The reason is to be found in the difference between the two brothers: Charles II, flexible and unscrupulous, above all a realist; James II, obstinate, bigoted, and blind to reality. Charles had learned a harsh lesson in 1672: that no matter how much he desired it, his subjects detested popery and would not allow him to impose it on them. He made no further attempt to do so, even during the years of his personal rule (1681–5). James ignored the lesson. He tried to repeat Charles' policy, as embodied in the secret Treaty of Dover—with disastrous consequences.

James was convinced that, as both the tories and Roman catholics were loyal to the throne, they were his natural allies. He ignored the fact that the tories were also devoted Anglicans, who hated popery as much as the nonconformists did. James' conviction was strengthened by his early successes.

His first parliament, which met in May 1685, was loyal and obedient due to the remodelling of borough charters. It voted him an annual revenue of £2,000,000 for life. This income was larger than any previous king's and it ended all his financial troubles.

Whilst parliament was still in session there came news of 2 whig rebellions. In Scotland the earl of Argyle rebelled in favour of Monmouth (May 1685), whilst in June Monmouth himself landed in Dorset and raised the flag of revolt. Large numbers of westcountrymen rallied to him: amongst them were nonconformists and poor or unemployed workers from the declining cloth industry.

Nevertheless, the revolts were doomed to failure. Although Argyle and Monmouth were whigs, they received no support from the nobles of their own party who preferred to play safe and remain loyal to the king. Thus their armies were largely undisciplined and badly-equipped rabbles, sorely lacking in cavalry. Argyle was quickly captured and executed. At first Monmouth appeared to be a real danger. His army of over four thousand marched through Devon into Somerset. There his way was barred by the king's army, encamped near the marshes of Sedgemoor. Monmouth attempted a night-attack, but it was ill-planned and confused—and the king's army cut the rebel force to pieces. Monmouth was captured and later executed (July 1685).

The government wrought a terrible revenge. Lord Chief

Justice Jeffreys went to the west country and presided over the trials of the rebels. His summary trials were known as the 'Bloody Assizes' because of the savage punishments which he meted out: one hundred and fifty were executed and eight hundred more were transported as slaves to the plantation of the West Indies. Jeffreys' brutality aroused deep resentment in the west—even loyal tories were surprised at his harshness. He became a hated and notorious figure—and has remained so ever since.

James took advantage of the rebellions to demand that he should have a standing army to defend him from further attacks. Parliament was willing enough. It was even prepared to permit a number of Roman catholic officers. But James wanted the repeal of the Test Act, so that all civil and military posts would be open to papists. When parliament refused, James prorogued it.

James acted foolishly, for his early successes had made him over-confident. The tories in parliament had been ready to give him money and even an army. But the Test Act gave them a monopoly of offices in Church and State. James was ignoring the fact that the tories were devoted to their Church as well as to their king. Furthermore, it was unfortunate for James that Louis XIV's persecution of Huguenots reached a peak in 1685. He revoked the Edict of Nantes which had protected their freedom of worship since 1598. To be a protestant in France was a criminal offence. Many Huguenots fled to England, bringing stories of brutal atrocities committed against them by Louis' catholic soldiery—and this at a time when James was trying to repeal the Test Act. It made a deep impression on Englishmen, as they watched their king advance popery.

As parliament would not give the king what he wanted he tried to achieve his ends without it. In Ireland an army of Roman catholics was created and the army which had been raised to defeat Monmouth was increased to sixteen thousand. It was encamped on Hounslow Heath, as if to over-awe London. James set about dismissing protestant officers and appointing papists. This was illegal, so long as the Test Act remained in force. However, the king's right to appoint Roman catholic officers was established by a test-case in the law courts. When Sir Edward Hales, a papist, was appointed governor of Dover, his right to hold the office was challenged. The judges decided in his favour. They argued that the king had the right to dispense with the law in certain cases. The appointment of papists to military offices now proceeded apace: the earl of Tyrconnel became commander of the Irish army and lord lieutenant of Ireland; Hales was made governor of the Tower; another papist, Sir Roger Strickland, was given command of the fleet.

The government, too, passed into the hands of the Roman catholics. At first Halifax had been James' chief minister. But he was an Anglican and no friend to France. James dismissed him when he refused to persuade parliament to repeal the Test Act (October 1685). After Hales' Case, the king removed the rest of his moderate ministers. Instead he gathered about him a group of catholics to govern the country—they included Judge Jeffreys and even a Jesuit, Edward Petre. His chief adviser, the earl of Sunderland, was an unscrupulous politician who became a Roman catholic in 1688.

James II did not stop there. He forced the colleges of Oxford and Cambridge to accept Roman catholic fellows. When the protestant dons of Magdalen College (Oxford) resisted, James dismissed 25 of them and put in papists in their stead. Oxford had always been loyal to the Stuarts. It had been Charles I's headquarters in the Civil War, and Charles II summoned the third 'exclusion parliament' there in preference to London (1681). But this act of James alienated the university.

The king was also driving the Anglican Church into opposition. It was clear that he was moving rapidly towards the establishment of Roman catholicism: monasteries were opened in London, and a papal legate was welcomed at his court. Finally a court of commission for ecclesiastical causes was set up with the power to suspend and excommunicate clergymen. It was the same—in all but name—as the court of high commission. In 1641 the latter had been abolished by an act which forbade the creation of any similar institution in the future. Sancroft, the archbishop of Canterbury, and Bishop Compton of London, aware that the new court was illegal, refused to be members of it.

By 1687 James had turned the nation against him. The old English fear of popery quickly revived. Here was a king bent on re-establishing it—and the Bloody Assizes had shown how ruthlessly he would work to that end. The fear was heightened by James' armies, officered as they were by papists. Englishmen remembered Louis XIV's brutal treatment of the Huguenots. Why else did James need an army if it was not to persecute his protestant subjects? More serious for James, he had undermined the crown's alliance with the tory gentry. His policy threatened the continued existence of the Church of England. Most of the bishops were arrayed against him and the tory gentlemen followed their lead.

James looked elsewhere for support. In April 1687 he issued the Declaration of Indulgence. It suspended the Test Act and all penal laws against the nonconformists and Roman catholics. In this way he hoped to forge a new alliance of popery and dissent against the Anglicans. This was what Charles II had attempted to do in 1672. But unlike his brother, James lacked caution and tact. His previous behaviour made the nonconformists suspect he wanted to use them for his own ends. James could have little love for them, for most of them were whigs. No doubt as soon as he had triumphed over the Anglicans he would turn on the nonconformists and attack them in turn. So they refused to rise to the bait—and only a few became the king's allies.

James was blind to the fact that the nonconformists were unlikely to support him. He decided to get parliament's approval for the Declaration—for then people would be less likely to criticise it. However, he knew that his first parliament still prorogued—would not give its approval. So he dissolved it (July 1687) and summoned a new one, to meet in November 1688. In the meantime more borough charters were remodelled to ensure a more compliant house of commons.

In May 1688 a second Declaration of Indulgence was issued. The king ordered the parish clergy to read it in their churches. The archbishop of Canterbury and 6 other bishops petitioned him to withdraw his declaration, on the ground that he had no right to suspend the penal laws. Subjects had always had the right to petition their king. Nonetheless James imprisoned them in the Tower and charged them with seditious libel.[1] In June the 'seven bishops' were brought to trial. They were acquitted. London went mad with joy. Even James' soldiers on Hounslow Heath threw their caps into the air and cheered. This was an ominous sign indeed.

In the interval between the imprisonment and trial of the 7

[1] James thought that the petition was 'a call to rebellion'.

bishops a son was born to James and his second wife, Mary of Modena.[1] It changed the whole course of events. Until then James had been without a male heir, so after his death the crown would have passed to the protestant champion, William of Orange. Much as they had come to detest James' policies the English expected that on his death the rule of popery would come to an end. The birth of a prince changed all that: men had visions of a permanent Roman catholic regime under James' descendants. In desperation 7 men wrote to William of Orange inviting him to invade England to protect its political liberties and the protestant religion. Amongst them were 2 whigs, a Russell and a Sydney, a staunch tory, Danby, and a bishop, Compton of London; what better proof that James had united the country against him?

William accepted the invitation and prepared to invade England. However, there was one serious problem: what would Louis XIV do? Louis' relations with James were less friendly than they had been with Charles II. James had disliked his brother's dependence on a French pension and he preferred to be independent. Nevertheless Louis realised that, if William's invasion was successful, the two greatest maritime powers in Europe would be united against him. He warned the Dutch that an attack on England would mean war with France. But Louis was bluffing. He was preparing for a war in Germany and he could spare no forces to throw against the Dutch. In the summer of 1688 Louis' armies invaded Germany. Now William could safely go ahead with his plans.

News of William's warlike preparations alarmed James II. He took steps to restore his earlier good relations with the Anglicans. He promised to summon a new parliament from which Roman catholics would be excluded; and a protestant was appointed to command the fleet. As the prospect of French support faded and signs of disloyalty multiplied around him, James desperately carried out further measures to conciliate his subjects. The boroughs received back their old municipal charters. Many papists were removed from civil and military posts, and the ecclesiastical commission was abolished. However, the country was unimpressed by concessions which were made out of fear.

[1] His first wife Anne, daughter of the earl of Clarendon, having died The prince, christened James, is known in history as the 'Old Pretender'.

In late October William of Orange set sail. On 5 November he landed at Brixham in Devon—he carefully chose the west country which, with its memories of the Bloody Assizes, was hostile to James. With an army of eleven thousand foot and four thousand horse he slowly advanced towards London. Gentlemen, nobles, and clergy, men of all sorts and conditions rallied to William. In Yorkshire Danby raised revolt in his support; Cheshire and Nottinghamshire rebelled too.

James was not without courage. He prepared to resist William's advance at Salisbury. But his army's loyalty was doubtful—and at last he decided to retreat in order to defend London. Thereupon John Churchill, the king's best military commander, deserted to the advancing enemy; so did more peers, captains, even his daughter Princess Anne. Only a handful of catholics remained loyal.

As William advanced on London, James decided on flight. He sent his wife and infant prince on ahead to France. Then he fled too. It was a foolish move. If he had stayed and negotiated, he might have preserved his crown with some vestige of power. His flight meant that he had given up his responsibilities as king. He left his capital in a state of near-anarchy. The London mob plundered at will, attacked papists' houses, and nearly lynched Judge Jeffreys. William had to take charge of the government to restore law and order.

However, James did not leave England. He was caught by some Kentish fishermen and brought back to London. His presence was an embarrassment to William who wished to be rid of him. So he was allowed to escape a second time. No one stopped him as he embarked on a waiting ship, and on Christmas day in 1688 he arrived in France. England's king had gone and fateful questions of government had now to be decided.

XXXV

THE REVOLUTION SETTLEMENT

IN James II's absence, a group of nobles summoned a Convention Parliament, which met in February 1689, sat for three weeks, and during that time made a constitutional settlement.

The Convention's first task was to explain the recent events in terms which would satisfy all parties. After prolonged discussion a compromise was reached. The Convention declared that James (and his 'evil counsellors') had tried to destroy the protestant religion and the liberties of Englishmen; having failed to do so, he had fled the country and therefore had abdicated. It did not matter that this was not true. The whigs were happy, because it recognised that James was no longer king, whilst abdication suggested that he had not been forced to give up the throne—and so the tories too were satisfied.

THE BILL (OR DECLARATION) OF RIGHTS

The Convention next drew up and passed the Declaration of Rights. It contained no statements of theory or principle; it was a practical document which dealt with immediate needs only. Thus it redressed the many grievances caused by James II's behaviour: it condemned the suspending power, and the dispensing power 'as it hath been exercised of late'; the king was forbidden to raise a standing army in peace-time without parliament's consent; it abolished the court of ecclesiastical commission; the government was not allowed to impose cruel or unusual punishments, or fines which were too heavy; no taxes were to be imposed except by parliament. The liberties of the subject were safeguarded: frequent parliaments were to be held; elections were to be free; members of parliament were to have freedom of speech; protestants could possess weapons for their defence; subjects had the right to petition the king. The Declaration also made two radical changes: in future the crown could only be inherited by a protestant and all subjects might be required to take an oath of allegiance to the monarch.

It only remained for the Convention to offer William and Mary the crown, which they accepted together with the Declaration of Rights. They were declared to be king and queen. The crown was to pass to their heirs, failing which it would go to James II's other daughter, Anne. The Convention was dissolved and William called a genuine parliament, which confirmed the Declaration of Rights.

This was the sum total of changes which were made in the year of revolution. No one put forward theories about the powers and position of the new king (e.g. whether he held his throne by divine right or by the consent of parliament); awkward problems were ignored. In this way the men of the Convention avoided doing anything which might have caused a split between the whigs and tories. The majority of Englishmen approved of the Revolution. Only a few remained hostile: the devoted supporters of James II, henceforth known as the Jacobites, regarded William III as a usurper; the radicals, who had hoped to see the vote given to more people, were disappointed when power remained in the hands of the nobles, gentlemen, and merchants.

Much had been left unsaid. In the following years problems were dealt with as they arose, in some cases by statute, in others by a common understanding between king and parliament about the best way to get round a difficulty.

THE SUPREMACY OF PARLIAMENT

The Declaration of Rights forbade the king to raise a standing army in peace-time. But when Louis XIV recognised James II as the rightful king of England, it meant war in defence of the Revolution. The war lasted from 1689 to 1697, during which time William III needed a large army and navy. Parliament was as anxious as the king to preserve the recent settlement. It passed the Mutiny Act, which gave him the power to enforce military discipline. However, the law was only valid for 6 months, so frequent parliaments were necessary to renew it regularly. Furthermore, the Triennial Act (1694) required that no more than 3 years should pass without parliament being summoned, and that the life of a parliament should not extend beyond 3 years. Thus parliament had become a regular part of the constitution.

Parliament controlled the king, because it controlled his

money. The government's finances were modernised. William was given a civil list of £700,000 a year for life. From this he had to meet his personal expenses and the ordinary costs of government. Extra needs were satisfied by parliamentary grants. William was unable to wage war without its help. Thus it could control foreign affairs by simply refusing to pay for policies which it disliked. It should be noted, too, that the commons were now very much more important than the upper house. When, after the Revolution, they successfully denied the right of the house of lords to tamper with money bills, finance became solely their concern.

The commons exercised a greater degree of control over the administration. In the past many of their grants had been misspent. From 1690 onwards, however, the commons appropriated money for particular purposes, and they appointed commissioners to audit the king's accounts, thus ensuring that money was spent for the purpose for which it was voted. Gradually parliament was able to force the monarch to bend to its will. He hesitated to veto bills, for fear of offending it: William did so but rarely; Anne did so once, in 1707; thereafter it was never used again.

As parliament's control over the king increased, so the government's control over the subject decreased. The Licensing Act had strictly censored all publications in England. Printing presses were only permitted in London, Oxford, and Cambridge and no book could be printed unless it was licensed by a censor. However, when the Act lapsed in 1695 it was not renewed. The government's right to censor books had gone, and the freedom of the Press was limited only by the libel laws. Furthermore, a new Treason Act in 1696 gave the prisoner a better chance, for it ruled that proof of treason required 2 witnesses, not one as before.

THE TOLERATION ACT: 1689

The whigs and tories felt themselves bound to reward the nonconformists for their refusal to support James II. In 1689 they passed the Toleration Act. Nonconformists were still excluded from public offices, because the Test Act remained in force. But freedom of worship was granted to all those who accepted 34 of the Thirty-nine Articles, condemned popery, and took an oath recognising William as head of the Anglican

Church. Most of the nonconformists did so, and though they still suffered from disabilities they were free from the government's interference in their worship. The Anglicans kept their monopoly of public offices, but they had lost their monopoly in religion. They were not even united. Over four hundred clergymen, including several bishops, felt that, as they had previously sworn an oath of allegiance to James II at his coronation, they could not now take a fresh oath to William and Mary. These men, known as non-jurors, gave up their livings to men who were willing to do so.

THE ACT OF SETTLEMENT: 1701

The object of this Act was to settle the succession. Mary died childless in 1694. As William had no heirs the crown would pass to Princess Anne, but all her children had died. James II was still alive, but of course his claim was unacceptable. Indeed it was his claim that made the succession an urgent problem: a protestant heir must be named to avoid a disputed succession—from which James might profit—and to prevent the Jacobites from attempting to restore him. The best protestant claimant was Sophia, wife of the elector of Hanover. She was the daughter of Elizabeth, the tragic wife of Elector Frederick of the Palatinate—and therefore the grand-daughter of James I. The Act of Settlement settled the crown on Sophia and her descendants.

Parliament took the opportunity to insert some clauses which placed more restrictions on the king. In future he was to be an Anglican. After Anne's reign, England would not fight wars to defend the monarch's foreign possessions, unless parliament consented—this was aimed at William and his concern for the United Provinces. The monarch was not to leave the country without parliament's consent—this, too, was directed at William. In future foreigners were forbidden to sit in the privy council or to receive estates from the king. These clauses were no doubt inspired by dislike of William's Dutch advisers. No officeholder or pensioner of the king could sit in parliament. This was designed to prevent William from influencing it. It would have been disastrous if this had remained in effect, because it would have prevented ministers from explaining their policies to parliament; as a result it might have produced a deadlock between the executive and legislature, akin to that of Charles I's reign. Fortunately most of these clauses never came into force but were repealed before 1714.

Two changes were permanent: (*1*) Ministers who were impeached could not be saved by a royal pardon. Thus parliament established that the king's ministers were responsible to it. (*2*) Judges were to be appointed by the king as before, but they were to hold office 'during good behaviour', not for so long as it pleased him. In future a judge could only be removed by a petition from the lords and commons to the king. At last the judges became independent of the government, whilst the monarch lost a right which James I and Charles I had found so valuable.

THE SIGNIFICANCE OF THE REVOLUTION

It might be argued that James II alone had been guilty of attempting a revolution. He had tried to undermine the existing laws, in order to make himself absolute and to bring back Roman catholicism. The so-called 'Glorious Revolution' of 1688 was simply an act taken by the propertied classes to protect their rights and restore the laws as they had been.

Although the Declaration of Rights placed restrictions on the king, he was left with a good deal of authority: he was commander of the army and navy; he could choose and dismiss his ministers; foreign affairs, war, and the colonies were his concern. But in the years that followed he became completely dependent on parliament, and his power gradually diminished. Parliament was the new sovereign.

The king's new position was that set out by John Locke in his book *Essay of Civil Government*. Locke was a whig and the earl of Shaftesbury's adviser. He rejected divine right. Instead, he claimed that government was based on a kind of contract. The people had entrusted the government of the country to a king. They promised to obey him on condition that he ruled for the good of them all.[1] If he broke the contract and ruled only in the interest of a few (as James II did for the papists), the people need no longer obey him. Locke's theory, which was adopted by the whigs, triumphed in 1688; when James failed to observe the contract, the nation chose William in his place. William and Mary became rulers, not by divine right, but by the consent of parliament.

[1] By 'people', Locke meant only those who owned property.

The Revolution appeared to involve no more than a change of kings and a Bill of Rights, which was designed to remove some recent grievances. In fact, it was much more than that. It was the final shift of power from the king to the propertied classes. The seventeenth century had witnessed a long, drawn-out struggle between king and parliament, between prerogative and statute. The Revolution of 1688 resolved the conflict in favour of parliament, and of the traditional ruling class of nobles, gentlemen, and great merchants who sat in it.

IRELAND AND THE REVOLUTION: 1660–89

(*1*) *Charles II's reign.* The reign was one of peace, and steady improvement in agriculture. However, Ireland was economically backward; it had few raw materials and few industries; although it sent cattle and dairy products to England, the export trade was controlled by English merchants. Ormonde tried to develop the Irish woollen and linen industries, but without success. Furthermore, Ireland lost the free trade which it had enjoyed in Cromwell's time. In 1666 English farmers, afraid of competition, persuaded parliament to forbid imports of Irish cattle and dairy produce. Later the Irish were excluded from the important fishing grounds. England's economic policy was a purely selfish one, conducted in the interests of its own merchants.

Ireland was occasionally affected by English politics. When the Test Act was passed, a number of catholics were removed from the corporations. The archbishop of Armagh fell a victim to the Popish Plot. But for the most part, the lot of the catholics improved.

(*2*) *James II's reign.* Under a papist king the catholics naturally came into their own. The earl of Tyrconnel built up a catholic army; in 1687 he replaced the Anglican earl of Clarendon as lord lieutenant. The corporations were remodelled as in England. Catholics were admitted to the professions; they had religious toleration; by 1687 the Irish government was in their hands.

(*3*) *The Revolution.* When James II fled from England, he retained the support of Tyrconnel and the Irish catholics; so it was to Ireland that he came with French troops in March 1689. His hopes were dashed when William defeated him at the battle of the Boyne in the following year. He hurried back to France, whilst William's soldiers subjugated the rest of the country.

Thereafter Ireland was treated as a colony to be governed in the interest of England, or at least of the Irish protestant ruling class. That ruling class was a minority which always lived in fear of a catholic rising and it protected itself by harsh penal laws, passed by the Irish and English parliaments in which only protestants could sit. The seventeenth century had served only to magnify the 2 basic problems of land and religion; an irreconcilable gulf had opened between the native Irish and their English masters.

XXXVI

SCOTLAND: FROM RESTORATION TO REVOLUTION

SCOTLAND AND THE RESTORATION: 1660–7

THE Scots played no part in the events which followed the death of Oliver Cromwell in 1658. They did not stir even when General Monck marched from Scotland to London to put an end to military rule. Nevertheless they supported the Restoration. They were tired of being ruled by covenanters and English soldiers, and they welcomed the return of the king and their own parliament.

Three outstanding problems needed to be solved:

(*1*) *Anglo-Scottish relations.* Between 1603 and 1643 the 2 countries, though linked through their Stuart kings, had remained independent of each other. Each country had its own parliament, law-courts, and form of Church. The Solemn League and Covenant, and later Cromwell's victory at Dunbar, had brought England and Scotland together in a closer union, but this now came to an end. The Scottish parliament was revived and it repealed all the acts passed by it since 1633. Thus the Scots regained their independence but lost the free trade which they had enjoyed under Cromwell.

(2) The king's position in Scotland. Charles II aimed at an undisputed control of Scottish affairs. He ruled through a secretary (in London), a commissioner and a privy council (in Edinburgh), and the parliament (which he manipulated). He was so successful that royal rule in Scotland was unquestioned until the Revolution.

(3) The religious settlement. Charles II restored episcopacy (government of the Church by bishops) as it had existed before his father introduced the Anglican Prayer-Book into Scotland. The presbyterian general assembly was abolished, and the bishops took their seats in parliament once more. If he had let matters rest here, all might have been well. However, the presbyterians were not left to worship in their own way. They were forbidden to hold conventicles (religious services in private houses) and in 1662 the Covenant was condemned. All ministers were required to be reinstituted by the bishops; when two hundred and seventy refused, they were expelled from their livings. An act of 1663 imposed fines on presbyterian recusants. And the ejected ministers were forbidden to return to their former parishes. They did not take kindly to persecution. In the south-west of Scotland there were many extreme covenanters, who turned out in large numbers to hold their services in the fields. Others took part in a revolt, the Pentland Rising, in 1666, which was, however, easily put down by the government.

THE EARL OF LAUDERDALE: 1667–79

In 1667 Charles II appointed Lauderdale to be his secretary for Scottish affairs. An ex-covenanter himself, Lauderdale adopted a mild and conciliatory policy towards the presbyterians. In 1669 and 1672 Declarations of Indulgence were issued, allowing many expelled ministers to take up their livings again. Two years later a proclamation pardoned them for past offences. Unfortunately, Lauderdale was not dealing with moderate men but with fanatics who denounced him because he upheld the royal supremacy. When they went armed to the open-air services, Lauderdale feared that they were intent on rebellion. He abandoned his attempt to reconcile them and fell back on the old policy of harsh suppression. Several thousand highlanders were sent to the south-west to maintain law and order. Instead they made matters worse by plundering and killing (1678).

Force was met with force. James Sharp, archbishop of St. Andrews, was a covenanter-turned-bishop and now a savage persecutor of those with whom he had once worshipped. In 1679 he was dragged from his coach and hacked to pieces by some fanatics. Shortly afterwards a body of covenanters rebelled in the south-west. At Drumclog in Lanarkshire they defeated a government force under John Graham of Claverhouse. However, their success was short-lived, because their army was destroyed at Bothwell Brig by the duke of Monmouth. Victory was followed by a brief reign of terror: 7 leaders were executed and hundreds of their followers were sent as slaves to the plantations of the West Indies. Lauderdale's policy, at first conciliatory then repressive, had failed, so Charles appointed the duke of York in his place.

'THE KILLING TIME'

James ruled with a firm hand. He seized the opportunity to secure his own rights for the future. Thus parliament was persuaded to pass 2 acts: one recognised his right to the throne, the other required all office-holders to take an oath accepting protestantism and the royal supremacy and condemning the Covenant. When James returned to England in 1682 most of Scotland was firmly under royal control. The only exception was the south-west, where the protestant extremists had not been subdued. Led by a preacher, Richard Cameron (and therefore known as the Cameronians), they renounced their loyalty to Charles II and conducted a brutal campaign of violence against government officers. The government retaliated. Dragoons were ordered to shoot them on sight. In a clash Cameron was killed, but his followers fought on. So widespread was the violence that these closing years of Charles II's reign became known as 'the killing time'.

CHARLES II'S REIGN: AN ASSESSMENT

Charles II's reign was a sorry story of intolerance and bloodshed, yet it was not without its achievements. There were reforms in the law (including a new high court in 1671), and poor laws were passed in 1663 and 1672. The Scots also helped to colonise North America. In 1621 their attempt to establish the settlement of Nova Scotia had failed. Thereafter, interest in colonising projects lapsed, and the only Scots who went to

America did not do so of their own free will. After Cromwell's victories at Dunbar and Worcester hundreds of prisoners were transported to work on the plantations. In Charles II's reign paupers and vagabonds were rounded up and shipped to America, along with more rebels after Bothwell Brig. By then others were going of their own accord: covenanters avoiding persecution, and adventurers seeking their fortunes. Colonising projects were revived. In 1682 East New Jersey was founded; in the south the presbyterian settlement of Stuart's Town was established. Although the latter was destroyed by the Spaniards 2 years later, the northern colony flourished.

JAMES VII[1]: 1685–8

The Scots offered no resistance to the duke of York when he became king, despite his religion. They remained loyal to him when the earl of Argyle led a rebellion on Monmouth's behalf. Argyle failed and was executed; his followers were shipped off to America. Parliament displayed its loyalty by voting James the excise forever. However, it refused to grant toleration to the Roman catholics and for a while James had to content himself with persecuting the Cameronians.

Nevertheless he was determined to advance his faith. Protestant officials were dismissed and Roman catholics were appointed in their place. He treated the towns in peremptory fashion, simply choosing their governing councillors himself. It was not long before Scotland was seething with discontent. In 1687 James tried to form an alliance with the nonconformists in both his realms. Two Declarations of Indulgence were issued, giving toleration to all including catholics and presbyterians. However, the presbyterians, like their dissenting counterparts in England, did not respond. By 1688 James' government was supported by only a minority of catholics and devoted royalists.

SCOTLAND AND THE REVOLUTION

The Scots took no active part in the Revolution. Only when William had been proclaimed king of England did the Scots act. William summoned a convention of estates to Edinburgh in March 1689. This assembly declared that, as James had forfeited the throne, William and Mary were the rightful king and queen

1 He was James II of England but VII of Scotland.

THE HOUSE OF HAPSBURG

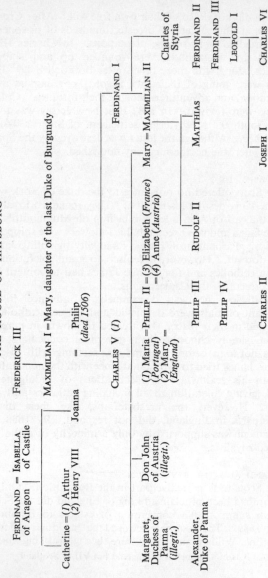

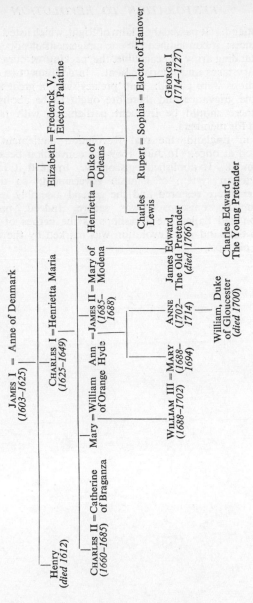

THE HOUSE OF STUART

JAMES I = Anne of Denmark
(1603–1625)

├── Henry *(died 1612)*
├── CHARLES I = Henrietta Maria *(1625–1649)*
└── Elizabeth = Frederick V, Elector Palatine

CHARLES I = Henrietta Maria
├── CHARLES II = Catherine of Braganza *(1660–1685)*
├── Mary = William of Orange
├── JAMES II = Ann(e) Hyde / Mary of Modena *(1685–1688)*
└── Henrietta = Duke of Orleans

Elizabeth = Frederick V, Elector Palatine
├── Charles Lewis
├── Henrietta = Duke of Orleans
└── Rupert = Sophia = Elector of Hanover

├── WILLIAM III = MARY *(1688–1702)* *(1688–1694)*
├── ANNE *(1702–1714)*
└── James Edward, The Old Pretender *(died 1766)*

Sophia = Elector of Hanover
└── GEORGE I *(1714–1727)*

William, Duke of Gloucester *(died 1700)*

Charles Edward, The Young Pretender

of Scotland.   It passed the Claim of Right, which listed Scotland's grievances: it condemned the encouragement of popery, the use of a standing army in peacetime, the 'packing' of burgh councils, arbitrary taxes and imprisonment.   In addition, two important resolutions were passed: that 'prelacy' was 'a great and insupportable grievance and therefore ought to be abolished', and that there should be frequent parliaments with freedom of speech for members.

As in England, the real Revolution Settlement was not achieved at once.   In June 1689 the convention became a real parliament.   It abolished episcopacy.   In 1690 it revived the presbyterian system of Church government;   so the ejected ministers were restored and the general assembly reappeared. In England episcopacy was secure.   Indeed, presbyterian London had hailed the 7 bishops as the heroes of the hour. But in Scotland the Revolution was marked by the overthrow of the bishops.

STUART ENGLAND

XXXVII

ECONOMIC LIFE IN THE SEVENTEENTH CENTURY

THE LAND

(*1*) *The price[1] rise.* The price rise which began in Tudor times continued until about 1640; during this time the same conditions prevailed as under the Tudors: producers benefited, but consumers suffered. Landlords were amongst the hardest hit, unless they could rack-rent, evict, and enclose. Some of the peers did so, and so increased their wealth. Furthermore, their numbers grew. James I created 60, and his son 30; some bought their titles, and others received them because they were the king's friends; few earned them. A number were rich merchants who helped to make the peerage a wealthier class. Below them the gentry prospered, though a few got into financial difficulties. Below them in turn came the yeomen and small farmers who had never been so prosperous. This is true only of the freeholders amongst them. Copyholders were less fortunate, and customary tenants were completely at the mercy of their landlords. Some of them saw their precious grazing lands enclosed while others were evicted. The number of yeomen fell at the same time as their class became richer and more important.

(*2*) *Enclosure and eviction.* Tudor landlords evicted and enclosed in order to obtain more land for sheep; this resulted in depopulated villages, more vagabonds, and less land available for growing wheat. By 1600, however, the boom in wool was

---

[1] The various technical terms used here are explained in Chapter XVII, 'The Price Rise.'

over, and it was less profitable to rear sheep. Landowners now enclosed for arable farming; enclosure meant greater efficiency, and the chance to experiment with new crops. Dispossessed peasants were still needed to till the land. Thus the old arguments against enclosure no longer applied. In any case the gentry would not enforce the many Tudor acts against it. In 1624 they were repealed—a sign that the government's attitude to the problem had changed. Although the old Tudor policy was briefly revived during Charles I's 11 years' personal rule, when Archbishop Laud fined enclosers, this ended in 1640. Thereafter landlords were helped rather than hindered by parliament in their attempts to evict and enclose. Nevertheless, most of England's open fields survived until the eighteenth and nineteenth centuries. In Stuart times more energy was devoted to draining fenlands and marshes, such as Sedgemoor and the great fens which stretched from Lincolnshire to Cambridgeshire.

(3) *Land and the Great Rebellion:* 1640–60. The Great Rebellion had two important effects. First, until 1640 the king had resisted the attempts of landowners to make their estates more productive and efficient. When his cause was overthrown, the gentlemen, yeomen, and the many merchants who bought land were free to apply business methods to farming. This harmed the copyholder (who was often evicted), and the wage-labourer (whose wages were kept low), but it made farming more efficient, and increased the nation's yield of food.

Secondly, much of England's farmlands changed hands. The estates of the king, the Church, and many royalists were confiscated and sold. Many other royalists had to sell their lands in order to pay the heavy fines which were imposed on them. In 1660 confiscated estates were restored to their original owners. But those who had been obliged to sell their lands lost everything. They were replaced by new men, who had purchased property during the 1650's—many of them were merchants, who brought plenty of money and a businesslike approach to farming. These new squires were not paternal and benevolent like many of the old ones. They did not care for the interests of their tenants and labourers and their wives did not visit the poor and nurse the sick. They cared only that their estates gave them a profit and a social position.

(4) *Landowners after the Restoration.* The Restoration benefited big landowners. First, feudal dues were abolished,

thus freeing their lands from irksome payments to the king. Secondly, the landlord's right to evict copyhold tenants was established. Thirdly, the Tudors and the early Stuarts had protected the consumer, and the small man who farmed for subsistence, but now parliament protected the man who grew food in order to sell it. Farmers were allowed to store corn, and sell it when it was scarce and prices had risen—this had been an offence in Tudor times. In order to encourage them to grow more, bounties on exported wheat were introduced (1673), the duty on corn exports ended (1689), and duties were imposed on imported wheat. More land was brought under cultivation, forests were cleared, fenlands were drained and the fen-dwellers evicted. Old and deplorable practices such as rack-renting and evicting were approved.

These changes had their bad effects. Copyhold tenants often became wage-labourers. Even if they owned their land small farmers declined or were driven out of business: they did not have the money to make improvements; they had no reserves to sustain them through bad times, and the land tax added to their troubles. The changes had their good side too. Men saw the profits to be made from farming, now that it was free from the restrictions which had hampered it in the past, so they were willing to invest their money in it. Bigger and therefore more efficient estates were formed, on which it was possible to experiment more freely with sainfoin, clover, and new and better varieties of peas and beans. East Anglian farmers, in contact with the Dutch who were advanced in these matters, grew turnips and clover. The so-called Agrarian Revolution of the eighteenth century had already begun.

INDUSTRY

England's industries were still organised in a variety of ways. Some articles were made at home by the family for its own use. The small craftsman still made his wares in his workshop, and sold them in his shop. But these were declining. More important were the domestic and factory systems. The latter was the system of the future: by collecting the necessary machinery and labour force under one roof, a manufacturer could cut down his expenses and save time. However, this required bigger sums of capital than the small master-craftsmen were able to provide. Many of the newer industries involved expensive operations, such as smelting iron, refining salt, and sinking shafts for coal-mines as the exposed seams were exhausted. Such enterprises could only be run by rich merchants.

The cloth industry, which was still the most important industry in England, was scattered throughout the country, but was particularly important in the West Riding, Wales, the West Country, and East Anglia. Some districts made fine cloth, others 'the new drapery' (a coarse cloth made from flax and cotton). It was organised in several different ways: 'one-man businesses', factories, and especially the domestic or 'putting-out'[1] system. The Merchant Adventurers of London, who already controlled the export of cloth, were extending their control over the industry too, providing the capital and operating the putting-out system.

These developments involved changes in the relationship between employer and employee. In the Middle Ages, the master-craftsmen worked alongside his journeymen and apprentices, who lived with him as members of his family. The entrepreneur, however, organised his business but left the manual work to his employees. His sole concern was to get the maximum amount of work from them. There was more specialisation too. Fewer men made and sold their goods. Instead, it was becoming common for one man to do one job: the hired hand who made the goods, the employer who hired him, the shop-keeper who sold them, the merchants who exported them, and the goldsmiths who provided the capital. Yet we must not exaggerate these changes: they were not of major importance until the eighteenth century.

Conditions (such as the price rise and a bigger home market) were suitable for the growth of industries (e.g. cloth, iron, coal-mining). But there were obstacles too: bad roads, which were often impassable in winter, the restrictive practices of the gilds, and the regulation of industry by the early Stuarts. After 1640, however, the crown ceased to be an obstacle. Monopolies were no more. The regulation of industry ended. Instead, there was greater economic freedom. Workers could move around the country in search of jobs. Employers hired unskilled men and ignored the Act of Apprentices. The governments of the

[1] 'Industry and Trade', Chapter XVIII, explains most of the technical terms used in this section.

interregnum did not hinder them. Indeed they helped, especially when they purchased large quantities of arms, ammunition, and food for the soldiers.

There was no attempt to restrict the freedom of manufacturers in 1660. Charles II was restored, but without the means to regulate industry, for there were no prerogative courts, and no monopolies. Merchants, moneylenders, and prosperous gentlemen were free to invest and expand industry at will. The Act of Apprentices became a dead-letter. Gilds limited their membership, but they were now in rapid decline. Most of the new industries did not have gilds, nor did old ones which had spread to new areas (e.g. the cloth towns of the West Riding). This enabled industries to grow more rapidly, but it left the employees without the protection which the gilds had afforded—and it was not until the eighteenth century that they began to organise trade unions.

Parliament assisted the manufacturers. To encourage the sale of cloth, it enacted, in 1666, the famous statute which required that the dead were to be buried in woollen, and not in imported textiles. In Stuart times, however, it did little to improve communications. What was done was largely the work of private enterprise: many of England's rivers were made more navigable, and fast stage coach services from London were inaugurated in Charles II's reign. The 'transport revolution', however, was still nearly a century away.

THE POOR

In the early seventeenth century conditions grew steadily worse for the poorer wage-earning classes. During the price rise wages rose more slowly; they bought much less in 1640 than they had in 1500. The Act of Apprentices prevented unskilled workers from improving their lot. Monopolies and later the excise fell heavily on the poor. Enclosures and evictions increased the number of wage-earners. Although there was a steady growth of population, there was not a corresponding increase in the number of jobs available. Some families chose to emigrate. But the basic problem remained: the country could not provide work for everyone unless the economy expanded. Even the fortunate ones—those with jobs—still had to face the normal hazards of life. Plague might carry off the bread-winner. Bad harvests resulted in high prices and famine.

12

For the unemployed there was only the Elizabethan Poor Law, by which 'idle rogues' were harshly punished, but the 'deserving poor' were given a certain measure of relief. Until 1640 this was reinforced by the Stuarts' interest in social justice. Under James I and Charles I, and especially between 1629 and 1640, the Poor Law was enforced, wage-rates were fixed, clothiers were compelled to pay fair wages even during a depression, and enclosers were fined. This was well-meaning but unsuccessful. Much more was done by the private charity of puritan merchants and gentlemen. When the Stuarts' paternal government collapsed, the care—and punishment—of the poor passed to the middle classes.

The puritans believed that poverty was a sign of sin; they were always preaching the virtues of hard work. Many of them treated the poor as idlers and sinners, not as the unfortunate victims of economic change which most of them were. On the other hand, a large number of puritans did distinguish between the deserving poor and the sturdy beggars, and they continued to operate the Poor Law. Indeed the poor were better off in some ways during the interregnum: they were free to move about the country to seek work, and the Act of Apprentices was no longer in force.

In 1660 large numbers of disbanded soldiers swelled the ranks of the unemployed, whose lives became harsher and unrewarding. The Act of Settlement (1662) empowered justices of the peace to send back any unemployed person to the place of his last residence or birth. Thus, if there was no work available, the poor were prevented from seeking it elsewhere. There only remained the workhouses, grim and forbidding. Many more people were dependent on wages which were low, whilst food prices were often high. The working week was very long, and all the family were forced to work. The lot of the poor was indeed a hard one, even before the Industrial Revolution depressed an even larger section of the community.

TRADE

Spain was Tudor England's most serious trading rival. In James I's reign many merchants and gentlemen still wanted war with her for economic reasons: once again they would be able to plunder her treasure fleets and richly-laden merchant ships, and to defy her claim to a monopoly of trade in her empire.

Therefore, it is hardly surprising that the Stuarts' policy of friendship with the Spanish king was very unpopular. However, a string of defeats at the hands of France, and Portugal's successful rebellion against Spanish rule showed that the power of Spain was a broken reed, and the capture of Jamaica by Penn and Venables enabled England to break into the very heart of her empire. Thereafter she ceased to be a dangerous rival. Portugal was in decline as well. In 1654 Cromwell extorted from her the right of English merchants to trade with her colonies; before a decade had passed, they controlled her carrying trade.

New rivals were emerging: France, trading in the Mediterranean and colonising in North America, and the Dutch in the Americas and the Far East. English merchants could not forgive the massacre of Amboyna; they retaliated with the Navigation Act (1651), which was aimed at the Dutch carrying trade. It was the first step towards the 'old colonial system'. Three wars with England and prolonged resistance to Louis XIV sent the United Provinces into decline. London, not Amsterdam, became the world's mart and banking centre. The Dutch colonies in North America were annexed, and her leading role in Baltic trade was wrested from her. As a result of these developments the nature of English trade changed. There was a greater emphasis on colonial products (in which London, Bristol, and Liverpool took the leading part) and the carrying trade, and less dependence on the export of cloth.

At home English merchants had to contend with an unsympathetic government. Foreign policy was determined, not by trade, but by family and dynastic interests. The idea of merchants being free to trade without restraint was repugnant to both James I and his son. They preferred to restrict trade to monopolistic companies, which they in turn could control. However, parliament was much more sympathetic to the needs of the merchants. Throughout the century, as it gradually gained the upper hand over the king, so commercial advantage became the key-note of foreign policy. This is clearly indicated by the Navigation Act of 1651 which was re-enacted in 1660, the protective tariffs (customs duties) which parliament imposed, and the growth of the old colonial system.

Some powerful trading companies still had monopolies in the later seventeenth century. But parliament favoured the view that all merchants had the right to trade wherever they chose. The Merchant Adventurers were deprived of their monopoly. The East India and Africa companies only kept theirs because they were engaged in intense rivalry with the Dutch, and organised companies were more likely to succeed than individual merchants.

THE ECONOMIC POLICY OF THE STUARTS

James I and Charles I regarded trade primarily as a source of royal revenue. One merchant complained that nowhere in the world were traders 'so screwed and wrung' as in England. The Stuarts were more concerned to control commerce (in order to get what they regarded as their fair share of the profits), than to protect it. Thus the navy was neglected. Barbary pirates preyed on English ships and coastal villages with immunity, although the situation improved with the ship-money fleets in the 1630's. Ralegh's Guiana venture and the Providence Island Company failed, because the government looked with disfavour upon anything which threatened to disturb its harmonious relations with Spain. And when James I learned of the massacre of Amboyna, he wept crocodile tears, but did nothing more.

As we have seen, the Stuarts did not believe in a free economy, that is one which expands without restraint to meet growing demands. They preferred a stable and static society, in which the trade, industry, and agriculture were regulated. Thus enclosures and evictions were condemned because they caused social unrest. The craft-gilds, the prerogative courts, and the Statute of Apprentices were used to restrict and control economic growth. But the commonest instruments were the monopolies. Trading companies and gilds exercised them. Others were sold to groups of courtiers, who purchased the sole right to make or sell a particular commodity.

Sometimes the government's love of monopolies had disastrous effects. The Merchant Adventurers exported most of England's unfinished cloth to Flanders where it was dyed. Sir William Cockayne advised James I that it would be more profitable if the dyeing was done in England. James agreed, and in 1614 a company controlled by Cockayne was formed. It was given a monopoly in the export of dyed cloth, whilst the privileges of the Merchant Adventurers were withdrawn. The scheme was a miserable failure. When the low countries retaliated by excluding all English cloth, the new company was unable to provide the facilities to dye all the cloth being made. The clothiers stopped making it, and hundreds of men were thrown out of work; hungry and desperate, they rioted. By 1617 James had to acknowledge failure and restore the privileges of the Merchant Adventurers. He made shifty excuses, but they did not disguise the fact that his meddling had been well-nigh calamitous.

The Stuarts' attempt to regulate the economy was doomed to failure. They had no paid corps of local officials to enforce their will. Instead, they had to rely on unwilling and unpaid justices of the peace. The end of Charles I's personal rule also saw the end of his economic schemes. Thereafter, parliament, the gentry in the country, and the merchants in the towns, were powerful enough to impose the free economy which they desired.

LONDON

London increased rapidly in size and population, despite James I who forbade it to expand beyond fixed limits and clapped a heavy fine on it when he was ignored. Its population in 1600 was about 200,000 (Bristol, next in importance, had a paltry 30,000); by 1689 it had probably risen to half a million or more. It provided an enormous market for English goods, and the counties around it went in for market-gardening and dairying to cater for its needs.

Despite London's importance[1], conditions of life there were primitive. Commercial facilities were equally so: the Bank of England and marine insurance only appeared at the end of the century; and there were no large wet docks for another hundred years. Not until the nineteenth century did the biggest and richest city in the world obtain the facilities which its importance justified.

CONCLUSION

The seventeenth century was an important period of change, which made possible the great economic revolution of the next two hundred years:

[1] This importance must not be over-emphasised. Indeed, London's share of the country's trade declined in Stuart times, though in actual amount it grew enormously.

(*1*) England gained a colonial empire, and evolved the old colonial system to protect her interests in it.

(*2*) The regulated economy of the Tudors gave way to a free economy, which was operated by the ruling class of gentry and merchants.

(*3*) Capitalism and the factory system grew in importance.

There was a less attractive side to the picture. Most people still worked on the land and lived in villages or market towns. But the dark satanic mills were already making their ugly mark on England's green and pleasant land. Economic greatness was being bought at a terrible cost: the decline in standards involved in the decay of gilds and apprenticeship laws; the paupers, the evicted small farmers, the underpaid wage-earners were at the mercy of the manufacturer with the capitalist spirit. The rich were getting richer, but the poor were getting poorer.

XXXVIII

THE ORIGINS OF THE BRITISH EMPIRE

In 1603 England was not a colonial power. The Elizabethans, otherwise so successful at sea, had failed to establish any colonies. Yet they had pointed the way, and Stuart England fulfilled their greatest hopes.

WHY COLONIES WERE FOUNDED

The Stuarts could not afford to colonise, nor, unlike Elizabeth, were they particularly interested in doing so.[1] Therefore the State did not play an active part; the empire was the work of private enterprise. It was a national effort in which all classes took part. But different people did so for different reasons. The founding of a colony required the co-operation of two

[1] With the possible exception of Charles II.

groups: men who were prepared to finance the venture (the investors); men, women, and children to populate the new settlement (the colonists). There were plenty of nobles, gentlemen, and merchants ready to invest money. Their motive was profit. A new colony would be a source of raw materials, and a market in which the merchants could sell their goods. Some investors were more high-minded. They believed that England was over-populated;[1] colonies would provide the surplus population with a new life of opportunity in America, at the same time making conditions easier for those who remained behind. Finally, puritans and catholics helped to establish settlements as refuges for their persecuted brethren.

The investors were naturally to be found amongst the richer men in England. The colonists came from all classes, though most of them were poor. They left England for a variety of reasons:

(1) Some men could not find work. Others did not have enough food. The land-hunger in England prevented them from obtaining farms. They were joined by evicted peasants, disbanded soldiers, vagabonds, and men thrown on to the streets by a slump in the cloth industry.

(2) Religion drove others abroad. After the failure of the Hampton Court conference, the puritans were harried first by James I then by Charles I and Laud. Persecution reached it height during the 11 years' personal rule—so did the puritans migration. Between 1630 and the outbreak of the civil war nearly 60,000 men, women, and children left English shores, and 20,000 of them were puritans on their way to New England. Roman catholics migrated too, though in smaller numbers. After the Restoration English and Scottish dissenters followed their forebears. However, not all of them went simply to seek a refuge in which they could practise their religion without interference. Some were fired with missionary zeal to spread their beliefs in a new continent

(3) The government soon came to appreciate the value of the colonies as a dumping ground for unwanted persons, such as criminals and sturdy beggars. Enemies of the state were dealt with in the same way: royalists after the Civil War, Scottish covenanters after the Restoration, and the victims of Judge

1 In a sense it was. The amount of food grown and the work available were not enough for England's population at this time.

Jeffrey's Bloody Assize. Most of them went, not as free men, but as slaves to work on the plantations of the West Indies and North America.

THE GOVERNMENT OF THE COLONIES

A recognised procedure for founding a colony was soon established. The investors would obtain a charter from the king. This charter made them a grant of land, on which they were to establish a settlement. They were empowered to share the land amongst the colonists and to maintain law and order. The rights and powers of the colonisers varied with each charter, but this much was clear: the Stuarts were not prepared to allow the new settlements a free and independent existence. Charles I set up the first commission of plantations to regulate colonial matters. Some of the early North American settlements were given the right to look after their own internal affairs. Later, the Stuarts preferred what was called the proprietary colony. The king would make a grant of land to an investor who would be regarded as the proprietor or owner. He would act as the king's representative in the colony, thus enabling the government to exercise control over it. Despite the prolonged resistance of New England, this system of royal 'governors' was extended gradually to the older colonies, which had previously managed their own affairs.

Whilst this is true of the North American colonies it does not apply to all the settlements founded during the seventeenth century. Those in India were simply 'factories' (depots for storing goods) of the East India Company. The land did not belong to the company, but was rented from Indian rulers. The factories were peopled not with permanent settlers but with traders who had come to buy and sell.

THE NORTH AMERICAN COLONIES

(*1*) *Virginia*. It is fitting that Virginia, the site of Ralegh's shortlived settlement, should have been the first permanent English colony in America. In 1606 James I granted charters to 2 Virginia companies, one of London merchants, the other of west country merchants from Plymouth. Their object was to found colonies for trade and profit. The Plymouth company, which made the first attempt, failed. The London merchants were more successful. Their expedition landed farther south in

Chesapeake Bay, and founded Jamestown (May 1607). However, the colonists suffered many hardships, famine and disease

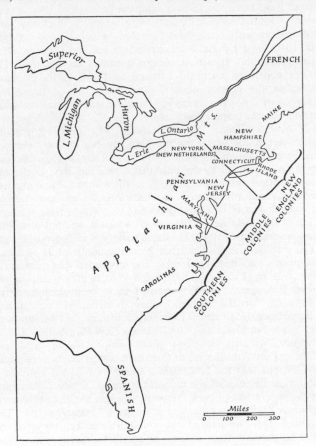

ENGLISH COLONIES IN NORTH AMERICA

reduced their numbers, and they contemplated a return to England.

Relief expeditions were sent. One, led by Sir George Somers in 1609, was shipwrecked on the Bermudas. He claimed them

12*

for England, and soon there was a flourishing settlement there. But this did not help the Virginians, who were only saved by 2 things: food from the Indians, and the courage of their leader, Captain John Smith. By imposing a strict discipline and making them work hard, Smith enabled the colonists to survive.[1]

In 1610 Lord De La Warr arrived to become Virginia's first royal governor. It was a turning point it its history. The settlers began to cultivate tobacco and sell it to England. Thereafter the colony never looked back. As it prospered, hundreds of colonists, many of them Anglican royalists, came out to swell the population.

(2) *New England: New Plymouth.* The next settlements, which were made along the northern reaches of the American coast, were known as New England. They were, with one exception, colonised by the puritans, whose industry, thrift, and tenacity fitted them admirably for this work. Puritans had already figured prominently in the Virginian venture—one of the chief investors was Sir Edwin Sandys, who led the puritans in James I's parliaments. However, Virginia was not a puritan colony as such, the settlers holding a variety of religious opinions.

The establishment of puritan New Plymouth in 1620 was a venture of a very different kind. The separatists (independents), persecuted by Elizabeth, had taken refuge in Leyden in the United Provinces. James I granted them permission to settle in America. So the 'Pilgrim Fathers' returned to England and in September 1620 sailed from Plymouth in the 'Mayflower'. They landed in December and founded New Plymouth. Under Governor William Bradford they farmed, fished, and cut timber. They worshipped in their own way, free from persecution. Theirs was the first puritan colony. Without a doubt it is the most famous of the colonial ventures in North America. Yet the separatists of New Plymouth are less important than the puritans who founded the next settlement, Massachusetts. The Pilgrim Fathers wanted only to worship in peace; they had no desire to expand their colony or convert others. Thus New Plymouth grew but slowly, and in 1691 it was finally absorbed into Massachusetts.

[1] On one occasion Smith was seized by Indians whose chief Powhatan ordered him to be executed. He was only saved by the plea of Powhatan's daughter Pocohontas, who later married him. When he returned to England, his wife became a 'seven day wonder', but she soon succumbed to disease and died.

(3) New England: Massachusetts. The Massachusetts Bay Company was promoted in 1628 by puritan gentlemen and merchants. Their object was to provide a home for their persecuted brethren and at the same time to encourage trade. Whereas they looked for profits, the settlers were simply seeking a refuge. Naturally, the different aims of the 2 groups led to disagreements, which were only resolved when the settlers broke away from the investors and managed their colony themselves. These puritans were very different from the New Plymouth brethren. They were disciplined, intolerant, and of an independent temper. Under their energetic rule the colony rapidly grew.

(4) Other New England colonies. During the great puritan migration 20,000 people settled in New England. However, not all of them went to Massachusetts. The intolerance of the puritans there caused some men to seek homes elsewhere in the wilderness. Roger Williams founded Providence (Rhode Island) in 1647; other refugees from Massachusetts migrated to the settlements of New Hampshire and Connecticut. These new colonies were puritan, but none was as intolerant as Massachusetts. One other New England colony, Maine, was not a puritan venture. It resulted from the devotion, effort, and money of one man, Sir Ferdinando Gorges.

(5) Maryland. During the same period, religious persecution produced a colony of a very different kind. In 1633 Lord Baltimore, a Roman catholic, founded Maryland (named after Charles I's wife, Henrietta Maria), where toleration was practised.

MERCANTILISM[1] AND THE COLONIES

The Stuart kings and the merchants thought alike in colonial matters: colonies existed for the benefit of England and her traders; they provided raw materials and a market for English goods. Therefore the government could not allow merchants of other countries to trade with them. Between 1642 and 1660 parliament pursued the same policy. In 1651 it passed the Navigation Act, which laid down that colonists could only send goods to England in ships owned by English or colonial merchants. The Dutch were trading freely with the English settlements in North America, and this act was directed against them. The wars against the United Provinces (1652–4 and

1 See Chapter XVIII.

1665–7) were fought partly to enforce it. In the second of these wars England acquired the New Netherlands (renamed New York), a Dutch settlement which lay between New England and Maryland. It gave her a continuous stretch of coastline from New Hampshire to Virginia which made it easier to enforce her trading monopoly; far more important, she gained control of the important fur trade route up the Hudson and Mohawk valleys to the Great Lakes.

Of all the Stuarts, Charles II was the only one to show a real interest in the colonies. He upheld the 'old colonial system', whereby the interests of the settlements were subordinated to those of the mother-country. They were expected to grow food and make articles which were not produced in England; likewise they were supposed to purchase their requirements from her merchants. The Navigation Act was the chief instrument for maintaining this system. Charles also tried, with some success, to exercise a greater degree of royal control. When he granted charters for new colonies they were of the proprietary type: Carolina, New York and New Jersey, Delaware (granted to Lord De La Warr) and Pennsylvania (granted to a quaker, William Penn[1]).

THE AMERICAN COLONIES: 1689

By the end of our period the North American colonies were thriving. They varied in their climate, geography, and way of life. In the cold forested colonies of the north the puritans lived. They were strict and intolerant men, but energetic and with the belief that all men were equal even if they did not observe it in practice. The middle colonies were a melting pot of peoples and religions: the Dutch Calvinists of New York, the quakers of Pennsylvania and the Roman catholics of Maryland. In the southern colonies there existed an Anglican and aristocratic society ruled by landowners, whose farms and plantations were worked by negro slaves from West Africa. With such great differences it is perhaps understandable that the colonies were suspicious of each other. They lacked a common interest, and they were unwilling to work together. Furthermore, they faced many difficulties and dangers: famine, disease,

[1] Penn, who insisted on religious toleration and fair treatment of the Indians, was responsible for the most enlightened colonial government yet known.

Indians (some were friendly, some naturally hostile or made so by ill-treatment at the hands of the colonists), the French in Canada, and relations with the English government. But their future was assured, because they were of great economic importance. Their growing population provided a large and expanding market for English goods, whilst the fur and fish of the north and the tobacco of Virginia were highly prized in England.

INDIA

The Elizabethans, searching for new markets, turned to the east, where they learned that trading prospects were good. This led to the founding of the East India Company by a charter from Elizabeth (1600). Despite great hazards—Dutch opposition, uncharted seas, and storms—the first voyages of the company made great profits.

It had to contend with two dangerous rivals, the Portuguese and the Dutch. Portugal had once had a monopoly of trade in India and the Far East, but she was now too weak to defend it. In 1612 Jahangir[1] allowed the East India Company to set up a trading station at Surat. The Portuguese settlers at Goa resented this, and there was constant friction. However, in 1642 they agreed to recognise the right of the English to trade in India; Cromwell's treaty with Portugal extended this right to all her colonies. So conflict between the two countries came to an end.

The Dutch had been the first to break down the Portuguese monopoly. They had wrested control of the Spice Islands from them and gained Ceylon and Malaya as well. When English merchants set up a trading station at Amboyna in the Spice Islands, the Dutch massacred them (1623). It was an event which made a deep impression on England; her merchants nursed a desire for revenge until the first Dutch war. The East India Company was forced to confine its trade to India and it did not venture into the Far East again until the late eighteenth century. However, it maintained good relations with the Mogul emperors, because it traded peacefully. Thus Sir Thomas Roe was able to obtain further concessions for it. New factories were established at Madras (1639) and in Bengal in the following decade.

[1] He was one of the Mogul emperors who ruled India.

The company appeared to be on the verge of a prosperous era. However, it fell on hard times during the political upheavals in England. There were disputes between royalist and presbyterian merchants, and trade was disturbed by war. But Cromwell saved the company when its fortunes had reached their lowest. After the first Dutch war, he compelled the United Provinces to compensate both the company and the relatives of the dead for the Amboyne massacre. He also granted a new charter: the company had consisted previously of a small number of shareholders, but the new charter made it into a joint stock company; anyone who wished to invest in it could do so. Many merchants did, and with the extra capital the company was able to expand its business. Thereafter it grew rich, selling textiles and metals in India in return for spices, silk, and indigo.

During the second half of the century the character of the East India Company changed. The Portuguese owned Bombay; they did not have just a factory there. In 1662 they gave it to Charles II as part of the dowry of Catherine of Braganza. Six years later Charles leased it to the company for a small rent. The company also received St. Helena from the crown; it was a useful stopping-place on the route round the Cape. And it acquired Calcutta in 1690. At the same time, the Mogul empire began to decay. It was no longer able to maintain law and order, and the company's factories were subject to attacks by rioters and rebels.

These two facts—the ownership of Indian territory and the need for self-defence—changed the whole nature of the company from a trading organisation to a colonial power. The king allowed it to make alliances with Indian rulers, to keep its own law-courts and even an army. In fact it was given the power of a sovereign State, and in the eighteenth century it came to rule India.

THE WEST INDIES

In the West Indies only Bermuda and Barbados had been colonised by 1653. Then Cromwell began to pursue a conscious imperialist policy. Jamaica was acquired (1655), and England became the most important naval power in the Caribbean. She had destroyed at last the Spanish monopoly in that sea, the monopoly which the Elizabethans had first challenged.

Thereafter buccaneers, many of them English, preyed on what was left of the Spanish merchant navy. They were even employed by the government to defend Jamaica against the Dutch (1665–7). One of them, Henry Morgan, was not only knighted, but also governed Jamaica for the king. The government thought it worth its while to do this. It prized its possessions in the West Indies above all others, because they produced such very profitable commodities as sugar and tobacco.

OTHER COLONIES

Elsewhere the work of territorial expansion continued. The French colonised Newfoundland and the Scots abandoned Nova Scotia (New Scotland)to them in 1629, but both colonies were ceded to Britain in 1713. Further north the Hudson's Bay Company, which was engaged in the fur trade, acquired land and built several forts to protect their interests. Forts were erected on the west coast of Africa to protect the important slave trade.

Some English ventures failed. Sir Walter Ralegh's journeys to Guiana in search of the gold mines of Eldorado led only to his execution, whilst his appeals to the government to set up a colony there went unheeded. John Pym and other puritans formed a company to colonise Providence and Association in the West Indies, but by 1641 the Spaniards had seized them. The attack on Spanish Hispaniola ended in fiasco. Despite these failures the men of Stuart England made great advances. They succeeded to Portugal's position of primacy in India; they broke into the Spanish monopoly in the West Indies; they drove the Dutch from North America and broke their commercial power in a series of wars. The efforts of the seamen, merchants, and colonists of Stuart England paved the way for the country's imperial career in the following two hundred years.

XXXIX

THE ARTS AND SCIENCE IN THE SEVENTEENTH CENTURY

THE ROLE OF THE COURT

WITH the possible exception of James I's liking for masques, he and his courtiers were hardly noted for their artistic pursuits. They were more interested in spirited and drunken junketing; morals and good taste were marked only by their absence. When Charles became king, there was a complete change. Out went the coarseness of his father's reign. The court became, like the king himself, dignified and cultured. Charles patronised the arts and collected paintings. He persuaded Van Dyck to settle in England, and his agents scoured the continent for 'old masters' until he had the finest collection in Europe.[1] His queen was more interested in the theatre. Players were frequently summoned to perform at court. Expensive masques were staged; when the Inns of Court produced one in the king's honour it cost £20,000. All this was frowned on by puritans. One of them, William Prynne, wrote *Histriomastix* ('The Scourge of Actors'), in which he criticised the queen's love of play-acting.

The court left Whitehall in 1642. It only returned with Charles II in 1660. His court was noted for its light-hearted attitude to life, its gambling, immorality, and frivolous courtiers. Nevertheless it was a centre of learning and culture. Science[2] interested the king; so did architecture—he wanted to re-design London after the Great Fire, but simply lacked the money and power to do so. He was fond of music, especially as performed in Louis XIV's court. His special love was the theatre. Unlike previous kings and queens, he did not summon the players to court. Instead he went to them, especially to the Theatre Royal, Drury Lane. But he was the last of the great royal patrons amongst the Stuarts; James II, William III, and Anne had less time or interest for such matters.

[1] The paintings were sold by parliament after the king's execution, and only a few were recovered at the Restoration.

[2] Prince Rupert too displayed an active interest in science and colonisation.

PROSE

The early seventeenth century was marked by two great prose works. One was the *Authorised Version* of the Bible. It had beauty and dignity, and it was written in simple language; at the time it had no equal in English prose. The other was Sir Walter Ralegh's *History of the World*, which was written whilst he was imprisoned in the Tower. It was more than a history; it was also an attack on James and his advisers, so much so that the king forbade its sale 'for being too saucy in censuring princes'. The puritans naturally loved it, and the book continued to sell.

In James I's reign men still wrote in ornate and flowery English. Some did not use English at all. Sir Francis Bacon was the greatest essayist and philosopher of the time; a true Elizabethan, he was interested in a great many subjects and wrote on them, but he preferred to use Latin. However, things were changing. More literate Englishmen were writing in their own language. Whereas in the sixteenth century English had been the language of poets and playwrights, it was now being used widely in the everyday world of business, law, and government. Weekly news letters reported the fortunes of both sides in the Civil War. Political pamphleteers aired radical ideas, mocked and insulted opponents. Histories, personal memoirs, letters to friends and relatives, diaries, sermons, political tracts, legal arguments, all were written in English. The language changed to suit the new uses to which it was being put. It lost its frills and became simpler.

This is true of the spoken word as well. The pulpit was used both by the government and by the puritans to express their different views. Anglican clergymen like Lancelot Andrewes (the bishop of Winchester) and John Donne (the poet) delivered sermons which were works of art; the common people preferred the plain blunt speech of the puritans, whom they could understand.

Throughout the century the change went on. The language became more vigorous, clear, and brisk; it was no longer intricate and learned, full of suitable classical or Biblical allusions.[1] It needed to be simple when roundheads and cavaliers, whigs and tories were attacking each other in pamphlets, sermons, and broadsheets.

[1] Milton was the great exception.

The second half of the century was notable for the many personal records which were written. Men published their memoirs to justify their part in the recent great struggle. Lucy Hutchinson published a biography of her husband, who had been a parliamentary colonel. The duchess of Newcastle wrote her version of the duke's role in the Civil War. Others kept diaries, the most famous of which is that of Samuel Pepys. He became clerk of the navy board at the Restoration. By dint of energy, honesty, and ability, he rose to control the navy in James II's reign; his efforts laid the foundations of the powerful British navy of the eighteenth century. His diary, a personal and private record, is a vivid portrait not only of Restoration London and the great events of Charles II's reign, but also of the man himself. There was John Evelyn too: vain, slightly pompous, moralising, writing his diary for all the world to read. And there were many others, amongst them the journal of George Fox, who was the leader of the quakers.

During the century new books were published on all manner of subjects. Amongst the more notable were the first serious histories in the English language, written by the earl of Clarendon and Bishop Burnet. Political thinkers published their theories. In his *Leviathan* Thomas Hobbes argued that a government has the right to exist only if it is strong enough to rule and put down all opponents. But John Locke thought that government rested on a contract. Science, mathematics, geography, music, and manners were the subjects of other volumes. But amidst all this, very few novels were published. *Pilgrim's Progress* was the only great one (if we can call it a novel). It was written by John Bunyan, the son of a Bedford tinker. His puritan views landed him in prison, and it was there that he wrote this remarkable book.

POETRY

Shakespeare apart, John Donne was the most important poet in early Stuart England. Although he had led a gay life in his early years, he ended up as an Anglican clergyman noted for his sermons. He turned against the verse of the Elizabethans whose sweet sonnets, about the lover who worships his lady from afar, were full of chivalrous sentiments. His poems were those of a religious thinker; they were written in a serious vein about man's spirit and his emotions.

The seventeenth century had its immortal poet too. John Milton was a man of enormous learning, whose poems reveal his love of the classics and of the Bible. Although he was an ardent puritan and an opponent of Charles I, his early verse, which was written in the 1630's, contained few political references.[1] During the Civil War, however, he wrote pamphlets in support of parliament. His love of liberty led him to attack its censorship of the Press, yet he remained loyal to the parliamentary cause. He approved of the execution of the king, and during the interregnum he worked for the government. At the Restoration Milton went unpunished, despite his extreme views. He was shocked at the collapse of his cause; in bitterness and blindness he returned to poetry to write his finest works: *Paradise Lost*, *Paradise Regained*, and *Samson Agonistes*.[2]

After 1660 poetry was chiefly used for political purposes; for example, John Dryden's *Absalom and Achitophel* was a vicious satire, which was aimed at the whig leaders, Shaftesbury and Monmouth. There was no great poet to take Milton's place.

DRAMA

Elizabethan drama did not die with the old queen. Tragedies and dramatic poetry remained very important; indeed Shakespeare wrote his greatest tragedies in James I's reign. His company, along with others, continued to perform at the Globe and the other theatres of London—and of course at the king's court. His plays (and this applies to most of the Elizabethan and early Jacobean playwrights) required no scenery; they depended upon the power of the spoken word, the ability of the actors, and the imagination of the onlookers. But now a rival appeared in the masque. This was a play which consisted chiefly of songs, dances, and intricate scenic effects. It was an elaborate and often beautiful affair, but as drama it was usually worthless. However, Shakespeare bowed to the new fashion; thus the storm in *The Tempest* called for scenic and sound effects, and its songs and dances reflect the influence of the masque.

The most popular playwrights of early Stuart England were Beaumont and Fletcher. Ben Jonson was the most talented (after Shakespeare's death). Jonson introduced a new kind of

---

[1] The fact that he wrote a masque, *Comus*, at this time illustrates that he was not a narrow-minded puritan.

[2] Milton, like Shakespeare, wrote in blank verse. The poets who followed him preferred to use heroic couplets.

play, the comedy of humours. Each of his characters had one dominating humour or emotion (such as cunning or hypocrisy) and the play was concerned with one human weakness, such as greed or lust. Jonson was learned and witty; he was also versatile, for he wrote the masques for James I's court. Apart from Jonson, however, the standard of drama was declining; characters were carelessly drawn; vulgarity was creeping in.

Although the theatre was very popular under James I and his son, it had powerful enemies. Outbreaks of the plague frequently closed the theatres. More dangerous were the puritans, who mounted a savage attack on them: theatres encouraged wickedness and idleness; they were a waste of money and a cause of riots. The playwrights retaliated by ridiculing their opponents; for example, in Ben Jonson's *Bartholomew Fair*, Zeal-of-the-Land-Busy was a narrow-minded puritan busybody who saw wickedness in the most unlikely places and things.

When the Long Parliament met, the puritans gained their revenge by closing the theatres. The popular view of the puritans, as strait-laced killjoys with no taste for beauty, is not entirely true. Nevertheless many of them had little interest in poetry and a particular loathing for the theatre, though they objected less to the plays than to the disreputable actors and playwrights who laughed at them. Consequently, it was not until the Restoration that the theatre revived.

The drama of the Restoration period was very different from that of the years preceding the Civil War. The plays contained no dramatic poetry. Tragedies were less important than comedies, especially comedies of manners which were full of clever talk and intrigue and whose characters were shallow. In keeping with the mood of London after the puritan rule, the theatre scorned moral restraint and accepted sin. Plays were vigorous and coarse, cynical and witty.[1] Women's parts were played by actresses (such as Nell Gwynn), instead of by boys, as in the Elizabethan theatre. Even the theatre-design was new. Gone was the Elizabethan apron stage, its simple settings and few 'props'; in its place was the indoor theatre with the French picture-frame stage and elaborate scenery.

ARCHITECTURE

The influence of ancient Rome and Greece on English

[1] John Dryden alone did not follow the prevailing fashion.

architecture was first felt in Tudor times. In the seventeenth century it became supreme. The mansions of nobles and great gentlemen were built with porches, pillars, and other classical decoration. Public buildings were influenced in the same way; a good example is the banqueting hall of Whitehall Palace, which was designed for James I by Inigo Jones, the finest architect of early Stuart England.

Houses were becoming more beautifully furnished; tapestries, paintings, and four-poster beds were common. Formal gardens, which were laid with paths, groves, flower-beds, fountains, and statues made their appearance. Such luxuries were only for the spacious homes of the rich. Though rural dwellings were more substantial, even for the lower classes, their furnishing was plain and simple. Townspeople crammed themselves and their belongings into tall timber-framed houses with overhanging upper storeys; these dwellings were inflammable and gloomy, cramped and unhealthy.

It was an age of building activity. The Civil War brought to an end the work of builders and architects, but it recommenced in 1660. London, in particular, expanded rapidly; after the Great Fire, many new churches and public buildings were erected. Elsewhere bigger and more beautiful public buildings were appearing: for instance the hospitals of Chelsea and Greenwich, the colleges of Oxford and Cambridge.

There were fine architects too, befitting a period of such great opportunity, above all Sir Christopher Wren. But there were few schools for training them. Inigo Jones began by designing scenery for the court masques. Most of them learned by experience. Wren came to architecture as an amateur, for he was better known as an astronomer and mathematician. The most important influence on Wren was Palladio, an Italian who built in the ancient Roman style. The notable feature of his Italian churches was the large space in the centre. Wren adopted the idea when he designed St. Paul's with a central dome, despite the bitter opposition of the more old-fashioned clergy. The same influence was present in some of his churches. Wren was an architect of genius. The Great Fire gave him his opportunity to design many beautiful buildings for London. His epitaph gives the best estimate of his achievements: 'If you seek his monument, look about you.'

PAINTING

Foreign painters dominated the English scene. When James I built his new banqueting house, he invited Peter Paul Rubens, a Dutchman, to decorate the ceiling. Anthony Van Dyck painted many portraits of Charles I, other members of the royal family, and courtiers. The only English artists of any note were those who painted miniatures. Nicholas Hilliard had set the fashion in Elizabeth's reign, and a whole school of artists was copying his techniques.

Painting, like the other fine arts, did not entirely disappear during the troubled times between 1642 and 1660. At Whitehall, where Van Dyck had painted the king and his courtiers, another foreigner, Peter Lely, painted Cromwell and his puritan generals.

The Restoration brought with it no great change. England was still devoid of good native painters, apart from Samuel Cooper, who painted miniatures—and he died in 1672. Foreigners continued to take first place, and the court painter was the Dutchman Peter Lely, whom Charles II knighted (just as his father had knighted Rubens and Van Dyck). Two features of seventeenth century painting are worth observing. The famous artists painted portraits, not landscapes. Secondly, nearly all of them worked within the circle of the king's court where the only important patrons were to be found. But the eighteenth century was to see a remarkable change.

MUSIC

Although the great age of Elizabethan madrigals and church music overlapped into Stuart times, it ended with the death of William Byrd (1623) and Orlando Gibbons (1625). Church music was still written because it was an essential feature of worship, especially under Laud. But secular music was also important due to the popularity of masques. Musical developments were arrested by the upheaval caused by the Civil War. Parliament forbade music in church services, and puritans enjoyed themselves destroying organs. However, not all puritans disliked music, which was often heard when Cromwell held court at Whitehall. Furthermore, opera was introduced into England during the interregnum.

The Restoration led to a musical revival. Cathedral choirs reappeared, and organs were installed in churches once more.

Opera was in vogue, and due to Henry Purcell, who composed *Dido and Aeneas*, it became established as a new form of art in England. Purcell wrote not only for opera, but also for the theatre, the court, and public ceremonies. He was a great English composer, and the last for many a long day.

More important than great composers was the nation's love of song and dance. Families held musical evenings; prosperous people learned to play the spinet and the lute; folk-songs were universally popular; morris dances were still performed; even poor men had their flutes and fiddles. Unfortunately the nation's musical tradition declined. People played less and listened more. Foreign influences—Italian, French, German—became more important, especially after the early death of Purcell in 1696.

EDUCATION

The Stuarts were not ardent patrons of education. The real impetus was provided by the middle class. Merchants and gentlemen established many free grammar schools, and endowed them with scholarships. They carried on their good work to such effect that a considerable number of the more talented members of the poorer classes were able to obtain an education. Indeed, in Stuart England there were more educational opportunities than at any other time before the late nineteenth century.

This must not be exaggerated. At first there were obvious restrictions on education. The kings gave no help. Education was a monopoly of the Church: clergymen staffed the universities; teachers had to be licensed by the bishops. However, the Church lost its control when the Civil War broke out, and during the puritan revolution many more children went to school. A few would-be reformers, like Milton, wanted a schoolmaster in every parish. Some of the puritans genuinely believed in equality; they demanded that education should be given to talented boys, regardless of their parents' class or income. Fresh ideas about the curriculum were aired: Latin was of little use, far better for boys to learn mathematics and history. It was a time of advance and experiment. But it did not last long.

The Church regained its control of education in 1660. The Act of Uniformity revived the bishops' right to license teachers.

Nobles and courtiers, clergymen and many gentlemen remembered that, after the Civil War, many of the revolutionaries had
come from the lower classes. They came to the conclusion that
'a little learning is a dangerous thing', and closed many of the
new schools. They argued that it was economically harmful
and politically dangerous to take men from their daily labour
in the field or the workshop in order to study. Despite this
attitude the position improved. Although the Corporation Act
forbade nonconformist schools, they grew up just the same.
Well-meaning members of the middle class continued to endow
grammar schools. At the end of the century charity schools
first appeared.

Education differed in kind from class to class. The nobleman's
son had a private tutor, went on a grand tour of Europe to
broaden his knowledge and outlook, and then spent sometime
at a university. Boys of the middle and lower classes went to the
writing school to learn writing, arithmetic, and reading. This
was followed by the grammar school, where Latin, Greek, and
Hebrew were studied. The free grammar schools usually
taught local boys of all classes, though some were beginning to
take in boarders; a few, such as Winchester and Eton, were
becoming restricted to the sons of rich parents. For orphans
there were the orphanage schools, of which Christ's Hospital
was the most famous.

Above the schools stood the universities. In the Middle
Ages Oxford had held first place, but the Reformation brought
Cambridge to the fore. It was at Cambridge that the puritans
flourished under Elizabeth and the early Stuarts. Thus it was
inclined to support parliament, whereas Oxford was a royalist
stronghold. Most of the teachers and lecturers were clergymen.
The undergraduates, however, were more of a mixture: the sons
of nobles and gentry, ministers and businessmen, and a few sons
of yeomen and traders. A few of the poorer students were
'servitors', who 'worked their way through college'. The two
universities were not keeping pace with all the changes which
had occurred in science and thought. Mathematics were less
important than Latin, and astronomy was neglected. However,
the universities were not simply schools; they were more
important as great seats of learning, where the teachers were also
scholars who engaged in advanced studies and research. This
was the glory of Oxford and Cambridge and has been ever since.

SCIENCE

The Renaissance had caused men to question traditional authority. But they did so in an unscientific manner. Renaissance man was 'universal', that is, he studied everything. Ralegh was such a man, with a profound interest in geography, ships, colonies, poetry, and history. He pursued his interests haphazardly, without any order or system. And while men rejected old ideas they grasped eagerly at new ones without testing them to see if they were accurate. Ralegh swore that he had seen mountains nearly 30 miles high.

In the seventeenth century this began to change. The universal man began to give way to the specialist. Science became divided into its component parts of mathematics, physics, chemistry, biology, and so on. There was a new habit of scientific observation, too; men began to test traditional authority by reason and experiment. Much of this was due to the writings of Francis Bacon. He argued that man could only advance his way of life by advancing his knowledge, and this was to be done by observing, collecting facts and analysing them, and carrying out experiments. It was in this spirit that William Harvey, Charles I's doctor, studied and so discovered the circulation of the blood. John Napier constructed the first logarithm tables. The invention of the microscope enabled scientists to study insect life and diseases. Even a puritan like William Prynne was imbued with the same spirit; he collected hundreds of Biblical references as proof that play-acting was the game of the devil. And in the greater conflict between king and parliament, both sides marshalled their precedents and scoured old histories for evidence to support their theories.

The Civil War heralded an open attack on traditional authority which swept away the Anglican Church, the monarchy, and the lords. Everything was open to question, in science and philosophy no less than in religion and politics. People had much greater freedom to write and say what they thought (unless they upheld king or pope). In the universities the conservative clergymen were replaced by men with fresh ideas. During the interregnum Christopher Wren, Robert Boyle, and John Locke studied at Oxford. Wren applied mathematics to architecture; Boyle was the father of chemistry; later in the century Locke's theory of contract was to replace that of divine right. Each of them was, in a way, typical of the new spirit.

At the Restoration the clergymen moved back into Oxford
and Cambridge. The ejected scientists and thinkers came
together to form the Royal Society. As its title indicates, its
patron was Charles II, who was himself a product of the new way
of thinking. He was tolerant, liberal, and scorned most of the
current superstitions; he had his own laboratory and observa-
tory, and was the patron of scientists. His courtiers were taken
up with science, too, though often because it was the fashionable
thing to do.

With such encouragement and patronage, scientists made
advances in many fields. Hans Sloane added to existing
knowledge in botany. Edmund Halley was noted for his study
of comets. The greatest scientist of the age was Sir Isaac
Newton, who not only established the famous theory of gravity
but also laid down important principles in mathematics, astronomy, and physics. His influence was recognised by Alexander
Pope, who jested:

> Nature and Nature's Laws lay hid in Night.
> God said, Let Newton be! and all was Light.

Old ideas died hard. The ideas of the ancient Greeks, in
philosophy and medicine, geography and astronomy, gave way
but slowly before the new scientific methods and discoveries.
The new way of thinking did not obtain universal support. The
clergy resisted it; so did their strongholds at Oxford and Cambridge. Nor did the ordinary people lose their prejudices
quickly. Quack doctors found a ready market for their
medicines which cured all ills; there were still alchemists who
vainly tried to turn lead into gold; astrologers cast horoscopes
for the great men of the land. Witches were very real and
dreadful for most people and James I wrote a book on them;
hundreds of deformed or lonely old women were put to death
on the charge of practising magic. Belief in the monarch's
power to miraculously cure those who suffered from the king's
evil (tuberculosis) survived as late as Queen Anne's reign.

Nevertheless, the new way of thinking had its effect. Experiments and a more rational and common-sense outlook were
disproving both old ideas and superstitions. Although the
advances of the seventeenth century did not amount to a
scientific revolution, they had laid the foundations of one which
would be carried through at the end of the following century.

TABLE OF EVENTS

<table>
<tr><td colspan="2">HOME</td><td colspan="2">ABROAD</td></tr>
<tr><td>1399</td><td>Richard II deposed</td><td></td><td></td></tr>
<tr><td colspan="2">*HENRY IV. 1399–1413*</td><td></td><td></td></tr>
<tr><td colspan="2">*HENRY V. 1413–22*</td><td></td><td></td></tr>
<tr><td colspan="2">*HENRY VI. 1422–61*</td><td></td><td></td></tr>
<tr><td>1422–37</td><td>Minority of Henry VI</td><td></td><td></td></tr>
<tr><td>1453</td><td>End of the Hundred Years' War</td><td>1453</td><td>Turks capture Constantinople</td></tr>
<tr><td></td><td></td><td>1455</td><td>Fra Angelico dies</td></tr>
<tr><td></td><td></td><td>1460</td><td>Prince Henry the Navigator dies</td></tr>
<tr><td colspan="2">*EDWARD IV. 1461–83*</td><td></td><td></td></tr>
<tr><td>1476</td><td>William Caxton sets up first printing press in England</td><td></td><td></td></tr>
<tr><td></td><td></td><td>1477</td><td>Last duke of Burgundy killed</td></tr>
<tr><td colspan="2">*RICHARD III. 1483–5*</td><td></td><td></td></tr>
<tr><td>1485</td><td>Richard III defeated and killed at battle of Bosworth</td><td></td><td></td></tr>
<tr><td colspan="2">*HENRY VII. 1485–1509*</td><td></td><td></td></tr>
<tr><td>1485</td><td>Henry marries Elizabeth of York</td><td></td><td></td></tr>
<tr><td>1486</td><td>Prince Arthur born</td><td></td><td></td></tr>
<tr><td>1487</td><td>Lambert Simnel's rebellion crushed at battle of Stoke
Act against Livery and Maintenance
Star Chamber Act</td><td>1487</td><td>Bartholomew Diaz rounds Cape of Good Hope</td></tr>
<tr><td>1488</td><td>James III of Scotland murdered</td><td></td><td></td></tr>
</table>

HOME		ABROAD	
1491	Perkin Warbeck claims to be Richard, duke of York		
	Prince Henry born		
	Treaty of Medina del Campo	1492	Spain conquers Granada
1492	Treaty of Etaples		Columbus discovers West Indies
1494	Poyning's Laws	1494	Italian Wars begin
			Treaty of Tordesillas
1495	Sir William Stanley executed		
1496	James IV of Scotland helps Warbeck		
	Magnus Intercursus		
1497	Cornish rebellion	1497–8	Vasco da Gama reaches India
	Perkin Warbeck captured		
	John Cabot discovers Newfoundland		
1499	Earl of Warwick and Perkin Warbeck executed.		
	John Cabot's attempt to find north-west passage		
1501	Prince Arthur marries Catherine of Aragon		
1502	Prince Arthur dies		
1503	James IV marries Margaret Tudor		
1506	Malus Intercursus		
1508–9	Sebastian Cabot's attempt to find north-west passage		

HENRY VIII. 1509–47

HOME		ABROAD	
1509	Henry marries Catherine of Aragon	1509	John Calvin born
	Empson and Dudley executed		
		1510–11	Portuguese capture Albuquerque and Malacca
1512	Act against benefit of clergy		
1512–14	War with France		
1513	Battle of Flodden; James IV killed	1513	Battle of the Spurs
			Balboa reaches Pacific
			Machiavelli writes *The Prince*

HOME		ABROAD	
		1514	Louis XII succeeded by Francis I
1515	Wolsey becomes lord chancellor and cardinal	1515	Ferdinand of Aragon seized part of Navarre
			French victory at Marignano
1516	Sir Thomas More's *Utopia*	1516	Death of Ferdinand
			Concordat of Bologna
			Erasmus' Greek Testament.
		1517	Luther's 95 theses
1518	Treaty of London		
		1519–22	Magellan circumnavigates world
			Cortez conquers Aztecs of Mexico
		1519	Leonardo da Vinci dies
			Emperor Maximillian dies; Charles V elected
1520	Field of Cloth of Gold	1520	Raphael dies
	Wolsey's alliance with Charles V		Luther excommunicated
1524	Amicable Grant	1524	Peasants' revolt in Germany
		1525	Charles V's victory at Pavia
1526	Wolsey's alliance with France		
1527	Problem of the annulment of king's marriage first becomes important	1527	Charles V's troops sack Rome.
1528	Papal commission of Wolsey and Campeggio		
1529	Wolsey dismissed	1529	Peace of Cambrai
	More becomes chancellor		
	Reformation parliament meets		
1530	Wolsey dies		
1531	Clergy recognise Henry as Supreme Head		
	Rise of Thomas Cromwell		
1532	Supplication against Ordinaries	1532	Pizarro conquers Incas of Peru
	Submission of the Clergy		

	HOME		ABROAD
1532	First Act of Annates		
	Archbishop Warham dies		
	Sir Thomas More resigns chancellorship		
1533	Thomas Cranmer consecrated archbishop of Canterbury		
	Henry's secret marriage to Anne Boleyn		
	Act 'in restraint of appeals'		
	Cranmer annuls Henry's marriage to Catherine		
	Princess Elizabeth born		
1534	Second Act of Annates	1534	Society of Jesus founded
	Act for submission of clergy		
	Act of Succession		
	Nun of Kent executed		
	Act of Supremacy		
	Treason Act		
1535–36	Revolt of the Geraldines		
1535	Sir Thomas More and Bishop Fisher executed		
	Cromwell's commissioners survey monasteries		
	Miles Coverdale's Bible		
1536	Smaller monasteries dissolved	1536	Calvin's 'Institutes'
	Pilgrimage of Grace		
	Act abolishing franchises		
	Welsh government remodelled		
	William Tyndale martyred		
	Anne Boleyn executed		
	Henry marries Jane Seymour		
1537	Prince Edward born		
	John Rogers' Bible		
	Council of the North established		
1539	Act confirming dissolution of larger monasteries.		
	Act of Six Articles		

HOME   ABROAD

	HOME		ABROAD
1540	Henry marries Anne of Cleves		
	Thomas Cromwell executed		
	Henry divorces Anne and marries Catherine Howard		
		1541	Calvin's rule in Geneva begins
1542–46	Wars with France and Scotland		
1542	Catherine Howard executed		
	Scots routed at Solway Moss		
1543	Henry marries Catherine Parr	1543	Copernicus publishes his discoveries
	Treaty of Greenwich		
	Act of Succession		
1545	Duke of Norfolk and earl of Surrey condemned to death	1545	Council of Trent meets
			Potosi silver-mines discovered
1546	George Wishart martyred	1546	Death of Luther
	Cardinal Beaton murdered		

EDWARD VI. 1547–53

	HOME		ABROAD
1547–49	*The Duke of Somerset's rule*		
1547	Somerset becomes lord protector	1547	Francis I dies
	Thomas Seymour marries Catherine Parr		
	Invasion of Scotland and battle of Pinkie		
	Heresy laws and Act of of Six Articles repealed		
	Chantries dissolved		
1548	Somerset's enclosure commission		
1549	First Prayer Book		
	Act of Uniformity		
	Prayer-Book Rebellion		
	Ket's Rebellion		
	Catherine Parr dies		
	Thomas Seymour executed		

HOME		ABROAD	
1549	Fall of Somerset		
1549–53	*Duke of Northumberland's rule*		
1552	Somerset executed		
	Second Prayer Book		
1553	Expedition of Willoughby and Chancellor		
	'Device for the Succession'		
	Queen Jane's rule		

MARY TUDOR. 1553–58

1553	Northumberland executed		
	Mary's first parliament: catholicism restored		
1554	Wyatt's rebellion		
	Lady Jane Grey executed		
	Mary's second parliament		
	Mary marries Philip of Spain		
	Mary's third parliament: papal supremacy restored		
	Heresy laws revived		
1555–58	Marian persecution		
1555	Mary's fourth parliament		
	Stephen Gardiner dies		
	Muscovy Company founded		
	Guinea Company founded.		
	Philip departs for Spain		
		1556	Charles V abdicates
1557	War with France		
1558	Mary's fifth parliament	1558	Mary Stuart marries the Dauphin
	Loss of Calais		

ELIZABETH I. 1558–1603

1558	Hanseatic League expelled		
1559	Act of Uniformity	1559	Treaty of Câteau-Cambrésis
	Act of Supremacy		
	John Knox returns to Scotland		Henry II of France dies
	Revolt of Lords of the Congregation		Mary Stuart becomes Queen of France

	HOME		ABROAD
1560	Mary of Guise dies Treaty of Edinburgh Elizabeth reissues the coinage	1560	Francis II of France dies
1561	Catherine Grey marries earl of Hertford. Death of Amy Robsart		
1562	John Hawkins' first voyage to New World	1562	French Wars of Religion begin
1562–66	Rebellion of Shane O'Neill		
1563	Act of Artificers (apprentices) Elizabeth aids Huguenots	1563	Council of Trent ends
1564	William Shakespeare born Mary Stuart marries Henry, Lord Darnley Hawkins' second voyage	1564	Calvin dies
		1565	Michelangelo dies
1566	Archbishop Parker's 'Advertisements' Rizzio murdered	1566	Religious riots in Spanish Netherlands
1567	Lord Darnley murdered Mary Stuart marries earl of Bothwell Mary defeated at Carberry Hill Hawkins and Drake ambushed at San Juan de Ulua	1567	Alva sent to Netherlands to restore order
1568	Battle of Langside Mary Stuart's flight to England	1568	William Allen founds English college at Douai
1568–9	Commission to investigate charges against Mary Stuart		
1569	Norfolk marriage plot Northern Rebellion		
1569–72	Revolt of the Geraldines		
1570	Pius V's Bull of Excommunication		
1571	Ridolfi Plot	1571	Don John of Austria defeats Turkish fleet at Lepanto
1572	Duke of Norfolk executed Treaty of Blois	1572	Sea-beggars seize Brill Revolt of Netherlands begins

13

HOME		ABROAD	
1572	Drake's attack on Nombre de Dios	1572	Massacre of St. Bartholomew
		1573	Alva recalled from Netherlands
1575	Seminary priests begin to arrive in England		
	Archbishop Parker dies		
1576	John Oxenham killed	1576	Requesens dies
	Martin Frobisher's search for north-west passage		The Spanish fury
	Archbishop Grindal suspended		
1577–80	Drake's voyage round the world		
1578–9	Elizabeth's courtship of the duke of Alencon	1578	Don John of Austria dies
			Battle of Alcazarquivir
1578–82	Sir Humphrey Gilbert's attempts to colonise in North America		
1579–83	Revolt of the Geraldines	1579	Southern Netherlands reunited with Spain
1579–80	Papal expedition to Ireland		English college founded at Rome
1580	The Jesuits begin to arrive in England	1580	Philip II becomes King of Portugal
	Court of high commission established		
1581	Levant Company founded	1581	Edmund Campion executed
			Act against recusancy
1583	Throckmorton Plot		
1584	Bond of Association	1584	William of Orange assassinated
			Duke of Alencon dies
1585	Ralegh's first attempt to found Virginia	1585	Henry III's alliance with Guises
	Dr. Parry's plot		
	War with Spain begins		
	Elizabeth's military alliance with Dutch		
	Leicester's expedition to Netherlands		
	John Davis' attempt to find north-west passage		
1585–6	Drake's raid on West Indies		

HOME		ABROAD	
1586	Battle of Zutphen Babington's Plot Trial of Mary Stuart	1586	Philip II's alliance with Guises
1587	Mary executed Ralegh's expedition to Virginia Drake's raid on Cadiz		
1588	John Field dies Spanish Armada Earl of Leicester dies	1588	Santa Cruz dies Duke of Guise assas- sinated
1588–9	Marprelate letters		
1589	Counter-armada	1589	Henry III assassinated Henry of Navarre be- comes king Catherine de Medici dies
1590	Sir Francis Walsingham dies		
1590–95	John Norris' army in Brittany		
1591	Epic of the 'Revenge'		
1592	Earl of Essex's campaign in Normandy Ralegh disgraced	1592	Duke of Parma dies
1593	Christopher Marlowe killed		
1595	Expedition of Drake and Hawkins to West Indies Ralegh's voyage to Guiana		
1595– 1603	The earl of Tyrone's rebellion		
1596	Cadiz expedition		
1597	The Islands Voyage		
1598	Lord Burghley dies	1598	Treaty of Vervins Edict of Nantes Philip II dies
1599	Essex in Ireland		
1600	East India Company founded		
1601	Rebellion and execution of earl of Essex Commons' attack on monopolies Elizabethan Poor Law		

JAMES I. *1603–25*
1603   Bye Plot

HOME		ABROAD
1603	Main Plot	
	Millenary petition	
1604	James I makes peace with Spain	
	James' first parliament	
	Bucks' election case	
	Hampton Court conference	
1605	Gunpowder Plot	
1606	Bate's case	
	James' first parliament: 2nd session	
1607	Jamestown founded	
1608	Calvin's case	
	James' book of rates	
	Ulster planted	
1609	Bermuda colonised	
1610–11	James' first parliament: 3rd session	1610 Henry IV of France murdered
	Great Contract	
1611	Authorised version of Bible	
1612	Bishops reintroduced in Scotland	
	James joins protestant union of German princes	
	Salisbury dies	
	Prince Henry dies	
1613	Elizabeth marries Elector Palatine	
1614	Addled parliament	
1615	James opens negotiations for Spanish marriage	
1616	Trial of earl of Somerset and his wife	
	Chief Justice Coke dismissed	
	Shakespeare dies	
1617	Ralegh's Guiana expedition	
1618	Articles of Perth	1618 Thirty Years' War begins
	Ralegh executed	1619 Battle of White Hill
1620	Pilgrim Fathers colonised New Plymouth	
1621	James' third parliament: Mompesson and Francis Bacon	

	HOME		ABROAD
1621	impeached; Commons' Protestation		
1623	Massacre of Amboyna Journey of Charles and Buckingham to Spain William Byrd dies		
1624	James' fourth parliament: Cranfield impeached; Act of Monopolies; enclosure acts repealed	1624	Cardinal Richelieu becomes Louis XIII's chief minister

CHARLES I. 1625–49

1625	Charles marries Henrietta Maria Charles' first parliament War with Spain: Cadiz expedition Orlando Gibbons dies		
1626	Charles' second parliament	1626	France and Spain make peace
1627	War with France: La Rochelle expedition Five Knights' Case		
1628	Charles' third parliament: 1st session Petition of Right Buckingham assassinated Wentworth becomes president of Council of North		
1629	Charles' third parliament: 2nd session Commons' 3 resolutions		
1629–40	Eleven years' personal rule		
1630	Charles makes peace with France and Spain	1630	Gustavus Adolphus invades Germany
		1632	Gustavus killed a Lutzen
1633	Wentworth becomes lord deputy of Ireland Laud becomes archbishop of Canterbury		
1634	1st levy of ship-money		
		1635	France declares war on the Hapsburgs

HOME   ABROAD

COMMONWEALTH AND PROTEC-
  TORATE. *1649–60*
      (*1*) *Commonwealth*
1649–50 Cromwell in Ireland
1650 Montrose executed
      Charles II signs Cove-
        nant
      Battle of Dunbar
1651 Battle of Worcester
      Navigation Act
1652–4 First Dutch War
1652
 and 54 Treaties with Portugal
1653 Rump expelled
      Barebone's parliament
      Instrument of govern-
        ment: Cromwell be-
        comes protector

      (*2*) *Protectorate*
1654–5 First protectorate par-
        liament
1655–6 Rule of major-generals
1655 Penruddock's rising
      Expedition to West
        Indies: Jamaica cap-
        tured
1656–8 Second protectorate
        parliament
1656 Humble petition and
        advice
1657 Rising of fifth monarchy
        men
      Blake dies
      Cromwell's alliance with
        Mazarin
1658 Battle of the Dunes
      Cromwell dies
1659 Richard Cromwell abdi-   1659 France and Spain sign
        cates   Peace of Pyrenees
      Commonwealth restored
1660 Monck's march from
        Scotland
      Long parliament dis-
        solves itself
      Declaration of Breda
      Convention parliament
      Charles II restored

HOME		ABROAD
CHARLES II. 1660–85		
1660	Act of indemnity	
	Settlements of land, finance, and government	
	Irish land settlement	
1661	Rising of fifth monarchy men	1661	Mazarin dies
	Cavalier parliament meet	
	Corporation Act	
1662	Act of Uniformity	
	Dunkirk sold to France	
1664	Triennial Act	1664	Philip IV of Spain dies
	Conventicle Act	
	New Netherlands Captured	
1665–7	Second Dutch War	1665–7	Louis XIV at war with Spain
1665	Battle of Lowestoft	
	Five Mile Act	
	The plague	
1666	Fire of London	
1667	Dutch attack in Medway	
	Fall of Clarendon	
	Treaty of Breda	
	Cabal formed	
1668	Triple alliance	1668	Louis' secret partition treaty with emperor
	Bombay leased to East India Coy.	
1670	Secret treaty of Dover	
	Hudson's Bay Coy. incorporated	
1672–4	Third Dutch War	
1672	Declaration of Indulgence	1672	Louis invades United Provinces
1673	Test Act.	
	Break-up of cabal	
1674	Treaty of Westminster	
	Milton dies	
1677	Mary marries William of Orange	
1678	Popish Plot	1678	Peace of Nymegen
1679	Cavalier parliament dissolved	
	First exclusion parliament	
	Habeas Corpus Act	
	Archbishop of St. Andrews murdered	

HOME   ABROAD

1679	Drumclog and Bothwell Brig		
1680	Second exclusion parliament		
1681	Oxford parliament		
1683	Tangier abandoned Shaftesbury dies Rye House plot		

JAMES II. 1685–88

1685	James' first parliament Rebellions of Monmouth and Argyle Jeffreys' 'Bloody Assizes'	1685	Edict of Nantes revoked
1687	First Declaration of Indulgence		
1688	Second Declaration of Indulgence		
1688	James Edward born Trial of seven bishops William's expedition to England	1688–97	War of the League of Augsburg

WILLIAM and MARY. 1689–1702

1689	Convention Parliament Bill of Rights Toleration Act Battle of Killiecrankie		
1690	Battle of the Boyne Presbyterianism established as State religion in Scotland E. India Coy. acquires Calcutta		
1694	Bank of England founded Triennial Act Mary dies		
1695	Licensing act lapses Bank of Scotland founded		
1696	Treason Act Purcell dies		
		1697	Peace of Ryswick
1698	East India Coy. lose monopoly		
1700	Duke of Gloucester dies		
1701	Act of Settlement James II dies		

INDEX

References in roman figures are to chapters

. What famous
Person 1 would
like to meet.
describe his
or her qualities
& achievements

or

my family
at
breakfast time.